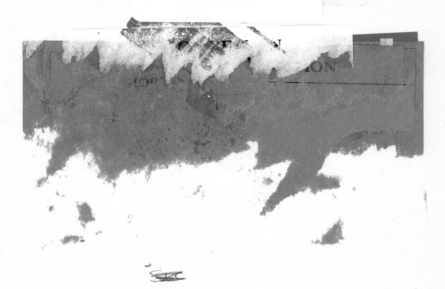

Dudley Docker

Dudley Docker

Dudley Docker

The life and times of a
trade warrior

R. P. T. DAVENPORT-HINES

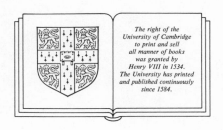

The right of the
University of Cambridge
to print and sell
all manner of books
was granted by
Henry VIII in 1534.
The University has printed
and published continuously
since 1584.

CAMBRIDGE UNIVERSITY PRESS
Cambridge
London   New York   New Rochelle
Melbourne   Sydney

Published by the Press Syndicate of the University of Cambridge
The Pitt Building, Trumpington Street, Cambridge CB2 1RP
32 East 57th Street, New York, NY 10022, USA
10 Stamford Road, Oakleigh, Melbourne 3166, Australia

First published 1984

Printed in Great Britain by the University Press, Cambridge

Library of Congress catalogue card number: 84–9444

British Library cataloguing in publication data

    Davenport-Hines, R. P. T.
    Dudley Docker.
    1. Docker, Dudley 2. Businessmen –
    Great Britain – Biography
    I. Title
    338.7′092′4 HC252.5.D5/
    ISBN 0 521 26557 6 c C

60 0357617 8

For
BLAIR WORDEN
and
CLIVE TREBILCOCK

Contents

List of illustrations, figures and tables

Illustrations

Figures

Tables

Acknowledgements

I have collected many debts in writing this biography. I owe particular thanks to Mr H. E. Scrope for giving me access to the Vickers microfilm collection, from which my first interest in Dudley Docker was drawn. Mr S. W. Alexander, the late Lord Barnby, Mr George Docker and the late John Docker have all assisted me with personal memories or private information, and I only regret that the latter's death in January 1982 prevented him from seeing the publication of a book which his recollections have enriched. Dr Luciano Segreto of Florence and George Behrend of Jersey gave useful information on Sofina and the International Sleeping Car Syndicate; C. A. Boardman, Foundation Archivist to the Schools of King Edward VI in Birmingham, sent me an account of Dudley Docker's education.

Professor Leslie Hannah arranged financial and other help in preparing this book for publication. He and John Armstrong both read the manuscript, and their criticisms were invaluable. Without the wise and ruthless advice of Professor Donald Coleman I could not have satisfied the publisher's wish for a major reduction in the length of the text, and I thank him for persuading me to eliminate several reckless or tasteless passages. Dr David Jeremy also gave generous encouragement during the preparation of this book. Above all, my wife Jenny Davenport financed much of my research and writing, criticised early drafts with microscopic severity, used her business expertise to elucidate some technical matters and her artistic talents to provide the diagrams. If this book has any vitality, it is due to her infectious gaiety and merriness. Andrew Best of Curtis Brown literary agents has also been put to some pains on my behalf during the writing of this biography.

For permission to quote from copyright or unpublished material I must thank Lord Addison, the Confederation of British Industries, Vice Admiral Sir Ian Hogg, Lady Lloyd George of Dwyfor, Mrs D. M. Maxse, the Midland Bank, the Librarian of New College, Oxford, Angela Raspin, Mrs R. M. Stafford, A. J. P. Taylor and Vickers plc.

Archivists who gave exceptional help were Edwin Green of the Midland Bank, Richard Storey of Warwick University and the late Geoffrey Dyer of Sheffield University. I also acknowledge with pleasure the friendly aid of the staff of the London Library. It would be unjust to those who facilitated the writing of this book if I did not record that my work was made harder and less pleasant by the arrangements of the Public Record Office.

This book is dedicated to Clive Trebilcock and Blair Worden, although they have done their best to prevent its completion. It has been written in the intervals of unemployment which are now the lot of most young historians: unemployment that my two mentors often tried to prevent or interrupt. This book only appears because the hopelessness of the cause defeated even their resources. The joy of being taught by them as an undergraduate, and the wish to emulate them as historians, are the real origins of this book; only those who have been their pupils or their friends can begin to imagine what I owe them.

Kensington, November 1983

Abbreviations

AEG	Allgemeine Elektrizitäts-Gesellschaft
AEI	Associated Electrical Industries
Airco	Air Transport and Travel Co.
BCU	British Commonwealth Union
BEA	British Engineers Association
BEAMA	British Electrical and Allied Manufacturers Association
BEPO	British Empire Produers Organisation
BSA	Birmingham Small Arms
BST	British Stockbrokers Trust
BTC	British Trade Corporation
CEB	Constructions Électriques de Belgique
Chade	Compania Hispano-Americana de Electricidad
CIWL	Compagnie Internationale des Wagons-Lits
DD	Dudley Docker
DOT	Department of Overseas Trade
EEC	English Electric Co.
EEF	Engineering Employers Federation
Elrafin	Electric and Railway Finance Corporation
EPA	Employers Parliamentary Association
ESC	English Steel Corporation
FBI	Federation of British Industries
FO	Foreign Office
GEC	General Electric Co.
GKN	Guest Keen Nettlefolds
ICI	Imperial Chemical Industries
MCWF	Metropolitan Carriage Wagon and Finance Co.
Metrovic	Metropolitan-Vickers Electrical Co.
NCEO	National Confederation of Employers Organisations
SEM	Société d'Électricité et de Mécanique

SGE   Société Générale d'Entreprises
Sidro   Société Internationale d'Énergie Hydro-Électrique
Sofina   Société Financière de Transports et d'Entreprises Industrielles

1

Dudley Docker and his world

The surname of Docker, insofar as it is remembered at all today, is associated with the adventures in the 1950s of Sir Bernard Docker and his wife Norah. For a generation of newspaper readers, they epitomised capitalism at its more irresponsible, riches at their most tasteless, and publicity-seeking at its most avid. Their 863 ton yacht *Shemara* and their gold-plated Daimler were outstanding pieces of conspicuous consumption amid post-war austerity. Their drinking bouts and public rows were the staple of every gossip columnist. Lady Docker seizing the microphone at a night-club and pouring out a torrent of her grievances, or being expelled from Monaco for dancing on the principality's flag, made her the cynosure of all sensationalists. Sir Osbert Lancaster commemorated the Dockers' notoriety in his cartoon of a bemedalled princeling saying into the telephone: 'Is that Luxemburg? Lichtenstein here – old boy, Monaco says Lady D's heading your way.' Sir Bernard had been a quiet and somewhat repressed man until his marriage at the age of fifty-two in 1949: he owed his eminence, as chairman of Birmingham Small Arms and as director of the Midland Bank, entirely to his father, who had joined the boards of both companies before the first world war. But if the origins of Bernard Docker's power were obscure, its eclipse was not. First, in 1953, his co-directors at the Midland Bank united to force his resignation. On that occasion he went quietly. But in 1956, when the the BSA board ousted him from office, he fought back; and the board-room battle that followed, with Bernard Docker buying time on commercial television to appeal to his shareholders, was the most resounding of the decade. Docker lost, not without inflicting terrible injuries on BSA; and the furore surrounding his departure can only be compared in magnitude to the takeover battle between ICI and Courtaulds in 1961–2, or to the board-room feud at Lonrho in 1972–3.

Paradoxically, though Bernard Docker is remembered for having lost the family millions, his father Dudley Docker, who made them, is forgotten.

1

Yet he was much the more interesting and extraordinary man. He was, by turns, county cricketer, captain of Midlands industry, leading exponent of the British merger movement, political intriguer, newspaper proprietor, banker and international financier, and founding president of the Federation of British Industries. He was, in H. G. Wells' description of Cecil Rhodes, 'a very curious mixture of large conceptions and strange ignorances',[1] a mystery man whose dislike of limelight obscured his importance and influence from all except a small circle of insiders. None of his private papers survive, and it is impossible to re-construct all his activities, or trace the full range of his interests. This biography seeks to sketch the life *and times* of Dudley Docker; it is an attempt at industrial portraiture; it describes many of the deals which he fixed, it recounts the rise and fall of the companies which he directed, but it also tries to re-create the milieu in which he worked, and to portray British social and economic history from his standpoint.

One of the main features of Dudley Docker is that he was a man of *influence*. He was 'the mainspring of the manufacturers' movement',[2] whose enthusiasms and dislikes typified those of other big manufacturers of his time. He was a man of vigorous, and sometimes imperious, opinions; and even when his opinions were nonsense, his reasons for holding them remain instructive. Marxists would say that Docker personified British monopoly-capitalism in the first half of the twentieth century; but this book is not a Marxist exercise, and prefers to show Docker as an example of the British big business man. Walter Rathenau, one of the leaders of the German electrical industry, observed in 1909, 'three hundred men, all acquainted with each other, control the economic destiny of the Continent',[3] and Docker was at the core of those of the three hundred who were British.

Docker's central attitude to life is easily expressed. 'We must produce as we have never produced before, and larger production means larger wages.'[4] As far as he was concerned, the experience of the USA proved that alleged evils of over-production were 'purely imaginary': 'The more produced, the greater will be consumption, as consumption creates consumption.'[5] For sixty-three years of active business life, Docker devoted himself to the cause of productive consumption. His formative years coincided with those between 1860 and 1900 which, according to Hobsbawm, witnessed 'the crucial question of British economic history', with the 'sudden transformation of the leading and most dynamic industrial economy into the most sluggish and conservative', and Docker's anxious resentment of this decline was critical to the pattern of his life.[6] Throughout the first half of his adult life, he was a strong imperialist who wanted the British Empire to unify into one trading unit which would thrash all other comers in the markets of the world. In the decades before 1914, he was virulently anti-German, and issued many warnings about Hohenzollern militarism and the threat to British industrial hegemony posed by Germany's new industrial might. He wrote in 1918

> that the outbreak of the present European war occurred at a very critical period in the history of Great Britain. There was immediate danger of civil war in Ireland, and throughout England, Scotland and Wales class antagonism had reached an acute stage. A long period of prosperity threatened to produce...something like industrial decline; a spirit of slackness was becoming apparent, keenness of competition was not appreciated, nor was the growth of inventive genius...the trading efficiency of the country was waning, and distrust and suspicion between masters and men had produced friction which might easily have developed into warfare.[7]

Docker regarded the war as a modernisation crisis providing Britain's final opportunity for social and economic reconstruction to preserve its world leadership. He was active in reconstruction plans, and their abandonment amidst the opportunistic improvisations of the Lloyd George coalition caused him abiding bitterness. Contemporaries might criticise obsessive accumulation of capital as irrational, but to Docker the accumulation of wealth was the natural object of all men.

Other Birmingham industrialists and politicians recur throughout this book. One of the most important was Docker's friend, Arthur Steel-Maitland, a Conservative politician who explained to Lord Milner in 1910 that he had chosen to represent a Birmingham constituency because 'I believe the town is potentially capable of corporate effort more than any other town in the kingdom...it is big enough to set a very important example, yet, unlike London, not so big as to be incapable of being got hold of.'[8] One singularity of the Midlands was that 'the gradation of classes in the manufacturing community of Birmingham remained a gentle one, and that consequently it was easier for the leaders to reach the masses': for this reason, Birmingham, in the first quarter of this century, became the centre of British corporatism, with Docker as one of corporatism's leading exponents.[9] He was an advocate of a manufacturers' political party, of a businessmen's government, and of an extra-parliamentary chamber, to be called the Business Parliament, to legislate on industrial and commercial matters. He believed that the development of large combines and trusts was necessary 'in the interest of the British race',[10] and the ferment caused by the first world war encouraged him to hope that British society could be reconstructed in a corporatist pyramid. As one writer has described:

Docker was committed to the establishment of a system of organisations which would represent industrial interests and speak for industry at every level, from individual firms to the entire nation. Industrial associations of all types would be joined in a national industrial federation whose primary purpose would be to provide a voice for industry as a whole in dealing with the government. Beyond this, Docker envisioned a completely integrated society and economy, in which each industry would have its own organisation of workers and managers, the two sets of organisations united by peak federations, and all finally capped by a great national forum of workers and managers and employers, embraced by the protection of an Imperial Tariff.[11]

Among British manufacturers of this period, none equalled Docker in the vigour with which he tried to impose the logic and structure of business upon political life and social organisation.

It is not coincidental that the names of Lord Milner and Steel-Maitland have been invoked. Docker respected both men – to the extent of offering them directorships in his companies[12] – and held the beliefs of other Milnerites such as Leo Maxse, Leo Amery, W. A. S. Hewins, W. L. Hichens, Clinton Dawkins, P. L. Gell or F. S. Oliver. All of these men were imperialists seized with that fanatical zeal which H. G. Wells called 'Prussian Toryism'. The Milnerites, despite their Germanophobia, were themselves curiously un-English in their dedication; despite attacking German methods and attitudes, their own policies seemed inexorably drawn to follow German patterns. What, for example, was Milner's dream of Imperial Federation but an Anglicised version of *Zollverein*? The Milnerites recognised this themselves. Amery wrote to Milner in 1903 that in his ideal vision of the Empire's future development, 'the underlying principle of the Prussian General Staff system [would be] applied to the whole of Imperial policy', Dawkins advocated an 'Imperial Council or Reichstag' under Milner's guidance, whilst Maxse conceded in 1902 'that in education, in business, or in public departments and particularly in the organisation of the Army and Navy, we have much to learn from Germany'.[13]

Docker was industry's leading Milnerite. His violent attacks on German organisation and success were usually accompanied by calls for Britain to imitate German methods. While he claimed that the success of 'Germany's world-wide business campaign' before 1914 had turned 'the heads of the German people and made them an only too easy and willing accomplice' of their militarists, and spoke of 'our foe [characterised] by a callousness, a cruelty and a fiendish malignity unparalleled in the world's history', he also praised the 'alliance between organised finance and organised industry' as 'marvellously advanced in Germany before the war', and promised, 'what the manufacturers of Germany can do, the manufacturers of Britain can do better'.[14] It did not trouble him that British manufacturers might turn the heads of their people and produce equally undesirable ends.

He spoke for heavy industry during the period when industrialism was at its most politically aggressive and self-confident stage in Britain, when the cult of the business man was strongest. Docker's friend Hugo Hirst of General Electric told a meeting of Cambridge undergraduates in 1914:

> You cannot think of the greatness of America without at once bringing to your minds the names of Morgan, Rockefeller, Vanderbilt, Carnegie and the other industrial kings of the Republic – if I may be permitted the paradox. You may not know of even one German general or admiral, but you cannot think of Germany without conjuring up the titanic figures of Krupp or Ballin, Rathenau, or Henkel Donnersmark; and it is these men, these captains of industry, men who turn hundreds of thousands of unskilled labourers into skilled workmen for the benefit of their country, who add to the strength and power, the prosperity and dignity, of the modern State. Today they form a bodyguard around the constitution of a country similar to that which a century or so ago gathered around the former kings with the difference that the nobility of industry has replaced the nobility of birth.[15]

These were the authentic terms in which Docker and his business friends considered themselves, and this hubris heightened after the bungling of the Boer War, when 'amateurism' became a national bugbear and Britain developed a temporary fetish for 'experts'. The military defeats of December 1899 and January 1900 humiliated the country, and the 'universal impression of fatuity, inadequacy [and] incompetence given by the Cabinet' and the Army caused a national revulsion. 'There is a very far-reaching feeling growing up that the Aristocracy make bad Generals and worse Administrators', one correspondent told Milner in February 1900. 'There is a cry in the City "Give us Men of Business" – a growing conviction that the men of fashion – however clever – are broken reeds.'[16] 'Never did I dream that educated gentlemen *could* be so out of touch with *realities* as some of the War Office people', wrote the same well-placed observer in April, 'They are just on a level with Dons and Schoolmasters & clerical Clergymen.'[17] The cult of the business expert reached its apogee in the next eighteen months, but continued to attract votaries for over another decade, as Docker's campaigns against administrative amateurism and for 'business government' demonstrated in 1910–14. Ironically a cause which was begun by the mal-administration of one war on the dusty veld of Africa was discredited by the mal-administration of the next war fought in the mud of Flanders. Following the munitions crisis of 1915, hundreds if not thousands of business men were seconded to government departments in the belief that the traditional officials, although honourable, laborious and loyal, lacked initiative or wide outlook. 'We want a sane and thoroughly capable man of the hustling species to have charge of progress', as one minister wrote,[18] but the entrepreneurs he recruited were not consistently sane, thorough, capable or hustling. Thus he found Sir Percy Girouard of Armstrongs 'anxious to get things into his own hands and...more concerned with his title and functions than with the business in hand', 'no manager and spends his time fussing about instead of sitting down and seeing that all the departments are doing their work'. Sir Eric Geddes of the North-Eastern Railway proved an abominable 'source of mischief' with his disposition 'to grab other men's work mainly for the sake of grabbing it', while Sir James Stevenson of Johnny Walker's whisky, 'cannot seem to work with other men and instead of putting his back in and getting on with his work...is far too much inclined to run from one to the other lamenting his difficulties'.[19] These examples of jealousy, bickering, intrigue and disloyalty could be almost infinitely multiplied, and destroyed the myth of the business expert. As one former railway manager wrote in 1917,

> We have howled for years for the appointing of 'business men' to regulate government affairs, but before such men have been in a warm berth for a month they become just like the old red-tape article and adopt all the old rotten obstructive methods and impossible English in their notices... The chief aim of all is to shove the blame for any action or delay upon some other.[20]

The business men in wartime government proved as fallible as anyone else, with the extra disadvantage that their co-directors constantly 'badgered' them to use improper influence;[21] and Docker, who had been one of the loudest howlers, grew cynical about business men in government after the war experience.

Docker failed, too, to convince his countrymen that production and money-making were the proper and primary aims of Britain. Still less did he win agreement – except from Leninists – for his proposition that the interests of the state, of industry, and of finance were identical, and could be developed without incompatibility. As Sir Keith Joseph complained in 1975, 'Britain never had a capitalist ruling class or a stable *haute bourgeoisie*', with the result that 'capitalist or bourgeois values have never shaped thought or institutions as they have in some countries'.[22] 'Again and again, over the course of this century in Britain, industrialism has been disparaged and economic growth disdained, not as in America solely by alienated intellectuals or religious enthusiasts, nor chiefly by extremist ideologues as in Germany, but by mainstream cultural figures addressing a wide middle-class audience.'[23] Industrialism's advocates urged their cause in terms which attacked British traditions of individualism so vigorously as to render the cause hopeless. Docker's dream of a corporatist state, dominated by big industrial trusts, was anathema to most of his fellow citizens, who knew too well the pleasures of individuality, and respected its contribution to Britain's historic greatness. Lionel Hichens, the chairman of Cammell Laird who had graduated from Milner's kindergarten, wrote in 1918: 'it is better for a country to have a large number of small manufacturers than a few big trusts: this also accords more with the genius of our race, whose sturdy independence and self-reliance has built an Empire containing a quarter of mankind'.[24] This was the opinion of one of Milner's own protégés, a man in charge of one of Britain's largest combines, manufacturing ships, steel and armaments, and there were many other adherents to this view in the commercial and financial communities. The politicians and administrators who were assured that a rationalised new order would sack them had every reason to frustrate its coming. The anti-democratic spirit which animated Docker and his friends fortified opposition to their corporatism among democratic-minded politicians, journalists, bureaucrats and voters. Docker was defeated, as between the wars his continental counterparts sometimes were not, by the depth with which democracy had been instilled into his countrymen. His activities were more insidious and more intelligent than the violence of Sir Oswald Mosley, but they were both foiled by the British preference for parliamentary conditions.

Electricity was 'the consummation of the industrial revolution'.[25] From early in the twentieth century Docker was involved in developing British electro-technology, and this stimulated his corporatism. The necessity in electrical engineering for large, multi-unit enterprises and for massive capital backing fired political corporatism across Europe. It is not co-incidental that several of the most vocal corporatists in early twentieth-century Europe were directors or promoters of electrical combines. In Britain, as this book shows, there was Dudley Docker; in Italy, there was the Milan manufacturer, Ettore Conti, president of Confindustria in 1920; in Scandinavia, Marcus Wallenberg; in Spain, Francisco Cambó; in France, Louis Loucheur; and in Germany, Walter Rathenau and Wichard Von Moellendorff of AEG. Loucheur, for example, was the corporate financier who organised the electrical industries of North France before entering government and who, during and immediately after the first world war, evolved with the Minister of Commerce, Clementel, a monopoly strategy designed to preserve France's international competitive position through large companies and strong industrial associations. Similarly, Rathenau and Moellendorff, who were both recruited from AEG to government work during the war, tried to establish an 'organic economic order in which wasteful competition was to be eliminated by industrial self-government based upon regional and industry-wide associations'. They believed that an 'interlocking basis for a true industrial commonwealth' would grow from collaboration between labour and employers, producers and consumers, and representatives of government.[26] Such schemes corresponded to Docker's plans for Britain, and although none of them were ever properly launched, they crystallise a moment in western European history when 'the business of the producer' was believed to be 'the greatest colonising asset of any State',[27] and when the interests of industry and state were more tightly enmeshed by war than at any previous date.

Docker's public life had three distinct stages. In the first, lasting from 1881 until 1914, he was preoccupied with building up his position as an industrialist in the Black Country. He drove himself hard, and although he expressed apprehensions about British progress, he remained fundamentally hopeful, with a reputation for being jovial, frank and outward-going. The second stage of his career spanned the Great War and the reconstruction period until 1920. On top of heavy business responsibilities, he undertook other work intended to transform Britain into a model corporatist state, and he seems to have had every expectation that he would succeed. By 1920, it was evident that all his wartime hopes were dashed, and his reaction to this included despair at the future of British industry. He withdrew from executive industrial responsibility, and became a financier who placed much of his hopes on British participation in multi-nationals. His interventions in British industrial management were henceforth confined to trouble-shooting forays and setting up merger talks, and in this sphere he remained active until his death in 1944. Although the condition and prospects of the British industrial economy partly caused these changes of Docker's direction, there was also a personal dimension to them.

From at least 1910, the pitch of his responsibilities affected his physical health. Thus, in 1912, as an attempt to recover his strength, he arranged 'to loaf for a year' on a Scottish estate, shooting, fishing and playing golf,[28] but the arrangements collapsed. When war broke out in 1914, he had to be summoned back from the middle of three months' recuperative holiday,[29] with the result that he was soon complaining of being 'tremendously rushed and not at all fit',[30] and felt, by January 1916, 'depressed and weary'.[31] At this stage, his mental condition appears to have become morbid, and claustrophobia to have set in. For example, one of the red-letter days of Docker's life was 27 July 1916, when he chaired the first meeting of the General Committee of the Federation of British Industries, but he had to hurry out before the meeting terminated, later offering the excuse 'I have been so overcrowded and feel so unwell that I really could not help it.'[32] It was from this stage that his dislike of limelight, and taste for acting through nominees, became really pronounced; so that by March 1920, the then President of the Federation of British Industries wrote of him: 'he is a constitutionally lazy man, and is inclined...to allow others to do the work, having once set the movement on foot'.[33] Apart from heavy colds, Docker suffered from gastritis,[34] an illness whose effects include irritability, and this may have increased his disgruntlement with his former associates which led to his resignations and public withdrawal around 1920–1. He himself believed that in picking men for power, one should take men in good health who would preserve a better balance, and by his own criterion, he was defective in the decade after 1910.[35]

Docker was a bundle of paradoxes. Though he could be painstaking and patient, especially in the preliminaries of a deal, he was also restless and changeable, lacking persistent application in seeing business through. His enthusiasms were sudden and fitful. He had excellent judgement of people so far as their material self-interest went, but seldom understood motives that were not pecuniary. He was both an opportunist and a pessimist: he had a low opinion of human nature, and despised idealism, yet held ambitious social ideals, although to modern tastes they may seem deformed. He spoke of co-operation and industrial reconciliation, but could be rancorous and thrived on reviling his opponents. Astute manipulation of newspapers and local opinion had a large part in creating his business reputation and influence before 1914, and he was keenly aware of his public image: yet he despised publicity and political acclaim for its own sake, and took increasing pleasure in escaping limelight. While notionally he was wedded to industrial democracy, and was famous for his imaginative recruitment of younger men to industrial power, he was in fact a peremptory employer who raged at subordinates who disobeyed instructions. At board meetings or committees, he was exceptionally silent, but informally, between meetings, he spared no pains to coax or cajole his colleagues to his point of view. He affected to be taciturn and inarticulate, but in fact possessed great persuasive powers, and produced many emphatic and memorable phrases in his speeches and writings. Tall and heavily built, his physical appearance sometimes vested his opinions with extra weight and force. A manager of the Southern Railway, of which Docker was a director in 1923–38, has described him attending meetings on the company's great electrification programme.

> D.D., shrewd and ruthless to a degree, looked like an amiable owl. Behind small, thick glasses his bright eyes stared at you. His small head seemed to be held immobile by an old-fashioned 'stick-up' collar. He rarely turned his head, keeping his unblinking glare straight in front of him. His

approval came with a short 'Yes', more often with a grunt and a kind
of hiccough. It was enough. Another three or four millions had gone
through.[36]

He could effortlessly resume a casual conversation at exactly the point
where it had been interrupted six months earlier, while his humour was
gruffly facetious: he always called the Midland Bank's general manager,
Astbury, by the nickname 'Raspberry'. If the moving letter he sent Leo
Maxse on the death of the latter's wife is a guide, he could be compassionate
and affectionate.[37] Though Docker spoke of himself as an industrialist and
claimed to represent the manufacturing interest, his talents in fact lay as
a financier who made money out of industry. Although authoritarian in
his own dealings, his dislike of governments and established order, if
sometimes naive and destructive, betrayed a real streak of rebellion in him.
He was indifferent to orthodox opinions, and pursued his way regardless
of the common herd: in this, at least, he showed his mettle.

However one chooses to interpret the enigma of Dudley Docker, this book
will show why contemporaries like Edward Hickman, the Wolverhampton
steel manufacturer, considered him 'one of the best commercial heads, if
not the best, in the country', and why his shareholders believed 'they could
go to sleep on their shares so long as Mr. Docker was at the head of
affairs'.[38]

2

Domestic life and early career

The immediate progenitor of the Docker family was a Moseley brass founder named Thomas Docker, who preferred, in later life, to be described as 'a gentleman' in official documents. He had six sons and three daughters, whose descendants were established throughout the Midlands in the professions or as gentlemen of private means. The ramifications of Thomas Docker's descendants need not detain us. Although his grandson Dudley was a man of strong family loyalties, who sought to found an industrial dynasty, he had no patience with genealogies. The editions of *Burke's Landed Gentry* which were published in 1921 and 1937 both contained entries headed 'Docker of the Gables' about Dudley Docker. They were among the shortest entries in either volume, with their details supplied by himself. He mis-stated the years of his father's birth and death, the year of his mother's death and the name of his maternal grandfather. He was not prone to ancestor-worship, or to dwell in the past, and this shows in the casual inaccuracies which he supplied to the editors of *Burke*.

His father Ralph Docker enrolled as a solicitor in the early 1830s, and practised in Smethwick and Birmingham for over half a century. In 1837 he was elected Coroner for East Worcestershire in a contest which he claimed cost him £10,000, because the voters had to be transported from all over the division to one polling station at Worcester. Afterwards, he became Coroner for North Worcestershire, and when he retired from that post, two days before his death, in 1887, he was the oldest and longest serving Coroner in England. He became, in the 1840s, Clerk to the newly established Kings Norton Board of Guardians, and until his retirement from that post in 1885, was said not to have missed more than half a dozen meetings. He was Registrar of Births and Deaths at Smethwick, and Clerk to the Smethwick Board of Health, which for many years held its meetings at his office in Rolfe Street, and only retired when his health declined in 1885. As an expert shot, he was a long-serving officer in the Smethwick

Rifle Corps. Ralph Docker 'was one of the best known men in Birmingham and district' whose collection of public appointments meant that he became 'styled as the Lord High Everything of his district'.[1] He was the chief promoter of the Northfield and Yardley Gas Act, which freed those districts from reliance on Birmingham's gas supply, and saved local consumers some £1,500 per annum in the late 1870s. He also fought a celebrated lawsuit, on behalf of the Smethwick Board of Health, which established their right to levy highway rates on the property of the London and North-Western Railway in the area. In youth he was a good athlete, whose forte was the high jump, and in later life, he rode to hounds. He was a life-long Tory, and was not identified with the Midlands manufacturing interest which embraced the Liberalism of the Birmingham Political Union.[2]

In July 1845, he married at Stourbridge, Mary Ann Sankey (1826–49), of North Harborne, Staffordshire. Her father, Richard Sankey, a horse-dealer, was a witness, together with one Henry Dudley. By this marriage, Ralph Docker had three daughters, Jane Isobel (1846–1917), Sarah Louise Caroline (1848–1937) and Mary Ann (1849–1936); but after only four years of marriage, his wife died of fever at the early age of twenty-three. He remained a widower for only a few years, and at some date in the early 1850s, married his young sister-in-law, Sarah Maria Sankey (1830–1900). Marriage by a man with his deceased wife's sister was prohibited by law, and although in the 1860s there were several attempts to repeal this law which were supported by the Prince of Wales, such marriage remained illegal until 1907. Defiance of the law was sustained by Victorian public opinion, for it was estimated in 1882 that there were 5,000 couples in London who had married despite the prohibition, and some twenty such couples in a little place like Stratford-on-Avon;[3] little notoriety would have attached to Ralph and Sarah Docker's marriage, which produced another nine surviving children. Apart from four daughters, there were five sons: Ralph (1853–1910), Edwin Sankey (1854–1926), William (1858–1923), Ludford Charles (1860–1940), and Frank Dudley, the subject of this biography.

Frank Dudley Docker (familiarly known as DD) was born on 26 August 1862 at his parents' home, Paxton House, at 130 South Street, Smethwick. He was educated privately,[4] before following his brothers to King Edward VI Grammar School at Birmingham in September 1873. King Edward's had been endowed in 1552, and enjoyed a high reputation, although the entrance standards were not arduous.[5] Docker was admitted to the Classical School of King Edward's (as distinct from the English School which taught more practical rather than classically orientated subjects), but was not a success. At Christmas 1874 he was marked last in general work in a class of twenty-one pupils, and twelfth out of twenty-one at French. Thereafter his name vanishes from the school list, and it is likely that he was removed to a private crammer. There are signs that he remained resistant to schooling and educational authority. He half-jokingly claimed in 1910: 'the only bit of Latin I remember is that bonus means good',[6] and certainly, if he learnt grammar and punctuation as a schoolboy, he speedily unlearnt them as an adult. The letters surviving in his own hand-writing are generally ill-punctuated and ungrammatical, and look as if they were written in hurried spasms. He used dashes rather than commas or full stops, and his scrawl was almost indecipherable. One surprising archaism, which he shared with Arthur James Balfour, was to write the letter S as a long f.

DD went into his father's office as a youth to train for the law. His elder brother Edwin was already in the firm, and eventually succeeded their father both as its senior partner, as a Worcestershire Coroner and as Clerk to Kings Norton and Northfield urban district council until the extension of Birmingham's boundaries in 1911. Apart from his partnership in the family firm of Docker and Hasgood, Edwin Docker had business interests, serving as a director of the Habilis Patent Self-Opening Umbrella Company in 1895–6 and of the Elkington electro-plate company from 1915. Unlike Edwin, young Dudley quickly found the law uncongenial, writing in 1916, 'my business mind is always opposed to *law*!!'.[7] In later life, he often abused the legal profession, and the lawyer's mentality. He despised the 'unravelling of legal subtleties', and considered that 'the legal intelligence' was only good for 'the making of black [into] pure white – or at any rate a nice, delicate shade of brown'.[8] The law seemed to him pettifogging and irrelevant, and he was impatient of its niceties and pace; as another Milnerite wrote, 'A lawyer's mind is naturally academic, and is satisfied with anything which makes a good contract *on the paper*.'[9] One speculation must be that he and his father found that they could not work in proximity to one another. There is no suggestion of how they treated one another; but an aggressively ambitious, impatient young man was likely to be frustrated by work with his septuagenarian father.

In 1881, when DD was eighteen or nineteen, he left his father's firm and joined his elder brother William in opening a varnish business. In doing so, he entered a long-established local trade. Varnish makers had first set up in Birmingham around 1770 to supply the needs of the town's dozen or so japanners, and the later development of the Midlands metal trades gave further impetus to the varnish and lacquer business. Many of the original firms which had made japanning lacquer switched to the manufacture of varnish when, towards the end of the eighteenth century, platers began to supersede japanners. Cheap japan goods (that is, lacquered hardware) were pioneered at Bilston; Wolverhampton became another japanning centre, where the Mander family made a fortune; and there were many japanners in Birmingham too. Edward Docker was a japanner and button-maker at Legge Street, Birmingham, in 1830, and Charles Docker was a japanner at 134 Great Hampden Street throughout 1830–50. With the introduction of electro-plate (patented by the Elkington brothers in 1838), decorative japan waned, and in the mid-nineteenth century, japanning became increasingly export-orientated, with the home market restricted to cheap lines such as tea-caddies and coal vases.[10]

Dudley Docker was a self-consciously forward-thinking industrialist who put some of his greatest working efforts into developing electro-technology, and even, in 1909, spoke longingly of his factories building aircraft and airships.[11] It is therefore paradoxical that his first business venture was in an industry which, however deeply rooted in Birmingham's industrial greatness, was small-scale, and associated with declining sectors of the metal trades such as japanning. Possibly William and Dudley Docker plumped for the varnish business in 1881 because of prior family connections. The historical antecedents of Docker Brothers were certainly known to its founders, for the telegraphic address of their business was the single word 'Japan'.

The brothers' first premises were a couple of arches under the Great Western Railway in Allcock Street at Deritend in Birmingham. They began with capital of about £1,800, and the balance sheet for December 1881 shows stock valued at £654 and plant at £225. Initially, they were merchants and not manufacturers, and dealt in only one material, Stoving Black Varnish. This they bought from a manufacturer in the Black Country in 40-gallon barrels, and then put into 1-gallon cans for re-sale to manufacturers of hollow-ware, cycles, bedsteads, umbrellas and the like. On occasions DD persuaded the carter who delivered the barrels to wait while the varnish was transferred to 1-gallon cans, and then re-deliver to Dockers' customers. When his persuasive powers were unsuccessful on this point, the cans were delivered by horse and float driven by one of his earliest employees, Herbert Preston.

In 1886, the intermediate brother between William and Dudley Docker, Ludford, joined the business, by which time its capital had risen to some £8,000 and the stock to £1,250. More capital was probably ploughed into the business at the end of 1887, for Ralph Docker died on 10 November in that year, and bequeathed his entire estate, worth £4,121, in equal shares to his two younger sons, Ludford and Dudley. Certainly the growth of Docker Brothers accelerated after 1887. The Black Country was one of the few areas in Victorian England where a young man who had abandoned the security of a solicitor's office for the hazards of small business, whose father was a High Tory lawyer and whose grandfather was a gentleman, would not be considered a disgrace for setting up in trade under railway arches. That Dudley Docker was not cut out from his father's will, but instead made its main beneficiary, indicates the exceptional values held by his father and by Midlands professional men in general.[12] Although black varnish continued throughout the 1880s to be the staple of their trade, the staff and sales both expanded. A varnish consultant called Hunt was recruited from the rival firm of Tabor Trego, and he supervised the actual making of varnish on the Allcock Street premises. Hunt had under him a man named Stack, and Stack's two sons, and with this workforce of four employees, Dudley Docker became a manufacturer rather than just a dealer. The Midlands metal trades consumed a great variety of paints and varnishes, and the Birmingham area specialised in several types of varnish which were not produced elsewhere in Britain. Docker Brothers, in their first decade at least, apparently only worked at the cheaper end of the market, supplying the needs of manufacturers of household goods and cycles.

Dudley Docker's business life in the 1880s remains obscure, but his other activities, as a sportsman, are better documented. The contribution of the Docker brothers had earned Smethwick Cricket Club the nickname of 'Dockershire', and all the brothers kept up the sport after they had left school. The best and most dedicated cricketer of them was Ludford, known to the Smethwick newspapers as 'The Local Leviathan', who joined Derbyshire in 1881, and was captain in 1884.[13] When Warwickshire Cricket Club was formed in 1882, young Ralph Docker, together with his brothers Ludford and Dudley, were among the twenty men shortlisted for the County XI of 1883. DD thereafter played regularly for the team. Warwickshire was not reckoned among the nine first-class cricketing counties; but among the second league of clubs, few had a brighter reputation, especially after the opening of the new ground at Edgbaston in 1886. In the inaugural match there, played against Middlesex on 7 June, Dudley Docker had the pleasant experience of being Warwickshire's man of the match. He also played against Australia when they paid their first visit to Birmingham in 1886.[14]

The cricketing of Ludford and Dudley Docker helped their varnish business. After Ludford had joined his brothers in 1886, he took over most of the responsibility for sales, and found that he could get inside the offices of potential customers by his fame as a sportsman. He would talk cricket for a while, and having got himself past the office door, would then start trying to sell his products. This ploy was regularly successful. DD also used his cricketing celebrity as an aid to business, very shrewdly since he lived in an age in which the ideal of the British sportsman was almost a fetish. One newspaper description of him in 1907 said 'Mr Dudley Docker looks in no way oppressed by his extensive commercial responsibilities. He wears a happy face and a genial manner...and in all respects he is what he looks – a   jovial,   kindly-natured,   straightforward,   sport-loving Englishman.'[15] This public image, although only partially accurate, was useful in many ways, including trade union negotiations; and it originated with his early cricketing prowess. He and Ludford were not the only talented amateurs to turn their sporting reputations to good use in business. William Morris (later Lord Nuffield) exploited his fame as a champion cyclist when he was a cycle-maker in the 1890s, and later, to a lesser extent, used his success as a hill-climber to promote his motor-cars. Hugo Hirst of GEC exploited his athletic prowess when trying to win the confidence and loyalty of his customers and his employees, and the sporting reputation of Selwyn Edge of Napier Motorcars was also valuable in business.

Cricket was responsible for Docker Brothers' first investigations of overseas markets. In the winter of 1887–8 Ludford went with Arthur Shrewsbury's team to Australia, but played disappointingly (perhaps because he heard shortly after his arrival that his father had died). After the tour was over, Ludford remained in Australia to sell paint and varnish, together with his brother William who had joined him. Shortly afterwards, William retired from partnership in Docker Brothers, and emigrated to Australia, where he went into business in Sydney. In 1892 both Ludford and Dudley resigned from the committee of Warwickshire Cricket Club after a row about its management, although both remained devoted to the game, and Ludford was later the county's president.[16]

Around this time Docker Brothers out-grew the railway arches in Allcock Street, and bought a small freehold factory in Rotton Park Street, Ladywood, for just under £2,000. It had previously belonged to Badham Brothers, and included white lead-grinding mills and colour-making plant. Even with these enlarged facilities, Docker Brothers could not meet their customers' demand for varnish, and continued to buy quantities from makers in Derby and Merton, Surrey, for re-sale in the Birmingham area. The works staff at this time comprised a works manager, nine men making varnish, four men making paint, and Herbert Preston with his horse and float. In 1890 they appointed a travelling salesman, W. Brockwell, in the Sheffield   area,   although   both   Ludford   and   Dudley   Docker   were   also involved in sales. A typical example of DD's bargaining shrewdness is remembered in his family. Whilst still a young man, he went to an old-established wagon-maker in Scotland, and said scornfully that he doubted whether the Scottish firm could afford to buy Docker Brothers' paints. The proud old Scotsman became very indignant at this, as DD intended, and to prove that he had a prosperous concern, did not haggle, and gave a big order, for which he paid too much. It was with similar adeptness that Dudley Docker built his business.

In 1894 Docker Brothers opened a London office and depot, at New Street, near Bishopsgate, of which Brockwell was put in charge. This London branch was one measure of their rapid expansion, and of their increasing success in winning export contracts, and orders from railways, rolling-stock makers and, to a lesser extent, shipping companies. The rolling-stock connection was enhanced after Ludford became a director of the Metropolitan Railway Carriage and Wagon Company, of Saltley in Birmingham, in 1898.

Docker Brothers and cricket were not DD's only interests at this time, for he apparently also had a side-line as a metal-broker. Certainly someone called Dudley Docker (probably not his cousin, Dudley Thornley-Docker) had offices at 18 and 19 Exchange Buildings, in Stephenson Place, Birmingham, from which he operated as a metal-broker. He was also a director in 1900–3 of W. A. Laycock Ltd, a newly founded company which produced railway plant and stores and gas and electric light filters. Through Laycocks, Docker increased his familiarity with the supply of components and other equipment to the Midlands rolling-stock manufacturers who were Docker Brothers' main customers.

On 17 August 1895, a fortnight before his 33rd birthday, Dudley Docker married, at St Augustine's in Edgbaston, Lucy Constance Hebbert. She was the daughter of one of Ralph Docker's most distinguished contemporaries in the Birmingham legal fraternity, John Benbow Hebbert (1809–87), by his wife, Lucy Julia, daughter of John Aston of Edgbaston and Rowington, and sister of a prosperous Birmingham manufacturer, George Lyttelton Aston. Hebbert had enrolled as a solicitor in 1831, and as he remained active until his death, his professional longevity surpassed that of Ralph Docker by two or three years. Indeed, as he became Clerk to the West Bromwich Justices in 1840, and Clerk to the Birmingham Justices in 1856, holding both posts until his death, he was one of the most prominent legal worthies in the Victorian Black Country. Hebbert was a die-hard Tory and Birmingham's leading Tory manager in the early Victorian period. His political blooding came in 1832, when he acted as agent when W. S. Dugdale seized the North Warwickshire parliamentary seat from the

Liberals. Subsequently, in 1835–47, Hebbert was 'the life and soul of Toryism in Birmingham', and its main organiser in parliamentary elections. He founded in 1834 a local political organisation, the Loyal and Constitutional Association, which served to counteract the Birmingham Political Union, and he was the Association's secretary until 1839. He had the satisfaction of seeing the Association achieve considerable political impact, although it declined in mid-century. For a time, he acted as manager of the *Advertiser*, a newspaper which was the mouthpiece of Birmingham Toryism, and was one of its regular contributors. Although Hebbert was one of the movers of the Tory's embittered and unsuccessful campaign to stop Birmingham's charter of incorporation, he had his measure of local pride, and helped to promote both the Midland Institute and Birmingham's Masonic Hall. He attended the first drill of the Birmingham Rifle Volunteers in 1859, and rose to the rank of Major.

Hebbert was the intimate friend of many of the Black Country's plutocracy, such as J. D. Goodman, the chairman of BSA. He named as one of his executors Sir Henry Wiggin, MP and former Lord Mayor of Birmingham, a nickel and cobalt refiner who was connected with the Adkins, Muntz and Nettlefold industrial dynasties; and this friendship was typical of his connections with the big manufacturers of the Birmingham conurbation. As he left an estate valued at £14,283, he evidently made several well-judged investments himself. Ralph Docker and Hebbert died within six weeks of one another in 1887, and sons of each man attended the other's funeral. The families' intimacy is shown by the fact that the third signatory to the family settlement, in 1888, on the young Lucy Hebbert, together with her brother Arthur and her uncle G. L. Aston, was her future husband, or else his namesake first cousin.

After their marriage, Dudley and Lucy Docker set up home at Rotton Park Lodge, in Rotton Park Road, hard by Docker Brothers' varnish factory, and it was there, almost exactly a year after their marriage, on 9 August 1896, that their only child, Bernard Dudley Frank Docker, was born. Early in the new century, the Dockers moved from Rotton Park Lodge to another home, The Gables at Kenilworth, where they lived until 1935. The Gables was an oddly built house, on two levels, with some reception rooms on the upstairs floors. Its previous owner, who had built it, had apparently run out of money, because most of the ceilings were left unplastered on the ground floor, leaving the wooden flooring of the upstairs storey exposed. Though the appearance was eccentric, it was not unsightly, and did not distort the acoustics of the house. Dudley Docker was indifferent to furniture and paintings, and John Docker suspected that his uncle probably sent a cheque to a department store like Maple's, and instructed them to furnish The Gables as they chose. In 1913 two portraits of Dudley and Lucy Docker were exhibited at the Royal Academy, but their nephew John had no recollection of either picture hanging in their homes. It is unlikely that DD took much interest in the portraits, except as status symbols, and it is significant that the artist he commissioned, Stanhope Forbes RA, was a brother of Sir William Forbes, General Manager of the London, Brighton and South Coast Railway, with whom he had business connections. In matters of art, as in everything else, DD used people within his own immediate circle of contact whenever possible.

Lucy Hebbert inherited almost half of her father's estate of £14,283, and was heiress to a comfortable patrimony when she married in 1895. Her money and connections consolidated Docker's social position, and were invaluable in developing and strengthening his business contacts. Industrial influence in the Midlands, then as now, relied on insiders' knowledge and the fixing of deals within a small, closed circle, perhaps more than anywhere else in Britain. This proved to be Docker's forte, and was the basis of his later reputation as the epitome of a Midlands industrialist. Docker's marriage enhanced his position in every respect.[17] Docker's status was confirmed when he became a Warwickshire Justice of the Peace in 1909, and his family's importance in county life was emphasised when his brother Ludford served as its High Sheriff in 1923 and his son Bernard was appointed as a magistrate in 1924.

He liked the outdoors, and took up shooting and golf after he became too old for cricket, to which was added membership of the Royal Thames Yacht Squadron when he had grown sufficiently rich. In the period 1910–20, he complained regularly about his health, and seems to have strained himself with over-work. In the summer, he went away whenever possible, either to Scotland or to a hotel at Lake Bala in the peaceful remoteness of Merionethshire. From 1918 until about 1924 he rented from Lord Forester the latter's exceedingly beautiful Shropshire house, Willey Park; and Docker spent as much time there as he could manage. In the 1920s, too, he usually took a house at Dunalastair in Perthshire for the shooting. On the moors, he was a fierce walker, who often tired his companions out, and refused to walk more slowly in case he caught cold.

In 1923 he acquired a spacious flat at 25 Berkeley Square, and this remained his London base until 1941. The Berkeley Square flat was in a particularly smart block, one of the first erected in Mayfair. The neighbour with whom he had most in common was Sir James Buchanan, the whisky distiller who left £7,150,000 in 1935. The well-known story by which Buchanan bought a peerage from Lloyd George's honours brokers, and ensured delivery of the goods by signing his cheque 'Woolavington', which was the title he intended to adopt, is certainly one which would have appealed to Docker. For much of the inter-war period, Bernard Docker lived nearby in North Audley Street, and Ludford's son, John, had a flat at 40 Berkeley Square for a time. In 1935 Dudley Docker sold The Gables at Kenilworth, and moved to Coleshill House, perched in the Buckinghamshire Chilterns, above Amersham. This was under thirty miles from central London, on the outskirts of the commuter belt known as 'Metroland', which Bernard and Dudley Docker, by their association with Metropolitan Railway Estates, helped to develop. Coleshill House was an airy and elegant building finished in white stucco and dating from the late eighteenth or early nineteenth century. It was large enough to convert to eight luxury flats in 1978.[18] Once again, Bernard had a home near his parents at Great Missenden.

Lucy Docker's character does not penetrate anywhere in her husband's career. She was not gregarious, and kept in the background. She liked the theatre, and later the cinema, and was a painstaking housekeeper who kept meticulous accounts. It is not known why she had only one child, but it is clear that both parents invested great hopes in the boy. Bernard Docker was sent to Harrow in 1911, at the age of fourteen, but after an attack of pneumonia, left in 1913. When his health had improved, he wasted some time with an inadequate coach before being crammed for Oxford University entrance by no less a scholar than A. L. Smith, the future Master of Balliol, to whom DD was introduced by Steel-Maitland. Bernard originally failed the Greek paper, but Smith 'gave enormous time and trouble to the boy', and was rewarded by seeing his pupil pass in the autumn of 1915. At this moment, it occurred to DD that Bernard, as an undergraduate, was unlikely to avoid conscription when, as seemed inevitable, compulsory service was introduced; and DD was naturally concerned to protect his only son and heir. He determined to get Bernard exempt from fighting by involvement in munitions production, and recruited him to Metropolitan Carriage. This decision horrified Smith, who protested to Steel-Maitland in terms which evoke DD's strengths and weaknesses as a parent. Bernard, so Smith wrote,

> wants above all things a year's discipline, moral and mental; his father wants to take him into the business, now, and send him to Oxford later! i.e. he'll have another year of shooting, golfing, motoring & the mud-honey of wealth, with a perfunctory few hours a week at 'business'...it is really a critical decision for the Boy's character. The Father is all that cd. be desired, to talk to; but in action, changeful and indulgent.[19]

Neither Smith nor Professor A. L. Lindsay could dissuade Docker, when he visited them in Oxford, and for the duration of the war, Bernard undertook munitions work at Saltley.

Bernard was put into business too early, and was pushed up to responsibilities too young (he joined the board of Metropolitan Carriage in 1918). He felt the pressure keenly, and went in awe of his father, whom he referred to (even in DD's death notice in *The Times* in 1944) as 'The Chief'. His handwriting, even in his late twenties, was immature, sloping in all directions, and he was not at ease with himself. He would have been a happier, and ultimately more successful, man if his father had not been so impatient to groom his lieutenant. Though DD got his son onto the board of almost every company with which he was associated (Metropolitan Carriage, Vickers, Metropolitan-Vickers, the Metropolitan Railway, the Midland Bank, and others), neither their co-directors nor outside observers mistook Bernard as having inherited his father's business genius.[20]

One example of Dudley Docker's influence on his son occurred after the latter's marriage in April 1933 to an actress with the stage-name of Jeanne Stuart. In September of that year, the couple went to stay with DD who was shooting in Scotland. After a few days there, the bride announced her intention to return to London for a few days to shop, and Bernard agreed to this. His father said very little, as was his wont, but had his new daughter-in-law shadowed by private detectives from the moment her train reached London; and before her return to Scotland, DD possessed a dossier on her activities in a mews-house with an actor called David Hutcheson. Bernard separated from her immediately, obtained a divorce in June 1934, and was so hurt by the episode that he did not re-marry until 1949. (Jeanne Stuart was re-married in 1952 to Baron Eugene de Rothschild, a retired Austrian financier then living in Long Island.)[21]

Returning to DD's prosperity as a paint manufacturer, Docker Brothers was registered as a limited liability company in May 1899. Its authorised and issued capital of £150,000 was in £5 shares, divided equally between Ordinary and 5 per cent cumulative Preference shares. The Company articles provided that, in the event of it being re-constructed or amalgamated, the Preference shareholders would be entitled to further payment of £2 per share out of surplus assets, once the Ordinary shareholders had been paid. This provision operated when, in 1907, Docker Brothers amalgamated with Britain's largest rolling-stock makers, of which DD was then chairman. The Docker family themselves held a large portion of the Preference stock, and from the outset in 1899, DD was alive to the possibility that the paint and varnish business would eventually be absorbed into a large combine. Certainly the merger of 1907 considerably enriched him.

With the conversion of Docker Brothers into a limited company, outsiders were introduced as directors. The first chairman was John Pierce Lacy, one of Birmingham's best known business men. Having moved there from Wexford as a teenager, Lacy had become a partner in 1860 with Joseph Ash as galvanisers and iron merchants, and was one of the most prominent members of the Birmingham Iron Exchange. In the late 1880s, together with Arthur Chamberlain, he had bought the shares of George Kynoch in the then unsuccessful ammunition makers, Kynochs. In the following years, Chamberlain and Lacy exercised predominant influence at Kynochs, and greatly improved its earnings. A few years later, he had performed similar resuscitation of the Patent Shaft Company of Wednesbury, and of the Birmingham rolling-stock makers, Brown Marshalls. He became chairman of both companies at a critical stage, and his financial reforms won wide admiration.[22]

With Lacy as chairman, and Dudley and Ludford Docker as joint managing directors, the other two members of the board were executives who had both been in the business for some years, A. G. Bone the works manager, and Brockwell, manager of their London branch. The directors were temporarily disturbed by a quarrel in 1900 between DD and Lacy,[23] but this did not check the success of the company. In June 1906, when Lacy died, Docker Brothers' £5 shares were being quoted at £20 each, and its growth was described as 'phenomenal'. One of the attractions for shareholders was the company's financial reputation. It pioneered a practice which several Birmingham firms, such as Guest Keen Nettlefolds, later made famous, but which was 'not in favour of other parts of the country'.[24] Its directors were empowered to accumulate internal and *secret* reserve funds, without disclosure to the shareholders, which could be used without competitors discovering its size or purpose. The existence of such powers led investors to assume that the declared asset value of the company was under-stated, and made investment more alluring. Provisions for secret reserve funds characterised several other Docker companies, sometimes not without controversy among the shareholders. In 1906 an injunction was obtained to prevent the BSA board from establishing a secret reserve fund as they wished, and there was criticism of Metropolitan Carriage's practice by a minority of shareholders in 1909–10. Perhaps the more important factor in the quadrupling of Docker Brothers' share value in 1899–1906 was that its three senior board members had all become directors in 1902 of one of Britain's biggest combines, the Metropolitan Amalgamated Carriage and Wagon Company. The likelihood that a generous takeover-bid would eventually emerge created a bull market for Docker Brothers' shares, which proved well justified. In 1907 the long-anticipated deal was concluded, and Docker Brothers was bought by Metropolitan for an estimated £264,375.

Docker's involvement with J. P. Lacy was tightened when, in 1899, the latter recruited him as a director of the Patent Shaft and Axletree Company of Wednesbury, a crippled giant of Midlands heavy engineering. Originally supplying patent axles, the company rose to prosperity on the tide of the railway age. It was privately owned until 1864, and after 1866 expanded into mining, smelting, constructional metallurgy, Bessemer steel and wrought iron. In 1879 embezzlement by the company's accountant and cashier obliged a reduction of capital by £90,000, and even then, accounts procedures remained utterly inadequate. No allowance for depreciation was made, and when certain shareholders forced a proper valuation in 1889, a deficiency of £265,000 was found. The capital was again forcibly reduced, but the ensuing reconstruction had only limited success, and the average dividend paid to Ordinary shareholders, during 1892 to 1902, was only $4\frac{1}{2}$ per cent. Particularly severe conditions were encountered in 1892–5, when the company reached the brink of dissolution; but an improvement occurred after the outbreak of the Boer War. Various of their products were required for the war effort, and one of their proudest moments occurred in 1900, when they completed, within two months, the seven-span Tugela bridge for the Natal.[25] As one of the Patent Shaft's directors at this time, Docker had first-hand experience of the stimulus to heavy engineering in time of war, and must also have absorbed many lessons about the organisation and management of large-scale enterprises. His wider application of these lessons is described in the ensuing chapters.

3

Birmingham's industrial titan 1902–14

The reputation of 'Mr Dudley Docker the great industrialist',[1] his personal and political influence and his business power all originated from his success in 1902 in arranging the merger of five large rolling-stock companies. With this deal Docker emerged as a mainspring of the British merger movement, and within a decade was the largest and most influential employer in the Midlands. This chapter recounts the background to the merger of 1902, and the achievements of Docker in the years before 1914 as chairman of the Metropolitan Amalgamated Carriage and Wagon Company (hereafter called by its later initials, MCWF).

Docker was a self-consciously modern capitalist who, by early middle age, had rejected many traditional attitudes of Victorian England as epitomised by the writings of Samuel Smiles, the author of *Self-Help* and the *Lives of the Engineers*. Smiles' gospel of work, with its emphasis upon individual effort and personal thrift, had encapsulated the spirit and outward aims of the mid-nineteenth century entrepreneur; but by the end of the century, it was a creed that seemed decreasingly relevant. One observer commented in 1890, 'The future Smiles will write "The Lives of the Market Riggers", or "The History of Trusts, Syndicates and Corners"', and the 1890s saw a series of huge, highly capitalised mergers in the cotton textile, brewing, cement, tobacco, chemical, soap and armaments industries, with 1899 the peak year for mergers.[2] Theoretically the merged companies should have used labour and capital equipment more intensively, have rationalised management and transport costs and have co-ordinated supply of materials more closely with demand, thus achieving an overall reduction of costs. In practice the mergers were preceded by minimal thought about organisational reform, with the result that there was little integration between the different constituent units of the amalgamated companies. Instead of the mergers resulting in the desired economies of scale, they often resulted in dis-economies: without central

24

co-ordination the different factories of the same combine continued to duplicate one another's functions, or a new layer of managers was required to impose the necessary centralised co-ordination.

The rolling-stock merger of 1902 avoided some of these pitfalls, and under Docker's supervision became a showpiece of what could be achieved. As one commentator noted in 1911:

> but for Mr. F. Dudley Docker's striking personality and remarkable genius for organisation, the task of amalgamation would never have been carried through. He was quick to see the advantages that would follow the directing of interests, formerly antagonistic, into one channel...and he set about merging these interests...almost a super-human task since there was no financial necessity on their part to assist him.[3]

The discussions which resulted in the merger were conducted by Docker with characteristic secrecy (although they were rumoured by January 1902), and as the settlement was announced in March 1902 with the minimum of publicity, the workings of his merger diplomacy are unclear. He was not a director of any of the five rolling-stock companies concerned, and his entry to them was through Docker Brothers which was their main outside supplier of paint and varnish for carriages and wagons. His brother, Ludford, and J. P. Lacy, both co-directors of Docker Brothers, were on the boards of rolling-stock manufacturers involved, and these connections enabled DD to make his initial soundings about the possibility of amalgamation, and to act as a trusted intermediary between the different interests.

The task of persuading the directors of the five companies to renounce their independence, and submerge their businesses in an amalgamation, was one which required of Docker 'the mingled qualities of a bold initiative, mastery of detail, resolution of purpose and discreet finesse'.[4] It is certain that his approach must have differed with each company. The works of the Oldbury Railway Carriage and Wagon Company, for example, had recently been badly damaged by fire, and needed complete re-building: to the Oldbury directors the prospect of merger into a powerful combine, which could provide the finance for reconstruction, would have seemed like salvation. Similarly the Lancaster Carriage and Wagon Works, for which £87,442 was paid in the merger despite its book value of £128,692,[5] had antiquated factories, and its demoralised directors welcomed rescue from unrelenting adversity. Brown Marshalls of Saltley in east Birmingham were also enfeebled. For the Ashbury Railway Carriage and Iron Company in Manchester the attraction was probably to seek security in a large and strengthened combine during the anticipated depression in rolling-stock orders after the Boer War. Finally, for the Metropolitan Railway Carriage and Wagon Company of Saltley in Birmingham, the merger promised the chance to be the dominant constituent in the largest and most powerful rolling-stock manufacturers in Britain.

Docker was a business man whose deals always carefully reflected his view of the drift of national economics and politics: and the rolling-stock merger of 1902 was no exception. Though it may be that the anticipated decline in the demand for rolling-stock and railway material at the conclusion of the Boer War was one of the arguments he adduced in favour of amalgamation, it is likely that he used even more forcibly the catchcries of 'professionalism', 'specialisation' and 'the expert' which had character-ised 'the quest for national efficiency' begun in 1899 after the traumatic British humiliations in South Africa during 'Black Week'. All the assump-tions, spoken and unspoken, which Docker brought to MCWF were rooted in the Edwardian 'Efficiency' movement of which he later became a spokesman. 'The most notable social fact of this age', declared the *Spectator* in 1902, 'is a universal outcry for efficiency in all the departments of society...from the pulpit, the newspaper, the hustings, in the drawing room, the smoking-room, the street, the same cry is heard: Give us efficiency, or we die.'[6] Everything that followed in Docker's career suggests that he raised this cry in the rolling-stock boardrooms, and that the agreement to his amalgamation scheme was secured by his issuing the fashionable ultimatum of Edwardian modernisation, be efficient or die. Of course there were solid financial inducements too. The combined net profits of the five companies for the previous financial year had been the equivalent of a dividend of 17 per cent in the amalgamated company, while the amount actually distributed had been £82,287, or the equivalent of 11 per cent. It was the succulence of a dividend nearer 17 than 11 per cent that attracted the rolling-stock shareholders.[7]

Opinions differed on the financial terms of the merger. *The Times* in an article inspired by Docker, judged that the five businesses were acquired 'a long way below the intrinsic value', whilst *The Economist* felt that, despite the high market values commanded by the shares of the five businesses, there was stock-watering in the merger.[8] In 1902 the combine had issued capital of £864,802, and Docker gave priority to paying off all debentures. Only £30,000 in debentures were outstanding by November, compared with £107,250 eight months previously. His motive in ridding himself of debentures seems to have been to free himself of the need to service the interest annually, and thus to have greater long-term flexibility in the financial strategy of the company. This was an unusual decision in 1902, which twenty years later the boards of most British steel and heavy engineering companies were to wish their predecessors had also taken.

Even in 1902 MCWF was not heavily geared compared with some retailing companies with gearing of 13:1; while contemporaries of Docker like Jesse Boot the chemist and William Lever the soap manufacturer still welcomed high gearing as a method of raising outside capital without losing control of their companies.

From the outset, it was rumoured that the Patent Shaft Company of Wednesbury would join the combine. The circular to the rolling-stock shareholders, received on 27 March 1902, denied the Patent Shaft rumours; but this was a feint. With Lacy as chairman and Docker as one of its directors, it was unlikely to stand outside for long. The shareholders' meeting gave no hint of a merger, although Lacy's speech, complaining of 'an American and German invasion of the iron and steel trades' because of British free trade policies, and warning that 'the next war would be a trade war', covered some of the economic developments to which the rolling-stock amalgamation was responding.[9] Merger plans, however, were announced later in the year, and were accepted by shareholders in November. Patent Shaft shareholders received shares in MCWF on an exchange basis: ordinary shareholders received $3\frac{1}{4}$ £1 shares in MCWF for each Patent Shaft share at a time when the latter were quoted at £6-17s-6d each. Docker, who had been elected chairman of the new Metropolitan Amalgamated Railway Carriage and Wagon Company in April 1902, saw the purchase of Patent Shaft as a major piece of backward integration. He wanted to make the combine self-sufficient, and although the rolling-stock companies made wheels, they had not hitherto made Patent Shaft's speciality of tyres or axles, and he wished to buy them a commanding position in that market. Patent Shaft's factories were said in 1907 to produce twice as many wheels and axles as anywhere else in Britain, and their acquisition was hailed in *The Times* as 'a master-stroke'.[10] One incident during the Patent Shaft merger talks shows how little the principles of amalgamations were yet understood in Britain. Lacy asked Docker for a letter promising that MCWF would assume all Patent Shaft's responsibilities. Docker initially resisted this request as absurd and ignorant. 'Who can be responsible but ourselves?' he asked, if Patent Shaft was to trade as a subsidiary of MCWF. But Lacy continued to seek a written commitment, and as a personal favour, Docker ultimately wrote such a letter, despite considering it superfluous nonsense.[11] In point of fact, Lacy's attitude was justifiable, and Docker was wrong, for companies were not liable for the debts of their subsidiaries when the latter, like Patent Shaft, were limited liability companies.

The rolling-stock merger of 1902 was an historic moment in Midlands business. Together with the contemporary amalgamations of Guest Keen with Nettlefolds, and of Lloyds with the Glasgow firm of Stewart and Menzies, Docker's scheme transformed Britain's industrial structure. The result was, for the first time, to link the Midlands with other parts of British industrial organisation and management. The Black Country had hitherto been a self-contained industrial area, but the quickening pace of large-scale industrialisation obliged the region to integrate its heavy industry with interests based elsewhere in the country.[12] Docker was a forerunner of this process. The merger was less defensive in origin than most mergers of the Edwardian period, and Docker sought economies of scale, through full-scale integration, in a more positive fashion than the bulk of his contemporaries. All orders were handled at the group's Saltley headquarters, and distributed among the different factories according to their circumstances.[13] With centralised planning and budgetary control at Saltley, the supply of raw materials to the various factories was better tuned to their needs, whilst costs were rationalised and reduced. Rolling-stock makers are considered Britain's first real assembly industry,[14] and Docker, at the head of the largest company in the sector, was determined to create a showpiece of modern, rationalised combination.

The combine was dominated by the personality of its chairman. Birmingham's leading solicitor, R. A. Pinsent, speaking of MCWF in 1915, said 'that the people there were not first-rate and not one was fitted to be chairman' except Docker.[15] He over-shadowed his co-directors and senior managers, and the company's successes reflected his strengths and interests, whilst its failings stemmed from his omissions. The board itself was large and unwieldy, with sixteen members in 1902. Each of the constituent companies had three representatives on the board, such as J. T. Sanderson, Arthur Shackleford and his son William from Lancaster; John Kershaw, Percy Wheeler and Herbert Wheeler from Oldbury; J. P. Lacy and Charles Hazlehurst from Brown Marshall; or Walter Hodgkinson and Ludford Docker from the original Metropolitan company at Saltley. The other directors received compensation of £500 each for loss of office. The first deputy-chairman, Sir George Scott Robertson, was a taciturn Scot who had trained as a doctor before entering the Indian Medical Service in 1878. During 1888–96 he was in the Indian Foreign Office, and had a varied and violent career on the frontiers, living for a year among wild hillmen in Kafiristan, and later being besieged and wounded by rebellious natives. After his retirement to Britain, he was elected Liberal MP for Central Bradford, and collected directorships in Yorkshire. He made a bizarre deputy to Docker.[16] After J. P. Lacy's death in 1906, his son Pierce Lacy, Birmingham's foremost stockbroker, joined MCWF's directorate, and gave help on financial strategy. Other board

Ill. 1 Lincoln Chandler (1865–1950)

appointments included J. R. Greg (son of Albert Greg, past chairman of the Lancaster company) and Lincoln Chandler. Chandler was 'a very able man with ambitions' who became firmly identified with Docker, and showed conspicuous loyalty to his interests through many years, although their relations were momentarily strained in 1915. At different times, Chandler was put by Docker on the boards of the United Electric Car Company, BSA, Vickers and various MCWF subsidiaries. In the period after 1910, the pair were hand-in-hand in Midlands political matters, and Chandler acted as Docker's mouthpiece in the councils of the Federation of British Industries and of the Midlands Employers Federation. He was a leader of the wartime National Emergency Committee of the latter body, and Sir Harris Spencer, its President, recalled that Chandler 'was forcible at times, yet always breezy, and while he never shirked responsibility, he always brought a broadmindedness to bear'.[17] The board and senior management of MCWF was, in short, dominated by Docker, with many of the original family controllers of the merged companies (such as Shackleford, Wheeler, Lacy or Greg) remaining powerful, but with some outside managers recruited (such as Chandler).

Years later, in 1924, Docker reflected upon his 'experience of the various changes I made at the Metropolitan Carriage...without producing results as satisfactory as one would expect from the outlay in money', and concluded, 'I have found that with all old works', by which he meant well-established factories and companies, 'what is wanted principally is an outlay of *Brains*.'[18] He found the resources and scope of British management were limited, and that the calibre of available men was disappointing. Professor S. B. Saul has attributed the managerial weakness of Britain's mechanical engineering sector before 1914 to the fact that its prominent men were trained in the highly traditional atmosphere of railway company workshops, and therefore had little capacity to absorb the benefits of modernised production processes. Men trained in railway workshops loved the technical product, but not the technique of production, and were careless of all forms of factory management except the engineering perfection of the product. Organisation, costs and labour use all suffered. Docker's remarks in 1924 occurred in a discussion on the ill-organisation of the Neasden workshops of the Metropolitan Railway, of which he had been a director since 1915, and were meant in the same sense as Professor Saul's comment. It was an experience which Docker had not only in rolling-stock, but in other engineering companies. Saul argues that mechanical engineering was more efficient in the Midlands than elsewhere because 'there were no major railway works in Birmingham and the Black Country to impress their traditions of engineering there'.[19] but MCWF unfortunately drew all their skilled men from the same pool as the railway companies,[20] and the *malaise* diagnosed by Saul in the railway workshops partly contaminated rolling-stock makers too.

As chairman of MCWF Docker proved talented at finance and public relations, but less successful in organising or understanding his subordinates. His twenty years running Docker Brothers, which for all its success was a comparatively small company, had not equipped him to manage such a big and scattered enterprise as MCWF, whose estimated total workforce of 13,868 in 1907 made it the ninth largest manufacturing employer in Britain. (The others, in order, were Fine Cotton Spinners and Doublers with 30,000; the Royal Dockyards; Armstrong Whitworth; Vickers; Calico Printers; the Great Western Railway; John Brown; and the Royal Ordnance Factories with 15,651.)[21] One measure of the combine's size is the area covered by its individual factories: the Britannia works of Brown Marshall were 11 acres; Lancaster was 15 acres; Oldbury and Ashbury were 20 acres each; the Saltley headquarters were 48 acres; and the Wednesbury property was 475 acres. It was a recurrent failing of Docker's to conceive a loose and abstract idea and to make furious but ineffectual efforts to apply it to his business. This failing appears as clearly in his attempts to manage a multi-unit enterprise like MCWF as in his political campaigns.

Docker's managerial problem is illustrated by a row of 1904–5. Sir Edward Holden of the London City and Midland Bank (hereafter called the Midland Bank) obtained for MCWF a contract to supply the American tramways magnate Charles Tyson Yerkes with carriages for the electrification of the London District Railway and for the first 'tube' construction. When the delivery dates were being prepared for the tender, the MCWF director responsible for rolling-stock production, William Shackleford, falsely assured his colleagues that he had reserves stored of the necessary timber. He privately expected to make good the deficiencies in raw materials without delay, and without his co-directors discovering. This, however, he failed to do, and deliveries fell steadily behind. Yerkes told Holden in January 1905 that MCWF 'were the biggest humbugs he had ever met...[one] could place no reliance on what they said...the management is not right, and the chairman is being bamboozled'. A week later, in an unusual intervention by a joint-stock banker in industrial management, Holden advised Docker to appoint someone to scrutinise all the works managements, and report on what was wrong. Docker responded to the hint, and made a searching review of his company's procedures. He was furious with Shackleford, initially demanding his resignation; and recognised the affair as a warning that there was a lack of frankness and trust at senior level in the company.[22]

'One of the greatest successes of this company has been its finance',

Docker told MCWF shareholders in 1919, 'we have found as much money can be made out of finance as by manufacture.'[23] His achievements in the Edwardian period were less in industrial production than in industrial finance, and his methods were copied by other Midlands manufacturers. Rolling-stock companies had always required sophisticated financial direction, not so much because, as the first assembly industry, they were highly capitalised, but because rolling-stock makers hired out a proportion of the wagons they produced and sold other wagons on deferred-purchase terms. A total of 517,407 newly made private wagons were registered in Britain in 1888–1917, comprising about 45 per cent of aggregate wagon production.[24] It was therefore a crucial part of Docker's business to obtain reasonable hire-purchase terms on wagons (especially with hard-bargaining coal owners), and to win a reputation for the financial facilities provided for his customers. Apart from these traditional characteristics of the rolling-stock industry, Docker's financial stewardship of MCWF had other features. The Articles of Association approved in 1902 vested the directors with the power to build up secret internal reserves which were not published in the balance sheet. Docker used these powers comprehensively, and by November 1910 had accumulated £450,000.[25] As Docker told shareholders in 1909: 'our exceptionally excellent financial position has been the most potent factor' in the company maintaining an Ordinary dividend of 15 per cent during 'a year of great commercial depression'.[26] This view was shared by outsiders: according to *The Times* in 1907, 'the absence of debentures, the huge sums spent on betterment [of the factories] and the admittedly strong internal reserves have all tended to give the shares a value that bears favourable comparison with even Government securities'.[27] Docker also wrote off to revenue all improvements to the company's land, buildings and plant. Oldbury, which had been wrecked by fire, was re-built in 1902–4; the Saltley works were next consolidated; a 10 acre site at Hadley was equipped to manufacture tram-cars on a large scale from 1905; and in 1902–12 some £300,000 was spent on Patent Shaft's facilities at Wednesbury.[28] Despite all this investment, the valuation was kept low in the accounts, and in 1919, when MCWF was bought by Vickers, its balance sheet still showed land, buildings and plant at the 1902 figure of £1.69 million. This absence of a depreciation policy, and the use of secret internal reserves to maintain dividends during adverse trading years, were perfectly proper and legal practice at the time; but they were much discredited by the collapse of the Royal Mail Packet shipping empire in 1930, and the trial of its chairman Lord Kylsant in 1931, after which accountants and successive Companies Acts treated them cautiously.[29] It was not an empty gesture which made

Docker have the company's name changed in 1912 to the Metropolitan Carriage Wagon and Finance Company.

Good relations were enjoyed with the company's bankers. Most of their business was transacted with the Midland Bank, chaired by Sir Edward Holden, although Lloyds Bank received a share too. Holden originally allowed MCWF overdraft facilities up to £100,000 in 1903, and when Patent Shaft transferred their business from Lloyds to the Midland in 1905, they were extended a separate maximum of £200,000.[30] Docker and Holden had a high regard for one another,[31] and worked closely together, especially after Docker was elected as a director of the Midland Bank in 1912. One sign of the intimacy between the company and its bankers was the latter's prompt provision in 1913 of a loan of £250,000 at $4\frac{1}{2}$ per cent,[32] and another was the favourable terms on which the bank handled its business. On company accounts it was customary for the bank to charge commission on turnover: from 1902 onwards, Holden however took only £200 commission on MCWF's turnover to £1 million, and £20 for every £100,000 thereafter.[33] When, in 1937, BSA asked the Bank for the same rate of charges, citing MCWF's Edwardian precedent, Astbury, the general manager, was incredulous at Holden's liberality.[34] It was a common complaint of manufacturers (especially between the world wars) that British bankers were aloof and uncomprehending of their needs, but the relationship between MCWF and the Midland Bank does not support this criticism. Docker felt that industrial borrowers had little to complain of,[35] and although the size and security of his companies secured him privileged treatment, Holden was an outstandingly helpful, sympathetic and constructive banker to many other industrial clients, including GEC and Daimler. Nevertheless, MCWF's intimacy with their bankers did not compete with that enjoyed by one of their competitors in South American markets, the Standard Steel Car Company of Butler, Pennsylvania. This was formed in 1900–1 by Andrew Mellon on the principle that rolling-stock buyers would borrow money from the Mellon National Bank to spend at the Mellon carriage and wagon factories, and such close co-ordination of finance and manufacturing facilities achieved considerable success in later years.[36]

One British financial practice which Docker execrated for its effects on MCWF was 'the insensate abuse of our credit facilities' whereby loans floated in the City of London 'for development and productive purposes all over the world' contained no stipulation 'that as much as possible of the new credit would be worked out by purchasing from [British] producers'.[37] As Docker told his shareholders in 1907, 'Our splendid isolation and superb cosmopolitanism is no doubt very pretty indeed, and very flattering to our vanity, but it is playing the very deuce with our business.'[38] Britain was supplying the credit facilities for its industrial rivals to develop the world. For example, the South African government raised a loan in Britain, in February 1914, of £4 million, mainly for rolling-stock. MCWF sent a director to South Africa to procure orders, but the proceeds of the loan were promptly spent in Germany. In March 1914 Ludford Docker wrote to Bonar Law, leader of the Conservative party, expressing

> our chagrin on learning that the money raised in this country is to be spent upon products from our keenest rivals in the foreign and colonial markets – rivals who will not even allow us to tender for the same class of manufactures in their own country if the necessary money should have been raised by loans in Germany...in such cases we are even barred in a neutral market.[39]

It was not only the Germans who profited from the City of London's view that so-called 'tied loans' were inherently vicious. The French, too, exploited it. No quotation could be granted on the Paris Stock Exchange without the leave of the Minister of Finance, and the French minister would not allow a loan raising money for expenditure abroad to be issued or quoted until it had been agreed to spend a portion of the loan in France upon French products.[40]

British manufacturers were constantly cut out of international contracts by competitors who were protected by tied loans in their own country, but profited from the more promiscuous issues of the London money market. Docker realised that the proceeds of London's loans did return to Britain, mostly in services; but as he wrote in a long letter to *The Economist* in 1914, 'Almost daily I, myself, have to decline all sorts of propositions...from all parts of the globe, because, if I passed them on to financial connections, the result would only be some new issue of capital unaccompanied by the required stipulations on behalf of home manufacturers.' British commercial policy was 'to worry through somehow', he contended; 'We are ill-organised as a people; and...the three great divisions of the business world – industrial, mercantile and financial – pay little regard to one another's interests.'[41] Indubitably Docker was correct in his point that Britain's international position was weakened by the promiscuity of the London capital market. 'Money is *the* great force in modern politics, and it is absurd that we should allow it to be directed by persons whose only inspiration lies in their pecuniary interests', wrote J. O. P. Bland in 1912, urging that the City would 'agree to government direction of foreign loans' if the danger of the present system was made clear, though 'the Jew-German element might object' and the 'FO has never understood' the problem. Sir Edward Grey, the Foreign Secretary, lamented British powerlessness in the

Middle East in 1913 with the comment: 'the real difficulty is the British investor',[42] but this was question-begging. The difficulty was that the British government, adhering to nineteenth-century *laissez-faire* ideals, declined to exercise the slightest supervision of the British investor. It was left to imperialist-minded financiers like Sir Vincent Caillard to introduce tied loans voluntarily to Britain: the £1.1 million loan which he negotiated with Turkey in 1914 stipulated that the proceeds be spent on orders in Britain.[43]

If industrial finance was Docker's forte, he also had a talent for publicity, and was attentive to his public image. Both the 1902 merger, and the subsequent performance of MCWF, were considerable personal achievements; but his reputation for business infallibility, the belief of some investors and journalists that he had the faculties of Midas, were exaggerated, and moreover exaggerated with his encouragement. Partly, at least, this was an attempt to reach and influence his workmen. From the outset Docker tried to improve the 'psychological atmosphere', as he called it, between the company and its men, and to remove mutual suspicion and disinclination to co-operate. Increasing production and economic growth were the unquestioned ends in Docker's view of the world, and restrictive practices were anathema. He believed 'A man is entitled to all he can earn...the material point is the cost of the article produced, and not the amount paid to the man', and he deplored employers who drove trade unionists into restrictive practices by 'the discreditable device of cutting the piecework rate as soon as the workmen have attained sufficient proficiency in the use of a machine'.[44] He was obsessed with absenteeism. At two of his factories, in 1913–14, workmen lost the equivalent of ten full days' working pay per annum (excluding illnesses, overtime and holidays), worth over £11,000. By modern standards this is a low absenteeism rate of about 4 per cent: a figure over double that is common nowadays, and 20 per cent is found in some British motor-car factories. Docker, in May 1914, nevertheless offered bonuses if his men would keep full time.[45] Another dislocation to production which Docker attacked was the observance of Wednesbury's summer-time Wake Week. This interrupted output, and by 1914 Docker's pressure on the town council and newspaper had undermined this local tradition. His success in suppressing the Wake Week showed the extent to which, in 1902–19, Wednesbury resembled a 'company town' in the United States, with Docker as the 'boss' who regulated it. As part of this attitude to Wednesbury, he wrote that 'Good houses are not luxuries, but necessities', and recommended that employers should not leave housing to local authorities.[46] He urged that employers should provide good recreational facilities for their men, and as a rather middle-class earnest of this, Patent Shaft donated the site in Wednesbury on which a nine-hole golf course opened in 1909. The whole Docker family were interested in medical charities (Bernard became chairman of the Westminster Hospital in 1936), and free nursing was provided for employees and their families.[47] Other benefits were offered to the families of employees, notably Docker scholarships for the children of MCWF workers at Birmingham University, of which Docker was a Life Governor.

Nevertheless, MCWF had several strikes, to which Docker applied his blend of ruthlessness, careful publicity and good timing. In 1904, for example, Patent Shaft received a large steel order for docks in South America. The company determined to make the necessary half-inch plates at Wednesbury, and asked their steelworkers to consider a fresh classification of wages so that they could be manufactured at a competitive price. The men declined to discuss the matter until a special meeting had been called of the Wages Board, and at that meeting, they declined to negotiate with the company's draft proposal. Docker could not countenance prevarication of this sort: he promptly placed the order in South Wales at a loss in wages to Wednesbury of about £5,000. He found it incredible that men could voluntarily spoil their chances of earning more money.[48]

Further trouble at Wednesbury in 1908 was caused by the blundering of middle-management, and revealed Docker's isolation from the practices and problems of his subordinates. On 29 July some 1,200 workmen at Patent Shaft's Old Park works struck in protest at the dismissal by an under-manager of a marker-off. The organiser of the Engineers Society, George Ryder, struck a popular chord when he complained that working conditions were everywhere becoming 'more irksome and stringent', and one of the strikers' prime complaints was a recurrent humiliation offered to their dignity. As part of Docker's interest in health, workers were obliged to attend medical examinations, at which they were examined publicly together in groups. When Docker met a strikers' deputation on 10 August, he assured them that neither he nor his co-directors had realised that the medical examinations were not conducted singly and in private; and undertook that this would happen in future. Nevertheless, the strike continued for three weeks, agreement only being reached on 19 August. Throughout this strike, Docker cultivated his public image. Wednesbury's local newspaper, the *Midland Advertiser*, which Docker always kept sweet, described his mood at the meeting of 10 August as 'conciliatory and fair-minded'; 'Mr Docker met the men in a very frank and straight-forward manner, and gained their confidence in the way he set them all at ease, and by a disposition to come if possible to a settlement'. When work finally resumed, Docker arrived at the factory gates at 6.50 am to demonstrate publicly to the returning workers his intention 'to exercise his own personal management' in the next difficult few days when the factory was returning to normal.[49] This gesture, imaginative in its way, nevertheless shows the fatal defect in his approach: instead of making a show of intervening to bring Wednesbury temporarily under his personal control, it would have been more constructive for him to improve the organisation, calibre and authority of the managers already there. His actions in a sense undermined them.

Docker's reputation with his fellow industrialists was enhanced by his handling of the strike, although only insiders knew the secret of his success. If the *Midland Advertiser* averred that Docker 'behaved most handsomely and consistently throughout', he himself confidentially admitted that 'he dealt with it *inter alia* by telling the men when on strike that there was no work going, whereas in reality he had diverted orders which would normally have been executed at Wednesbury to Saltley and Ashbury'.[50] One of the benefits of amalgamation had long been recognised as the apportionment of orders and raw material supplies between the different factories of a combine, so as to obtain the most economic working; the benefits in strike-breaking were less often admitted. Docker recognised that absence of employee communication in his company caused the strike of 1908, and brooded considerably on the problem in following years.

Another prolonged strike showed Docker in the role of outraged victim. In September 1911 MCWF concluded an agreement with the Engineers and Allied Trades Societies, including the Workers Union, of three years' duration until July 1914, whereby the company paid an increase of 1s weekly in time-rates of wages under 42s, plus $2\frac{1}{2}$ per cent on piece rates. In March 1913 John Beard of the Workers Union obtained a further understanding outside the 1911 agreement, which effectively created a minimum wage of 23s weekly. Docker soon came to regret this generosity: as he said in June 1913, 'our concession was taken by official agitators, who live on labour troubles, as a sign of weakness and squeezability'. On 28 April 1913 the Workers Union struck in the cause of a minimum wage of 23s at the Smethwick works of MCWF's competitor, the Birmingham Railway Carriage and Wagon Company; and at the end of May, MCWF men came out in sympathy. Docker was furious that just 'because one of our competitors has a dispute, the Workers' Union say, in this arbitrary manner, that no other men shall work'. He devoted much of his speech to his shareholders on 4 June to attacking 'this new form of strike, instituted without rhyme or reason, in defiance of agreements, forced on by gross intimidation, the beginning of a reign of terror'. It was, he said, 'an abominable breach of contract' by unions which 'do not yet know the meanings of the words "honesty" and "honour"', and he promised that 'until they are prepared to keep their contracts with us, let the cost be what it may, we shall not again open our works'. He deplored as 'a distinct step towards industrial anarchy' the Trades Disputes Act of 1906 which had 'by a most lamentable *volte face*' repealed the effects of the Taff Vale judgement of 1901 and had 'freed Trades Unions from liability to the law of the land'. After a month's strike, 37,000 men were idle, £250,000 wages had been lost, and the weekly wage loss was continuing at the rate of £58,310.[51]

The strike for a minimum wage of 23s, in which MCWF were embroiled despite having already a minimum wage agreement, spread across the Midlands like wild-fire during the summer of 1913. Apart from the settlement finally reached, it had one positive result. On 14 June a new organisation, the Midland Employers Federation, was launched in Birmingham under the presidency of Harris Spencer, of Wednesbury's Globe Tube Works. Its first secretary was Arthur Warne Brown, who had been an official of MCWF for eight years, latterly as secretary of Patent Shaft. The Midland Employers Federation, in 1913–18, worked hard at developing negotiation procedures with the labourers and unskilled of its area, and had marked success in repairing relations with the Workers Union. Docker succeeded Spencer as its president in 1918.[52] The minimum wage strikes of 1913 hardened Docker's conviction that 'a serious conflict between...Labour and the employers was imminent'.[53] It is true that British trade union membership rose by two-thirds during the labour unrest of 1910–14, but industrial strife was mostly confined to two categories of workers: the unskilled, who had been hit by inflation, and workers in the mines, railways and docks, where unusually reactionary employers over-resisted wage rises and provoked confrontation. Docker's view of the trend was chiliastic, and he blamed the Liberal government's inter-ventionist legislation whenever possible. After Patent Shaft's miners at Wednesbury had struck as part of the national campaign in 1912, he wrote in the *Daily Mail* that the recent Miners' Eight Hours Act, which introduced minimum working hours, had 'quickly proved its utter futility' and had aggravated tension in the industry.[54] Certainly the Act did not work smoothly and was followed by falling productivity, but he exaggerated the impracticability of the legislation and ignored the obscurantism of the coal owners in a period of rising costs and insufficiently rising prices.

It was characteristic of Docker's big ideas, and remoteness from the feelings of lesser beings, that in the midst of the great bitterness and tensions of 1913, he offered a workers' shareholding scheme to MCWF's employees. Not surprisingly, they rejected his idea, although a renewed offer was accepted in 1916–17, and with Docker's panache for public relations, the spokesman of the worker shareholders was given prominence second only to Docker at the meeting in 1919 which approved the group's acquisition by Vickers. Another group associated with Docker. BSA/ Daimler, also introduced a workers' shareholding scheme in 1916, and by October 1918, the participants had saved some £500,000 for use in it. Docker urged, 'Let [the employee] come in on the ground floor, and save him from the fluctuations of the Stock Exchange; let the firm advance him the money to take up his shares at a low rate of interest, and give him time to repay by instalments.' His belief in worker shareholders should not be confused with support for profit-sharing schemes. He condemned as 'fallacious' the view that it was the workers who made business profits by their manufacturing effort. The profits of an order were made by experienced salesmanship, or in adroit financing of the contract, or in careful buying of raw material; 'but it is very seldom that work in the factory has anything to do with increasing or making a profit on an order, although the profit may be adversely affected by slack time-keeping or restricted production'. The fact that, with two adjoining competitors, drawing on the same labour at identical rates, but with one factory well-managed, and the other not, profits would be earned at the first, and losses made at the other, satisfied Docker that labour, as such, did not *make* profits. For these reasons, he opposed profit-sharing, as not involving workers in bearing any share of losses, and put all his weight behind worker shareholders.

He appreciated the need for good employee communications, so that workers comprehended the reality behind company figures. Docker wrote that workers felt they were mere 'adjuncts to machines', and

> only hear of the successes disclosed in the balance-sheets, which make no mention of the losses which have occurred in the year's trading. The men hear of the millions, and compare them with the shillings or pence they earn. Then comes the opportunity for the agitator, who imbues the idea that the working class are being exploited, and that syndicalism is the appropriate remedy.

Docker, instead, wanted the workers fully informed of their company's trading prospects, with an understanding of 'some of the complexities of selling', and of the general position of their industrial sector: 'The first essential is to get rid of suspicion and distrust. Let there be light!'[55]

Docker also tried to drill militarism into his workers. One of his greatest *bêtes noires* was Richard Burdon Haldane, the lawyer turned Liberal politician. H. G. Wells' description of Haldane shows clearly the characteristics which Docker found exasperating and provocative: 'a self-indulgent man, with a large white face and an urbane voice that carried his words as it were on a salver, so that they seemed good even when they were not...he floated on strange compensatory clouds of his own exhalation [and] rejoiced visibly in the large smooth movements of his mind'.[56] Haldane epitomised everything about Britain which the taciturn Birmingham manufacturer detested; but as Secretary of State for War, he was responsible for one measure which Docker liked and adopted for the improvement of MCWF's profits. Haldane was a Germanophile, and, using his knowledge of German organisation, introduced the Territorial and Reserve Forces Act of 1907. Its provisions included the merger of the yeomanry and volunteers into a new Territorial Army of fourteen divisions and fourteen mounted brigades. Straight away in 1907, MCWF formed its own heavy artillery battery, and the driving enthusiasm behind this was Docker. He also arranged for Territorial Army recruitment meetings to be held in the combine's factories, and in April 1910, a rifle range was opened at the Saltley works for its employees. The company paid for these last facilities, although the rifle club was thereafter financially self-supporting and two Martini rifles were donated by the local MP, Steel-Maitland. The club's president was J. R. Greg, a recently elected director of MCWF, who was also the officer commanding their artillery battery, and the rifle club was intended to complement the company's Territorial activities. The Saltley club opened with almost 500 members, and rifle clubs were later started in the other factories, concluding with Wednesbury in 1914. Docker himself was a fair shot, and both his father and father-in-law had pioneered Volunteer Rifle Corps at Smethwick and Birmingham in the 1850s; so it is not surprising to find that he was the force behind his factories' rifle clubs. Whether rifle clubs made any contribution to national preparedness is doubtful, and Professor Marder opined that circuses would have been as helpful to home defence as the rifle club movement, which was mere amateurism exhumed from the 1850s.[57] Docker told his shareholders in 1909, 'times of great national trial are rapidly approaching', and undertook this expense for preparedness against Germany. Although some people joked that the battery's main purpose 'was to furnish a little amusement for the chairman',[58] Docker's services were officially recognised by the Crown. In the Coronation Honours announced in June 1911, Docker was created a Companion of the Bath – the only civilian so honoured in the list – for his support of the Territorial movement. Docker's interest in national defence was absolutely sincere, but there was another aspect to his artillery battery. Many productioneers like Docker explicitly recognised the benefits of having a workforce that had been militarily trained. Hugo Hirst of General Electric told Sir Vincent Caillard of Vickers apropos compulsory military service in 1904:

> When a man has read to him once a year and once in a lifetime (as when he joins the Army) that unless he does this or that he will be shot, he learns amongst other things to get up regularly in the morning, and after a while regards it as a crime to be five minutes late. After he has practiced these habits for two or three years, the feeling works itself right into his constitution.[59]

Well-regimented artillerymen, it must have seemed to Docker, would also be well-regimented rolling-stock workers.

Docker met surprisingly little resistance from his workers in his more ruthless attempts to rationalise the MCWF combine. For example, in 1908 he closed the old Brown Marshall factory at Saltley, which became redundant after the adjacent Metropolitan site had been re-built. The Lancaster works were also shut in 1908, despite inducements offered by Lancaster Corporation to keep it open. The rolling-stock factory was the second largest in Lancaster, after Lord Ashton's linoleum works, and the town was hit badly by the closure. Finally, in 1908, the Hadley tramworks in Shropshire was closed due to lack of orders, and remained empty until 1910 when it was sold to Joseph Sankey and Company. Docker was not reluctant to use the threat of closure against other municipal authorities. When Wednesbury raised its rates by 1s to 8½s in the pound in 1905, he made minatory noises in public about possible closure, and was warm in Wednesbury's praise when the rate was cut by 2d in 1907. Incidents in 1908–9 led Docker to threaten closure at Ashbury, because 'of the Manchester Corporation's attitude towards us in the matter of smoke nuisance, they having caused us great annoyance by harassing us with expensive prosecutions (which I am more than half inclined to term persecutions), notwithstanding that we are doing everything possible to avoid sullying the pure air of Cottonopolis'.[60]

It was not only in Britain that MCWF integrated its productive capacity. Docker also opened a works at Manage in Belgium. He had several related reasons for doing this. MCWF estimated that wage rates were 30 to 50 per cent lower in Belgium than Britain, although productivity was also 30 per cent lower, and Docker claimed that restrictive practices were less troublesome in Belgium. It was certainly a fact that Patent Shaft's steelworks were not situated in an area suited to low-production costs in the common-grade trades;[61] and the antiquated plant and methods of other potential British steel suppliers rendered their prices uncompetitive. It was a pioneering step by Docker to open a Belgian steelworks to feed his British factories, and a measure of British decline that this was economically worthwhile, despite the increased distances involved. There was no novelty in British companies opening foreign subsidiaries to supply export markets cheaply, but MCWF was apparently unique at this time in buying a foreign factory to process materials for British manufacture. Docker's admiration for Belgian financial and industrial policy was well entrenched before 1914, and if war had not erupted, he would have extended Manage's operations considerably. As described in later chapters, Docker's Belgian interests were extensive after 1918.

MCWF's immense productive capacity could not be sustained on domestic orders alone. Indeed home orders for carriages all but vanished, as British railway companies' workshops became self-sufficient in their needs. Rolling-stock and other material were sold to many parts of the world, but no foreign market was more important than the Colonies of the British Empire. The principal colonial customers were Egypt, India, New Zealand, Nigeria, Rhodesia, South Africa and the Sudan. In 1913 Docker described the Colonial Office as 'the greatest business department of our Government',[62] and there were many dealings between its officials and the management at the Saltley works. The cordiality between the two would not have surprised the economist J. A. Hobson, who had defined in 1902: 'Imperialism is the endeavour of the great controllers of industry to broaden the channel for the flow of their surplus wealth by seeking foreign markets and foreign investments to take off the goods and capital they cannot sell or use at home.'[63] Although nowadays Hobson's analysis of economic imperialism needs modification, the outward activities of his contemporary Dudley Docker often seemed to prove the pertinence of his views on capital accumulation and colonialism. Docker himself was convinced that the colonial markets were indispensable for continuing national prosperity, and looked forward to some form of federated trade organisation within the Empire. Speaking of the Colonies and Dominions to his shareholders in 1907, be warned, 'These sturdy sons will have to be taken into partnership, or...before many years have gone by, they will be making their commercial alliances elsewhere, and their political alliances will not be long in following'; the British Empire had reached a turning-point which was 'an extremely grave one in every way'. In 1909, he concluded his chairman's speech by appealing for the success of the forthcoming Imperial Conference,[64] from whose deliberations he hoped imperial tariff reform would result.

The different products of the combine had different dispersals. MCWF had no European export market in wheels and axles, but exported 'a great deal' to Argentina, Brazil, Chile and the Colonies; 'a little' to Canada and only 'a very little' to the USA (the last two markets were both decreasing because of the North American predilection for the chilled cast-iron wheel). In rolling-stock, the great continental powers, such as France and Germany, had powerful rolling-stock capacity of their own, and the lesser European nations were already committed to French or German products.[65]

Much business was conducted with South America. Argentina, Brazil, Chile, Mexico, Paraguay, Peru and Uruguay were all customers. Docker 'supplied all the Chilean railways with rolling-stock', and it was reported in 1910 that Argentina had given orders worth £5,000,000 to MCWF during recent years. In 1910, Argentina celebrated its centenary, and to commemorate the event and steal attention at the International Exhibition at Buenos Aires in May 1910, MCWF presented the President of Argentina with a private saloon carriage of sumptuous finish.[66] Ludford Docker described Argentina as 'almost the *only* country where we get any sort of show', and felt that Whitehall's slackness, compared with Berlin, in the export drive was exemplified by the fact that Britain did not originally intend to be represented at the Argentine Centenary Exhibition by anyone 'of more importance than the nearest admiral'. Indeed, his brother mobilised Neville Chamberlain and three MPs (Norton-Griffiths, Steel-Maitland and MCWF's deputy-chairman, Scott Robertson) to press for more high-powered and flattering British official visitors to the Exhibition, commensurate with the Hohenzollern princeling sent by Germany.[67] Their exports to South America were not only in rolling-stock. The Great Southern Railway of Buenos Aires ordered two large bridges from Patent Shaft in 1908, and a swing bridge, worth £10,000, over the River Riachuelo, in 1910.

Losses were sometimes sustained. In 1909–10 MCWF had to write off £24,000, which had been supplied in goods to Mexico, for which payment was not forthcoming, and for which the security deposited with the Midland Bank (bonds worth $105,000) turned out to be worthless. There was no recourse for Docker in such a case, as was shown in its aftermath, in 1910, when MCWF won a rolling-stock order for the Brazil North-Eastern Railway. They unsuccessfully approached Commercial Union Assurance, Midland Bank and Lloyds underwriters in search of someone who might insure the risk on the contract, and it was this sort of experience which, some ten years later, prompted Docker's support at the Federation of British Industries and the British Trade Corporation for schemes to insure exporters' risks.[68]

One of the imperial orders received by MCWF was to supply the rolling-stock and special locomotives for the Benguela Railway. Work started on building this railway in 1905, and its route went from the Atlantic coast of Angola up the steep escarpment to the central plain. It then traversed 1,000 unexplored miles until it reached Katanga, and it there had connections with the great African mining areas, including the Rhodesian copper-belt, as well as the projected Cape to Cairo line. The contractor was Docker's friend, John Norton-Griffiths, and by 1908, he had built 250 miles of the railway, to the summit of the Angolan plateau, with further progress looking comparatively easy. A slump in the price of copper shares in 1908 hit the Tanganyikan interests which were financing the railway, and although Crown Prince Louis of Portugal opened a section of the line, work was all but abandoned until after the Great War.[69] Docker does not seem to have travelled abroad himself to handle the more valuable tenders, but his co-directors often did. J. R. Greg visited Egypt in 1906, for example, and Chandler went to Canada in 1910. Foreign royalty was often entertained at Saltley as a preliminary for winning orders, as witnessed by the visits of Prince Tsai Tse of China in 1906 and of Prince Carol of Roumania in 1911.[70]

It was to establish the constructional engineering products of Patent Shaft in one Dominion market that MCWF formed a Canadian subsidiary, the British Empire Bridge Company, in conjunction with the Cleveland Bridge Company of Darlington. Docker later wrote that it had been their intention to establish works in various parts of Canada, and their first step was to submit a tender for a steel bridge over the River St Lawrence. The design for the bridge had been agreed by a committee of engineers appointed by the Canadian government, and the British Empire Bridge Company's tender was the lowest of four submitted, but the contract went to a Canadian company. What enraged Docker was that the successful tender was for a railway bridge only, for which no tenders had been invited; and in several respects, the successful tender broke the specification to which the British Empire Bridge Company had kept. To add insult to injury, the British company's deposit of £100,000, required with their tender, was kept by the Canadians for six months, and then was returned without interest. Docker attacked this 'exceedingly shabby treatment' both in a speech of 1 June 1911, and in a dispute with Sir Wilfrid Laurier, Liberal Prime Minister of Canada 1896–1911, conducted in the correspondence pages of *The Times*.[71]

Docker's publicly ventilated anger over the Quebec Bridge Affair was not entirely due to the losses which MCWF had sustained. As he admitted privately, the affair came at 'an excellent moment', and he hoped to drum up around it an agitation which would unite the business community in insisting upon a Dominion reciprocity agreement emerging from the conference which met in London during 1911.[72] This once again showed the inextricability of Docker's business and political aims, and his insistence that they were synonymous, as well as his capacity for turning adversity to constructive ends. Many other industrialists, even as late as 1911, still believed that business and politics were compartmentalised, and resisted admitting that each reacted on the other. The industrialists who had least illusions on this point were armament manufacturers, whose profits almost entirely depended upon government policy; and Docker's early understanding of the relation between state and industry may have been enhanced by his directorship of BSA in 1906–12, and MCWF's own involvement in wartime industrial mobilisation. As rolling-stock manufacturers well knew, they held an important place on the margin of the defence sector. Patent Shaft had received valuable contracts for constructional work during the Boer War, and the rolling-stock makers had also aided Sir Percy Girouard in diminishing the British Army's transport problem in South Africa.

When the Russo-Japanese war erupted in February 1904, MCWF received a rush order for 1,800 huge vans to be supplied to Japan for use in Manchuria. The combine was able to re-apportion work within its factories to accommodate this sudden influx of work, and the Hadley factory was given over to supplying the Japanese. Within three months, they had done so. Docker was very partisan about the Far Eastern war, and unusually frank in his welcome of a check to Russian expansion in Manchuria which had threatened British industrial markets in China. He told MCWF's shareholders in June 1904:

> the great war now waging in the Far East possessed...supreme interest and importance. Its results...had been extremely gratifying, both to this country and America, not as being unfavourable to Russia, but as being so many blows struck for the open door. The prowess of the Japanese had indeed been phenomenal, and their ultimate victory would mean the independence and territorial integrity both of China and Korea, and the means of securing the open door in those countries and equal opportunities for development, their capacity for which was enormous...It would prevent the sordid struggle for territory, for spheres of influence, for trade exclusiveness and trade restrictions, which have held those two countries in bonds for centuries...The development of China...would be best effected by a great progressive people with whom China had a strong racial affinity, aided in every way by the great Anglo-Saxon Powers...he had no fear of the yellow peril...Macaulay's New Zealander was [not] at all likely to be displaced by a gentleman with a pigtail. To them Japan had always been a good customer...They looked to the opening up of China under Japanese auspices and American and European supervision with great hope.[73]

Docker's remarks suggest racial condescension towards the Japanese, and ignorance about Chinese conditions: nor did he foresee the extent to which, in little more than a decade, several of his best-informed contemporaries would perceive Japan as out-menacing Germany in potential industrial competition. His admiration of the Japanese was, moreover, typical of those business men, politicians and publicists who campaigned against amateurism and individualism after the Boer War. They regarded Japan as a 'paragon of National Efficiency' which 'could be admired without the shudder of apprehension that a contemplation of German efficiency so often evoked', and interpreted 'the events of the Russo-Japanese War as a triumph for collective regulation over the old *laissez-faire* creed'.[74]

Perhaps the best evidence of Docker's success, with which to conclude this account of MCWF before 1914, are an American attempt to buy the combine and Docker's attempt to merge with Guest Keen Nettlefolds. The American initiative came from Andrew Mellon, head of the Mellon National Bank of Pittsburgh, and later Secretary of the United States Treasury (1921–32) and Ambassador to Britain (1932–3). The Mellon Bank was heavily involved with the Pennsylvania steel industry, and financed many customers of the Standard Steel Car Company, a rolling-stock maker formed by Mellon in 1900–1. In the summer of 1913, Mellon sent an emissary from the United States to suggest that MCWF should be amalgamated with the Standard Car Company, and be floated as an international combine by the New York financiers, Kuhn Loeb and Company. On being approached, MCWF declined to give any of their operating figures to the Americans until a definite offer was forthcoming. The British added – and it is not fanciful to see Docker's ruthless bargaining touch here – that they would not consider any offer below £5 cash for every £1 share. This would have involved a minimum, for the Ordinary shares alone, of £7,123,560. The unaccommodating British attitude owed something to the view that it would be a shame to sell 'such a magnificent English concern to an American company', but it is striking that Mellon continued negotiations for some time longer,[75] and proof of the prosperity and strength which the amalgamated wagon companies had achieved in the first decade of Docker's stewardship.[76]

· Docker himself hoped that MCWF's growth would prove illimitable, and was working in 1914–15 towards an amalgamation with Guest Keen Nettlefolds. GKN had also been created by a merger in 1902, and was the only Midlands combine which compared in size to MCWF. The death of Arthur Keen senior in February 1915 interrupted Docker's plans, for his son and successor proved to be 'so nervous [and] so full of settling his father's affairs and taking over the business' that Docker decided that for the time being, 'it would be premature to push him'.[77] If such a merger had been concluded, the resultant company would probably have been the largest engineering company in Britain, and it is likely that Docker would have been chosen as the industrial titan to control it. The idea disappeared in the ferment of war, but its conception was a measure of Docker's restless ingenuity and fertile ambition. MCWF's production, he hoped, was an infinitely multipliable quantity.

Docker's rolling-stock success raised his prestige to such heights that his expertise was sought by other businesses. He joined the boards of several other companies, either with a view to arranging mergers, or to provide his general business judgement. In 1904–5, for example, he sat on the board of O. C. Hawkes Ltd, a prosperous Birmingham company which manufactured wholesale and retail looking-glass and had an interest in the Birmingham Plate Glass Insurance Company. The company was still controlled by O. C. Hawkes himself, and the explanation of DD's involvement is unclear. After he left the board in 1905, his brother Ludford joined it until 1908, which suggests that DD's interest continued. Around the same period he was a director of a Midlands rolling-stock fittings company headed by W. S. Laycock. Another company of which DD was a director in 1904–5 was John Wilkes, Sons and Mapplebeck Ltd, Birmingham metal-rollers, copper-smelters and copper-refiners, formed in 1891. Once again, Ludford Docker succeeded to his brother's directorship in 1905, and served as the company's chairman in 1907–8, whilst years later, in 1930, Bernard Docker was also recruited as a director. It seems that Dudley Docker was an active operator on the Birmingham Metal Exchange in this period, and possibly his interest in the Wilkes, Mapplebeck company was complementary to his playing on the metal market. In 1906 he became director of Birmingham Small Arms, a company with which he, his son and nephew Noel were associated for over half a century, and the activities of which are described in this chapter, and chapter 11. In 1908 he became a director of W. and T. Avery Ltd, Smethwick manufacturers of weighing-machines, which, with some 3,000 workers, ranked as the hundredth largest manufacturing employer in Britain at that period. Sir Gilbert Vyle, an electrical engineer who was appointed as Avery's managing director became one of the most influential leaders of Birmingham business opinion in 1915–33, and will be mentioned later for his support of Docker's call for a revolution in the administration of Britain. Docker was also a director of the Stratford-on-Avon and Midland Junction Railway in 1909–12, the Metropolitan Railway in 1915–33 and the Midland Bank from 1912 until his death. At the end of the war he became a director of the London, Brighton and South Coast Railway, and after it was absorbed by the new Southern Railway in 1922, sat on the latter's board until 1938. This list of outside directorships throws up several features. The longest that he stayed on any of the five industrial boards was six years (at BSA), but in each case except Avery's, he retained intimate links with the companies' direction. In three cases (Hawkes; Wilkes and Mapplebeck; and the Stratford-on-Avon Railway) he was succeeded as director by his brother Ludford, whilst at BSA, Chandler acted as his replacement. Though the pressure of his duties at MCWF was probably one cause of this, it may also have been evidence of the restless, fitful nature of his enthusiasms and application.

Turning to the company with which he was longest associated, and for whom his work became nationally eminent, BSA was formed in 1861 with the encouragement of the War Office, which provided the Birmingham company with free access to their facilities and technical drawings at the Royal Small Arms Factory at Enfield. The BSA directorate was drawn from a small and geographically localised circle of business men, who soon found that the government's small and fluctuating orders made the business precarious. Their first War Office contract was not agreed until 1868, and in 1879 the factory was shut for a year through lack of work. In an attempt to diversify the business into more stable civilian markets, BSA began producing bicycles (1880), bicycle components (1893), motor-cycles (1895), and by 1901 the capital invested in their cycle component branch alone amounted to £307,139. Their withdrawal from reliance on government arms orders continued during the Edwardian period, and by 1910 the proportion of BSA's turnover represented by armaments was only 21.3 per cent, rising to 28.9 per cent in 1911, 25.5 per cent in 1912 and 33 per cent in 1913.

The circumstances of Docker joining BSA's board in the autumn of 1906 are unclear. His election coincided with the appointment as chairman of Sir Hallewell Rogers, a former Lord Mayor of Birmingham, who had joined the BSA directorate in 1904. One colleague wrote in 1951 that Docker 'took a warm interest' in Rogers and was 'responsible for making him chairman of BSA'.[78] Any truth in that story is now unascertainable, but Docker certainly had considerable influence on the selection of BSA directors, for in 1907 the board was augmented by his junior colleague at MCWF, Chandler. Indeed in October 1908, when Docker discussed his 'dis-satisfaction' with the running of BSA with Sir Edward Holden, he had 'decided that if the chairmanship was offered to him, he would accept',[79] which indicates a major commitment to the company. A reliable source, writing in April 1906, hinted that certain people had recently made a killing in BSA shares. For some time, a 'war to the knife' had been fought between BSA and its rival, the National Arms Company, but the latter's directors finally decided to sell up, and 'Those with early information rushed in and bought BSA shares'.[80] One hypothesis – it is no more than that – is that Docker was one of those whose foreknowledge enabled him to buy up BSA shares at the right time. That would account for some of the weight which he carried as a director.

In the autumn of 1906, BSA was on the brink of difficulties. The period 1907–11 was the leanest interlude of armaments orders throughout 1905–39, and BSA suffered particularly from the War Office's broken promises. In 1906, they had bought from the government the Royal Small Arms Factory at Sparkbrook in Birmingham. The number of rifles manufactured annually there over the preceding fifteen years had averaged over 16,000, and the contract signed by Haldane, the Secretary for War, undertook that in return for buying Sparkbrook, BSA would get a quarter of all War Office trade orders for Lee Enfield rifles in 1906–9, and that the order for 1906–7 would not be worth less than £20,000 (at average trade prices).[81] The War Office did not adhere to this undertaking for long. In 1908, Sparkbrook was allotted an order of only 6,250 rifles, and in 1909, some 5,572 rifles. This completely defeated the plans which BSA had made for Sparkbrook, for as they told the Director of Army Contracts, they could 'without any especial effort and working ordinary hours supply the whole of our share of this order in about four weeks'. The Rifle Department's potential output was 1,500 rifles weekly, directly employing 1,750 men; but in June 1910, their output on government contracts was the equivalent of 235 rifles weekly, employing 300 men. Moreover, they could not make up the shortfall by exports, because there was no overseas demand for Lee Enfields and Lee Metfords for which they were tooled at the War Office's request. They had no capacity to meet foreign enquiries for Mausers or Mannlichers.[82]

As an attempt to utilise Sparkbrook's surplus facilities, BSA developed a motor-car department there. It was, however, badly organised and ill-equipped, and because of the constant experimental adaptations of models, there was no proper scheduling or planning of work. In October 1909, for example, current work in progress or on the stocks comprised no less than four models with a total of only sixty-five vehicles. This confused and over-extended product line caused managerial strain, and it is mind-boggling that BSA submitted tenders at that juncture to supply 500 taxis in London, fifty cabs for South America, and ten charabancs and ten lorries for Argentina.[83] An investigatory committee's report, tendered to BSA's board on 22 June, was a searing indictment of previous methods. 'There has been great laxity in all departments and quality of work has not been properly considered', they reported. Parts were stocked 'irrespective of proportion or eventual requirements.' Inspection was neglected, assembly workers were overstaffed by 160 and office hands by 40, while the department was 'too liberal in free repairs' on old models. There was no proper stock-taking and no standardisation of parts, so that cost controls were impossible. Baguley had proved incapable of organisation, his only solution for bottlenecks being to employ more staff; he had presided over anarchy, not only in design, production and after-sales service, but in essential and simple matters like stock-taking and supplies of parts.[84]

Docker's reaction to this uncompromisingly negative report was characteristically positive. If, as it seemed, BSA could not find proper management for its motor-car division from internal sources, then it would have to buy outsiders' skills. He had become deputy-chairman of BSA in 1909, and from this vantage, set about arranging a merger with the Daimler Motor Car Company of Coventry with a view to grafting the latter's expertise onto BSA's ailing motor department. This merger strategy was, however, complicated and vitiated by other, more personal considerations. Docker seems to have felt the need to repeat in the motor-car industry a merger that would set Midlands business men talking as the rolling-stock merger had done a few years before, and this influenced his actions. He also thought of industrial mergers as inherently productive, and equated bigness with strength. He therefore did not appreciate the need – or perhaps was too lazy or busy – to ensure that the Daimler/BSA merger created a combine distinguished throughout by even and consistent management, whether in finance, marketing or development. As a result, the combine was never adequately balanced or co-ordinated. A final personal factor was Docker's cupidity, which led to financial arrangements in the merger which were thoroughly unfortunate.

The British Daimler company was less than fifteen years old, but its production of about 500 cars in 1906 made it, together with Rover, the largest British car producer at that time. By 1907 the Daimler company employed between 2,000 and 3,000 men and had a maximum productive capacity of sixty cars per week on a site covering 14 acres.[85] Docker himself owned a Daimler car from at least 1906, and was also a close associate of Daimler's executive management, Percy Martin, Edward Manville and George Flett. Martin was a forceful American who was Daimler's managing director in 1906–34.[86] His professional pride as an engineer was immense, and made him somewhat contemptuous of other skills: the remark of another motor engineer, Herbert Austin, that 'financial experts [should] put on their thinking caps and try to catch up with the engineers, [so that] slump periods, like plagues, will be a thing of the past', typified Martin's attitude.[87] Manville was a British pioneer of electro-technology, and partner in the Westminster electrical engineering consultancy which had advised on the electrification of the London, Brighton and South Coast railway, for which MCWF and AEG provided the equipment. He and Docker were later co-directors of the Metropolitan Railway, and were political adherents during the war period when Docker was president of the FBI and Manville led the Association of British Chambers of Commerce. Manville's election as MP for Coventry in 1918 was financially backed by the British Commonwealth Union, of which Docker was a leader, and his name will often recur in this book. The third power in Daimler was Docker's co-director at MCWF, George Flett, another pioneer of tramways and electrical engineering, and an enthusiastic and reckless motorist, who was killed in 1910 when a Daimler carrying Ludford Docker, J. F. Cay and himself crashed after leaving a board meeting of MCWF.[88] Flett and Manville had been outstandingly successful collaborators at Daimler after capital reconstruction in 1904. On an issued capital of £142,568, they earned profits of £83,167 in 1905 and £213,469 in 1906, respectively 57 and 150 per cent of the invested capital. These figures excited the envy of competitors, the avarice of investors and the respect of bankers.[89]

The terms of BSA's purchase of Daimler leaked in September 1910, and were published at the end of the month. BSA paid over £600,000 for its new subsidiary: they issued five full-paid BSA Ordinary shares of £1 each in exchange for every four of the 200,000 issued Daimler Ordinary shares of £1 each; whilst the owners of 80,880 Daimler 6 per cent Preference shares of £1 each received £1¼ in cash, plus accrued dividend. The deal was welcomed in the financial press. *The Economist* judged that 'Daimler shareholders have little to complain of, for their profits have fluctuated enormously and their security is much improved by the share they obtain in the old established Small Arms company'; whilst BSA, in one fine stroke, 'assume[d] a very important place among motor engineering companies'. *The Financial Times*, too, hailed the 'combination [a]s one of the most important ever affected in the motor industry'.[90]

This complimentary tone about the merger has prevailed ever since, but the truth was less favourable. One of the provisions included by Docker was that Daimler should pay to BSA dividends worth £100,000 a year. This sum represented as much as 40 per cent of the capital which BSA had put into Daimler, and left the motor company with no spare cash to develop its commercial car business or other lines. Docker was insistent that this dividend payment should be maintained, even if this meant extending Daimler's overdraft at the Midland Bank. In February 1912, Daimler's debit at the bank was over £200,000, and Holden had to warn Manville that the bank directors 'were getting a little fractious'. Though Docker liked to compare the BSA/Daimler merger with MCWF's purchase of Patent Shaft, Holden did not accept the comparison. Whereas the latter had ample resources to lend Patent Shaft, BSA were not in a position to finance Daimler, and neither BSA nor Daimler had ample liquid resources.[91] Under pressure from the bank, the group made a capital issue in 1913 of 300,000 Preference shares paying 6 per cent,[92] which relieved the liquidity problem for a time, but further watered the group's capitalisation. This is the first clear example in Docker's career as merger-maker of the cloven hoof that bedevilled most of his later deals: over-tortuous schemes of inter-indebtedness leading to over-capitalisation. The Westinghouse/MCWF/Vickers mergers of 1917–19 recounted in chapter 8 were the most grievous case of this, and showed Docker as sharp on the main chance as any unscrupulous City company promoter.

Docker retired as deputy-chairman of BSA in 1912, perhaps because he felt over-worked or because he was a restless man inclined to delegate details and administration once he had set general ideas in motion. He installed Chandler in his place on BSA's board, but there was not an integration of the facilities of Daimler and BSA as occurred after the rolling-stock merger. There was minimal re-organisation of either company, and, absurdly, in view of the Baguley crisis of 1909–10, BSA continued producing undistinguished models of their own fitted with Daimler engines. One sign of inefficiency is that in 1913 Daimler employed 5,000 workers (out of a total of 100,000 in the British motor-car industry) to produce only 1,000 cars, which suggests muddled management and misallocation of resources.

Daimler's problems, though aggravated by the terms of the merger, were a microcosm of the weakness of the motor industry at the time. There was an 'absence of commercial acumen', as Professor Saul has written, 'the passion for technical perfection and individuality for its own sake which was embodied in an institution as uneconomic as the consulting engineer, cast its baleful influence' over the whole British motor industry. Martin's subordination of costs and marketing to the technical finish of the model, and the background of Manville and Flett as electrical consulting engineers, tell their own story in support of Saul: as described in chapter 11, Daimler's need was for business administrators and not inventors or engineering wizards. In the period before 1914, Martin and Manville involved the BSA/Daimler group in 'several rather grandiose schemes such as a petrol-electric motor 'bus, the Renard motor train etc, all of which were successful technically but proved to have little or no commercial value'.[93]

Saul's suggestion that a 'general weakness of the early industry was the persistence of control in particular hands through large blocks of shareholding [which]…contributed to the excessive individualism [and]… quickly deteriorated into ignorance and insularity' is again supported by the case of Daimler.[94] Thus one of the biggest shareholders, subscribing £33,618 Preference shares in 1907 alone, was Arthur Wood who as a director of Daimler from 1904 until 1934 lacked any acuity or judgement except on the end of a fishing-line. Such men were ill-equipped to cope with Daimler's dilemma in 1910–36: whereas in 1904–7 they had marketed a first-class product at the right moment, thereafter Daimler cars were steadily more vulnerable to the competition of more exciting and imaginatively marketed cars. The penultimate chapter of this book shows just how ill-equipped they were.

The final area of Docker's industrial power was electrical engineering, where he believed previous British efforts were 'directed to strangling a key industry'. Manufacturers betrayed 'Victorian ideas and narrow outlook', resting content with output of small wares. 'Our legislators and municipal rulers by their narrow and jealous attitude have prevented any large distribution scheme by which current could be supplied to a consumer at a price that would be useful to him and be a real incentive to the saving of coal', he wrote in 1919. 'Our universities and technical schools have failed to discover and train a proper supply of first class electrical brains that could be pressed into the service of industry and make competition with foreign manufacturers possible…financial houses have been backward, for they have failed to use their power of bringing together sporadic manufacturers and co-ordinating them into an organised industry.' This he contrasted bitterly with Germany where manufacturers devised combinations and working agreements backed by 'a strong financial group which supplied the sinews for war and largely controlled policy'.[95] Behind the scenes Docker was active in resisting these tendencies. After 1904 he was concerned with Flett in the United Electric Car Company, on whose board Chandler and Ludford Docker also sat; but only opaque references survive to his role in pre-war electro-technology. An elliptical remark in Holden's diary for November 1913 reads, 'I saw Mr Dudley Docker with regard to the German Electrical Syndicate, but I told him I would prefer to keep out of it.'[96] Other entries in 1912 refer to meetings with Docker, Hirst and a man called Hampsphon; and an electrical engineer spoke in 1916 of Docker's pre-war 'coquetting' with the Germans.[97] One surmise is that Docker, in 1912–13, was working towards treaties with the German electrical giants, Siemens and AEG; another possibility is that he was involved in the scheme of the pro-German Belgian electrical utilities trust,

Sofina, in which he was a shareholder, to buy the chief tramway and lighting companies in India: a plan which collapsed after the invasion of Belgium in 1914.[98] It is also known that in January 1916 Docker declined an invitation from Rathenau of AEG to 'a Conference at Amsterdam to renew their business co-operation stopped by the war',[99] but once again the details are lost. The only certainty is that Docker's experience of the stunted growth of British electrical engineering fortified his political activities before 1914: to these we turn in the next chapter.

4

Business Leagues and Business Newspapers 1905–14

Dudley Docker would have been affronted to be called a political man, and yet he was a man of intense political feelings. To some he appeared a black reactionary anti-parliamentarian and to others he resembled a guild socialist. The truth is that he had the politics of a true plutocrat. Docker, like the Texan oilman Hugh Roy Cullen in one description, 'opposed government regulation that in any way might conceivably sandpaper business profits but he joyfully favoured any sort of government regulation, interference, intrusion, intervention, support or action if it was price-raising or promised to be directly profitable to business'. He thus evinced 'the actual principle governing the [plutocrat], who is at bottom an unconscious anarchist, hostile to all government not his personal instrument'.[1] This chapter examines the workings of Docker's unconscious political anarchism, and shows him as a foremost example of the attitudes and lobbying of the big manufacturers of the Edwardian Midlands. In doing so, sidelights are shown of Lord Milner's non-commissioned men in action fighting for what H. G. Wells called 'Prussian Toryism'. The activities of Milner's trusted lieutenants have often been described: Amery, Sir William Ashley, J. L. Garvin, W. A. S. Hewins, Leo Maxse, Sir Halford Mackinder or G. E. Morrison left ample records of their struggles for Imperial Defence, Imperial Tariffs, Imperial Federation and Imperial Efficiency. Little, however, has been written of the financiers and manufacturers who comprised the mass of Milnerites, providing the movement with some of its greatest opportunities for executive influence during the Great War. Docker led the industrial Milnerites in the Midlands: and the following chapters examine his attempts to achieve the political corporatism and national re-organisation that Milner desired.

Despite – or because of – the High Toryism of his father and father-in-law, Docker's Conservatism was never orthodox, nor directed to orthodox ends. He considered that 'he had never absolutely belonged' to what he

55

called 'the old Tory party', and hoped for 'more enlightened and progressive' policies from the new Unionism.[2] Balfour's leadership was not to his taste. Balfour's aphorism that 'Nothing matters very much, and little matters at all' was the antithesis of Docker's beliefs; and by Docker's first criterion for judging his fellow men, their success in their own business affairs, Balfour performed lamentably (he lost over £250,000 of his family's fortune by fatuous investments in bankrupt companies to promote powdered peat as a commercial fuel). In the aftermath of the Liberal victory in the general election of 1906, Docker fulminated 'Isn't it quite time the Unionist Party woke up – my view is that their present condition is lamentable.'[3] Docker's home at Kenilworth was in the Rugby constituency, and although in 1906 he lent one or two Daimler motor-cars to the campaign of the Unionist candidate, Arthur Steel-Maitland,[4] he declined Steel-Maitland's invitation to join the Executive Committee of the Rugby Conservative Association. He wrote in April 1906:

> I cannot make up my mind to be a Conservative, as I think they wld wish, in fact I am seriously thinking of an association with Labour – it appeals to me, and I think in my case it is natural. I am sure it is wrong to leave them (i.e. Labour gentlemen) alone as they are – they can't do without capital – we can't do without them – unless we go abroad – Why be a Conservative?[5]

This opinion that it was more natural for a big manufacturer to join the modern, materialistic Labour movement, and that the Labour leaders could be tamed by big capitalists, was also reflected in the private views of Birmingham Milnerites such as Amery and Steel-Maitland.[6]

Protection was at the heart of Docker's politics. At the time of the merger in 1902, *The Economist* commented that although it was 'all very well to invoke the bogey of foreign competition', judging by the rolling-stock companies' results, they had not hitherto suffered it severely.[7] Whatever the truth of that opinion for the period before 1902, as we have seen, it had no application to the next decade, and Docker, as an aggressive man who thrived on fighting external enemies, became an outright and enthusiastic tariff reformer. His co-director George Flett was a member of the Tariff Commission, the body set up at Chamberlain's request in 1903, by Professor Hewins of the London School of Economics, Sir Vincent Caillard of Vickers and other protectionists. The Tariff Commission called a multitude of witnesses from business and agriculture, circularised a detailed census of production, and in the light of these, issued a series of reports supporting Chamberlain's fiscal plans. MCWF was involved in all this. Flett put Docker in contact with Hewins in 1904, and in the following year, after Docker had donated £250 to the Commission, he was invited to Hewins' house in Worcestershire to inspect the voluminous data on British industry which was assembled there.[8] John Cay, MCWF's director in charge of Patent Shaft's iron and steel department, testified to the Tariff Commission in November 1904, and a year later, he returned with William Shackleford, the managing director responsible for rolling-stock construction.

Before examining their evidence to the Commission in detail, some general comments should be made. The Birmingham area had been the first in Britain to be widely affected by the rise of German industrial might. In 1885 the Royal Commission on the Depression in Trade and Industry had identified German competition as the cause of decline in several Midlands trades. This process accelerated, and whereas the average annual value of German exports in 1880–4 was 65 per cent of that for British exports, by 1899 the figure had risen to 78 per cent, and Midlands industrialists (such as J. P. Lacy in his speech to Patent Shaft's shareholders before their merger in 1902) bewailed the dumping of foreign surpluses in Britain which undercut domestic production.[9] In certain circumstances it made sense for producers of any nationality to off-load their productive surpluses abroad. Manufacturers, especially those whose domestic markets were protected by duties, could collaborate in marketing their products at home at high prices which defrayed the cost of cheap exports. So long as the home prices covered the prime costs of production such as labour, materials and fuel, the returns from exports would reduce such fixed charges as depreciation or interest on loans. This, of course, enhanced profitability, and where the factories were working at full output, the prime costs of production decreased the more that output increased. It would therefore be well worth manufacturing more than the domestic market would absorb, and 'dumping' the surplus abroad. One illustration on which the Tariff Commission delightedly pounced was where the labour-cost in converting pig-iron into steel rose from 14s 6d per ton to 17s 3d when output diminished by 25 per cent from full capacity; fuel, in the same instance, rose from 6s to 8s per ton. To British, and indeed American, industrialists dumping was regarded as a German menace. A related German export practice, which was feared and resented, was the payment by primary producers of bounties upon finished export goods made from their own high-priced half-finished goods. The cheap 'through-rates' which German shipping companies were compelled under government pressure to adopt for goods *en route* abroad, were also regarded as 'unfair' by British business.

There were also incontrovertible examples of Germany trying to abort nascent branches of the English electrical industry (such as Osram light bulbs or dynamos) by dumping before 1914. Indeed, in no area was Docker's insecurity and anxiety about Britain's industrial power more justified than in electrical engineering. It is barely exaggeration to say that British electrical markets were colonised by German and American interests for much of the quarter century before 1914. To men like Docker, Caillard, Flett, Hirst or Manville, with interests in the British electrical industry, this foreign suzerainty was intolerable because they had to submit to harsh terms or outright depredation. Among Docker's circle, the policies of the German big banks and electrical trusts produced both Germanophobia and admiration, and the achievements of the German electrical giants, Siemens-Schuckert and AEG were crucial to the development of their thinking. The strong finance power and the intimate co-operation in export business which the latter received from the German banks became an obsession with Docker, and led to his launching in 1916–18 of the British Trade Corporation and the Metropolitan-Vickers Electrical Company. Docker was unmindful, or perhaps unaware, of the losses which some bankers sustained by their aggressive support for German electrical engineering exports, and before 1914 praised the financial policies which had given Siemens-Schuckert and AEG their commanding position in world business. It also seemed important in Docker's judgement that both Germans and Americans had the benefit of a protected home market in this most capital-intensive business.

Joseph Chamberlain's espousal of tariff reform led to violent political controversy, but Docker deplored these party fights, and in 1904 wanted the subject to be examined in more detached fashion by a Royal Commission.[10] His initial desire was for immediate and practical defences to be erected against foreign dumping, especially in steel and electro-technology. In practice his wishes would have been met by the introduction in Britain of a measure resembling section 6 of the Canadian Customs Tariff Act of 1907. This instituted a duty of up to 15 per cent, which was imposed on individual items by comparing the market price in the country of origin with the market price at which it was dumped in Canada. The minority recommendations by Docker's dissident acquaintances on the Balfour of Burleigh committee (of 1916–17) on Commercial and Industrial Policy, such as Lord Faringdon and Sir Gerald Muntz, were based on the Canadian example, which would have appeased all but the most die-hard protectionists.[11]

Docker's managers, Shackleford and Cay, in their evidence to the Tariff Commission in 1904–5, described how foreigners with 'the monopoly of their home trade...for the sake of keeping their concerns in good swing will rush in and take a contract at a very unremunerative price'. Foreign competitors also reaped the benefits of stable domestic markets, which enabled them to use their productive power in an even and efficient fashion. Whereas MCWF's business was 'very fluctuating; sometimes... very busy and at other times very slack', continental rolling-stock makers 'know almost exactly what they are going to get in their own country during the year...the orders are practically apportioned...and they know what they have to depend on at good prices'. Docker's wish for Britain's Colonies to exercise an unwritten favoured-nation policy originated from this point. Krupps, for example, had the 'best of trade' in tyres, axles and wheels in Australia, India and other dependencies, although it was Cay's opinion that the British Colonies were 'so much more successful than German Colonies or French Colonies' precisely because 'our Colonies are able to buy in the cheapest markets and so progress'. (Krupps dumped in India some 15 to 25 per cent beneath the British price.)

Personally, Cay was agnostic about the benefits of protection. He suspected that a duty sufficient to keep out foreign material would at once raise wages and hence the price of materials, and would also drive Germans and Americans to invade other British markets such as South America, where MCWF did much business. Neither Shackleford nor Cay pretended that MCWF's problems were entirely fiscal. The rolling-stock sector, and Patent Shaft too, were adversely affected by the increasing tendency of railway companies to manufacture their own components: Cay particularised the North-Western Railway's carriage-works at Wolverton, and their Crewe depot which made rails, tyres and axles. This was not their only criticism of the railway companies. Like many British manufacturers, they complained that freight rates were fixed irrationally, and that the railway companies had shut down a valuable and necessary canal network. Shackleford and Cay identified other important British divergences. The wage rates in their Belgian and German competitors' factories were 30 to 50 per cent lower than in Britain, where the daily wage rate was about 6s; although they believed that foreign workers were only 70 per cent as productive as British. According to Cay, most German and many Belgian steelworks 'were much more modern' with 'everything of the most recent invention', whereas most British works were 'antiquated', with 'only those who have amalgamated and got fresh capital' undertaking modernisation. Moreover, Shackleford and Cay denied that any benefits could derive from having workmen with technical education.[12] In short, neither Shackleford nor Cay were whole-hoggers when it came to protection. They explicitly identified as causes of Britain's relative loss of markets the changing structure of MCWF's home market, the expense of railway transport, labour costs and the technical backwardness of plant. In Cay's mind, too, there was a real fear of retaliation if Britain introduced protective tariffs. Nevertheless, the burden of their evidence showed that in the short-run, MCWF suffered from foreign dumping. For a business in which 'Trade is not good all round at one time', the lack of a stable and protected home market, whose supply could be planned in advance, was deleterious.

The testimony of Shackleford and Cay has been described at such length to demonstrate that there were solid reasons for Docker to believe his companies were adversely affected by free trade, both because it affected what he called 'the margin of profit and anxiety on the score of dependable output',[13] and because other manufacturing nations profited by it. But his combative character was also attracted by the aggressive nature of tariffs. He described them as giving 'a power to bargain', by which he meant a power to coerce Germans and Americans in trade wars. Books such as Ernest Williams' *Made in Germany* (1896) represented his view that British manufacturers were endangered by a rout in international markets and that commercial rivalries should be seen in political or military terms. The £2½ million spent by Krupp on armaments extensions in 1908 were soon well known in engineering circles, and the celebrated warnings of Krupp's capacity in 1906–9 by H. H. Mulliner of Coventry Ordnance would certainly have confirmed Docker in his view that an Anglo-German confrontation was inevitable. Statistics also supported his apprehensions that British growth and rate of profit on capital was declining. There was no reason, if war had not supervened, why German exports should not have exceeded British by the end of the decade, for already by 1913, when Britain exported 14 per cent of world goods, Germany exported 13 per cent. Moreover the nature of German exports was transformed. In the early 1890s, sugar beet and woollen goods were the major produce sent abroad, but by 1913 the leading export sectors were chemicals (worth £52m), machinery (£34m), and ironware (£32.5m). Germany also seemed to be winning the race for the greatest productive capacity in key industries: for example, in steel production, in which MCWF had factories, German capacity rose by a factor of 46 from 300,000 to 14 million tons in 1870–1914, while British steel production rose by a factor of only 9 from 700,000 tons in 1870 to 6½ million tons in 1914.

Such tendencies seemed extremely menacing to Docker, who was convinced that any distinction between Anglo-German commercial and political rivalry was false. This rivalry created tragic misunderstanding and great bitterness. Thus Albert Ballin, head of the great Hamburg-Amerika shipping line, who was execrated by British protectionists accustomed to the Union Jack dominating Atlantic passenger and freight traffic, wrote to Kaiser Wilhelm after visiting England in 1910, 'Tariff Reform and a

Zollverein with the colonies are the catchwords on everybody's lips, and the anti-German feeling is so strong that it is scarcely possible to discuss matters with one's oldest friends, because the people over here have turned mad and talk of nothing but the next war and the protectionist policy of the future.'[14] Docker was one of those business men who, in Ballin's coinage, 'turned mad' and created an atmosphere in which war, caused by European political breakdown, became a seductively familiar prospect.

It remains to scrutinise Docker's political activities in detail. Within a few months of Steel-Maitland's defeat as Unionist candidate at Rugby in 1906, Docker urged him to seek adoption in the East Birmingham constituency where MCWF's Saltley factory lay.[15] Docker thought the inefficiency of the Conservative Association there was 'shocking',[16] but when in 1907 he tried to meet the Association's chairman about constituency organisation, the latter in offensive terms refused to meet him.[17] The chairman, Norris Foster, an undistinguished barrister on the Midland circuit, seems to have feared that his control of the Association would be impaired if a big hustling local employer like Docker became involved. Docker did not forgive the insult. Some time later, when Steel-Maitland was indeed adopted at East Birmingham, he was aghast to find that Docker intended to sponsor an independent candidate. He recorded in 1909 that Docker and some of his co-directors 'considered the behaviour of the party had been such in Birmingham that it needed a lesson'. Docker told him that 'the whole of the Conservative officials in Birmingham were such a poor lot', and the Liberal Unionists only 'a trifle better'. He thought that Foster 'might have been ordinarily civil...he wanted to hit back and was thinking of running a labour man...he wanted as a representative someone who could do [MCWF's] business for them [in political circles], instead of having, as at present, to go to members on the other side sometimes'.[18] Austen Chamberlain and Docker's friend, Edward Goulding, one of the most influential Unionist backbenchers, were equally critical of the effectiveness of several lazy old Unionist MPs for Birmingham seats who fancied themselves 'the actual hubs of the Empire' and refused to retire;[19] and Docker was exasperated that members for industrial constituencies did not more energetically represent the interests of the big factories in their area. Walker, another MCWF director, reportedly said that the company 'wanted a man who could get government orders for the firm and "would make himself unpleasant to the leaders of his own party" unless this were done', and approached a local man J. J. Stephenson, promising 'him all the support they could secretly give, on the understanding that he would come out as a Labour man and...as a Tariff Reformer, that they would do this privately, and that they were going to do all they could to wreck the

Ill. 2 Sir Arthur Steel-Maitland (1876–1935)

Conservative party'.[20] Stephenson was an official of the Amalgamated Society of Engineers, a member of the Labour party's national executive and chaired the party at its Belfast conference in 1907. He was adopted as Labour candidate at East Birmingham ('the weakest corner of the phalanx of Birmingham Unionism') in January 1909,[21] but seems to have been forsaken later in the year by Docker, whose colleagues helped

Steel-Maitland to a handsome victory in the general election of January 1910.

Nevertheless, Docker's encouragement of Stephenson during 1909 proved his sincerity in telling Steel-Maitland in 1906 that an association with Labour appealed to him as 'natural', and presaged his help of other Labour men in Birmingham in the general election of 1918. Regardless of party or principles, he wanted to cultivate the political support and personal obligations of politicians so as to secure his business operations. 'If the word "subversive" refers to efforts to make fundamental changes in a social system, the business leaders are the most subversive influence in the United States', so one American observer wrote.

> The primary loyalty of the businessman has been to profits, and he has willingly sacrificed the general and abstract principles of free competition and free enterprise in circumstances which promised a pecuniary advantage...the interests of businessmen have changed, to a considerable extent, from efficiency in production to efficiency in public manipulation of the government for the attainment of preferential advantages.[22]

Docker's subsequent career often proved the truth of this observation.

It was not until 1914, when Steel-Maitland had completed his re-organisation of the East Birmingham Conservative Association, that Docker was formally reconciled with the constituency party;[23] but he then became a vice-president of the Association, and by 1916, he was the only 'considerable subscriber' supporting Steel-Maitland's organisation.[24] Steel-Maitland never compromised his independence in the manner which Docker and Walker had expected of Stephenson, but he was at pains to gratify the largest employer in his constituency, and was always a diligent adviser to MCWF in their dealings with Whitehall and Westminster. Indeed, in the spring of 1915, Docker arranged for Steel-Maitland to become a director of the company, with a hint that the chairmanship might revert to him after Docker's retirement; but on the eve of Steel-Maitland's board election on 25 May, he was offered the job of Under Secretary of the Colonies in the new coalition government and withdrew his acceptance *ad interim*. He remained keen to collaborate in business with Docker, and only accepted the official post with reluctance.[25] As late as 1919–20, when MCWF had merged with Vickers, he still hoped to become a director of the combine.[26]

Docker had even greater parliamentary influence at Wednesbury, where Patent Shaft was based. He was the biggest employer in the town, the most generous subscriber to its charities, and as he wrote in 1920, had 'practically run the place'.[27] In 1908 he declined the Conservative parliamentary candidature at Wednesbury (at a time when his name was

Ill. 3 Sir John Norton-Griffiths (1871–1930)

also being rumoured at East Birmingham), presumably feeling that his work in industry was more powerful and important than anything he might achieve in Parliament.[28] As his newspaper lamented in an editorial of 1914, 'The businessman who enters the House of Commons makes a sacrifice, while the lawyer who enters the House of Commons gains.'[29] In Docker's place, a young imperialist named George (later Lord) Lloyd (of the banking and iron family) was adopted officially, but he abruptly resigned as candidate; and early in 1909, Docker (who had succeeded Lord Dartmouth as president of the Wednesbury Conservatives) secured the adoption of John ('Empire Jack') Norton-Griffiths, a man with a bad financial record with whom he had collaborated in railway and public contracting in southern Africa and South America.[30] Docker's approach to Norton-Griffiths had an arcane motive to it. The sitting Liberal member for Wednesbury, Clarendon Hyde, was a partner of Sir Weetman Pearson in the great firm of public contractors, S. Pearson and Sons; and Norton-Griffiths was Pearson's keenest British competitor, who was obsessed with staying even with Pearson. (Characteristically, when Norton-Griffiths wrote to Stanley Baldwin in 1929, asking for 'fair play' in receiving a peerage like Weetman Pearson, he explained 'it is not so much a personal matter as it is one of pique.')[31] The first speaker invited by Norton-Griffiths to the constituency was Laming Worthington-Evans, the Unionist candidate at Colchester, where the sitting Liberal MP was none other than Sir Weetman Pearson; and there can be no doubt that the contest between Hyde and Norton-Griffiths was not only a trial of rival fiscal doctrines (Hyde's free trade against Norton-Griffiths' protectionism), or of Liberal against Conservative, but also a contest between deadly business competitors.

Docker and Lincoln Chandler were Norton-Griffiths' backers from the outset, and were the strongest speakers at his public meetings during the election campaign in December 1909 and January 1910.[32] Chandler, indeed, was effectively the campaign manager (although he had voted Liberal in 1906, was the grandson of a Chartist and had been named after the American President who liberated southern slaves), and his populist approach, with its torchlight processions, raised the pitch of excitement. Chandler and other Unionist speakers emphasised the number of contracts which Norton-Griffiths had placed with Patent Shaft in the past, and hinted that more work would arrive in the future if he was elected. This feature of the campaign, coupled with the theme of imperial pride, corresponded with J. A. Hobson's observation in 1902 that 'local specialisation of industries places a formidable weapon in the hands of the protectionist politician', and that 'Panem et circenses interpreted into English means cheap booze and Mafficking.'[33] Docker's costs at Wednesbury and East Birmingham may be surmised from the fact that Sir Francis Newdigate-Newdegate, the Warwickshire colliery owner, spent over £5,000 running himself and Sir Henry Maddocks as the parliamentary candidates at Tamworth and Nuneaton in January 1910.[34] In Wednesbury, at any event, Norton-Griffiths polled 6,636 votes (beating Hyde by 596 votes) and was returned to Westminster. There he was identified with imperial causes and trade policy (notably the institution of a Ministry of Commerce); but his parliamentary status is indicated by the description in 1917, by Sir Maurice Hankey, the Secretary of the Cabinet, of 'a small group of ultra-Imperials, of which Norton-Griffiths MP, a clever man in a technical sense but stupid, unpractical and visionary in his ideas, appears to be the centre'. Other ultra-imperials, according to Hankey, included Laming Worthington-Evans (Norton-Griffiths' ally in the general elections of 1910), Patrick Hannon (a Conservative populist who was Secretary of the Navy League), General G. K. Cockerill (then Director of Special Intelligence at the War Office), Leo Amery, 'and a number of minor MPs. Nearly all of this group are insufferable bores. Their aim is Imperial Federation, but their ideas are woolly to the last degree. They wine and dine at intervals. I do not think they exercise any serious influence.'[35] One of Norton-Griffiths' main efforts to gain influence was made in 1911, during the Imperial Conference in London (in which Docker also took a close interest).[36] He rented a house in Berkshire at which he lavishly entertained politicians from the Dominions and Colonies, both to further his business connections and to propagandise about Imperial Federation. His work necessitated long absences abroad, which limited his parliamentary impact, and led to neglect of constituency interests; and in 1914, he announced that he would not seek re-election, probably because his business went into liquidation at this time with heavy losses to everyone except himself.

Docker was involved in the selection of a new Conservative candidate, a tinned-meat manufacturer named Maconochie, a Tariff Commissioner since 1904 who had fulfilled his food contracts with the Army during the Boer War somewhat unsatisfactorily. In typical populist technique, he was dubbed 'Fighting Mac' as quickly as Norton-Griffiths had been nicknamed 'Empire Jack';[37] but because of the outbreak of war, and the postponement of the general election, he did not contest the seat until December 1918. He was then roundly defeated by the Labour man, and Docker was so angry about the apathy and bad organisation of the Wednesbury Conservatives that he resigned as their president. Although he was secretly responsible for the Conservative candidature at Wednesbury in 1923 of Herbert Williams, secretary of the Machine Tool Trades Association, he ostentatiously refrained from any public aid to Wednesbury Conservatives until the end of his life.[38] In addition to his activities in East Birmingham and Wednesbury, he was active in other Midland constituencies. He raised big subscriptions in the Coventry area for the Unionists: at Nuneaton, Newdigate-Newdegate could not afford to continue running Maddocks as the Conservative candidate, and Docker was the intermediary in finding a new candidate who would be supported by industrialists' subscriptions. In 1911, Albert Eadie of BSA was apparently settled as the next candidate, but when this arrangement failed, J. R. Greg of MCWF was adopted instead in 1912.[39]

Along with these orthodox forms of political organisation, Docker's hostility to the 'amateurism' of Whitehall and Westminster also led him to launch an extra-parliamentary pressure-group aimed against the conventional order. He harnessed the enthusiasm raised by Norton-Griffiths' campaign to launch, in February 1910, the Business League of Wednesbury. Drawing its members from 'both masters and men', its objects were listed as 'a Business Government with business men' in the Cabinet, particularly at the Exchequer and Board of Trade; 'a Minister of Commerce who would be independent of Government changes'; 'The entire re-arrangement of our Diplomatic and Consular Service'; an Imperial Conference to implement imperial preference tariffs; tied loans; and counter-tariffs against competitors.[40]

Most of these aims reflected Docker's conviction that only business men were useful in the quest for national efficiency, or continued his campaigns for fiscal and tied loan reform. But in singling the consular and diplomatic services for re-organisation, Docker was responding to a widespread, indeed international, complaint by business men that the consuls and diplomats of the various exporting nations were unhelpful or ignorant in trade matters. In the British case, though many individual cases could be cited of snobbish, lazy or unbusinesslike members of the foreign service spoiling chances of foreign business, the manufacturers' complaints should not be accepted *prima facie*. All too often, the representatives sent abroad by British firms were themselves snobbish, lazy, chauvinist or unbusinesslike, careless of the language and customs of the countries they visited and ready to cheat both their foreign customers and their British principals. Quite as many orders were won by diplomats despite bad handling by local representatives as were lost by diplomats during negotiations in which the business representatives had proved adept. The generally lamentable quality – morally, emotionally and mentally – of the men sent abroad by British manufacturers in 1880–1939 is very striking, and would be a profitable subject for further study. One frequent complaint was that the consular reports on local trade conditions which were published in Britain were too obscure and diffuse to be useful to business men. This was an absurd and unjust criticism, which only demonstrated the low calibre and initiative of the exporters. One example of their inferiority occurred around 1913 when the British Commercial Attaché in Berlin organised a large conference in London of furniture manufacturers and urged on them the immense opportunity awaiting in Germany where a craze for imitation English antiques was sweeping bourgeois circles. He provided them with details of splendid market possibilities, and besought them to write to him for further help and introductions. In the event, he received only one letter, addressed to the Commercial Ambassador, British Embassy, Berlin, France.[41] Such downright stupidity, of which another aspect was the practice of sending out foreign advertisements and quotations in British currency, weights and measures, was common. If the dual responsibility for exports shared between the Foreign Office and the more insular Board of Trade was inefficient, many of the criticisms of government trade facilities were self-exculpatory, or the product of uninformed and almost visceral antagonism by manufacturers towards any branch of the state.

These jeremiads were not unique to Britain. In the USA, the consular corps was staffed by political hacks appointed by successive administrations from the ranks of supporters too notorious for domestic berths. There was no continuity or experience, so that for example President Cleveland in 1893 replaced 164 of the USA's 218 consul-generals, consuls and commercial agents, and in 1897–8 McKinley superseded 238 out of 272 salaried consuls. These consular placemen had a well-earned reputation for laziness, incompetence and corruption, with only 20 per cent of US consuls submitting reports in 1898. The traditions of the system continued to hamper American exporters even after the Lodge Act of 1906 introduced the principle of meritocratic selection and promotion; and the fees levied by consuls were resented and sometimes extortionate. The relative merits of the US and British consular systems are indicated by the preference of British American Tobacco, 'a Company American in its enterprise and boldness', which was entitled to appeal to either consular body in China, but invariably turned to the British because they were more efficient and did not charge fees for consular work.[42] Though Docker might have been hard to convince, the British consular system was in every respect better adapted to exporters' needs than the American.

Another source of British exporting weakness lay with the calibre and quantity of British Chambers of Commerce abroad. There were few of them compared with France or Germany, and 'due very largely to the *laisser faire* spirit', so Victor Wellesley testified in 1916, 'there is always a strong feeling among British subjects abroad that by coming together they are merely introducing competition against themselves'. During his time as Commercial Attaché in Spain after 1908, Wellesley found that Chambers of Commerce were 'very often got together for the glorification perhaps of one or two individuals', and did no serious work. In other cases he 'noticed a very strong disposition on the part of influential members against the Commercial Attaché visiting them at all...interested parties did not wish the Commercial Attaché...to introduce competition in markets where they were already firmly established'.[43] This attitude remained common, even in the inter-war period. As the British consul in Lima lamented in 1929:

> The great British houses in Peru, the backbone of the trade, are described euphemistically as 'conservative'. Exports are their principal interest. Their general attitude was perhaps epitomised by one of their chiefs at a meeting at which all the leading houses were represented; a lone voice suggested that a local British Chamber of Commerce was needed, and he replied that it was *not* wanted, because it would 'only increase competition'; there was no sign of dissent...the only way to maintain our present position, let alone improve on it, is for many more British firms to send out travellers to examine local conditions on the spot...it is extraordinary that, apparently from conservatism, apathy, suspicion or fear, British firms should prefer to select some local agent, probably holding some 20-50 existing agencies, of which he is able to give proper attention to but few, rather than appoint a joint direct representative. Thus the Incas of old, formidable individually, but divided, were slaughtered by the Spanish invader.[44]

Docker's Business Leagues were a practical expression of a rhetoric that had been swelling in Britain since the Black Week of the Boer War in December 1899. The bungling amateurism of Sir Redvers Buller – at its most devastating at Spion Kop in 1900 when two different officers each believed they had sole command of the attack – led to a national revulsion which was kept alive in the next six or seven years by the reports of successive committees and Royal Commissions on the South African débâcle. In the words of Kipling's poem 'The Lesson 1899–1902',

> Let us admit it fairly as a business people should,
> We have had no end of a lesson; it will do us no end of good...
> All the obese, unchallenged old things that stifle and overlie us –
> Have felt the effects of the lesson we got – an advantage no
> money could buy us...
> It was our fault, and our very great fault – and now we must
> turn it to use.
> We have forty million reasons for failure, but not a single
> excuse.

Until 1899–1901 this current of thought remained obscure in British life, voiced only by outsiders such as the South African politician John Merriman, who in 1884 had attacked 'the dawdling, the inefficiency and the delay which reigns supreme' in Whitehall and Westminster, instancing Joseph Chamberlain and Sir Charles Dilke as the only 'business men in the whole company'. 'Circumlocution here and red-tape there; constant delays; universal procrastination until the opportunity has passed..."Too late, too late, always too late"...because you don't put businessmen to do your business [but] appoint ministers who go out of town for six weeks at a time'. After 1900 such views were mainstream. Lord Rosebery in that year compared the state to 'a great joint-stock company with unlimited liability on the part of its shareholders...[which] depends on incessant vigilance, on method, on keeping abreast of the times'. A year later he advocated a Cabinet of business men headed by tycoons like Andrew Carnegie and Sir Thomas Lipton who would force state bureaucracy to reach the efficiency of private business. As late as 1910 Lloyd George speculated privately about forming a business men's government with men like Alfred Mond and Sir Christopher Furness, who 'carry enormous weight in the country'. (He added revealingly, 'They are very simple, these Captains of Industry. I can do what I like with them. I found that out at the Board of Trade.') This grossly simplified view of government – resurrected in the 1960s by Lord Robens with his call for a business government with the Prime Minister as managing director of 'Great Britain Limited' – remained mere minatory rhetoric until given tangible form by Docker at Wednesbury in 1910.[45]

From 1911 other branches of the Business League were opened in the Midlands, and Docker's speech launching the League at Bristol in November 1912 'was regarded by his friends as his greatest success in public'.[46] He and Chandler were the animating forces of the Business League, which was reputed to enjoy great, if discreet, local influence.[47] Docker's own description of the League betrayed something of his political simplicity; in 1911 he complained indignantly, 'There was not a single thing in connection with the League that any sound, sensible man could object to, or could call political. That was one of the things they had tried to avoid.' To Docker, the aims of the Business League were so obviously right, so essential to secure industrial growth and spread prosperity, that they were the antithesis of politics; he promised, 'if our League spreads, politics would be done for. This is my object...Politics often come between masters and men. Business – a common interest – can only bring us closer together.'[48] Clearly, he was enfolded in a comprehensive semantic failure – in which several thousand Midlands business men joined.

They joined him because, in an age of accelerating world industrial competition they could no longer tolerate the weakness of Britain's industrial elite, which in the nineteenth century had always been 'less wealthy either collectively or individually', as W. D. Rubinstein has shown, 'than the commercial elite and vastly less influential than the landowners'. As the mercantile and landowning interests grew 'associated ever more closely in politics and in social life' during 1886–1922, the grievance of manufacturers at their comparative powerlessness and neglect became increasingly bitter.[49] Industrialists particularly resented the indifference of London investment bankers and issuing houses to the lengthening British depression after 1873 and to the poor return on industrial capital. The City eschewed long-term finance for industry in favour of foreign loans, government issues and public utilities, while enjoying a privileged position in its relations with government which did not reflect the reality of British industrial structure. As clearing-house bankers were ineligible for directorships of the Bank of England, the London investment bankers held a self-perpetuating control over its Court, and hence over the money supply: this control made them almost invincible at a time when 'the economic weapons acceptable to the politicians were confined to monetary and fiscal techniques – just the matters in which the special competence of the City was thought to lie'. This influence which major financiers held over politicians in the late nineteenth century was enhanced by their cosmopolitanism, their lavish hospitality and by a personal elegance that many cultivated.[50] The Business League represented industry's attempt to readjust the balance of influence at a critical moment in British manu-facturing history.

The foundation of a Ministry of Commerce was often mooted by industrialists at this time, and denoted their widespread disillusion with the prevailing political culture. Docker wanted a Minister of Commerce, because, like other industrialists such as Hugo Hirst, he realised that protection in Britain would require a government body, such as a Ministry of Commerce, constantly comparing the conditions in Britain's various industries with those abroad, and adjusting tariff rates and commercial treaties accordingly.[51] A Ministry of Commerce was required to prepare the ground for tariff reform, just as Docker wanted a Federation of British Industries for the same reason in 1916. But Docker also wanted a Minister of Commerce, 'aided by a strong advisory board and independent of party changes and exigencies', because he considered, with some justification, that the Presidency of the Board of Trade and the Chancellorship of the Exchequer were jobs treated merely as 'political rewards for skill in Parliamentary debate' whose 'holders are seldom men who possess large views on national business policy'.[52] It was for this reason, Docker felt, that government policy on industrial matters was always indecisive, inconstant and unrealistic. Viewed purely from a business man's point of view, these criticisms were just, and the need for a Ministry of Commerce was over-powering; but Docker over-simplified the problem with his usual impatient extremism. He persuaded himself that a business man as minister, with few party links, possibly even without a parliamentary seat, was a realistic proposition and could make effective reforms; and his credulity highlights his utter miscomprehension of the political world, and his lack of democratic instincts. (He said in 1910, 'I can...imagine a community...doing itself remarkably well under a really able and powerful tyrant; only this I should insist upon – that he must be a first-rate businessman'.)[53] This view, because it was monolithic, had no concept of politics as a reconciliation of opposing views and interests. The metaphor of government as a business reflects Docker's mental confusion: whereas a business has one aim – to make money – a nation is so varied and divided in its aims as to be almost aimless. Docker's own industrial power relied on using nominee directors and 'warehoused' investments, and he never grasped that these were inefficient instruments of political power. His frustration in dealing with politicians finally hardened into outright hostility. This miscomprehension was mutual. It was not necessarily self-interested cant when industrialists of Docker's stature approached government about policies to expand markets at home or abroad: they were sincere apostles of growth, who equated material progress with trade supremacy. But often, they were defeated by the widespread official attitude that business men's lobbying on commercial matters was narrow and selfish; and these tensions increasingly alienated Docker from Britain's political and administrative leaders, or 'mandarindom' as it was dubbed by Leo Maxse in the *National Review*.[54]

Balfour's leadership of the Unionist party was another stimulus to Docker and the Business Leagues. The manufacturers with whom he associated found Balfour's manner and policies every bit as exasperating as Asquith's. 'Our party has no earthly [hope] with AJB', wrote Goulding in 1909, 'The country don't understand or believe him and they know that he is a loser and they are right.'[55] Men like Docker and Goulding feared that the Balfour or Cecilian brand of Unionism would never dislodge the Liberals, and sensed the distaste of Whittinghame and Hatfield for factory owners and their needs. They saw too that Balfour excelled in the elaborate parliamentary rites which they so hated, and in which enemies like Asquith and Haldane also revelled. The polysyllables, abstractions and smooth Oxford manners of these lawyers and amateur philosophers enraged Midlands manufacturers, for rather the same reasons that Milnerites who hated 'the wobbly rush and gush of upper class London' found it 'infinitely refreshing to escape from the shilly-shally quidnunc talk of clever people at Brooks's. Parliament or the West End to the indomitable ''put-it-through'' line of the City'.[56]

The self-regarding rituals of the ruling caste equally excited Docker's resentful impatience; in frustration and despair, he therefore formed an extra-parliamentary organisation to create conditions in which national decisions could be taken without worrying about the impenetrable arcana of Balfour and his sort. A counterpart to Docker's views can be found in Maxse's attacks on Balfour as 'The Champion Scuttler' and his 'BMG' campaign (Balfour Must Go) in the *National Review*.

Working-class participation in the Business Leagues was essential to Docker's purposes, and indeed was an established tradition of Midlands political organisation since the mid-nineteenth century. As he wrote to Asquith in 1912, 'manager, clerks and mechanics can meet on neutral ground' and discuss the whole of national business life. 'The level-headed, slow and sure man, who does not particularly appreciate possible Utopian blessings...will find a rallying point and refuge in such bodies, while the agitator will gain the stimulus of mutual respect and a tolerance of respective weaknesses may...be hoped for.'[57] Lincoln Chandler claimed that as high as 77 per cent of the League's membership was working class, so their potential in this respect was immense. Docker's speeches apparently influenced John Beard, leader of the Workers Union in the Birmingham area. 'Control of industry by the workers', Beard said in 1916, 'means that we must shoulder responsibility...by partnership...between Employers' Unions and Workmen's Unions', and he urged 'The one thing that the workers must aim at is to allow the machine to be used to its fullest capacity.' These were exactly Docker's sentiments, and those of many another Midlands manufacturer: Beard and Docker collaborated on munitions committees in 1915, and agreed on the need for higher production and corporatist social structures to unify the material interests of employers and employed. Though Docker may not have been so naive as to believe in the possibility of unanimity between employers and their workers, he found that his constant rhetorical emphasis on this point paid dividends. If G. D. H. Cole regarded collectivism as 'at best only the sordid dream of a business man with a conscience', it was a dream to which Beard succumbed.[58]

It was not coincidental that Docker, Steel-Maitland and Amery were all working from a Birmingham power-base in this direction. In the first place, they all agreed with Steel-Maitland's view that radical Toryism 'may be able to do something in Birmingham on lines that even Chatham would have approved of';[59] that it could become the centre of a radical-minded alliance of employers and employed committed to working for high production and greater, shared prosperity. Historically, too, the so-called Birmingham Alliances of the 1890s served as partial inspiration for Docker's concept of the Business Leagues as combinations of employers and workpeople. They had shown that the interests of employers and employed could be allied to mutual benefit in small-scale industries and created a tradition of collaboration in the Midlands which the Business Leagues followed.[60] Docker's idea of the Business Leagues acting as forms of industrial education of the workers was imitated by Steel-Maitland, who, after becoming chairman of the Unionist party organisation in 1911, launched a national network of clubs to recruit and train working-class men as Unionist political speakers. Another Birmingham MP, Amery, tried to develop the Trade Union Tariff Reform League into a 'Unionist Labour Party' after 1909, while a future Birmingham MP, Oliver Locker-Lampson, ran a Unionist Working Men's Candidates' Fighting Fund.[61] The idea was continued after the war by the British Commonwealth Union of which Docker was president and Patrick Hannon, another Birmingham MP, was director.

The Leagues rapidly attained political power within their own localities and made their aims explicit. It was known that they were ready to intervene in the municipal elections at Wednesbury in 1911 if the candidates appeared insufficiently business like;[62] the Leagues' motto was *Pro patria; imperium in imperio* (For our country; a Government within a Government); and Docker said he wanted an industrial party of some twenty to forty members in the House of Commons. He told a smoking concert of the Wednesbury Business League in April 1912 that 'the hard-headed businessman... was long chalks ahead' of left-wing agitators or professional politicians, and that as few as twenty such MPs 'who knew really what they wanted' could revolutionise the House of Commons.[63] Docker believed anyone who had made money had given ample proof of omniscience.

Elsewhere in the British Empire there were contemporary counterparts to Docker's business movement. In the two decades before the first world war, the frustration of Canadian business men at a series of political decisions taken in the interests of labour or other groups, led to vituperation of

> 'professional politicians' as a distinct and disreputable social class. Most of them were lawyers or doctors, what J. B. Maclean called 'the sediment of the learned professions', who went to Parliament because 'it is the best

paying job their mediocrity will allow them to obtain'. To preserve their comfortable incomes professional politicians became abject slaves of their political parties, the machines that existed solely to capture and divide the spoils of office...The antidote to the professional politician was the businessman in politics – the practical, honest, patriotic man who knew that the business of Canada was business and was also wealthy enough not to be influenced by mere pecuniary considerations. Everyone who meditated on business matters called for more business representation in politics. No one knew how to encourage a most reluctant business community to dirty its hands with the muck of electioneering.[64]

In 1912 two MCWF directors were adopted as Unionist candidates in Warwickshire constituencies, J. R. Greg in the Labour-held marginal seat of Nuneaton, and Ludford Docker in the Conservative stronghold of Stratford-on-Avon. In the latter case, there was originally an understanding that the sitting member would retire to make way for Ludford Docker, but this was constantly postponed. By the time that the general election of 1918 was called, Stratford had been abolished as a constituency, and Ludford Docker was consoled with the promise that he might have the candidature in the adjacent Warwick and Leamington division on the retirement of Sir Ernest Pollock. He nursed this constituency too, but when Pollock became a peer in 1923, Anthony Eden was adopted instead. Ludford Docker took this disappointment with characteristic generosity.[65] Another of Docker's closest industrial colleagues, Sir Hallewell Rogers of BSA, who was adopted for a Birmingham constituency, was described as 'one of the first business candidates for Parliament',[66] and his parliamentary ambitions probably originated with the Business League agitation. The same applies to the candidature of Edward Manville, a friend of Docker and sympathiser of the League, who was adopted by the Coventry Unionists at a time when Docker was leading their fund-raising.[67]

These businessmen parliamentary candidates were intended by Docker to obviate a parliamentary evil which he particularly loathed: the rejection or talking out of private bills, especially those sponsored by railway companies, 'which are refused a hearing by the House of Commons for petty political reasons'. Schemes which had been rejected at second reading, without reaching committee stage, included those of the Great Northern Railway of Ireland (1906), the Great Eastern Railway Bill (1912), and five more railway bills in 1913–14. Labour MPs blocked all railway bills in 1909 in a campaign for higher wages, and the Midland Railway Bill of 1910 was almost wrecked on outside issues. The partisan obstruction of railway bills delayed orders for a rolling-stock manufacturer like Docker, and convinced him of the need for counter-attack.[68]

Docker's position as head of the Business League movement had national recognition. In 1912, for example, he was asked by Sir Algernon Firth, president of the Association of British Chambers of Commerce, to be part of the delegation which was analysing the labour unrest of 1911–12 with Asquith and a sub-committee of the Cabinet. Firth wanted Docker to tell the politicians about the importance of 'personal atmosphere' in industrial relations, but Docker was unable to attend, and instead sent a long memorandum, which was submitted to Asquith. His analysis is worth quoting:

> Today a factory cannot continue to exist without the greatest refinement of organisation. It would be humanly impossible to carry on without highly complex rules and regulations, piecework and other systems; and these...reduce the individual worker to...a mere cog in the wheel. Agitators and other impracticable people regard this as a diabolical contrivance of capitalists. As a matter of fact, complicated organisation is a sheer necessity, and it is the abuse, and not the use of it, that constitutes the evil...the devolution of responsibility and authority in factories where large numbers of men are employed has...almost entire[ly] eliminat[ed]...the human element...between...artisans and the heads of the concerns.

It was this development of large-scale enterprise that caused strikes, he felt: 'it is obvious to any practical person that the men do not act on intellectual impulse, and that the doctrines they parade are mainly catchwords'. With the exception of a minority of socialist theorists and 'the type of labour agitator who is a mere iconoclast', he felt that working-class militancy was 'essentially a reaction against...individual remoteness from the employer, of impotence in the highly organised life of which, as individuals, they form so small a part, and the uncertainty of the future which the trade cycle has bred'. His recommendations followed logically from this view. 'It will have to be recognised as an elementary business proposition that industrial success is impossible unless the employer studies and trains the sentiments of his workpeople with the same efficiency that he equips his...machinery', he wrote. 'Departmental managers must add to their technical ability a greater degree of tact and social qualification than is at present generally recognised as necessary.' He specified that managing directors 'too frequently' instructed their departmental heads to reduce costs, only to find later that the saving of a few hundred pounds had been made by methods which disrupted the whole works and were a false economy. It was not enough, though, for departmental managers to become more accessible. 'I doubt if any man who is on nodding terms with his Managing Director ever becomes a willing striker', he wrote, and urged managing directors 'to move freely about the Works, without being shadowed by the foremen'.[69]

Docker believed that educational reform was a crucial part of national reconstruction. In the mid-Edwardian period he had sat with manufacturers like Edward Hickman and Neville Chamberlain on the Advisory Board of the Faculty of Commerce at Birmingham University. Headed by the imperialist Professor W. J. Ashley, the Commerce Faculty tried to provide an astringent commercial training on the scientific German model: but its impact was limited by Ashley's policy of accepting only students from established business families. Indeed it was significant of attitudes to business education that about half of the students on Ashley's courses, during Docker's association, were Japanese. Docker was impatient of petty or piecemeal educational modernisation. 'Money must be spent freely to remodel our organisation and to make it serve the needs of industry', he wrote in 1918, 'The curriculum must be revised – the school-leaving age advanced – and last, but not least, the calibre and quality of the teachers improved, and greater emoluments and prospects offered to them.' He deprecated the tendency of brighter pupils to enter the professions rather than industry:

> The establishment of an Appointments Board at every university, similar to that existing at Cambridge, which would be responsible for retaining a complete record of the students passing through their hands, and personal comments on their general capabilities, would obviate this difficulty. A central clearing-house would be essential to which manufacturers could apply; this would be kept supplied by the Appointments Boards, with lists indicating the training and suitability of persons to various posts.[70]

Docker's admiration for the Cambridge Appointments Board was such that he had its head, H. A. Roberts, together with Sir William Pope, professor of chemistry there, to stay with him on holiday at Lake Vyrnwy in 1917; and he consented in 1919 to become one of the four external members elected to the first-ever Board of Engineering Studies at Cambridge University. In the following year, a building syndicate for a new engineering school at Cambridge was formed, and in the early 1920s Docker and Lord Esher were the most influential members of its Appeals Committee. The two men were temperamentally similar, and must have made a formidable partnership: the machiavellian fixer of British defence policy might have been speaking for Docker when he wrote in 1915, 'I am not going to put myself out. I never do. Nor am I going to "regularise" my position, which means that someone gives me orders – I never do.'[71]

Docker had a strong belief in the power of the local press. The *Midland Advertiser*, a Wednesbury-based newspaper, was replete with references to him during 1908–14. His speeches and activities were chronicled in such detail, and the editorial comment about him was always so laudatory, that one can only conclude that he had a financial interest in the newspaper. He put time and effort into cultivating his power in Wednesbury, and it is unlikely that he resisted consolidating his position by controlling the local press. His methods of achieving press influence are shown in a memorandum of 1909 by Steel-Maitland in which is recorded a story which had been blurted out by Morton, editor of the *Birmingham Gazette*, when drunk. Morton said that his newspaper had backed the parliamentary candidature of a Liberal called Brampton at Docker's behest, 'because Docker was proposing at the time to put £10,000 into the *Gazette*'. Although Morton does not seem to have been a reliable accomplice himself, he reportedly 'would not trust [Docker] as far as he could see him'.[72] Though Docker apparently never made this promised investment, he maintained his interest in the newspaper's future. He obtained an accountant's report on it in 1910,[73] and in 1911 was involved in attempts to guarantee the *Gazette* as a viable Unionist newspaper. These attempts were led by Lord Willoughby de Broke and by Lord Norton, and at one stage a company seems to have been formed, with shareholders including Dudley Docker, Norton-Griffiths, George Lloyd, Steel-Maitland, Newdigate-Newdegate, and Lords Dartmouth, Plymouth, Calthorpe and Willoughby de Broke. By this stage, Docker's interest in Midlands press power was such that he was a life member of the Birmingham Press Club, but after prolonged attempts to rescue the *Gazette*, he reluctantly concluded in June 1912 that it was impossible to run the newspaper.[74]

Docker did not only rely on local newspapers giving coverage to the campaigns for 'business policy' which he was running. He became himself an occasional contributor to the national press, writing an article entitled 'The Labour Unrest: The Businessman's View' for the *Daily Mail* in 1912. This article was part of a series of specially commissioned articles on the industrial situation, with other contributors of the celebrity of H. G. Wells. He first called for 'closer and more intimate personal relations and inter-change of ideas between men and masters', so that in time 'a tribunal of employers and men' could be established to settle questions that arose. But the main thrust of his article was that 'The policy of coddle can never be of permanent use, and great economic and business questions can never be settled by Act of Parliament.' He deplored the various legislative reforms of labour law, during 1906–12, as 'dangerous and mischievous innovations which merely exasperate the workers and increase the discontent by reason of their comparative ineffectiveness'; their worst evil was 'to make the workmen look outside themselves to a Government to play providence for them, which no Government can do if permanent amelioration is...looked for'. On all counts, he believed, 'the less Government interference we have', the better.[75] Docker also contributed to Midlands newspapers with which he had influence, and for example, in 1914, in the *Birmingham Gazette*, called on the City Corporation to increase the salaries of senior staff. 'Birmingham requires officers of superlative merit to serve it', he urged, 'It is only business, after all, to pay proper salaries to competent men.'[76]

In June 1911, Steel-Maitland was appointed chairman of the Conservative party,[77] where his duties included keeping influential London newspapers in sympathetic Conservative hands.[78] Two rich Conservative supporters who often helped him were Sir Alexander Henderson (afterwards Lord Faringdon), a stockbroker and railway chairman, and Davison Dalziel, head of the Pullman Car Company. Both men, apart from being business acquaintances of Docker, also subsidised newspapers which treated Conservative Central Office cordially; and it was this shadowy world of political favours and newspaper patronage into which Steel-Maitland introduced Docker in 1912.

The *Daily Express* had originally been owned by the Tariff Commissioner, Sir Arthur Pearson, but he went blind, and withdrew from active interest, leaving his editor, R. D. Blumenfeld the tariff reformer, saddled with debts. At Bonar Law's introduction, Blumenfeld managed to borrow £25,000 from the Canadian company promoter, Max Aitken, in 1911, and the *Daily Express* survived on this for a year.[79] This proved only an interim measure, and in 1912, it fell to Steel-Maitland to find a new proprietor for the *Daily Express* who could stabilise its finances and ensure its future. As Henderson wrote, it was 'essential that a strong commercial head should be found if the *Daily Express* is to be made a success'.[80] Steel-Maitland's first choice was Docker: he was later to write, 'I have always believed Mr Docker one of the ablest men I know, and I know him pretty well.' However, in June 1912, Docker declined the *Daily Express* overture.[81] This was not the end of his involvement in the matter, because in July 1912, Blumenfeld informed Bonar Law of Steel-Maitland's new scheme to save the *Daily Express*. This involved financial reconstruction, and a new board of directors including Henderson and Docker 'to represent the new money', or failing them, Sir William Bull the solicitor MP for Hammersmith, or John (later Lord) Gretton, the brewer.[82] In the final arrangements, Unionist party funds put up £10,000 in Ordinary shares, and Aitken himself provided a first mortgage of £40,000 in return for the newspaper inserting laudatory paragraphs about him.[83]

It was not long before Steel-Maitland succeeded in establishing Docker as a London newspaper proprietor, for in May 1914, Docker's company

Business Newspapers Ltd bought control of an evening newspaper, the *Globe*. This was the oldest evening newspaper in the world, having been founded in 1803 as a trade journal for booksellers. In 1874 it was bought by Captain (later Sir) George Armstrong, who subsequently owned, managed and edited it jointly with another die-hard blimp, Sir William Madge. This pair had a reactionary editorial policy, and supported tariff protection, while their rabid jingoism ignored Edmund Burke's injunction, 'remember so as to be patriots as not to forget we are gentlemen'.[84] In 1911, for example, when the majority of Conservative peers withdrew their opposition to the Parliament Bill under Asquith's threat to swamp the Lords with 500 new peers, the *Globe* wrote of the peers who had saved the Liberal government, 'that no honest man will take any of them by the hand again, that their friends will disown them, their clubs expel them, and that alike in politics and social life, they will be made to feel the bitter shame they have brought upon us all'.[85] Madge and Armstrong were both over-excitable men with a pompous belief in the power and justice of the journalists' pen, and indeed Madge's later life was a melancholy example of the illusory power of the press baron. After leaving the *Globe* in 1914, he became owner of *The People*, boasting in *Who's Who* that it became 'a phenomenal success under his management'. In 1921 *The People* was sold by the Madge family for £160,000 to a Canadian company promoter, Grant Morden MP, whom Docker incidentally detested. Yet after the sale Sir William Madge continued to think that he was proprietor, went daily to the office, drifting from desk to desk making suggestions and criticising as he had always done. The journalists politely ignored him, and he continued to think that his opinion mattered. This story should have served as a rebuke to self-important editors ever since.[86] After the death of Sir George Armstrong in 1908, the *Globe* was bought by Lord Northcliffe's younger brother, Hildebrand Harmsworth, who 'looked and spoke like a bookie with a purple face and brown boots'. He was lazy, died of cirrhosis of the liver, and lost £80,000 on the *Globe* in 1908–12.[87] In 1912 he sold it for £40,000 to a syndicate headed by Max Aitken, and in this deal, Unionist party sources provided £25,000 of the purchase price, and Aitken only £15,000.[88] Aitken re-installed Madge as editor and exerted little editorial influence, but the newspaper continued to lose about £25,000 per annum.

By 1914, Aitken, too, was restive, and in May, as Unionist Central Office reported to Bonar Law, Docker agreed to buy the *Globe* for £5,000, taking over the present staff. Aitken 'behaved remarkably well', releasing outstanding debentures, and paying £4,000 to Madge (whose son-in-law Colonel Bellamy remained business manager of the paper), on condition that the latter paid off at least £7,000 to the creditors.[89] The transaction was carried through in the name of Business Newspapers Ltd (whose other directors included Pierce Lacy), but the company was entirely Docker's vehicle. He can have had few illusions about the commercial possibilities of the newspaper, especially after Aitken made a bet of £500 with one of Docker's friends that Business Newspapers would not make the *Globe* profitable.[90] Although Docker remained acquainted with Aitken for years, his attitude was equivocal, and he regarded Beaverbrook's appointment as Chancellor of the Duchy of Lancaster and Minister of Information in 1918 as 'a perfect disgrace'.[91] Altogether he discounted millionaires who made their money out of newspapers as windbags altogether beneath '*real businessmen*' who were manufacturers: an attack on Austen Chamberlain by the *Daily Mail* was, he wrote, 'the height of bad taste and I do think we have had enough of the Northcliffe dictation – what on earth has he ever done but talk?'[92]

What were Docker's motives in becoming a London newspaper pro-prietor? They were identical with those of D. A. Thomas, a Welsh colliery owner, who, like Docker, 'attached exceptional importance to publicity on industrial matters'. Around 1914 he contemplated buying the *Pall Mall Gazette*, explaining that 'A newspaper in London is a source of political power and...I prefer that sort of hobby to the ownership of a yacht...my object being to influence the opinions not so much of the man-in-the-street but those of Parliament and Clubland.'[93] Docker had the same attitude. Clubland was also the *Globe*'s traditional target, and publicity on industrial subjects was Docker's interest. This was explicit in the announcement of the change of ownership which was published on 9 June 1914.

> The new Proprietary being deeply concerned in the maintenance of our national supremacy, are disturbed...by rash attacks upon the Con-stitution, by the ill-considered finance of impractical statesmen and by the setting of class against class for purely political ends. Having no connection with or support from any party or party machine, they intend to uphold...the real interests of the country, and to be untiring in criticism of the manoeuvres of professional politicians of any party...It will be our policy to urge unflinchingly that the control of the business affairs of the nation be placed in the hands of businessmen.

This disavowal of the influence of Unionist party machinery was false, but it would not have carried credence with anyone who read the paper anyway. Editorials were consistently hostile to the policies and personalities of the Liberal government. They considered Asquith's 'Administration of 1908–16 [w]as one of the most disastrous and demoralising, if not catastrophic, chapters in British history', whilst of the Prime Minister himself they wrote 'his legal training colours his every action and...his finesse and belief in...intriguing has been more in evidence than qualities of real statesmanship'. Asquith's ministerial colleagues fared no better.[94]

The *Globe* had been edited since 1912 by Charles Palmer, a staff member since 1886 described variously as 'a veritable dynamo of energy', 'a genuinely idealistic Kiplingesque imperialist' and 'a very able and energetic journalist who has conducted the *Globe*...with conspicuous ability.'[95] In 1914, it acquired a new literary editor, Harold Lewis, formerly of the *Nottingham Guardian*, and a new city editor, Herbert Harry Bassett. Bassett had been editor of the *Financial Review of Reviews* until 1913, and edited *Bradshaw's Railway Manual*, 1904–24. He had also written an intelligent and readable study of *British Commerce* (1913) and after Docker sold the *Globe*, became city editor of the *Birmingham Post*, a newspaper which Docker tried to buy in 1942. The editorial policies and news comment of the *Globe* changed distinctly after Docker became proprietor, and there is no doubt that he exercised close supervision. Palmer and his successor Foster received written instructions from Docker about which politician to attack,[96] and also reprinted at length Docker's own speeches and letters. Docker personally tried to drum up advertising from business acquaintances. Midlands friends of Docker could also be confident of sympathetic coverage: F. J. Nettlefold and Pierce Lacy were among those who benefited. Docker's peremptory control of his newspaper was not uncommon. Lord Rothermere boasted in 1918, 'I have six editors and if anyone of them dared to say something I disapproved of I should have him on the pavement in half an hour';[97] and other press barons practised similar autocracy. The choice of lead stories, as much as the editorial comment, in the *Globe* of 1914–19 reflected Docker's wishes.

Under Docker's proprietorship, the *Globe* opposed those who wanted 'a great constructive programme' from the Unionists: 'what the country really requires is a pause...that is the only programme which will carry the Conservatives into power, whatever the wiseacres of the Whips Office may say'.[98] Praise for the Unionist leaders was rare, although an exception was made for the party chairman, Docker's friend Steel-Maitland, who was boosted as a suitable Minister of Commerce. The *Globe*'s new political credo was explained in an editorial of 11 June 1914 headed 'The Party or the State?' This argued

> the party system has been carried on to unnecessary lengths...the last two years have seen such a tightening of party discipline and control over the minds and consciences and votes of members that the proceedings of the House of Commons have become deliberative only in name. There was a time when a case well put in the House of Commons could influence a number of votes. Today Demosthenes himself could not influence

two...Today the House of Commons largely consists of men who granted, are often clever, but more seldom wise...and still more rarely...efficient for the work of governing a commercial and industrial country.

The increasing rigidity of the party system...is one of the causes, and also one of the results, of so many lawyers and so few active men of affairs being in Parliament. It is the reason why so much of our legislation is inefficient, even when not injurious, to our commercial interests, on which after all the country depends.

Of more general dealings with officialdom, the *Globe* complained 'that because the businessman is their inferior in certain somewhat superficial arts', civil servants regard him as 'altogether on a lower intellectual level'. The *Globe* maintained, inaccurately in the case of some of its followers, that the 'businessman on the other hand does not arrogate all ability to himself' and by always employing experts and specialists, 'is certainly never guilty of those stupendous muddles which have resulted from politicians dabbling in law, orators in warfare and lawyers in finance'. As to defining the 'best businessmen', the *Globe* declared they were not 'discovered by the cheer of the voter; they discover themselves, and the discovery is endorsed by the opinion of their competitors'.[99]

These dissident noises from the *Globe*, no less than those from the Business Leagues, indicate the nature of Docker's political estrangement. At a time when both the labour movement and the Ulster interest in the Unionist party seemed to be pushing confrontation with the government to new extremes, Docker voiced equal disenchantment with the Liberal government's treatment of manufacturers, those 'industrial kings', as Hugo Hirst called them, who formed 'a bodyguard around the constitution of a country'. Docker felt that business men were not sufficiently respected or consulted by politicians, and set about largely destructive work upon the powers at Westminster. When the stroke of war fell upon the nation in the summer of 1914, he was launching a new propaganda assault through Business Newspapers and the Business Leagues: though the eruption of hostilities interrupted his plans, the war opened for Docker previously unimaginable opportunities for corporatist reform. As he wrote in 1918:

> After a period of disorganisation it dawned at last on Great Britain that the mechanics of warfare were as important as the personal element; that superior equipment would tell its own tale, and that the forces of industry of the belligerent nations must engage in as keen and bitter a conflict as the armies in the field. There was a wonderful reawakening – Mr Lloyd George says, 'We are a different people'.[100]

5

The Great War 1914–18

The Great War of 1914–18 was a time of immense importance to Docker. He worked at full pressure throughout, and in many important respects, was at the heart of national policy. He was an acknowledged leader of those vocal and influential industrialists whom Paul Barton Johnson has dubbed 'trade warriors' or 'productioneers', who saw the war, in Docker's words, as a 'mighty solvent' for the future,[1] a last chance to stop German and American rivals from spoiling British industrial hegemony. Key industries could be protected and British manufacturers unified, both in industrial units so as to increase productive efficiency, and their trade associations, so as to gain an equal footing with labour in governmental dealings. So thought the productioneers; and Docker's role in founding the Federation of British Industries and the British Trade Corporation, his advocacy of a Trade Intelligence Department at the Foreign Office, his industrial mergers and his support for business reconstruction made him foremost among productioneers. For Docker and his associates, expansion of overseas trade and the furtherance of British economic power were the main reasons for Britain's continuance as a nation, and the only purpose of the political system of any industrial society. As Sir Clarendon Hyde said in 1917, the potential 'growth of trade is almost illimitable, and the whole engineering trades of the world are still in their infancy'.[2] Lord Faringdon believed that Britain would be bankrupted by its surplus peacetime capacity unless exports were vastly expanded. The productioneers wanted British industry, after the victory over Germany, to reach a new exporting power, and to dominate world engineering.

The aims of the productioneers were frustrated both by the cultural differences between business men and professional politicians, and by the divisions among business men themselves. Docker was slow to appreciate (as we have seen from his Business League campaigns) that unanimity was impossible among both monopoly capitalists and petty capitalists, and his plans for a consolidated manufacturing interest were quickly defeated. He envisaged the Federation of British Industries, for example, as a 'Business Parliament', in which industrial policy would be made by the industrialists themselves, and also as a financial and marketing weapon for export warriors. Docker thought the war was being fought to make the world safe for British monopoly-capitalists, and looked to it as a means for introducing to Britain the corporatist organisations which he felt had been successful in Germany before 1914. Like other productioneers, he felt that British organisation was deficient and that traditional British individualism would have to be abandoned for the collectivism and regimentation which had made Germany and the USA such deadly rivals. 'Just as individualism stands for opportunism and national aimlessness, so collectivism stands for policy, and all policy implies a national aim', Victor Wellesley told Steel-Maitland in 1918. 'Just as Germany is the home of collectivism, so Great Britain is the home of individualism, and that is why in the past Germany has had a policy and we have had none.'[3] The productioneers wanted no less than the total transformation of Britain: a great work of destruction had to precede the reconstruction for which they struggled. National aimlessness had to be eliminated along with British habits of empiricism and individuality. As one British electrical engineer said in 1916, 'the success of the individual Englishman all over the world has been largely due to the English method of developing initiative', but Britain's failures were 'the outcome of a spirit of independence and a want of discipline'.[4] Docker and his friends were ready to sacrifice personal independence, and to risk diminishing individual initiative, in return for more national discipline and unified purpose. They had their American counterparts in the commercial expansionists of the American Manufacturers Export Association and the National Foreign Trade Council, who used the excitement of the European War to obtain the Webb-Pomerene Act of 1916 permitting the formation of export combinations and pressed for corporatist reforms to obtain a united front by financiers, manufacturers and federal government in the world contest for export orders. For these American productioneers, too, the German model of corporatism was paramount.[5]

Docker perceived the Great War in similar terms to the British Electrical and Allied Manufacturers Association, of which he became a vice-president: as a 'commercial war' caused by 'economic conditions…there could hardly be any other immediate cause for it in this industrial age'.[6] He believed that economic factors dominated international relations, and that the Foreign Office had proved ill-equipped to assess the implications of other countries' trade policies. 'We were caught napping in the matter of the national and Imperial security and safety, and we are paying a very pretty price for our folly, our supineness and our senseless refusal to face facts', Docker declared in 1916, adding that economic diplomacy was historically 'a notable feature in our foreign policy, until we became so cosmopolitan and generally superior that such trifling matters as the care of our commerce were pricks to our pride and derogatory to our dignity.'[7] His one influential ally in the Foreign Office, Sir Victor Wellesley, had been Commercial Attaché in Spain, before serving as Controller of Commercial and Consular Affairs (1916–19) and Deputy Under Secretary (1925–36) at the Office; their working association lasted from 1916, when they served on a government committee on Commercial Intelligence, until the 1930s, when they collaborated in the formation of the Foreign Office's Economic Relations Section. They were in total agreement about the intimate connection between modern industrial development and international tension. Wellesley wrote in 1918 that 'The rapid evolution of Germany's internal organisation, the close interlocking and concentration of finance and industry, the consequent riotous acceleration of production, with its concomitant need of foreign markets and of new sources of raw material, provided [German militarism's] solid foundation', and criticised the Foreign Office in which he worked: 'we were ignorant of the economic forces which were so irresistibly impelling Germany to war, because we had never studied her internal conditions systematically, and preferred her military and naval developments as a surer index of her intentions'.[8] Docker concurred entirely and his view that foreign affairs were pre-determined by materialist forces was central to his work during the world war.

The influence of the productioneers on British society was considerable, although not in the form they wanted, still less in the manner attributed to them. For example, Professor Middlemas has argued that the insatiable demand for munitions and manpower during 1914–18 transformed British government structure, and permanently elevated trade unions and employers' associations into a new status of 'governing institutions'. Docker's Federation of British Industries was foremost amongst these governing institutions, which Middlemas believes 'share[d] some of the political power and attributes of the state' and were integral to the process, lasting from 1915 until 1979, whereby British governments were the first among industrial nations to make 'the avoidance of crises their first priority'.[9] There are two objections to this thesis of 'corporate bias'. First, the accommodation of interests is a feature of all liberal democracies, and Middlemas surely exaggerates both the novelty and the rarity of Britain's espousal of crisis avoidance. A more specific objection to Middlemas' version is that the 'governing institutions' fell far short, after 1919, of what Docker had conceived and other productioneers supported, and indeed in many important respects lacked the attributes of power which Middlemas himself posits of 'governing institutions'. In the inter-war period the FBI was little more than a clearing-house for technical advice and other consultancy work. Its political power, and parliamentary influence, had not one scintilla of the strength which Docker wanted; nor were the procedures by which the FBI was consulted by government as formally institutionalised as he expected. Indeed, he was embittered by the way in which some presidents of the FBI deliberately diminished its role. This decline was exemplified in 1925, when Churchill as Chancellor of the Exchequer, took Britain back on to the gold standard. Vernon Willey was then president of the FBI and went officially to the Treasury to explain why his members disliked the move. Churchill, however, received him unsympathetically, and took the attitude that the Federation was showing 'intolerable presumption' in complaining about Treasury policy.[10] Such checks to the FBI's influence were a disappointment which envenomed Docker's later years, and are irreconcilable with Professor Middlemas' views of events.

Moreover, Docker held no automatic agreement with the principle of crisis-avoidance. 'I am not the man to shirk a duty because it is not a very pleasant one', he said in 1913,[11] and his instinct was to welcome turmoil, during which creative reforms could be brewed. On several occasions, he saw positive possibilities in crises which most of his countrymen deplored as wholly destructive, and he despised shuffling compromises or timid expediencies, such as characterised the Baldwin, MacDonald and Chamberlain governments.

Turning now to the course of the war, and the part of Docker's businesses in its prosecution, its first effect on MCWF was the loss of their Belgian factory at Manage. On 17 August, when the Germans had almost reached Brussels, P. G. Bourne, the British works manager, left the works, and no further news was received until 20 November when they received a letter, dated 6 September, from the Belgian managing director at Manage, Taminiaux. In May 1915 the Germans appointed a Special Commissioner named Hinnenthal to supervise the works with Taminiaux as manager under him. Taminiaux refused to co-operate at first, and after some delay, the Germans sequestered the works on 2 December 1915. It was not until months later that MCWF heard of the sequestration, and then only indirectly, from the Henricot Steel Company of Court St Etienne in Belgium, with whom they had regular dealings before 1914. Docker immediately sent word to Taminiaux that all employees should leave the works and indeed that the factory should be destroyed rather than used by Germans.

Mr Henricot himself delivered the message to Taminiaux, but the latter had changed his attitude since May, and replied that he would remain at the works, even with the Germans. Henricot nevertheless induced all the principal workmen at Manage to resign at the end of April 1916, and in June, MCWF asked Henricot to pay half-wages to all good workmen at Manage to leave the works and stop work for the Germans on the basis that the Birmingham firm would re-pay Henricot after the war. This was done, and the factory effectively shut. Taminiaux was the only Belgian wagon-builder who continued to build and repair wagons for the Germans, and Henricot 'could only imagine he had gone mad'. He was dismissed by MCWF as soon as proper communications were re-established with Belgium after the Armistice in 1918.[12]

The other MCWF factory transformed by the eruption of war was at Lancaster. This had been shut for some years, and around 11 August 1914 was taken over for billeting soldiers and horses. However, in July 1915, the Admiralty asked Armstrongs and Vickers to establish jointly a factory with an output of at least ten torpedoes weekly, and the company which was then created, Caton Engineering, bought part of the Lancaster works for £25,000. Torpedo production began, and in October 1915, when Caton wished to expand further, MCWF offered to sell more of the works for £20,000. Caton were disposed to accept this price, but the Admiralty, which had sponsored part of their finance, was more cautious, and took the opinion of the Chief Valuer of the Inland Revenue. He replied that the factory area in question was not worth £20,000, and the Admiralty, rather than waste more time, annexed the Lancaster works on 18 October, under the Defence of the Realm Act, with the compensation to be settled later. Subsequent negotiations were dogged with misunderstandings between the industrialists and business men. Symbolically when MCWF's solicitor went by appointment to the Admiralty in November 1915 to discuss matters, by mischance he failed to find his way to the right department, and after wandering the corridors in furious misery, he left without seeing anyone. Disagreements about compensation terms were prolonged until June 1916, with Docker complaining that he had 'been buffetted from pillar to post' in 'the most unsatisfactory matter I ever had to deal with & the most unfair to us'. He appealed for assistance to Steel-Maitland, whose cousin Gerald was Private Secretary to the First Lord of the Admiralty, and who exerted himself in helping to reach a settlement. It was not until December 1916 that the Ministry of Munitions finally agreed to buy the Lancaster works and attached land for £26,300, with interest on £13,500 at £5 per cent per annum from October 1915. By the end of the war the Ministry had spent £255,760 on buying, equipping and maintaining Caton, for which they found no civilian buyer until December 1923.[13]

Hostilities had equally immediate and profound effects on Docker's interests outside MCWF. The war of 1914–18 was the highpoint of British presslords' political influence, and Docker was quite as determined as any greater presslord like Northcliffe that his wishes should prevail. In the first month of the war, the *Globe* was the wildest of all London newspapers in spreading spy-scares, and the authorities were so concerned by the effects, that the Press Bureau, in September 1914, officially asked Palmer to discontinue the campaign before panic started.[14] It was to the fore in dislodging Prince Louis of Battenberg as First Lord of the Admiralty in October 1914,[15] and campaigned against aliens in every sort of job. From October 1914 onwards, the *Globe* regularly carried a paragraph about 'the alien enemy in our midst' which promised 'to convey to the proper quarters for investigation any well-authenticated cases of [espionage] suspicion which may come to the knowledge of our readers', and this xenophobic fever infected many other articles. It clearly had Docker's approval, and he himself wrote a long letter to the *Financial News*, in October 1914, urging 'joint action by the manufacturers of the country...to establish at any cost and by any means an effective blockade of...[German] Finance'. He demanded statutory powers to hold all funds belonging to enemy aliens in Britain, and fumed at the Foreign Office and Board of Trade for adhering to 'legal etiquette' and 'mere punctilio'. According to Docker,

> Nowhere is the danger from the enemy within our gates more apparent than in the financial world, where...currents of sinister influence are secretly working. On all sides we see aliens with power and liberty to inflict vital injury upon us in our stronghold of money and credit. Germans and Austrians hold important positions in finance and have no difficulty as the law stands in transferring funds to the Continent.

Alien financiers, he warned, were obtaining 'most valuable' industrial knowledge which they were sending 'to their headquarters' through neutral states, by 'treacherous devices in the invention and use of which the enemy excel'.[16] Later in the war, in 1917–18, Docker's campaign against pro-German elements in the City of London took practical form when he helped to create the British Trade Corporation and the British Stockbrokers Trust, as described in chapter 7.

Another subject which exercised Docker was the running of existing contracts with the enemy. Trade with the enemy was prohibited by proclamation on 5 August 1914, and Parliament gave statutory backing to these prohibitions by Acts passed in September and November 1914. Steel-Maitland was one of the chief Conservative speakers in these debates,[17] and admitted that his speeches were prompted by 'his business friends', which almost certainly meant Docker. The two Trading with the Enemy Acts of 1914 dissatisfied Docker, for in December 1914, he asked

Steel-Maitland to speak to Sir John Simon, the Attorney General, about legislation to prohibit existing contracts with the enemy. Steel-Maitland referred the matter to Bonar Law, with the recommendation that a government committee be appointed to examine the problem. He added that such a committee would need 'one or two really high class commercial men who at the same time can see things from the general standpoint to serve on it, and Dudley Docker is just such a man'. Docker emphasised that the subject did not affect MCWF, 'but it does very much concern the working-classes and the trading community generally, as it involves at least a million of money in wages and materials'. It is unclear what omissions he can have thought there were in existing legislation, but he probably had in mind some of the agreements between British and German companies to manufacture under licence certain types of patented electrical or engineering equipment.[18] Docker's involvement in this controversy emphasises his belief that the world war was being fought to beat German industrialism.

Other public responsibilities followed as the demand for armaments became more urgent. In April 1915 Docker was appointed chairman of the Birmingham Munitions Output Organisation. The foundation work for this body was done by Captain (later Sir) Robert Hilton, who then worked for Birmingham Gas Department, but who was later recruited by Docker as managing director of the Metropolitan-Vickers Electrical Company, 1919–28. Hilton was responsible for the preparatory organisation, and suggested Docker's name to government officials on 11 April.[19] Subsequently, he called a meeting of manufacturers and trade unionists at the Midland Hotel in Birmingham on 19 April, which he attended with Lord Elphinstone on behalf of the War Office. Docker presided at the meeting, and emerged from it as chairman of the Executive Committee responsible for organising the munitions output of the Birmingham district. The other members of the committee were equally heavyweight. On the employers' side, there was Sir Gerard Muntz of Muntz Metals, Arthur Keen of Guest Keen Nettlefolds, Harris Spencer of the Midland Employers Federation, Sir Hallewell Rogers and Neville Chamberlain of BSA, and Arthur Chamberlain. The workers were represented by George Ryder of the Amalgamated Society of Engineers, John Beard of the Workers Union (who became chairman of the TUC in 1929) and Solomon Hill of the Allied Trade Federation (all of whom had led strikes at MCWF during 1908–13). The municipal authorities were represented on the committee by Hilton (who acted as its secretary) and by Ernest Hiley, the Town Clerk of Birmingham, whom Docker recruited in 1917 as a director of MCWF, and who served with Hilton until 1921 on the board of Metropolitan-Vickers.

The whole committee, then, was criss-crossed with connections between its members, and represented all the powerful interests of Birmingham. Its early work was handicapped by the disorder which prevailed in the Whitehall munitions organisation, especially in the unclear demarcation of responsibility. Docker was clear where the trouble lay, and in a letter published in *The Times* on 22 May 1915, at the height of the shell crisis, and following the formation of the Asquith–Bonar Law coalition, he called for a Ministry of Munitions possessing 'business experience and full executive power'. 'No one at present knows what the manufacturers of this country properly organised and with an accessible Minister who can say "Yes" or "No" can do, but I am one who believes they could respond to any claim made upon them.' By 22 May, the formation of a Ministry of Munitions by the new coalition was inevitable, given Whitehall's previous munitions record, and the press campaign about the shells shortage which Lord Northcliffe was orchestrating. The call for such a ministry, by an industrialist of Docker's stature, in the correspondence pages of *The Times*, however, prepared public opinion for the unprecedented administrative convulsion that followed. Docker considered the Conservatives' decision to co-operate in a 'coalition was most unfortunate – probably the worst day's work our party has done', and wished to be shot of the Liberal government altogether.[20] He was apprehensive that Bonar Law would take the new job of Minister of Munitions, and warned Steel-Maitland, 'if he does I predict failure & perhaps destruction – he is completely out of date as a businessman'.[21] His reaction on hearing that one of the detested tribe of radical lawyers, Lloyd George, had been appointed was surprisingly favourable.

Lloyd George took up his duties as Minister of Munitions on 26 May 1915 and on 28 May, a deputation from the Birmingham munitions group, comprising Docker, Hilton and Keen, met Lloyd George and two other Cabinet Ministers, the Marquess of Crewe and Lord Curzon, together with various officials of the new ministry. Birmingham was the first industrial city of the nation, and Lloyd George wanted to know why the munitions output committee there had produced nothing, although it had existed for over five weeks. Docker replied tartly 'that is quite simply answered', and explained that his committee had been waiting for a month for a reply to questions which had been sent to the War Office. In the meantime, they had been making plans for co-operative production in an area stretching as far as Wolverhampton. Docker explained that his committee felt that Birmingham's plant and skilled men were not suited to making either shells or fuses, and were better fitted for making other products needed for the war effort, such as munitions wagons, brass and copper. Lloyd George disagreed, and an interchange followed in which Docker continued to urge that Birmingham should be treated 'as an overflow place for shells' only. The discussion, indeed, became ramblingly acrimonious, and Lord Curzon had to intervene, although Addison, who was present, thought the Birmingham deputation much more impressive and constructive than one from Clydeside received earlier in the day.[22] Neither Docker nor Keen were clear what Birmingham's shell capacity was. The engineering sector was honeycombed with sub-contracting between firms, which made it impossible to get exact figures of productive power, and the labour situation was still irregular. Docker cited the Cadbury's chocolate factory and Tangye's engineering works which were keeping millwrights needed for BSA's rifle plant for civilian purposes, and at a meeting in June with Lord Elphinstone and Addison, explained that the Birmingham organisation was still unable to obtain all the available labour and machinery in its area because 'a good many of the brass finishers and others were inclined to hang back and take advantage of those who were loyal and willing to put their machinery at the nation's disposal'.[23]

Docker's subsequent views on the manpower question were typical. He was anxious always that skilled munitions workers, 'the army at home' as he called them, should not be called up and wasted as cannon-fodder, and worried lest indiscriminate conscription disrupt munitions production, or men be killed who were needed for the post-war battle of production. 'In my judgement the country would be useless if after the war we have not enough men to carry on and I think it is the first duty of the Americans to find *men*', he wrote after the USA entered the war in 1917, 'in addition to that they should send over a very considerable number of parts of machinery which could be assembled and the article produced here, thereby keeping money in the country...too much money and too many men are being unnecessarily sent out'.[24] He cultivated and admired the Minister of National Service, Auckland Geddes, and by April 1918 was convinced that everything reasonable was being done over manpower, except in Ireland. He believed shipbuilding was the only overmanned industry, and averred from MCWF's experience, 'it is far better to be understaffed than overstaffed...With a very much depleted staff of officials and men the output has been marvellous.'[25] More generally, he believed that the British Expeditionary Force had 'not learned to control big numbers' and was wasting life: 'the first three essentials are aeroplanes, tanks and gas', he wrote during the German offensive of April 1918, which 'are only just being properly exploited...[to] *save* life'.[26]

It became *de rigueur* for Docker to entertain celebrities on their lightning visits to inspect the Birmingham munitions effort. When King George V visited Birmingham in July 1915 he toured the Saltley works, and lunched there with Docker, his co-directors and members of the Munitions Committee. MCWF were originally selected to build some of the prototype landships which were to become known as 'tanks', but in the summer of 1915 were released from this contract in consequence of other important war work.[27] The first tanks were instead built by a Lincolnshire firm of agricultural machinery makers, but in 1916 MCWF resumed responsibility for spear-heading tank production, and ultimately made some 80 per cent of all tanks deployed by the British in the war. This made Docker even more of an attraction for visitors. 'Wd you care to come to B'ham with me', inquired Winston Churchill of his wife in February 1918, 'and see Tanks & munitions workers...& Mr Dudley Docker?'[28] The relations between Churchill and Docker remained cordial, for in March 1919, Docker gave a dinner at the Grosvenor Hotel in honour of Churchill's achievements whilst Minister of Munitions, and presented him with a silver model of a tank. Another guest at the banquet, Lord Birkenhead, the Lord Chancellor, 'proposed the health of Mr Docker, whose inventive genius had so substantially contributed to the success of British arms'; and altogether there seems to have been an orgy of mutual congratulation. Docker had indeed urged previously that Churchill and Lord Reading should represent Britain at the Versailles peace negotiations of 1919: 'They are really the only people I know with any imagination at all, and we don't want a repetition of Alsace Lorraine.'[29]

Docker was, however, far from being the complete darling of the Establishment at this time. The attacks of the *Globe* on the Asquith–Bonar Law coalition became increasingly sharp. Although its editor, Charles Palmer, had told Bonar Law in 1914 that he would be happy to follow his suggestions on editorial policy,[30] in the autumn of 1915, he became increasingly agitated about the government's manipulation of the press. On 11 October, Palmer splashed a story attacking 'blighting censorship' and 'the pernicious, degrading and dangerous influence of the Press Bureau', which had helped the politicians to develop '*suppressio veri* and the *suggestio falsi* to a degree of cruel artistry never before practiced'. This tone was maintained throughout the next three weeks, and on 3 November, its attitude was attacked in a speech by Sir Frederick Smith (later Lord Birkenhead), who was appointed Attorney General on the following day. Smith was a barrister-politician of a type which Docker despised, who had brought Britain to the brink of civil war during the Ulster crisis of 1913–14 and won the nickname of 'Galloper' as a consequence. He had been appointed the first director of the Press Bureau on the outbreak of war in August 1914, with his brother Harold Smith as its secretary: and resenting the *Globe*'s criticism of the Bureau he thought Palmer was a 'little swine'.[31] On 5 November, Palmer retaliated with attacks on Smith's appointment as Attorney General. Smith was 'the most perfectly developed type of the lawyer-politician', whose 'capacity for platform vituperation' and 'rhetorical vulgarity' had 'gained him his place in politics'. So much was true; but Palmer also imputed cowardice with the comment that Smith was 'a general's galloper in mock civil-war but an Eye-Witness when there is real fighting to be done'. Smith had in fact shown bravery whilst acting as Eye-Witness attached to the Indian Army at the front in 1914–15, and was sensitive to jibes of this sort. It proved a fatal remark for the *Globe* to have ventured.

The *Globe*'s lead-story on 5 November – the day of the attack on Smith – was sensational. Following information which they had been given mischievously by Max Aitken, they reported that Lord Kitchener, the Secretary of State for War, had been so sickened by recent political machinations that he had tendered his resignation to the King. Although the resignation had not been accepted, 'we understand Mr Asquith has resumed the reins at the War Office', they proclaimed. The story was untrue, but its fault lay in being premature, and it was not without substance. It was a notorious fact that Asquith and his colleagues wanted to be rid of Kitchener – indeed, when the soldier went to the Dardanelles in November 1915 to report on the Near Eastern situation, he took his seals of office with him to prevent his dismissal *in absentia*. There seemed little doubt that he would be removed in a matter of weeks. One of the few men whom Smith admired apart from himself was Kitchener. Indeed, Smith's biographer speaks of Kitchener in November 1915 as 'a once great man whose fingers had become enervate upon the wheel of power' whom Smith, almost alone, still hero-worshipped. Similar stories were published on 5 November by the *Daily Express*, *Evening Standard*, *Westminster Gazette* and *Star*, and the Central News Agency telegraphed the news of Kitchener's resignation to every London newspaper that afternoon. The Press Bureau officially denied the story, but this did not deter Palmer from repeating it in the *Globe* next day. Other newspapers were more cautious, and merely reported that Kitchener's resignation was very imminent. 'When the politicians were scuttling like rabbits in Whitehall, they called the soldier to their councils', the *Globe* told its readers, 'Lord Kitchener is no superman but he loathes the politician and the country loves and trusts him'. For security reasons, Kitchener's whereabouts were being censored by the Press Bureau, but in a provocative gesture, Palmer circumvented this by writing that the British people 'are tired of the little ways of the little men. They would gladly see them all, well – sent to report on the Near Eastern situation.' Palmer was unwise to repeat his allegation with such violence, as he promptly discovered.

Acting under the Defence of the Realm Act, police and soldiers raided the *Globe*'s offices, confiscating its printing equipment and all editions of the paper for 5 and 6 November. The raid was ostensibly instigated by the officer commanding London district, but Smith was responsible, and to many people it seemed 'a bad business if we are to free the Germans from militarism by introducing their *lèse-majesté* into England'.[32] The *Globe* was not permitted to publish again until 22 November, when its printing equipment was returned on the condition that it published an agreed statement that there were 'no grounds of dissension between Lord Kitchener and his colleagues, such as to effect their future ministerial co-operation'. This statement was framed by Smith and was utter humbug. Asquith had told the Secretary of the War Cabinet, Sir Maurice Hankey, on 1 November that the Cabinet 'were unanimous that Lord K ought to leave the War Office', and Hankey wrote on 8 December, 'The PM is very anxious to get rid of Lord K, who, he says, darkens counsel and is a really bad administrator.'[33] Even the War Office wore 'one broad contented smile' during Kitchener's absence at the Dardanelles.[34] But the statement which Smith wangled from the *Globe* was tantamount to saying that Kitchener's departure from the War Office would cause disaffection, and so Asquith remained saddled with Kitchener – who recognised that Smith's action had saved his job, and was grateful to him for the remaining months of his life. The whole incident was an ugly one which historians have previously always discussed from Smith's standpoint.[35] The Defence of the Realm Act was abused by a Law Officer of the Crown partly to score a personal revenge upon opponents who had called him vulgar and cowardly, but also to carry his point in a Cabinet intrigue which had nothing to do with national security. As one MP commented during the long Commons debate on the *Globe*'s suppression, a prime effect of seizing its editions was to prevent readers 'see[ing] its admirable piece of invective against the Attorney General', except in the British Museum's files.[36]

This was not the end of Docker's troubles at the *Globe*. During the fortnight it was banned, he dismissed Palmer, who then seems to have tried to extort money from him by threatening a lawsuit. As Lloyd George was told on 7 December, 'Palmer does not think the action will go into the Court, as, among other things if it does, he hopes to make public, instructions he received (and disobeyed) from the Proprietor, Mr Dudley Docker, directing him repeatedly to attack [Lloyd George] the Minister of Munitions.'[37] It is likely that a settlement was reached, for nothing more was heard of the matter. Palmer subsequently went to work with Horatio Bottomley, the yellow journalist, embezzler and MP for Hackney, and in a famous by-election of February 1920, defeated the coalition candidate and was elected as MP for the Wrekin in Bottomley's interest. A few months later, however, he caught pneumonia at the hustings and died. Palmer's editorial functions were temporarily undertaken by Edward Foster, the *Globe*'s business manager, and he promptly embroiled Docker in more trouble. On six occasions between 29 November and 11 December Foster published anonymous letters (signed 'Patriot', 'Indignant', 'Another Disgusted Englishman', 'Anti-German' and so forth) implying that Mrs Asquith, the Prime Minister's wife, had played tennis with German prisoners-of-war and afterwards had sent them Fortnum and Mason food hampers. She sued, and although Docker avowed that the *Globe* was 'perfectly innocent', and asked Steel-Maitland to get Sir Edward Carson for the defence,[38] this proved impossible, and she won damages of £1,000. In 1917, however, they successfully defended another libel action brought by a vicious and unscrupulous adventurer called Noel Pemberton-Billing, then recently elected as MP for Hertford. The *Globe*'s counsel so discredited Billing's financial dealings that the jury found against him after retiring for only ten minutes.[39] Billing learnt from this experience, and in 1918, used Business Newspapers' techniques when he was the defendant in a libel action brought by the dancer Maud Allen. This was the case in which Billing whipped up national hysteria with the allegation that there existed a 'Black Book' compiled by German spies which listed 47,000 English homosexuals who were undermining the 'stamina' of British sailors and soldiers. His cross-examinations comprised savage attacks upon the integrity of prosecution witnesses, which was precisely the method which Business Newspapers had used to break him in 1917.

Alfred Turner was made editor of the *Globe* early in 1917, but in September, Docker appointed Leo Maxse as additional editorial consultant. Maxse had been editor since 1893 of the *National Review*, 'a monthly which served as a bell-wether for anti-Semitic, anti-German xenophobia on the far right', and which enjoyed many aristocratic subscribers and contributors. Maxse was a protectionist, imperialist Francophile, and the author of a book entitled *Germany on the Brain*. His journalism 'in [its] best Maxsean form [was] extra pessimistic' in attitude; its tone was acerbic, but brilliantly readable and his instinct for power-politics was superb. Unfortunately, he deteriorated into reactionary, crankish spluttering, and his attacks on 'The International Jew' were rebarbative.[40] Maxse revivified the prose of the *Globe*, and had a private ear to many Westminster intrigues. He was a partisan of General Sir William Robertson, the Chief of Imperial General Staff, in his quarrels with the Prime Minister, and the *Globe*'s

Ill. 4 Leo Maxse (1864–1932)

attacks on Lloyd George in the autumn of 1917 were instigated by
Robertson. When Robertson was finally sacked in February 1918, the *Globe*
was quick to follow Colonel Repington, the military correspondent of the
Morning Post, in publishing stories to unmask Lloyd George's plot against
Robertson.[41] Repington was another brilliant, but unscrupulous, journalist
who had a high opinion of Maxse, and believed that the *Globe* was almost
the only newspaper which 'play[ed] the game by the Army'.[42] Repington's
contempt for the intervention of professional politicians in military policy
was almost identical to Docker's view of politicians meddling in business
policy; and the two men were natural allies. In the spring of 1918 Maxse
indeed wanted Robertson installed either as Prime Minister or even Dictator

in charge of the war effort. Docker demurred, writing that although he knew 'nothing of Robertson', he doubted that 'Robertson would be the best P.M.' though 'he *might* be used in a crisis'.[43] A further divergence between the two men concerned Churchill. Maxse abominated him, opining 'There is no more dangerous man in our public life', while Docker urged in April 1918 'it is *now* that Winston is needed & it is a thousand pities he can't be used'.[44] He particularly objected to '*very* improper' and partisan attacks on Churchill in the *Morning Post*: 'Heckling these people is very much the same thing as heckling the Generals at the Front, and after all these men ought to be the Generals at the Back.'[45]

Another of the *Globe*'s informants was Rear Admiral Murray Sueter, a pioneer of submarine, airship and tank development. Sueter had ordered his subordinates to arrange press 'puffs' of his achievements, and after writing to the King in 1917 asking for an honour in recognition of his tank work was put on half-pay by the Admiralty. He was never employed by the Admiralty or Air Ministry again (and had to wait until 1934 for a knighthood for political services), thereafter evincing bitter animus against his former service. The *Globe*'s articles on the Royal Naval Air Service, and on related aviation topics, were inspired by Sueter in 1918.[46]

Docker's instructions to Maxse sometimes tempered the latter's virulence, and occasionally asked that positive support be given to individual ministers. He admired the work of Sir Auckland Geddes as Minister of National Service in 1917–19, and after the latter had stayed with him at Kenilworth in February 1918 wrote that he was 'one of the refreshing people I have met connected with the present Government' and that Midlands business friends invited over to meet Geddes 'all came to the same conclusion'. Docker gave a further entertainment in honour of him in March, and in expectation of press attacks on him in April asked Maxse to support him journalistically 'in your usual judicious manner'. For good measure he also wanted support for Geddes' elder brother Eric, who was then First Lord of the Admiralty, while admitting that he knew little about him except his fraternal relations.[47]

Maxse made the *Globe* more sophisticated and prevented repetition of its worst solecisms, as for instance when the abdication of the Russian Czar had been hailed as 'a minor incident'; although he was unable to restrain an editorial of August 1918 which achieved an unintentionally ludicrous effect in accusing the Kaiser of homosexuality by using the word 'aural' where 'anal' was intended.[48] Docker's position as a press proprietor enhanced his influence with politicians. The *Globe* took a keen interest in food policy, for example, and when Lloyd George became Prime Minister in 1916, he suggested to Lord Devonport, the Food Controller, that Docker be appointed his deputy. Devonport was a grocery chain proprietor (of Kearley and Tonge) 'whose...bad manners were mistaken for strength of character',[49] and it is clear that he did not relish taking on another self-confident business man, like Docker, who would subtract from his power, or share in his anticipated glory. In the event, Devonport proved incapable of delegation, lacked a sense of proportion, and failed completely; his successor in 1917, Lord Rhondda, said, 'I stand between this country and revolution.'[50] One of the main lessons learnt from the introduction of business men into executive government during the war was that business men were every bit as temperamental, jealous and unreliable as professional politicians: the most violent antipathy in Lloyd George's Cabinet of the reconstruction period was between two former railway managers, Lord Ashfield at the Board of Trade and Sir Eric Geddes at the Ministry of Transport, who each felt menaced by the other.[51] Given the characters of Devonport and Docker, a similar enmity would have exploded if they both had been appointed to the Food Ministry.

The *Globe* also lauded Lord Derby as Director General of Recruiting in 1915–16, and he did not forget this when he became Secretary for War. In January 1917 he told Lloyd George that he wanted to appoint Docker to a specially created post, Controller of War Expenditure, 'with very full powers' and 'reporting directly to me'.[52] Nothing emerged from this suggestion, and it is unlikely that Docker would have had the necessary patience to grapple with the War Office's disordered finances. Another influential position for which Docker was urged was membership of the government committee on post-war trade policy, chaired by Lord Balfour of Burleigh;[53] considering the exhaustive deliberations and nugatory achievements of that body, he deserved congratulations on his escape from a pointless grind. For the most part Docker preferred an informal, advisory role. The crucial question of post-war reconstruction was for eighteen months left to a group of ramshackle committees superintended by a weak and neurotic Liberal politician, Edwin Montagu. This was an unsatisfactory arrangement, and by 1 May 1917, Montagu informed Lloyd George that 'Dudley Docker and many inside people are urging' the creation of a Ministry of Reconstruction.[54] A fortnight later, Lloyd George responded to such pressure by appointing Dr Addison as Minister of Reconstruction, and on 5 June, a dinner was specially held by Lord Reading, the Lord Chief Justice, for Docker and Lloyd George to meet to discuss reconstruction problems.[55] Reading was no doubt involved through his brother Godfrey Isaacs of Marconi's, who had been one of the FBI's most active supporters since its formation. Later, in 1918, Docker advised the Ministry of Reconstruction on a cause dear to his heart, the promotion of new Trade

Associations, and Addison described his guidance on the classification of groups as 'most helpful'.[56]

Docker abominated the statism of the Ministry of Munitions, and eventually became an implacable opponent of their activities in labour relations and in accounting. MCWF consistently refused to take any government contract stipulating investigation of their books by the Ministry to check that an excessive profit was not being made. They insisted instead that the certificate of their auditors be accepted as sufficient evidence that they were not profiteering, and they successfully maintained this attitude throughout the war. Docker feared that information obtained by Ministry officials who were business men seconded to government during the war might be exploited by competitors when the officials returned to civilian business in peacetime. This was not fanciful: Lord Kylsant, one of his co-directors at the Midland Bank, for example, had acquired a great shipping empire by exploiting confidential information gleaned as a member of the Royal Commission on Shipping Rings of 1906.[57] A particular clash between MCWF and the Ministry followed the placing of an order, in August 1916, for 1,000 tanks, some of which were to be fitted with six-pounder guns, and the others with machine-guns. The original contract price for these was £3,820 and £3,770 respectively; but in April 1917, Ministry accountants reached the conclusion that the profit involved was excessive. In June, the Ministry responded to an offer by Lincoln Chandler to reduce the contract price by £500 per tank in return for further guaranteed orders, by demanding a reduction of £2,500 per tank. Throughout the rest of July, extremely hard-bargaining and brinkmanship were carried on by Chandler, Hiley and Ministry officials, throughout which the company refused to disclose a breakdown of its production costs. The disagreement had deleterious effects, for while the price remained unfixed, the company did not order all the necessary materials and did not push the work wholeheartedly.[58] Eventually, on 31 August, Hiley and Chandler accepted an order of 1,600 tanks at £2,850, subject to no rebates and allowances, and with a Ministry break-clause.[59] The Ministry took the affair very seriously, because MCWF was 'an enormous and influential Company', and their refusal to submit to cost investigation would, if widely known, have made the relevant passages of the Defence of the Realm Act worthless.[60] Despite the pertinacity of MCWF's rebellion against the Ministry of Munitions, and the serious delays in production which resulted, MCWF remained the main supplier of tanks for the British Army.

Docker could seldom tolerate or comprehend opposition, and did not drop the question of the Ministry's accounts investigation. In September 1918, a special meeting of the Executive Council of the FBI was called to consider a memorandum submitted by Docker, and to debate his motion that the government should abandon current methods of cost investigation, and accept auditors' certificates from companies. Docker himself did not attend the meeting, where his case was put by Hiley (who complained of 'inquisitorial methods' and contraventions of secrecy) and Caillard of Vickers ('The action of the Government caused suspicion and irritation, and put a premium on inefficiency...it was time for manufacturers...to frighten these officials'). Docker, Hiley and Caillard wanted all FBI member companies to decline, in future, to produce their books to government accountants, and to insist that future munitions contracts should be remunerated on a sliding-scale during the period of the contracts. The plan was resisted by some other FBI members (notably Sir George Murray of Armstrongs who had once been Permanent Secretary at the Treasury) and whilst its wording was being argued and re-drafted, the Armistice of November 1918 and subsequent mass cancellations of munitions orders rendered it redundant.[61] Docker's attempted FBI rebellion against the government accountants would have caused a sensation had it been launched. An ultimatum of that nature would have led to exaggerated fears of profiteering and to suspicion that the FBI was only interested in accumulating more war-wealth for its members. The backlash might have ended in more determined efforts to expropriate industrial capital, and would certainly have proved counter-productive to Docker's wishes. It demonstrates the resentment and frustration at government control which had accumulated among large manufacturers that Docker found so many willing adherents to this policy of reckless confrontation.

The interruption of MCWF's supply of tanks in the summer of 1917 was extraordinary and unpardonable. The affair had no publicity, and was soon forgotten. When General Headquarters of the British Army in France wanted to arrange lectures on tanks, their first hope was that 'Dudley Docker would suggest a literary man at home to take up the job', and in April 1918, Churchill sent a long, confidential telegram to Docker on the realities of the military situation, intended to encourage the maintenance of tank output.[62] The latter was next dislocated, in the summer of 1918, when recruitment officers called up for the armed services between 200 and 300 of the company's employees before suitable men could be provided to take their places. The immediate effect, as Churchill complained to the Cabinet on 26 June, was that MCWF's weekly tank output fell from 50 to 15.[63] Churchill retained his good opinion of Docker, and in 1918–19, appointed him to two different bodies within the Ministry of Munitions. The first of these was Mr Justice McCardie's committee to investigate labour unrest in the Midlands, and the second was the Advisory Council, chaired by Lord Salisbury, on the liquidation of the Ministry of Munitions after the Armistice.

Docker owed his membership of the McCardie committee to his presidency of the Midlands Employers Federation, and the committee's remit typified the difficulties of wartime industrial relations. The atmosphere of war nerves and strain was acute, and the mushrooming of local shop stewards' movements and other rebellions against the trade union leadership led Docker to write in 1918 'that the rank and file of workers no longer place the reliance they formerly did on their Union leaders, but are inclined to break away from any bargain on small provocation'.[64] As a committee (including Douglas Vickers and other representatives of the Federation of British Industries) reported to the Ministry of Munitions in May 1917, many ordinary trade unionists felt their leaders were

> not up-to-date, or...[were] traitors to their fellows and bought by the capitalist. The Unions are now so large that it has become impossible for the leaders to retain their personal touch with the rank and file, with the result that they have lost their influence...and have the constant apprehension that they will be supplanted at the next opportunity by those who are willing to make any bid and the most outrageous promises to attain popularity.[65]

The involvement of trade union leaders such as George Barnes, George Roberts, Henderson, or John Hodge in central government made their followers deeply suspicious of a sell-out and correspondingly harder to handle. Their suspicions were at least partially justified and would have been confirmed, for example, if they had witnessed the maudlin spectacle which Hodge made of himself at a dinner of industrialists hosted by Docker at the Grosvenor Hotel in January 1917.

The strikes investigated by the McCardie committee stemmed from the use by some employers of an undue proportion of skilled labour. Daimler was one such company, and in February 1918, the Ministry of Munitions placed an embargo on Daimler's further recruitment of the skilled. On 8 June, the Ministry introduced a new scheme designed to embargo or control the employment of skilled workers in a larger number of factories. The Ministry thought of the measure as a restriction on employers and not employees, and disregarded a warning from the Trade Union Advisory Committee that in view of the improving military situation, it would be interpreted as conscription of industrial labour. On 1 July, embargo letters were issued against three Coventry companies, Hotchkiss Ordnance, Siddeley-Deasy Motors and Triumph Cycles, but obscurely phrased letters to the foremen gave the false impression that the companies were prohibited from engaging any skilled men except discharged soldiers and sailors. Other ambiguities arose, rumour and resentment spread, and the trade unionists of the Coventry District Engineering Joint Committee resolved that if the embargo was not removed, they would give notice with effect from 22 July. This was duly done, and although after much pressure, the Coventry Joint Committee on 21 July suspended notices pending a national conference on the subject, on 23 July, some 10,000 toolmakers and other workers struck in Coventry. The next day, 12,000 skilled men in Birmingham struck. Similar action was threatened in other industrial areas, and the national conference of engineering workers called for a general strike against embargoes on 30 July. Before that could happen, however, the Coventry and Birmingham workers were threatened with military conscription, and following advice from the Trade Union Advisory Committee, returned to work on 28 and 29 July.

The whole damaging affair reflected the bitter impatience felt by the skilled men for the restoration of pre-war conditions of employment, and was another pointer to their suspicion of their national leaders. It was aggravated by bad communications, most glaringly by the Hotchkiss management, but also by Ministry officials; and there is no doubt that a delicate position was exploited by agitators. Churchill immediately appointed a committee to investigate these so-called Embargo Strikes, under the chairmanship of Sir Henry McCardie, a publicity-conscious Judge who later shot himself. The committee included representatives of the Ministries of Labour and Munitions, together with three representative trade unionists and three employers, including Sir Allan Smith of the Engineering Employers Federation and Docker. The committee had twenty meetings, and examined seventy witnesses, between 2 August and 3 September, when it issued an interim report; but Docker only attended two meetings in that month, and only another three of the remaining eleven sessions up to 12 November.[66] It may be that Docker formed a low impression of the committee's value. Even Churchill wrote on 28 August to Lloyd George that McCardie was 'hopelessly at sea with his Committee, drifting over the whole Labour ocean and dipping his colours to every Bolshevik craft in sight...Labour politics come to him with all the charm of a new revelation.'[67] Certainly, McCardie's conclusions were unexceptionable: the Coventry dispute was caused by undue delay in redeeming the government's pledge to restore pre-war labour conditions, and expressed pent up rebellion against the whole system of manpower control. Its roots were not dissimilar from the rebellion against governmental account investigations which Docker tried to start among FBI members in September 1918. On all sides of industry, war nerves were getting rawer.

As mentioned before, the outbreak of war disrupted the expansion of the Business Leagues, and senior officials such as Chandler and Docker became too busy to arrange meetings. In any case, the main strut of the Business Leagues' platform – the superiority of modern business methods – was completely broken by wartime experience. In the peace of Edwardian England, Docker had sworn that if only business men were put into government, all petty frustrations, indecision and inefficiency would disappear. The war put this claim to the test, and found it hopelessly wanting. For example, one of the first business men seconded to Whitehall to help the munitions effort was Sir Percy Girouard of Armstrongs', who Docker wrote in May 1915, 'has already created an excellent impression'.[68] Yet by July 1915, Christopher Addison, the Deputy Minister for Munitions, was confiding in his diary, 'Poor old Girouard is never tired of talking about the "business man" but we are all struck by his very narrow outlook in arranging the business of the nation.'[69] Girouard proved to be a muddle-headed intriguer, incapable of efficient administration or of a long view of problems, whose mind was 'full of questions of procedure and military precedence...and...high-falutin nonsense as to the big business man's methods';[70] at the end of July 1915, he was dismissed. Other business men loaned to Whitehall proved less incompetent, but every bit as touchy, jealous and disloyal: as Addison wrote later in the war, after placating a business friend of Docker's called Sir Alexander Roger (then at the Ministry of Munitions), 'It is really astonishing the amount of one's time taken up with settling petty questions affecting personal dignities which are worth nothing even when they are settled.'[71] After these war experiences, claptrap about the superiority of the modern business man carried no credence, and the Business Leagues, needless to add, were not revived.

Docker nevertheless found time to help form other pressure-groups. The first of these, the British Manufacturers' Association, was launched in 1915 as a protectionist lobby of Birmingham industrialists. The Association apparently shared Docker's view that the Tariff Reform League had 'raised little beyond a very fine crop of actual and potential baronetcies', that the League's leader, Hewins, was a machinating nonentity and that Austen Chamberlain, though 'harmless', lacked grit as the political leader of Birmingham protectionism.[72] The Association hoped to put ginger on the tail of the Protectionist party, but during the quarter-century in which Docker was associated with it, its impact was nugatory. Of the wartime pressure-groups which Docker led to national influence, the Federation of British Industries and the British Commonwealth Union, more will be said in the next chapter.

6

The Federation of British Industries and the British Commonwealth Union 1916–22

The impetus to form the Federation of British Industries came from a meeting of the British Electrical and Allied Manufacturers Association (BEAMA) at the Birmingham and Midland Institute on 23 February 1916. Docker chaired the meeting, and his long speech on the need for business men's self-government – probably the most important speech of his life – was the progenitor of the Federation of British Industries. With electrical magnates like Rathenau, Cambó, Conti, Wallenberg and Loucheur leading the corporatist movement on the continent, it is not surprising that it was electrical manufacturers who fathered the first comprehensive and unified industrialists' federation in Britain; if Docker imparted to the FBI much of its original character, his thinking on the subject owed as much to his analysis of the methods of AEG and the German electrical industry as it did to the British rhetorical obsession with 'business government' which followed the Black Week of the Boer War in December 1899.

BEAMA had been formed in 1911 to represent the whole electrical manufacturing industry in discussions with civil servants, politicians and municipal or public authorities, but was also active in foreign trade promotion, and in collecting commercial intelligence. Its first triumph came when, in the aftermath of two colliery disasters, following official investigations which had exonerated electricity, the House of Commons welcomed a restrictive clause on the use of electricity in the ventilating shafts of mines, as if a naked light was less likely to cause gaseous combustion than heavily insulated electrical gear.[1] BEAMA mobilised a campaign which ultimately secured the withdrawal of this nonsensical clause: the episode not merely justified Docker's strictures on much recent industrial legislation, but also re-demonstrated the need for modern and efficient trade associations. During 1915, BEAMA moved closer to the Employers Parliamentary Association (EPA), an organisation which arose in 1912 under the leadership of Sir Charles Macara, a Lancashire cotton man, to fight what Macara called Lloyd George's 'German scheme of National Health Insurance'. Macara claimed that EPA 'was entirely non-political', and held other views resembling Docker's. 'He believed it was necessary if they were to maintain the prominent position that England occupied among the nations of the world, that commercial men should take a more active part in the administration of affairs.' Britain 'had had for a considerable time too many legal gentlemen in power, and unless they had more reasonable legislation than had been the case recently their position as the foremost industrial and commercial nation of the world could not be maintained'; according to Macara, 'As the example of Germany had been followed in the National Insurance Act, so the employees of England should follow Germany's lead in its Industrial Federation, which embraced all industries.'[2] Docker himself thought that EPA lacked driving force, but welcomed their pre-war approaches because he thought it useful to encourage any employers' association which attracted Liberals as members.[3] BEAMA and EPA both favoured manufacturers forming their own National Industrial Board, to act instead of a Ministry of Commerce,[4] and with this end in view, their presidents launched the Central Association of Employers Organisations in December 1915.

In his address to the electrical manufacturers in 1916, Docker complained that at a time when Britain was 'dependent for its safety on engineering industries', those industries were unrepresented in the government. If, when the war began, Britain had already possessed a Ministry of Commerce 'with a real business man at the head of it', then there would have been no need of a Ministry of Munitions, and

> none of the scandalous waste of men, money and brains which had been and was still seen, and but little of the labour trouble that had been experienced (hear hear). Such a Minister would have been in a position quickly to organise, with the aid of a comparatively few men, the great resources of industrial Britain, and also the vast army of workers...He would have understood instantly what was wanted and what could be achieved...it had been a painful revelation to many people in this country that its industries and its national defence were one and the same thing; and it was the duty of manufacturers, who did not create the war, but had got to win the war, and pay for it, to insist absolutely that in future their voices must be heard, and...have a representation in the Government (applause).[5]

Docker then turned to the tariff which he expected the government to introduce almost immediately. In the absence of a Ministry of Commerce liaising with industrialists, the government was incapable of establishing suitable rates and incidence of the tariff, and Docker therefore called for

Ill. 5 Dudley Docker *circa* 1916

the formation of a 'Business Parliament' to express the opinions of the industrial community. His speech was supported by T. C. Elder of BEAMA, who declared 'Either we shall have the biggest national scrap heap ever witnessed or we must make the biggest effort ever recorded in industrial reorganisation', and warned 'Financiers are a sort of separate nation apart, with the City of London for its metropolis, but possessing no territory and no sentiment.'⁵ Other speakers were Rogers and Manville of BSA/Daimler. Harris Spencer of the Midland Employers Federation, and Gilbert Vyle of W. and T. Avery (whose remark, 'we ha[ve] to upset the whole British constitution in order to get a Cabinet of businessmen', was a classic expression of the productioneers' views). The meeting was a rare convergence of northern and Midlands industrialists, and the conversations which Docker had after its formal adjournment spurred him to join with F. R. Davenport of BEAMA, Peter Rylands of EPA, F. J. Nettlefold of Courtaulds and A. W. Tait of Ferranti and British Aluminium in launching just such a Business Parliament as he had described.⁷

Docker's use of the phrase 'Business Parliament', and the terms in which he described the nascent Federation of British Industries throughout 1916, suggest that in Docker's mind the new institution was modelled on the Superior Council of Industry and Commerce which had been formed by the Belgian government in 1890. The Superior Council had sixty-six members, forty-four representing industry, and twenty-two from commerce. Of these, twelve industrialists and six commercial men were nominated by the King; the other forty-eight counsellors being elected by 480 delegates chosen by the chief manufacturers and traders of Belgium. The Superior Council was attended by delegates from the Foreign Office, Ministry of Finance and Public Works, and from the Ministry of Industry and Labour, who were entitled to speak, but not to vote. A third of the counsellors could request the government to summon the Council at any time. Its first major deliberations had been on the new Franco-Belgian customs tariff of 1891, and its other topics included re-organisation of the Consular Service (1893), the protection of patents and trademarks (1897) and petrol monopolies (1899).⁸ Docker believed that such an organisation was needed in England to prevent further legislation on financial and industrial problems such as had been passed by the Campbell-Bannerman and Asquith governments.

Docker did not borrow his ideas from Belgium alone. He also consulted Marcus Wallenberg, the financier responsible for many Scandinavian mergers, and founding president of Sweden's Industrial Union, who visited London in 1917 as head of an official Swedish commercial delegation. Wallenberg assured Docker that his Industrial Union was the only employers' organisation consulted by the Swedish government, and convinced Docker that Britain's Business Parliament must have a similar monopoly of relations between industry and Westminster. Wallenberg's experience was a misleading model for Docker, since his elder brother Knut was at that time Swedish Minister for Foreign Affairs, and the Wallenberg family had such power concentrated in their hands that one observer wrote in 1921 'they seem to run the whole country'. The unanimity which Marcus Wallenberg could orchestrate in Sweden was impossible to achieve in a country like Britain, which had begun industrialisation earlier, and whose industries were so fissiparous as to be almost incompatible.[9]

Speaking of his proposed Business Parliament to the MCWF shareholders in June 1916, Docker declared:

> 'Put not your faith in Prices' was the cry once. 'Put not your trust in Parliaments, in parties and in politicians' might well replace it now...For Heaven's sake, let us see to it that in matters we *do* know something about, our industries, our financial institutions, and so forth, we keep the politician at a respectful distance.[10]

In the months before the inaugural meeting on 21 July, the *Globe* carried many stories boosting the project, and indeed, Charles Palmer later described himself in *Who's Who* as 'originator of the idea which resulted in the formation of the Federation of British Industries'. The FBI's inaugural meeting was celebrated with a characteristic editorial:

> It is impossible to get rid of the politician, but it is not...impossible to guide him in the way he should go. He is the most amenable creature if the right stimulus is applied to him, for he regards nothing but votes, and they affect him precisely as a horse is affected by the sight of a sieveful of corn. The moment a combination of employers and employed, such as the members of the [FBI] contemplate, makes visible to him a great mass of organised voting power...he will be tumbling over himself to get it on his side. But this latent power must be made very plain. The manufacturers will have a great fight to wage with the importers upon whom so large a section of the professional politicians now depends, and every effort will be made to stimulate the senseless feud between Capital and Labour...But if they are relentless...they will win.[11]

By July 1916 Docker had persuaded 124 companies and trade associations to subscribe £1,000 each to join the FBI, and representatives of these formed the first Grand Council. Membership of the Grand Council eventually grew to about 450, elected by ballot annually, and divided into twenty-four groups comprising the leading industrial sectors. However, except in the cases of a few abnormally localised industries, these groups did not meet regularly for policy discussions as Docker envisaged, and the Grand Council did not become the all-powerful peak of the FBI's organisational pyramid. The difficulty of arranging well-attended meetings during the war, and the loss of impetus by the time peace came, was one cause of this failure; but it is also likely that Docker realised the impossibility of controlling developments through such a large and disparate body as the Grand Council, and preferred that initiatives during his presidency should come from the smaller Executive Council. Docker disliked forms too much to be happy using the inflexible structure of the Grand Council; his impatience, and his taste for fixing, made him prefer to seek his own way through personal persuasion of the Executive Council.

It is not coincidental that of the thirty original Executive Council members published in the *Globe* on 25 September 1916, none represented a trade association. The Fine Cotton Spinners and Doublers Association was, despite its name, a textile company, while the British Manufacturers Association was a Midlands protectionist lobby-group. All the thirty men were selected in their capacity as directors of manufacturing companies; no less than sixteen were involved in heavy engineering, while another four were from armaments or shipbuilding firms. The textile sector contributed only two men; the FBI was initially very much the interest group of large-scale heavy industry. Of these thirty men, four were closely identified with Docker: Lincoln Chandler, Edward Manville, Edward Hickman and Sir Vincent Caillard of Vickers, once described as 'fond of interfering like all people who have been thrust into positions for which they are not made'.[12] With Docker included, this group constituted a sixth of the Executive Council and were its hard-core of productioneers, although men like Godfrey Isaacs of Marconi's were also full of trade warrior's animosity. In 1916–19 they led much of the FBI's development and policies, with Caillard and Chandler especially active. Chandler, in FBI politics as in business, was Docker's all-purpose aide, while Caillard was tireless in attending meetings to which Docker sent apologies for absence, or letters for Caillard to read out. Docker and the productioneers all controlled large factories in the Midlands, and, as one historian writes, the FBI 'strongly represented Birmingham's interests' and marked the ascendancy of Birmingham opinion over Manchester's in British industrial policy-making.[13] Moreover, with the subsequent co-operation of the Docker companies with Vickers, Addison, the Minister of Munitions, was justified to write that 'the big armament companies are the most influential members' in 'the new monster association'.[14]

As the FBI's first president, Docker had decisive influence over the recruitment of full-time staff. The groundwork was done by Colonel W. C. Dumble, formerly general manager of the London General Omnibus Company to 1913 and a member of the Admiralty's Naval Construction Department when it was developing tanks for MCWF to build; Dumble was assisted by Major Maurice Caillard, half-brother of Sir Vincent, Private

Ill. 6 Sir Vincent Caillard (1856–1930)

Secretary to the Chief of General Staff at the War Office in 1908, and later Vickers' agent in Paris. Other administrative responsibilities fell on Sir Fitzjohn Oldham, a London solicitor associated with the Employers Parliamentary and Glassbottle Manufacturers Associations, who was used by Unionist Central Office to 'launder' bearer bonds paid in return for baronetcies and peerages.[15] Dumble and Caillard were diligent but un-inspired, and were soon replaced by Roland Nugent, Guy Locock and Charles Tennyson. Docker was 'sagacious and brave' in his recruitment of this trio,[16] for none had any commercial experience: Nugent and Locock were on the staff of the Foreign Office, and Tennyson came from the Colonial Office. Their recruitment was proof of the productioneers' view of the FBI as a means for trade warriors to increase the power of export monopolism by intimate collaboration with the Foreign and Colonial Offices; to attain 'the renaissance of the national and Imperial life' that Docker promised 'is going, if we all do our duty, to characterise the post-war age'.[17]

It was for this reason that Docker and the productioneers attached such importance to the Federation's Consular and Overseas Trade Committee. Formed in November 1916 with Caillard as its first chairman, it studied various aspects of commercial intelligence, reform of the consular body and international trade. Docker followed its deliberations keenly, and as a member of several government committees on overseas trade organisation, was decisive in helping the FBI committee to its conclusions. There was also close liaison between this branch of the FBI and the Department of Overseas Trade, established under Steel-Maitland in 1917. One of the FBI's chief aims was to organise British manufacturers into selling organisations for each sector of manufacturing, or to create a national selling agency divided into sections for each industry. It was felt that a more unified and corporatist sales structure would not only reduce the costs of overseas representation to individual companies, but would result in better economic intelligence, the elimination of wasteful competition and a progressive expansion of exports. These ideas were not new. BEAMA, on its formation in 1911, had been motivated by similar aims, and the British Engineers Association (BEA) had been launched in 1912, under the presidency of Douglas Vickers, to provide a sales and intelligence organisation for manufacturers interested in the export penetration of China. The BEA, at least, was staffed by ex-journalists and alcoholic soldiers, with no business sense or managerial competence, and its utter failure was evident by 1915. The FBI, however, avoided these pitfalls.

At the first meeting after the Armistice in 1918, the FBI launched a scheme, seemingly instigated by Docker, whereby it appointed its own Trade Commissioners to represent general British manufacturing interests abroad. The areas selected for the first appointments – Spain, Greece, the East Indies and Scandinavia – were all areas in which the productioneers were anxious to obliterate pre-war German dominance. The first Com-missioner, was appointed to Madrid on 24 January 1919, and the Spanish example illustrates what the FBI hoped to combat. German exports to Spain in 1913 were worth less than £7½ million, and imports under £3 million, but the Germans had thought it worthwhile to erect an elaborate and costly commercial mechanism and to conduct systematic propaganda. The dreaded AEG and Siemens had a profitable turnover in Spain, and the smaller trades had sent an army of commercial travellers throughout Spain in the years before 1914. Translations of German engineering textbooks had been circulated among Spanish students, and German plant was offered as cheap equipment in the engineering colleges. In 1913 alone some 200 tons of designs, plans and photographs were sent to Spain from Germany, and the German technical literature usually comprised studies of local conditions and the application thereto of German methods and equipment. The Spanish resented aggressive instruction, and British trade propaganda's crude glorification of its own enterprise, with its implied strictures on Spanish development, aggravated the evil it was meant to avoid. Moreover, in machine tools, the British had suffered ignominious losses. Almost every Spanish factory or workshop erected in the 1880s or 1890s used British-made lathes, drilling machines, planing machines or steam engines. The British held a priceless advantage over their competitors, which German ingenuity and British neglect turned into a weapon destructive of British trade. German salesmen took this old equipment as a theme for the antiquated, effete standards of British industry, and convinced Spanish engineers (educated in Germany or fed on German textbooks) that British patterns were twenty years behind their German counterparts.

It was to reverse these trends that the FBI appointed its first Trade Commissioner to Madrid, and by December 1919 Nugent was claiming that 'the Federation Office is in the eyes of all Spaniards an infinitely more important place than the British Embassy'.[18] Nevertheless, by July 1919, when Steel-Maitland resigned from the Department of Overseas Trade in frustration, it was clear that, in the absence of firmer co-ordination with government and finance, this aspect of the FBI's work was fatally weak. 'The Federation is doing work which they should be strong enough to insist upon the Government doing out of the revenues of the country', Lincoln Chandler complained in October 1919,[19] and the FBI's unilateral efforts lost momentum as the government got bogged down in the slough created by Lloyd George's preference for moral, intellectual and administrative irregularity. The Consular and Overseas Trade Committee's work petered into minutiae after Caillard's retirement from the FBI presidency in the autumn of 1919: indeed his departure marked the end of the productioneers' ascendancy in the Federation.

The beliefs of the productioneers can quickly be recapitulated. They were obsessed with German industrial rivalry and felt, in Docker's words, that the war was a turning-point: 'We must get on with our commerce...or sink into a second-class community.'[20] Industrial prosperity was perceived in terms of international economic combat, as shown in the FBI's letter of January 1917 to Lloyd George urging immediate steps to beat the post-war German *Zollverein*.[21] Apart from getting tariff protection, the productioneers wanted a merger and rationalisation movement on the scale characterised by German electro-technology and American machine tools; they wanted government, industry and finance to co-operate in rationalisation and export policy; and they wanted labour to aid, and benefit from, industrial reconstruction and export successes. Following from his belief that there was nothing 'political' or objectionable in the aims of his Business Leagues, Docker expected the FBI membership to agree on measures to these ends, and present them with sufficient unanimity and authority to establish the FBI as a Business Parliament acting in industrial and commercial matters in the fashion of the Belgian Superior Council. But however much he proclaimed that the 'occasion is a supreme one',[22] he was frustrated by dissent and jealousies. As Rylands told him in 1919, 'the difficulties of running a Federation' were 'almost insuperable' given 'the extraordinary and sometimes unreasonable variation in view among the Manufacturers of Great Britain'.[23]

The FBI's membership rose from about 80 in June 1916 to over 400 in June 1917, and membership income at the end of the first full year was £46,000 rising to £121,000 in the peak year of 1921. This expansion diluted the power of Docker and his adherents, as he expected, but he had not anticipated the strength of opposition to the productioneers' policies. Already in August 1918, Bonar Law was told that with the FBI, Docker had 'created a Frankenstein monster which he could not allay',[24] and which he was inclined to disown. The Frankenstein had many parts. Thus Sir Peter Rylands, late of the EPA, led opposition to the FBI becoming a manufacturers' political party, as Docker advocated. Rylands warned 'the cry that the capitalist with the money-bags is trying to rule the country would be fatal', and deplored Docker's efforts in that direction as 'pyrotechnical'.[25] The Lancashire cotton crowd, adherents to free trade and *laissez-faire*, opposed tariff protection and centralised regulation of reconstruction plans. Sir Allan Smith of the Engineering Employers Federation (EEF) and Sir Wilfred Stokes of the BEA were never 'particularly friendly' to the FBI, as both were anxious to preserve their own spheres of power.[26] Indeed, in return for the EEF's qualified co-operation, Smith extracted an undertaking that the FBI would eschew questions touching work conditions, or pay rates, except at the request of the relevant employers' federation or trade association. This instantly extinguished Docker's hopes of a Business Parliament comprehensively representing manufacturers in all dealings with government and labour. Though it remained possible for the FBI to secure major achievements in commercial and industrial policy, its scope was curtailed and the manufacturers' voice divided in a way which had no benefit, except to Smith's personal status.

Nevertheless, the FBI clashed heavily with the EEF in the winter of 1917–18, in circumstances which emphasised the different priorities among the manufacturing interest. The EEF emerged from the confrontation with its position strengthened, having threatened withdrawal of its members from the FBI. The threat was not idle, since there is evidence that the shipbuilders, for example, always evinced sympathy with Smith and gave their first loyalty to the EEF. The disagreement arose after the appointment, in the autumn of 1917, of a Labour Committee of the FBI, chaired by Rylands.[27] Its fifteen other members included Caillard, Chandler and Manville. The committee was of the highest calibre. H. G. Tetley of Courtaulds, Sir George Murray of Armstrong Whitworth, Sir Herbert Austin, Godfrey Isaacs of Marconi's and Sir Charles Marston of Villiers Engineering, to name a cross-section, were not men to be patronised by Docker, or rail-roaded by a Docker group. (Indeed, one of its most active and enlightened members, Frank Moore, a Leicester boot manufacturer, was living contravention of Docker's opinion that smaller employers were narrow-minded, 'pinching and screwing' their employees, and so aggravating labour relations as to be 'a justification in themselves for large amalgamations'.)[28]

The Labour Report, when completed, agreed with Docker that, before the war, 'it was becoming more difficult to preserve industrial peace', and that restrictive practices were now 'equally serious'. 'Unless our productivity can be greatly increased we have little chance of avoiding the economic disaster with which we are threatened by the prolongation of War conditions', because the 'enormous' burden of War debts 'must be borne by Industrial Production ... to avoid national bankruptcy and possibly revolution.' Like Docker, they discounted the value of profit-sharing schemes, and urged the use of Works Committees.[29] They made other minor recommendations which, like all their proposals, were *conditional* on trade unionists abandoning all pre-war restrictive practices. They observed that employers had hitherto generally

> not contributed anything towards what may be called the Conservation of Labour, and it is small wonder that the workers, who see capital laying by reserve funds for the repair, renewal and replacement of plant, and

> for the provision of dividends in times when Trade is bad, and Labour turned into the street, feel that they are being treated as machines...to be cast aside when broken down or out of repair.

The committee instead urged

> that some share of the burden involved in the Conservation of Labour ought, in each industry, to fall on Capital, and...that the voluntary assumption by Employers of some part of this charge would have far-reaching effects in persuading the workers that the interests of Capital and Labour are not antagonistic, but that co-operation with Capital is a necessary and profitable function of Labour.

On this basis they recommended that trade unions and trade associations covering each industrial sector should establish insurance schemes covering union members against sickness, under-employment and unemployment.[30] This idea followed Docker's concept of a pyramid-like structure of trade associations and trade unions for each industry, and had some resemblance to guild socialist plans. It also corresponded to views urged in 1919 by another Birmingham imperialist, Leo Amery. He judged that 'industry had been becoming more and more immoral and inhuman', and hoped that Whitley Councils would not only create 'industry based in justice and also humanly interesting to those concerned', but also that 'a council of all the Whitley Councils' would develop into 'the Second Chamber of the future and the way of meeting the element of real need which underlies Bolshevism'.[31] Although Rylands insisted that the Report was written from 'the social and national point of view', Smith and the EEF objected not only to the general recommendations but remonstrated that it was an exclusively labour matter outside the FBI's responsibilities.[32] There was a sharp exchange, with the EEF threatening to cease co-operation with the FBI, and Smith ensured not only that the report was ignored but that the FBI never again trenched on labour topics. Following Smith's new victory the National Employers Federation (of which Docker had succeeded as president) was absorbed into the EEF, and a new National Confederation of Employers Organisations was established under Smith's aegis. The NCEO was ostensibly a twin-body to the FBI representing all of industry on national labour policy, but in practice in its early years it remained subordinate to Smith and the EEF.[33] This arrangement extirpated the vestiges of the FBI's involvement in labour relations and crushed Docker's last hope of a Business Parliament concerned with every aspect of manufacturing policy.

Despite this frustration, Docker had further impact on labour policy during his presidency of the FBI by helping to launch the Whitley Councils scheme. This was a government-sponsored plan, whereby representatives of employers and employed in each industrial sector formed Joint Councils to discuss wages, working conditions, job security, participation, technical training, private grievances and any other relevant matters. Its framers envisaged a Joint Council for each industry with an hierarchy based on District Councils and Works Committees, and headed by an Industrial Parliament. Docker helped to launch the Whitley scheme in 1917, and after discussing the preliminary details with him, the Minister of Reconstruction wrote in 1917: 'There is a good deal of prejudice against Docker, but he has big ideas about providing security of employment, and I feel reassured after the interview.' Addison did not specify the root of the prejudice, which perhaps lay in the implacable and imperious way in which Docker urged a corporatist state. As it was the Whitley scheme resembled both the pyramid of industrial associations, topped by a Business Parliament, which Docker wanted, and the guild socialists' ideal community in which production was organised through associations of the workers in each industry, topped by a democratic body representing the guilds of all industries. The Whitley Councils were a mixed success. Those in some industries were very successful and still operate today at national level, while in other companies such as Colman's mustard and ICI they inspired flourishing consultative committees. But elsewhere in the inter-war period they failed at factory level, sometimes after sabotage by reactionary middle-managers, but more often because neither the managers nor the workers' representatives could understand their purpose and potential, and were dismissive of London theorists.[34] Like most projects with which Docker sympathised, the Whitley scheme did not take sufficient account of the ignorance and insularity of small men.

The final crucial area of FBI activity in which Docker's hopes were dashed was tariff reform. The EPA, despite Macara's opposition, was absorbed by the FBI in the winter of 1916–17, and its Lancashire members detested protection. Docker in his retiring presidential speech in October 1917 acknowledged that this made it impossible for the FBI to press for tariff reform.[35] His belief in the need for a 'power to bargain' remained undiminished, and a few months later he claimed, 'there is no manufacturer who fails to recognise that the German trade organisation is a war organisation, and can only be met and defeated by warlike methods; and unless the British manufacturer is armed with a tariff club he is impotent, and his brains, his capital and the labour of his workpeople are of no account'.[36] Caillard and Docker continued trying to draw various small imperialist and protectionist bodies into the FBI's orbit. Of these the most significant was the British Empire Producers Organisation, publishers of the magazine *Production*. As Nugent told Caillard in January 1919,

'BEPO...are neither a very powerful nor a very efficient body, but the removal of anyone else who is competing with us...is always a gain.'[37] In February the Executive Council Committee asked Docker, Caillard, Oldham and Nugent to finalise an amalgamation with BEPO, as previously discussed by Docker and Caillard.[38] Docker attended none of the subsequent negotiations, being represented by Sir Ernest Hiley of MCWF who was one of 'the Regular Gang' of Docker men in FBI politics.[39] The BEPO negotiating sub-committee reached terms which exceeded their instructions by embodying a resolution about Imperial Preference. Although this resolution did not commit the FBI to BEPO's fiscal policy, it collided as Rylands told Docker 'with the rigidity of Manchester opinion' as the cotton spinners asserted 'that it was the beginning of a movement to stampede the Federation in the direction of a Tariff'.[40] Liverpool and Nottingham followed Manchester in their opposition, and the FBI was forced to repudiate the terms negotiated by Hiley, Oldham, Nugent and the president, Caillard. On 2 August, Hiley warned Nugent that Docker would resign from the FBI, and withdraw his companies, 'if the Federation does not back up' Caillard over the BEPO merger terms.[41] Neither MCWF, Patent Shaft nor Docker Brothers paid their subscriptions, which were due in June 1919,[42] and various critical letters were exchanged between Docker, Nugent and Rylands, as Caillard's successor as president. In December 1919, Docker resigned from the Finance Committee of the FBI,[43] and Rylands recognised that Docker was 'disgruntled' with the FBI, possibly because Rylands, Nugent and the ex-EPA membership of the FBI had made clear their reluctance to participate in the ambitious parliamentary schemes of another body, the British Commonwealth Union.[44] Rylands succeeded in pacifying Docker to the extent that his companies quietly paid their FBI subscriptions in January 1920:[45] but from this stage the founding president disappeared almost entirely from FBI policy-making.

Lancashire's suspicions about the BEPO merger terms were not necessarily wrong. The evidence is non-existent, but it is plausible that the Imperial Preference resolution was an obscure attempt, during the presidency of such an outstanding imperialist as Caillard, to jump the FBI back onto the protectionist tracks which Docker had originally considered prerequisite for success. Such a coup would certainly have been in character with Caillard, 'one of those who does not know what is possible, fixes his heart on the impossible and then gives way to melancholy when he finds he cannot realise it'.[46] Docker was directly interested in the affair: as its outcome was a rout of imperialist protectionism, nothing remained in the FBI of Docker's original hopes.

The forces which combined to defeat Docker assembled to form, in July

1918, the Imperial Association of Commerce under the presidency of Lord Inchcape, the India merchant and chairman of the P & O Line. This association was the reaction of financial and shipping circles, merchants and brokers, to the agitation of corporatist manufacturers generally, and to the FBI in particular. Inchcape and his supporters were horrified at the impact which Docker and his sympathisers were having on government, and the prospectus which they issued declared that the new association would 'act as a medium of communication between all *bona fide* British traders and the Government... to procure the adequate representation of all sections of the business community upon all Government Committees whose deliberations affect... trade'. They also vowed to oppose 'any form of restriction or control of trade which threatens to crush and eventually destroy that splendid initiative and individual enterprise which has in the past so largely contributed to the strength of the Empire', and to combat propaganda or prejudice 'which menaces the individual in the successful prosecution of his legitimate business'. Contradicting men like Docker, the Association claimed that in August 1914 'nothing save the wonderful power wielded by British traders enabled this country to cope successfully with the crisis', that the 'influence and power of our mercantile classes was superb' and that 'vast and complicated trade' could only be 'carried on by men with lifelong experience'. Inchcape and his colleagues loathed the 'tendency to change the business methods of this country, and to attribute the evils of war to a system which has in truth made the splendid efforts of Great Britain and her overseas dominions and colonies both possible and practical'. 'Every banker and shipowner, every merchant, broker and distributor... has felt the relentless pressure which has threatened and is today threatening to limit his rights... as a trader': Inchcape predicted that if they did not 'face the issues which concern their very existence, they will be superseded by a new and costly machine which every day is becoming more powerful and more inimical to their interests'. The Imperial Association of Commerce, with its commitment to *individual* initiative and enterprise, its repudiation of change in British business efforts, and its hostility to wartime corporatism, represented the backlash to the 'trade warrior' rhetoric of 1910–19. It was proof for Docker that unanimity was impossible among the mass of British business men, and its formation foreshadowed the destruction by the early 1920s of all Docker's hopes for corporatist reform.[47]

It now remains to consider Docker's involvement in one final wartime pressure-group: the British Commonwealth Union.[48] Formed in December 1916 as the London Imperialists, under the leadership of Sir Trevor Dawson of Vickers, it was originally intended 'to ensure the better representation of industrial and commercial interests in the Metropolitan constituencies'. The original members included two other Vickers' directors who were FBI activists (Caillard and Barker), together with Frederick Orr-Lewis of Canadian-Vickers; they were soon joined by senior directors of Beardmore, Armstrong Whitworth and Nobel Industries. Armourers were again to the fore in imperialist organisation, and they swiftly extended their scope from London MPs to the general representation of the country. Unlike the FBI, the London Imperialists' influence was not dependent upon governmental recognition that they were truly representative of manufacturing interests, so they did not widen their membership to embrace industrialists who were unsympathetic to protection. Caillard, politically subtle and author of the monograph on *Imperial Fiscal Reform* which led Hewins to found the Tariff Reform League, was in unwontedly rough company. The other London Imperialists tended to betray that ignorance of both politics and economic theory which has already been identified as a weakness in Docker's political activity. They were, for example, vociferous supporters, like the *Globe*, of the Australian Prime Minister Billy Hughes, who was the hero of all British productioneers for his campaign against the Frankfurt metallurgical trust of Metallgesellschaft and Metallbank which had been represented in London by Henry Merton and Company.

In March 1917, Dawson approached Lincoln Chandler about co-operation between the London Imperialists and the FBI with a view to establishing an industrial group in Parliament, and later that month, eight FBI leaders (including Chandler, Manville, Docker and another MCWF director Alex Spencer) attended a meeting with the Imperialists. Docker was the only one of the eight who did not immediately join the Imperialists' Executive Council, characteristically preferring to receive 'notices of all meetings and to be entitled to attend them', but he was dominant in subsequent discussions. He moved cautiously, because the FBI had recruited on the basis of 'its being a non-political body, and free from any fiscal creed, [so] he might be charged with bad faith if we entered the arena of politics or economics'.[49] Opposition to the British Commonwealth Union (as the London Imperialists were re-named) organising with the FBI 'a body of Manufacturers...for the express and sole purpose of controlling Parliament' was strongest among former EPA leaders such as Oldham and Rylands. The latter feared that the scheme would alarm the public with visions of ruthless American trusts, and unite the opponents of the manufacturing interests. Unlike Docker, Rylands foresaw that the scheme might force the FBI into 'active support of members of Parliament pledged to policy in matters other than commercial which they might detest'; he counselled, 'Parliamentary influence ought to be sought very carefully, and without ostentation...through the medium of the Federation itself.'[50] As a result of this opposition led by Rylands, Chandler finally had to inform the BCU in June 1917 that the FBI had decided 'to take no direct parliamentary action in its corporate capacity'.

This defeat annoyed Docker, whose wishes for the BCU's parliamentary project soon suffered another check. Grant Morden, the Canadian specu- lator (described variously as a 'ruffian' and 'most impertinent') who was Dawson's deputy in the early period of the London Imperialists, wrote in 1932 of 'my controversy with Docker who wanted to make an industrial party, whereas...I got out my charts showing how we could be...an Industrial Party, but camouflage it...[so] as we would not be known as such'.[51] Morden won the argument, and Docker never forgave him. Later, in 1918, after the House of Commons Select Committee on Public Expenditure had published condign criticism of Morden for his activities with Dawson in floating the British Cellulose Company, Morden was obliged to resign from the Union to Docker's certain satisfaction. Subse- quently, in December 1919, Morden (by then MP for Brentford) was re-admitted to the BCU Committee, because his friend Hugo Hirst would not otherwise renew General Electric's subscription of £1,000. When a dinner was then given in Morden's honour, Docker proved that he had not forgiven old scores by broadcasting 'strong' objections to 'feasting' Morden at the BCU's expense.[52]

The BCU appointed as its executive director an Irishman, Patrick Hannon. Born in 1874 the son of an illiterate farmer from Kilfree, Hannon began his career as a photographer at Loughrea in Galway in 1894. He worked at promoting Irish agricultural co-operation, before acting as Director of Agricultural Organisation in Cape Colony (1904–7). He was afterwards a functionary in the Tariff Reform League, the National Service League, the Navy League, the National Aerial Defence Association, and the Imperial Mission. A busybody who revelled in gossip, Hannon later became a drinking crony of Beaverbrook with the requisite insincerity of that presslord's courtiers. He succeeded Sir Hallewell Rogers as a Birmingham MP in 1921, sat on the Executive Council of the National Union of Manufacturers from 1919 (serving as president 1935–53), was Secretary of the House of Commons' Industrial Group 1921–9, and also meddled in bodies as distinct as the Public Morality Council, the Institute of Exports and the Comrades of the Great War.

Docker's original hope was that the British Commonwealth Union would sponsor an industrial party along lines which he started with the Business Leagues in 1912–14. The closest existent parliamentary grouping to it would have been the National Party, led by

Brigadier General Henry Page Croft, MP for Bournemouth, and Sir Richard Cooper, MP for Walsall.[53] Once wartime tensions had abated, and the bi-partisan party system had been restored in 1922, it is improbable that an industrial party would have been electorally successful. The alternatives would have been for its members to re-join the Conservatives, as Nationalists like Croft and Cooper did, or to tend towards the reactionary corporatism which in Germany was associated with Hugo Stinnes and which would have been hopeless in Britain. Despite his defeat by Morden, as Bonar Law was told in August 1918, Docker after 'many lunches or dinners at the Ritz or Claridges' was persuaded to continue co-operation with the BCU, and did so 'with a vengeance!'.[54] In June 1918, a letter from Docker suggesting that parliamentary candidates seeking BCU backing 'should be expected to support the ideas of the Union' was read by Caillard to the General Purposes Committee, which passed a resolution to that effect; and on 11 July, another of Docker's letters was read to the committee, which then agreed to support them 'with all its influence on the definite condition that the policy of the Union in the case of all such candidates should take priority over Party Allegiance... [so] 'that on Industrial and Commercial questions in Parliament, members supported by the Union should give their support to Union policy as the first claim upon their Parliamentary vote'.[55] The BCU's support of candidates was, of course, made under conditions of 'strictest secrecy'. A week later, the first BCU candidate was approved: Arthur Beck, a Birmingham manufacturer of electrical accessories. He fought the Kingswinford constituency in Staffordshire, to which he was introduced by Docker, on a programme of complete home-ownership in Britain, a strong Aliens Act and an end to foreign dumping. Docker took a personal interest in Beck's candidature throughout the last six months of 1918,[56] and his influence is discernible in the BCU's other parliamentary protégés. Of the fourteen men on the 'Official List' of BCU candidates, Rogers and Manville were Docker's colleagues at BSA, Cunliffe-Lister was a director of MCWF heavily under his patronage, Norton-Griffiths had been launched in politics by Docker in 1909, and Maconochie had been selected at Wednesbury under Docker's aegis in 1914. Similarly, Alderman Jephcott who was elected as a Conservative at Yardley, and Alderman Hallas who was elected as 'patriotic labour' candidate at Duddeston, were both Birmingham trade unionists with whom Docker had dealt for years, and had possibly been encouraged to think of parliamentary candidatures in pre-war days when the Business Leagues were operating at constituency level. All fourteen save Beck and Maconochie were elected. Docker also wanted to sponsor 'a Midland Radical Labour man' in the East Worcestershire constituency represented by a Unionist called Leverton Harris. The latter was a shipowner and Parliamentary Secretary to the Ministry of Blockade; he was in fact highly effective in the post, and a Quaker by birth, but he was erroneously believed by right-wing Tories to be a German Jew giving treasonable information on the blockade to Germany. Docker seems to have shared this prejudice (although no specifically anti-Semitic remark by him has ever been traced), and 'felt sure Harris would lose the seat to *any* opponent who goes to the poll as an anti-alien'. In the event, Harris evaded Docker's threat first by joining the BCU himself in 1918, and then by leaving politics altogether in the autumn.[57]

The sub-committee which selected BCU candidates was chaired by Cunliffe-Lister, with Ludford Docker as a member; and one of its main criteria was ironic in view of Maxse's editorial policy at the *Globe*. A Black List was prepared of Free Traders, members of the Independent Labour party, pacifists and those who had opposed the government in the Commons vote on the Maurice debate in May 1918. That debate had been the culmination of the anti-Lloyd George intrigues of General Robertson, Colonel Repington, Leo Maxse and others, and had amounted to a vote of confidence in Lloyd George. Since Maxse had ranged the *Globe* so uncompromisingly on the side of the generals against the civilian government, it may seem paradoxical that the rebels in the Maurice debate should have been singled out for punishment. The explanation lies in the fact that the majority of the dissidents were Asquithian Liberals, and it was this group which the productioneers most wanted to crush in British political life.

In addition to the fourteen official BCU candidates, there were another ten candidates secretly funded by the BCU, of whom six were elected. The failures included Christabel Pankhurst, a Lower Deck candidate put up for a naval constituency in the hope of splitting the Labour vote and a National party candidate who was later a founder of the British Fascists. The successes included Sir Harry Brittain, a rumbustious imperial publicist; Percy Hurd, who had been Hewins' secretary at the Tariff Commission; the vain and bumptious Howard Gritten, refused official support by Unionist Central Office and regarded by them as 'a grumbling Bounder'; and Sir Park Goff, a former King's Messenger and self-styled expert on Eastern Europe, whose parliamentary manner is evoked by his speech on the Army Estimates in 1920:

> The Armenian is the evil of the East...the existence of Armenia is a calamity and a disgrace...The Greek is thoroughly untrustworthy and unreliable...the Ottoman Greek and the Armenian...is a murderer, a forger, a liar and a thief...The only claim to fame which Greece has is that it is the only country in the world where a Scotchman cannot live...I

would describe Romania as the House of Lords, Turkey as the House of Commons and Bulgaria as the London County Council.

Men like Gritten and Goff constituted the BCU's successes.[58] One continental counterpart of the BCU was the Curatorium for the Reconstruction of German Economic Life founded by the electrical magnate Carl Friedrich von Siemens in 1918. Siemens collected large sums through this body to back the election to the Reichstag of business men who would support the interests of industry and finance (*die Wirtschaft*). Siemens disbursed to individuals, not party organisations, and his beneficiaries represented the Democratic, Centre, German People's and German National People's parties. Siemens, like Docker 'treated *die Wirtschaft* [the business community] as if it were a monolithic unit that operated according to...immutable principles' and with unanimous fixed interests: an assumption that was palpably untrue, as, for example, Siemens differed sharply on most points of policy from his chief competitor in the German electric business Walter Rathenau of AEG.[59]

Docker's views were also felt on a sub-committee, appointed in October 1918, comprising himself, Caillard and Vassar-Smith, to consider giving the BCU direct parliamentary representation, through its director Hannon, and Allan Smith, the chairman of the General Purposes Committee; its deliberations must have overlapped with the FBI sub-committee, appointed in November 1917, also numbering Docker, Caillard and Vassar-Smith, to consider the Federation's potential influence at constituency level on MP's industrial attitudes. If Docker was not the sole inspiration for the BCU's activities during the general election of 1918, he was of prime importance both in developing the parliamentary strategy, and in the selection of candidates from his own business acquaintance. His own position was regularised when he joined the Council of BCU on 4 July 1918, together with Sir Hallewell Rogers and Leo Maxse. This was followed by his companies making generous financial commitments to assure the Union's future. On 25 July, Hiley and Rogers undertook that MCWF, BSA and Vickers (with which Docker was by then associated) would each donate £2,500 to cover current expenses, and subsequently Vickers and MCWF agreed to subscribe £10,000 per annum for three years although they were released from this undertaking later, and paid a total of £15,000 each in the three years to December 1921.[60] It was against this background that Docker could be described to Steel-Maitland, in May 1919, as 'probably the most powerful member of the British Commonwealth Union'.[61]

The object of all these manoeuvres, and of many of Docker's other reconstruction plans, was the general election of December 1918. Yet the suddenness with which this was called overwhelmed the BCU's constituency plans, and they were further disappointed that Caillard and Docker were unsuccessful in seeking an interview with Lloyd George so that BCU policy towards the coalition could be fully considered.[62] Docker's own rallying cry for the election, as he told an eve-of-poll rally at Wednesbury, was 'recognition for sailors and soldiers, keep the old flag flying, fair trade and no dumping, no Germans in the British Empire',[63] but his resentment that the BCU's plans could not be better laid because of the rush to the country was reflected in the *Globe*'s editorials. The general election summoned after the Armistice was attacked by the *Globe* as intending 'to ensure [party politicians'] opportunity to play their monkey pranks at Westminster for another five years'. In view of the influenza epidemic, according to a desperate editorial entitled 'Votes for Microbes', the election campaign created 'the possibility of a new Black Death', and should be postponed: certainly, if it had been postponed, the BCU would have had time to organise the extra candidates Docker wanted. The *Globe* advised readers, if confronted with several candidates who were all 'clean men', to vote for Page Croft's Nationalists. In the absence of a Nationalist, any independent coalitionist was preferable to a couponed coalitionist because 'a strong body of Independents' was needed in the Commons to prevent 'a Government with a subservient majority at their…call' approaching 'new problems on old party lines'.[64] This advice had been foreshadowed in August by the BCU telling Page Croft that there was no 'shred of difference' between themselves on industrial matters: 'We are both determined to keep out of power in the future the Party trickster and the bolshevik.'[65]

In 1919, with the Lloyd George coalition safely back in power the *Globe* rapidly moved into opposition to the 'pseudo-Bolsheviks…in the neighbourhood of Downing Street', and to those 'Labour mis-leaders [who] with the connivance of a cowardly Cabinet' were 'making frantic efforts in many places to convert the victory into defeat for the benefit of Germany'. But when, in June 1919, the lead headlines blazed 'The Alternative to Lloyd George, Leadership at Last!…A Man Who Will Not Run Away', the political messiah hailed by Maxse and Docker transpired to be no less absurd a figure than a long-term contributor to the *National Review*, the die-hard, coal-owning Duke of Northumberland.[66] Northumberland's attacks on the Sankey Commission investigating the coal industry, and on the miners' leader Robert Smillie, continued to be splashed during the summer of 1919, but were the last splutters of Docker's proprietorship. By August, Conservative party officials had heard that the *Globe* was for sale, and in October it was bought by Sir Robert Donald, a Liberal journalist with great personal animus against Lloyd George.[67]

Whether Docker decided that he could no longer support the losses which the *Globe* sustained, or whether he had become disillusioned with the possibilities of press power, is unknown; but some lessons can be drawn from the turbulence and bellicosity of Docker's reign at the *Globe*. As Roland Nugent of the FBI wrote in 1920 of the propaganda efforts of the BCU, 'the trouble is that people like Mr Docker, if they write a letter which is put in [a newspaper], think that this is propaganda which is having some effect and do not realise...the very fine and delicate art involved in getting a really consistent press campaign going'.[68] This comment was equally applicable to the vigorous, but not always constructive or consistent, campaigns of the *Globe*: the characteristics which had made Docker one of Birmingham's paramount manufacturers were not those of a great presslord, or a political adept, or a popular campaigner.

There is no doubt that Docker deplored the opportunism of the Lloyd George coalition. He had a particularly furious clash with its Minister of Transport, Sir Eric Geddes, who alleged in December 1919 that the state was obliged to become a large-scale rolling-stock manufacturer at Woolwich Arsenal because of the extortionate prices charged by private makers who preferred to supply the export market. Docker exploded at this, writing to Geddes and Lloyd George that 'The wagon builders are short of work and the Government know it', and publishing various press denials.[69] Geddes' figures were false, as when he gave the production cost of a 16-ton mineral wagon as £200 although the raw material alone cost £207; and Docker suspected that the minister, as a former railway manager, was using his official position to further the long-standing disagreements between some railway operators and some rolling-stock makers. MCWF consulted Edwin Docker's legal firm, and, following their advice, had by the end of the month approached Sir John Simon and Sir Edward Carson about a libel action against Geddes for heavy damages.[70] There is no doubt that the company was injured by Geddes' reckless statements, because shortly before Christmas 1919, the South African Dominion Agents broke off negotiations for a rolling-stock contract on the grounds that Geddes' figures suggested they would get bad value.[71] Though a writ was never served, Docker mobilised many of his allies against Geddes. Steel-Maitland published a rebuttal in *The Times*;[72] BCU members such as Manville took the matter up in and outside Parliament; and the FBI formed a special Wagon-Builders' sub-committee on 16 December. Its members included representatives of all private interests in the industry, as well as Steel-Maitland and, as chairman, Cunliffe-Lister. Nugent described the Federation as 'moving heaven and earth for the wagon builders, chiefly at Mr Docker's request', in what promised 'to be a most amusing little fight';[73] and in due course, a deputation waited upon Bonar Law. A long and increasingly complicated wrangle then ensued with the Ministry of Transport about the fashion in which relative costs between the public and private sector could be investigated by accountants. By July 1920, the momentum had left the controversy, although the FBI committee continued to meet until September. Geddes' threat of the government becoming a large-scale competitor of the private rolling-stock makers may not have been serious, but Docker certainly treated it as such.

His revulsion against the Lloyd George coalition was shared in many quarters, and several plots were hatched to supplant it. The prime movers of one such conspiracy, to launch a government of 'Constitutionalists' led by Lord Grey of Fallodon, the former Foreign Secretary, were Docker's two acquaintances, Steel-Maitland and Lord Robert Cecil. Early in 1922 they sent a memorandum to forty-nine men, including Docker, outlining the beliefs of the Constitutionalists and inviting comments and support.[74] Docker was one of the twelve respondents who replied that they were in agreement with the memorandum;[75] nineteen others were definitely against, and eighteen were doubtful. Docker was attracted by the Constitutionalists' appeal to moderate opinion, their bitterness about the collapse of reconstruction plans, by their call for retrenchment in government spending, and for reduced taxation. Their emphasis on industrial reconciliation and partnership ('Abuse of labour by Ministers of the Crown is as harmful as abuse of capital by the labour extremists') was also congenial to Docker. But later in March 1922 he apparently re-read the memorandum, and noticed that the Constitutionalists considered the League of Nations to be the keystone of foreign policy. His secretary informed Steel-Maitland on 15 March that in view of the references to the League of Nations, Docker withdrew his support: Docker was 'in entire disagreement with the methods adopted by advocates of what he considers an ideal impossible of attainment'.[76] Those who were familiar with the extremely pessimistic and materialist view of foreign affairs which he shared with Sir Victor Wellesley would not have expected any other answer.

Though Docker deplored the shadiness of the Lloyd George coalition, he was involved in at least one of their intrigues. After the railway strikes of 1919, the coalition Chief Whips arranged a meeting in August of industrial magnates to discuss 'educational propaganda'. The guest-list included Caillard, Docker, Faringdon, Cunliffe-Lister, Douglas Vickers, Vernon Willey and Vassar-Smith.[77] Some £100,000 was eventually subscribed to run a propaganda campaign against trade union militancy, and in favour of political gradualism; and the campaign was put in the hands of a reptilian former government undercover agent, Sidney Walton. Professor Middlemas considers that Walton's activities had 'prodigious' effects, but at least one extremely well-placed contemporary disagreed. Roland Nugent, director of the FBI, had inside knowledge of these conspiracies, and he wrote in 1920, 'propaganda work at the moment...stinks in the nostrils of the press, thanks to the clumsy methods of Mr Sidney [Walton]...If the press...thinks anything is propaganda, it absolutely refuses to touch it.'[78] Reading Walton's handiwork inclines one to believe Nugent rather than Professor Middlemas. Interestingly, in the original discussions of August 1919, Caillard on behalf of the productioneers insisted that 'it would be a grave blunder to give any appearance of Party or Coalition intervention' in the anti-Bolshevik propaganda campaign, and wanted the role of the Party Whips reduced to a minimum.[79] Co-operation with the Whips was objectionable to die-hard enemies of the political establishment, whether nationalist manufacturers or Clydeside Bolsheviks.

Further doubt is cast on the success of these propaganda campaigns by the intermediaries which were used. For example, the BCU made many of its approaches to the Labour movement through Havelock Wilson, head of the National Seamen's Union, and the only non-Unionist MP, apart from Page Croft, who was consistently puffed by the *Globe* under Docker's proprietorship. The submarine warfare of 1916 had made Havelock Wilson pathologically Germanophobic, and as a reaction to socialist pacifism, he became a virulent opponent of the parliamentary Labour party, whilst his Union became increasingly isolated from the rest of the trade union movement. His hostility to mainstream socialism was shown by his defence of the mine owners to the Sankey Commission on the coal industry in 1919; and the BCU showed their admiration for him with two payments of £500 each in February and May 1919. A more unrealistic intermediary with socialism could not be imagined, and indeed Keir Hardie had long before said that Wilson's influence, 'either in trade union or political affairs, is *nil*'.[80]

Other undercover work by the BCU was equally far-fetched. Various productioneers, including both Caillard and Docker, persuaded themselves that Christabel Pankhurst's Women's party was invaluable in combating Bolshevism.[81] Lloyd George shared this view and in November 1918 told Bonar Law that the Women's party 'fought the Bolshevist and the Pacifist element with great skill, tenacity and courage, and...in Glasgow and South Wales...produced remarkable results'.[82] Christabel Pankhurst was originally shortlisted for a Wiltshire constituency near Caillard's house, but eventually fought at Docker's birthplace of Smethwick, where the Labour candidate was the national organiser of the Ironfounders Society. The BCU contributed £1,000 to her election costs, subsidised the Women's party on a weekly basis until the spring of 1919, and she afterwards wrote that Docker was also 'very helpful and...more than kind' in organisational and strategic ways during the Smethwick campaign.[83] After the BCU ceased to support the party in July 1919, Caillard, Docker and Sir William Beardmore each paid £500 privately to keep Miss Pankhurst going, and further funds were contributed by the Coalowners' Association in return for campaigning in South Wales against nationalisation.[84] Once again it is hard not to feel that the impact of the 'Christabelligerents' was over-rated by the productioneers.

Another of the BCU's undercover 'business transactions' was with the super-patriotic British Workers League, which received £300 monthly from April 1919 until March 1920, and thereafter £125 monthly. A similar beneficiary was J. A. Seddon, National Democratic Labour MP for Hanley, who received £25 weekly until October 1920, and thereafter £25 monthly.[85] These so-called 'patriotic labour' groups owed much to the encouragement of Lord Milner,[86] and also had practical encouragements from his admirers such as Amery, Steel-Maitland and Worthington-Evans. A leader of the British Workers League described the movement to Steel-Maitland in 1916 as 'the only straight patriotic organisation, *sans phrases*, in the country',[87] but its impact was soon eroded in peacetime.

One of the greatest obsessions of the BCU's productioneers was that Britain would suffer revolution on the scale of 1793, 1848 or 1917. In a memorandum of 1918, Hannon identified BCU's enemies as the Independent Labour party, the Union of Democratic Control, the Shop Stewards Movement, the Irish in Glasgow and Liverpool, together with 'cranks, academics and faddists whose special quality is to minimise German barbarism'.[88] He foresaw 'grave danger' that when the Army was demobilised, the men would fall into the clutches of agitators, and in the period up to 1920, BCU put much effort into 'educational' propaganda work. They established a network of regional Economic Study Clubs, which resembled the pre-war Business Leagues in their aim of educating manual workers in business economics; and there was also an attempt made to train working-class political speakers, such as Steel-Maitland and Oliver Locker-Lampson had tried to develop in the Unionist party before 1914. Hannon's other pictorial and printed publicity for the manufacturers' interest (called the Economic News Service) was also disseminated until funds ran out in 1922. Allied to this, BCU also paid for surveillance of left-wing trade unionists, and for local reports on labour unrest. There was indeed some traffic in this sort of intelligence between Caillard and Lloyd George,[89] and the productioneers were prey to every sort of alarmist. During the coal-strike of October 1920, for example, Sir Hallewell Rogers wrote to Lloyd George that BCU considered Britain was in 'a kind of Civil War'.[90]

Professor Middlemas has described how the original arrangements of 1919 between the coalition whips and industrialists to provide Sydney Walton with £100,000 for propaganda work were followed by the formation of a new organisation called National Propaganda, chaired by Lord Inchcape, the shipowner. The new body had a budget of £250,000 and was directed 'to counter nationalisation, revolutionary and extremist activities, to safeguard private enterprise and promote increased production'.[91] One of the National Propaganda's luminaries was Admiral Sir Reginald Hall, a Conservative MP who had been Director of Naval Intelligence during the war and persuaded the Inland Revenue that company subscriptions to National Propaganda were a tax-deductible expense. By this stage, BCU had its own substantial propaganda organisation: demarcation between the activities of National Propaganda and BCU initially proved difficult, although they subsequently co-operated more closely.[92] It is hard to estimate the effects of propaganda, but it is likely that its power to influence its readers was exaggerated by men like Hannon and Walton with a predilection for boosting themselves. Much of their effort was otiose, as was the involvement of the Union in surveillance of left-wing trade unionists; and it is significant of the general distrust of Hannon that one Secret Service contact complained to Cunliffe-Lister that he 'can never hold his tongue'.[93]

The real achievement of the BCU in the period of 1918–22 was to provide the nucleus for the body of MPs which formed themselves into the Industrial Group. This Group far out-stripped in cohesion and influence such predecessors as the Unionist Business Committee, and within a short time no Chancellor of the Exchequer or President of the Board of Trade could afford to neglect it. In its early years, in particular, the Industrial Group was considered by ministers to be the mouthpiece of the FBI, although as we now know the BCU was the organisation behind it and because of Rylands' views the FBI had no direct responsibility for it. The Group was not always taken at its own evaluation. Thus Austen Chamberlain, the Chancellor of the Exchequer, wrote after presenting his Budget of 1920, 'The Federation of British Industries is very strong in the House and...I shall have a big fight with the Big Bugs...but they are a selfish, swollen lot, and if they think they can bully the Chancellor because there are so many of them in the House, they will find that they are mistaken'.[94] One member of the Chamberlain family, at least, was ready to resist the pressures of the business party. Nevertheless, BCU had considerable impact on other government legislation of the period. The first organised parliamentary compaign by BCU was against the Ministry of Ways and Communications Bill of 1919 which empowered the Ministry of Transport to acquire any transport facility that was judged necessary in the national interest. Business men regarded this provision as 'a monstrosity of collectivism, dictatorship and bureaucracy', and it was duly withdrawn; but it drew the first of several interventions by Docker and the BCU in national policy on railway organisation and electrification.[95] The Electricity Supply Bill of 1919, on whose Standing Committee the BCU had fourteen members, was another piece of legislation considerably whittled by their activity.[96]

Throughout, BCU retained the characteristic inter-relation of Docker's political and business interests. Its Parliamentary Secretary, for example, approached the Foreign Office in 1921 to elicit whether BSA could sell rifles and field guns to Lithuania despite the British government prohibition of such arms exports while the Vilma dispute continued with Poland (the Foreign Office replied that BSA could not).[97] The first chairman of the Industrial Group, during 1919 to 1921, was Sir Edward Goulding, a director of MCWF; and the most outstandingly successful politician among BCU supporters, Sir Philip Lloyd-Greame (better known by his later surname of Cunliffe-Lister), was also 'prominently associated' with Docker's companies.[98] 'His record is of the best, and he is out to win the peace', the *Globe* promised in 1918, 'Hendon's MC is becoming Hendon's MP.'[99] Within two years Cunliffe-Lister was a junior minister at the Board of Trade, before heading the Department of Overseas Trade in 1921 and serving as President of the Board of Trade for seven years during 1922 to 1931. Throughout he kept in close touch with Docker. Similarly, Hannon, the BCU's director, joined the BSA board in 1924, and was in 1932–3 the 'liaison between the Board and Mr Docker in the difficult days when Mr Docker save[d] the Company from…the brink of extinction'.[100] Hannon and Cunliffe-Lister were unusually suited, among BCU men, to political life. Hannon, certainly, could never resist the opportunity to speechify,[101] but his prolixity was not typical of the Union's businessmen supporters. They tended to the opposite extreme, like Docker's co-director Douglas Vickers, the most silent member of the Parliament of 1918–22, of whom *Hansard* records no speech or oral question.[102]

Of BCU's fortunes after 1922, and of Docker's political activity during the age of Baldwin, more will be said in chapter 9. What can be recapitulated here is that neither the FBI, which he helped to found, nor the BCU, which he helped to strengthen, formed the manufacturers' party which he had envisioned storming into political command. The whole idea was chimerical, as other industrialists had realised. 'In business one must act promptly, take risks, have a free hand, and talk as little as possible', so Lionel Hichens of Cammell Laird told the Industrial Reconstruction Council in 1918, 'A Government was handicapped in all those respects because of its responsibility to Parliament and the public...''State Management on Sound Commercial Lines" [or] ''a Business Government" were parrot-cries incapable of realisation so long as Parliamentary control remained a reality, and so long as the party system continues.'[103] In the last resort, few manufacturers were as revolutionary as Docker in wanting to transform the parrot-cries into the facts of daily British politics. The broader support for the productioneers was a temporary wartime phenomenon based on considerations of national security. The unexpectedly severe collapse of Germany at the end of 1918 nullified all previous assumptions about the bitterness of post-war Anglo-German trade rivalry, and undermined the support for a reconstructed corporatist Britain. Neither the FBI nor the BCU obtained the adoption of tariffs, or the obsolence of class war, or the abolition of restrictive practices. New administrative means had been introduced, which might make business policy more flexible and better-informed, but there were still lawyer-politicians in the Commons and faddists in the country who disavowed production for its own sake. For Docker, a man unused to defeat, it was intensely galling.

7

Diplomacy, the British Trade Corporation and the British Stockbrockers Trust 1916–25

Diplomatic and consular reform, and reconstructing British institutions for an export onslaught, were two of the main aims of Docker's Business League, and keystones of the manufacturers' movement during the Great War. It was therefore appropriate that Docker was at the heart of government plans to reform British commercial intelligence organisation, extend financial facilities to exporters and create a new government department responsible for exports. The proposals which he framed on these points were mostly too disruptive of the status quo to be accepted by government, and the single recommendation of his which was not butchered – that of a British Trade Corporation – was frustrated by Whitehall and by the prevailing conservatism of the City of London in the years immediately after the war. Nevertheless, the response which the proposals evoked at the height of the war not only illuminate the war psychology of the period, but illustrate an aspect of reconstruction plans which historians have neglected.

The beginning of Docker's influence can be traced to the evidence he gave, early in 1916, to a secret government committee on trade relations after the war. Chaired by F. Huth Jackson, the head of a City house with large South American business and a director of the Bank of England 1892–1921, its other members were Sir William Ashley, the imperial-minded professor of commerce at Birmingham University, Stanley Baldwin (then an obscure backbencher) and Sir Alfred Booth the shipowner (Lord Milner considered becoming a member, but decided against). Its remit was to consider the extent to which Germans and other foreigners should be permitted after the war to operate in Britain in any aspect of finance, industry, commerce or shipping; but it was also empowered to examine consular reform, better banking facilities for exporters and the thorny question of 'tied loans'. It is clear from these terms of reference that the committee was a response to the campaigns against German business power, and for a blockade of German finance, of which Docker was an important spokesman; and it was natural that he was one of the thirty witnesses who appeared before the committee. His evidence began by referring to the low German steel prices which made German wheels and axles so much cheaper than British, but he also spoke of the financial ambitions of the German big banks and commended their use of specialists and scientific experts. He urged that all issues on the London capital market should be subject to government permission – a point intended to establish an administrative framework for tied loans on the French model, which, although supported by other witnesses, was rejected by the committee.

Some witnesses before the Jackson committee were, incidentally, notable for identifying what fifteen years later became known as the Macmillan gap. The Macmillan committee on Finance and Industry, which reported in 1931, said little that had not been anticipated by the wartime productioneers; and the remarks for which it is most commemorated, about the lack of financing facilities for small and medium sized companies (which came to be known as the Macmillan gap) were not novel. As Lord Faringdon recalled, 'Before Mr Huth Jackson's committee, several of the witnesses said, When I was in a small way of business but doing a thoroughly sound business, I had great difficulty in getting the necessary credit or accommodation; now that I am in a large way of business and everyone knows that I am a moderately rich man, I can get any amount of money.'[1]

The three reports circulated by Jackson in the spring of 1916 avoided xenophobic references to foreign participation in legitimate business in Britain, but mentioned various possibilities for reform of banking and diplomatic facilities. Although these reports had no public circulation, they stimulated the Board of Trade and Foreign Office to appoint further committees to examine the Jackson proposals, and on these proliferating bodies Docker sat, as their verbatim minutes show, always taciturn but decisive.

Thus, in December 1916, Docker was asked by Sir Edward Grey, the Foreign Secretary, to join a committee on the re-organisation of British commercial intelligence, chaired by Lord Faringdon. The existing system, run by the Commercial Intelligence Department of the Board of Trade, had been widely criticised, and the committee was asked to report whether foreign trade could be promoted by reform of the consular service. The other men appointed with Faringdon and Docker were Victor Wellesley of the Foreign Office, Sir William Clark of the Board of Trade and Stanley Baldwin.[2] Baldwin, however, was appointed Financial Secretary to the Treasury in January 1917, and was replaced by a Liverpool cotton merchant, Sir de Fonblanque Pennefather, MP, who was nominated by the Association of British Chambers of Commerce.[3]

Docker professed to have joined the committee 'with an absolutely open mind', but together with Wellesley, formed the impression at the first meeting that Faringdon favoured the Board of Trade, and 'no amount of argument will move him'.[4] Various witnesses were called before the committee, including Sir Eyre Crowe of the Foreign Office, Laming Worthington-Evans of the War Trade Department, and Sir John Jordan, British Envoy to China. Docker seldom spoke before the witnesses; but he was of decisive importance in the committee's deliberations. He explained 'manufacturers could not agree to any kind of dual control' of commercial intelligence, as between the Foreign Office and Board of Trade, and wanted 'to bring the information to the power'. He had 'always conceived the power to lie with the Foreign Office' and asked, 'How can the Board of Trade help me if I want a concession abroad?'[5] The committee proved unable to agree. Faringdon and Clark submitted a minority report which would keep Commercial Attachés under the Board of Trade's aegis, whilst Docker, Wellesley and Pennefather called for a Trade Intelligence Department to be directed by the Foreign Office. The most interesting feature of their recommendations was their call for commercial intelligence counsellors who would be neither attachés, commissioners, consuls nor glorified commercial travellers. Their main function would be to 'investigate conditions, analyse their causes, observe recent changes and indications of impending changes'; and generally to do for industry what Military and Naval Attachés did for the Services.[6] This idea was subsequently developed in 1918, when the FBI began to appoint its own Trade Commissioners for selected overseas markets to perform somewhat similar functions.

Both the Docker and Faringdon reports were referred to the War Cabinet, despite Faringdon's retrospective complaints that his committee had been unfairly loaded with FBI sympathisers;[7] and sniping continued between the Board of Trade and Foreign Office throughout the summer. In particular, Lord Hardinge of Penshurst, Permanent Under Secretary at the Foreign Office, opposed the Wellesley–Docker plan because 'in the spirit of the Old Diplomacy [he] saw in trade and commerce something sordid – something unworthy of the Diplomatic Service'.[8] No direct decision was ever taken, but later in 1917, a new Department of Overseas Trade was established, under the dual control of the Foreign Office and Board of Trade. At least one of the politicians involved, Bonar Law, did not believe the system of dual control was workable, but supported the botched compromise as the only way of deadening departmental jealousies. Docker thought the new department's success would depend upon whom its first Comptroller was, and the choice of Steel-Maitland delighted him. He must have hoped, like many of his business friends that the new department would soon develop into the Ministry of Commerce which manufacturers had long sought.[9]

Steel-Maitland had an appalling time at the Department of Overseas Trade. He was given dreadful accommodation, and was absurdly under-staffed. He himself had to work an average of sixty-four hours per week on departmental business, and by March 1919, his two senior assistants, his Private Secretary and his secretary had all broken down through overwork, and were at sanatoriums or on rest-cures. Dual control proved to be unworkable, as Docker had warned, and both the Foreign Office and the Board of Trade were antagonistic and jealous of the new department.[10] In May 1919, Steel-Maitland complained to the Foreign Secretary that his Office was 'defective' in helping the new department, specifying that Lord Hardinge was 'absolutely incompetent' and snobbishly obstructive on trade matters (as might be expected of a former Viceroy of India who had been a favourite voluptuary of Edward VII). To Lord Robert Cecil, the Deputy Foreign Secretary, Steel-Maitland wrote that the Office wasted its talents 'because of the lack of method under which work there is carried on'.[11] One expression of this attitude was given by Duff Cooper, whose memoirs of his spell in the Foreign Office's Commercial Department at this time show considerable disdain for trade; whilst Lord Vansittart has recounted how Cooper spent his time there sleeping off hangovers.[12] If the Foreign Office was unhelpful, the Board of Trade was worse. Sir Albert Stanley, its President, was intent upon separating the Department of Overseas Trade from the Foreign Office, and re-absorbing it into his ministry; his successor, Sir Auckland Geddes, took this line even more hungrily.[13]

The controversy became so heated that yet another government committee was appointed to examine the government machinery for dealing with trade and commerce. It was chaired by Lord Cave, a dull political time-server who had been Home Secretary, and was later Lord Chancellor. Docker was one of its three other members, and in July 1919, he submitted a minority report which completely diverged from the majority. The crux of Cave's recommendations were that dual control of the Department of Overseas Trade by the two older ministries should continue, and that the Commercial and Consular Departments of the Foreign Office should be transferred to the department. Docker, on the other hand, thought that dual control was 'the root of the trouble' and 'must be eradicated'. He wanted the Foreign Office to be responsible for Britain's foreign commercial policy, and made many detailed suggestions for increasing expertise on this subject.[14]

Docker's recommendations were ignored, the status quo was not disturbed, and the makeshift compromise of 1917 was prolonged, despite Treasury moves to abolish the DOT, and revert to the old system, in 1922 and 1927. The Foreign Office attitude was represented by a minute of 1923 that the only result of a further attempt 'to define the line between commercial, diplomatic and political work would be waste of paper and irritation all round. Everyone is sick of fussy tampering.'[15] As a result, the ramshackledom of 1917 continued to give poor results until after the second world war, although vindication of Docker's criticisms of the system came from Austen Chamberlain, as Foreign Secretary, in 1929. At that time, Docker was leading a syndicate to develop hydro-electric power in Egypt, and Chamberlain complained of 'confusion, contradiction and misunderstanding' because the Foreign Office, Board of Trade and Department of Overseas Trade were all involved in independent discussions with Docker about the British government's attitude to the scheme.[16] This typified the inefficiency which Docker had forecast a decade earlier.

If Docker's proposals for overhauling the Whitehall machinery for aiding exports were aborted, he had more initial success in reforming British financial institutions to cope with overseas business. In July 1916, the Board of Trade appointed a committee to consider the best means of providing British firms with post-war financial facilities for trade, especially for big overseas contracts. This move was directly inspired by the references to German industrial banking in the reports of the Huth Jackson committee, for which Docker had been one of the informants. The subject was one which greatly excited the trade warriors, as shown for example by the calls in the British Empire Producers' Organisation's journal. *Production*, for an Imperial Bank of Industry capitalised at £40 million.[17] This new committee was chaired by the ubiquitous Faringdon, and its members comprised Basil Blackett of the Treasury, Sir William Clark then head of Commercial Intelligence at the Board of Trade, and eight bank directors, including Docker.[18] The most interesting witnesses heard were Frank Tiarks, a director of Schröder's and the Bank of England (1912–45), and Sir Vincent Caillard of Vickers who was accompanied by Baron de Nordwall, formerly AEG's representative in Britain; although characteristically Docker was silent throughout these and other cross-examinations. The committee's report was published on 22 September: its theme – 'If industry is to be extended it is essential that British products should be *pushed*, and manufacturers, merchants and bankers must combine to push them' – was one which Docker had been re-iterating for years, and was the *cri de coeur* of every trade warrior. Many phrases in the report resound like passages from Docker's speeches and writings since 1910, and it is probable that

Ill. 7 Lord Faringdon (1850–1934), by Sir William Orpen

he took a lead, under Faringdon, in drafting the proposals. Briefly, the committee called for the institution, under Royal Charter, of an industrial trading bank, capitalised at £10,000,000, imitating and competing with those foreign banks which had 'taken the labouring oar' in so much export penetration. The Bank was to include a Bureau d'Études, as a commercial intelligence centre; the middle management was dubbed 'the General Staff'; and employees were to be encouraged to start their own business, whilst remembering BTC was 'their Alma Mater', whose 'ésprit de corps' they had imbibed.[19] The vocabulary and attitudes of wartime permeated the report, and Docker's importance is indicated by Sir Hallewell Rogers' remark that if the government did not back the Trade Corporation sufficiently, 'no doubt Mr Dudley Docker would find some other means of tackling the finance of the country'.[20]

The Board of Trade accepted these proposals, and the British Trade Corporation (hereafter BTC) was constituted. Docker and another member of the Faringdon committee were the first subscribers to the issued capital, and a surviving list of the fifty applicants for the rest of the capital is very striking.[21] Ten banks applied, half of them associated with members of the original committee; and four other committee members applied individually, as did Vickers Ltd, Caillard and three other directors of Vickers; BSA, its chairman Rogers, two other past or future BSA directors, plus a Sheffield company which was shortly afterwards acquired by BSA; MCWF, and one of its directors; the Gloucester Carriage Company, and its chairman, Vassar-Smith; Armstrong Whitworth, and two of its directors; and Cammell Laird. Three successive presidents of the FBI (1916–19), eight of Docker's co-directors from three different companies, and four armaments companies were a formidable tally. They were, *prima facie*, confirmation of J. A. Hobson's contemporary view that imperialism was the product of capitalists seeking outlets for surplus capital. BTC was imperialist in every essential; in Docker's own words, after 'hostilities cease on the battlefield', the Corporation would 'cope with our adversaries' just as ruthlessly in the international market-place.[22] The German big banks would be supplanted from all their places in the sun, and though the areas of BTC operations need not be territorially annexed, the hope was that they would become trade dependencies. BTC was directed solely against German finance. United States banks, until the passage of the Federal Reserves Act of 1913, had been prohibited from either establishing foreign branches or accepting drafts drawn on foreign trade: and at the time the BTC was chartered, they had taken little advantage of the more liberal banking legislation.[23] If, as Hobson defined, 'The economic root of Imperialism is the desire of strong organized industrial and financial interests to secure and develop at the public expense and by the public force private markets for their surplus goods and surplus capital', then BTC was a prime expression of wartime imperialism. It was perceived as such by at least one contemporary anti-imperialist, who wrote that 'The Federation of British Industries... fathered the British Trade Corporation on the Government', and that the Federation itself 'was in its initiation very largely the creation of Vickers Ltd'.[24] Yet BTC's most damaging opponents were not pacifists, anti-imperialists or communists, but Docker's fellow capitalists in the City of London. In 1917 Steel-Maitland wrote of 'the hostility towards it which is manifested on many questions in the city', and a Board of Trade official noted, 'Bankers and financiers do not altogether realise the importance (from an Imperial point of view) of the...work which the corporation has been founded to undertake.'[25] The traditional role of the City in financing foreign and government loans scarcely extended to acting as a capital market for British industry, and in the nineteenth century British manufacturers were either self-financed or backed by local banks with few City contacts. As late as the world war most City men rested content with this situation. As one Milnerite complained,

> a considerable body of opinion in the City, not necessarily very conversant with modern industrial developments...regard our financial system, just as Burke regarded our Constitution, as something which grows and is not made, and which has by natural evolution grown almost to perfection. It is argued that every country evolves the system which suits it, whether it be the British or the German or the American. To these critics it is presumably 'natural' that the Germans should build Zeppelins and we should not; that we should invent aniline dyes and the Germans exploit them; 'natural', too, that the German and American steel industries should increase by leaps and bounds and ours should remain stagnant.[26]

It is indubitable that the City's conservatism at this time was 'a major factor in the chronic under-investment of British industry which continues to this day': indeed, 'anomalously among advanced industrial countries' British merchant banks did not begin widespread finance of home investment or encouragement of industrial rationalisation until the 1930s.[27] Lord Faringdon was himself aware that some of the most unreasonable difficulties in raising money were met by smaller and medium sized industrial concerns, and was keen to help 'new business and new men with...a small capital to begin with'.[28]

It was significant of the unenterprising and regressive views of the City that Gaspard Farrer, of Barings, the sole merchant banker appointed to the Faringdon committee, declined to sign the report which all the joint-stock bankers accepted. His attitude can be gauged from his reply to Frank Tiarks'

statement that the London 'issuing houses have many businesses brought
before them which may be excellent businesses but which require expert
examination and...technical knowledge, about which, though perfectly
good, we...say, We are not going to be bothered'. Farrer, speaking for one
of London's biggest and oldest issuing houses, replied: 'Yes, it is hardly our
business.'[29] It was this lazy amateurism and complacence which Docker
was fighting. His friend Caillard told the committee that 'a very first-rate
British financier' had replied to his pre-war complaint that the proceeds
of a big London loan to Argentina were being spent abroad: 'That does not
matter to us; we make our commission, the British public gets a good
investment and we do not care about British industry.' Caillard added,
'That is the spirit which I would like to see altered', and that was the spirit
which BTC attacked.

When BTC's enabling vote came before the House of Commons in May
1917, the voices of reaction were audible. The Bank was attacked as 'a
dangerous and mischievous innovation', 'an official bucket-shop', 'one of
the greatest insults to the British mercantile community', 'hopeless,
destructive and suicidal...perfectly monstrous...outrageous...thoroughly
indefensible' and 'bastard'.[30] The Government Front Bench was not
properly briefed for the debate, and in the face of this assault, panicked
and withdrew the motion. Docker, whose appointment as a director of BTC
had already been announced, responded to this débâcle by publicly
attacking his parliamentary critics for 'possess[ing] only the most
elementary business knowledge', and behaving like 'the deluded...Little
Englanders who before the war resisted any form of [military] preparation
and assured us that war was impossible'. For Docker, BTC was essential
if Britain was to thrash 'the German financier [who] permeate[d] every
artery of our trade' before 1914.[31] Eventually, in July 1917, after 'a final
splutter of venom and insinuation',[32] the Commons approved BTC's
enabling vote, and banking operations could start.

The parliamentary controversy was disastrous. Sir Edward Carson, who
was chairman of the Cabinet's Economic Offensive Committee, warned in
January 1918:

> the British Trade Corporation, the Non-Ferrous Metals Bill and the
> Imports and Exports Bill are all well calculated to disturb the minds of
> our enemies, providing they are carried through promptly and with clear
> evidences of practical unanimity in Parliament and in the nation. But if
> they are stillborn, or...whittled down...or if there is an impression
> abroad that they will not be seriously enforced, then they are likely to
> cause more harm than good. For in that case Germany will regard them
> as mere bluff. The German Government (quoting from the House of
> Commons debates and the press) will represent them to their people as

measures which are not seriously intended, and to which the trend of British opinion is traditionally and instinctively opposed.[33]

The evidence from the parliamentary record and the newspapers was already available for the Germans to conclude that BTC was 'not seriously intended', and that it was too alien to British methods to survive. BTC's subsequent career confirmed this.

Its original seven directors were headed by Lord Faringdon, the stock-broker, newspaper proprietor and railway director whose name recurs throughout this book. There were three bankers, Huth Jackson; Sir Harry Goschen, chairman of the National Provincial Bank; and Sir James Hope Simpson, of Liverpool and Martins Bank, who had previously been with the Bank of Egypt. Industry was represented by Docker, Arthur Balfour (later Lord Riverdale), a Sheffield steel manufacturer, and Sir John Noble of Armstrong Whitworth, once described as 'not *brilliant* in any way — He does not pretend to be – but he is sound and diligent and endowed with much common-sense – the nicest of men and *persona grata* with foreigners.'[34] Balfour, at least, joined the board 'at the urgent request of the promoters purely on public grounds', and represented the Association of British Chambers of Commerce of which he was a Council member.[35] Faringdon was Governor of the Board, with Docker initially acting as his deputy.[36] BTC appointed as its Manager, A. G. M. Dickson, a Scholar of University College, Oxford, who spoke French, modern Greek, Italian and Turkish. He had worked for the Imperial Ottoman Bank in 1890–8, had been Athens manager of the Ionian Bank in 1899–1904, before becoming the Alexandria-based Sub-Governor of the National Bank of Egypt. He had served in 1915 as Commissioner of Currency and Finance to the British invasion force in Turkey, and had a wide knowledge of the east Mediterranean and the Middle East.[37] Dickson's deputy Percy West, formerly London sub-manager of the Banco de Chile, was an experienced operator on the London money market.

BTC's first six months, until January 1918, were passed in arranging foreign representation, and in setting up the Information Bureau by which Faringdon set great store. It was naturally unable to start operations until after the Armistice, and 1919 was its first year of active business. One project of 1918 was a banking branch in Petrograd.[38] BTC's aim was to move into spheres of German trading influence, especially in the power vacuums left by the collapse of Romanov, Habsburg, Hohenzollern and Turkish imperialism. This strategic decision by the Corporation's trade warriors resembles the strategic decision taken by another group of productioneers, the board of Vickers including Caillard and Docker. Before

1914, Vickers had set up foreign arsenals in such countries as Spain, Italy, Japan, Russia and Turkey, and acted as suppliers of armaments to major powers. After 1918, however, they sited their new national arsenal projects in the new secession states of eastern Europe: in 1919 they sent an industrial embassy to Poland which led in 1920 to their participation with the Starachowice company in a Polish arsenal; in 1920 they took a holding in the Reşita company of Roumania, followed by an investment in a Yugoslav company, with a view to participating in the Balkans arms trade; and in 1921, they undertook to manage the naval dockyards and installations at Reval in Esthonia. These sites, on the borders of Bolshevik Russia, appealed to the armourers as places within future spheres of British political and strategic interest, quite apart from their potential for industrial development.[39]

BTC's main thrust was in the east Mediterranean, where Dickson, the general manager, had a quarter of a century's experience. Their activities were uniformly unsuccessful, for they found that the British government were instinctively equivocal and could not be relied upon to back the Corporation. Just as BSA, during Docker's deputy-chairmanship, had felt betrayed by the War Office after the purchase of the Sparkbrook factory, so BTC swiftly discovered that Whitehall was a faithless ally. BTC were led into various engagements which seemed to be in the imperial interest, in which they were not backed, and from which they sustained serious reverses.

The Corporation's first stroke was to buy almost all the stock in the National Bank of Turkey for £243,119.[40] That bank was itself a monument to the caprice of the British government, and should have forewarned Faringdon, Docker and Dickson of the treatment that BTC would receive. British interests had founded the Imperial Ottoman Bank in the mid-nineteenth century, but had not consolidated their position. In 1888, Vincent Caillard, who was then administering the Ottoman Public Debt, had written of 'that exasperating slowness which seems so often to seize city men',[41] and by the twentieth century, the Imperial Ottoman Bank was controlled by French interests. In 1907–8, the Foreign Office sponsored various attempts to establish a new Turkish trading bank in which Britain would be more evenly represented. This culminated in the formation in 1909 of the National Bank of Turkey, in which the financier Sir Ernest Cassel was associated with Lord Faringdon and later with Lord Revelstoke, of Barings. Though the idea of a new bank had been encouraged by the Foreign Office originally, the latter took little part in the mechanics of its foundation, and was scarcely consulted. When the National Bank encountered intense opposition from the Imperial Bank in 1910–11, the

Foreign Office gave 'only lukewarm backing',[42] and the faintness of Whitehall's support only made the matter worse. The hopes of Cassel, Faringdon and Revelstoke that the National Bank of Turkey would mastermind the development of public works, railways, industries and communications were soon punctured, most noticeably when the Foreign Office did not back a scheme for British capital to participate with the Deutsche Bank to extend the railway south of Bagdad. As the president of the National Bank told the Foreign Secretary in 1913, 'The impression has been produced in the minds of our competitors and of the Ottoman Government, that we are not trusted by the British Government, or regarded as the appropriate agency for taking the lead in British enterprises.'[43] By the outbreak of war, the Bank was almost dormant.

The Turkish collapse in 1918, and the end of hostilities, created a position in which, as Caillard informed Lloyd George, 'His Britannic Majesty is the greatest ruler of Mahommedans in the World', controlling 'a much greater number of Mahommedans than did the Sultans of Turkey in the days of their most extensive power.'[44] It was natural that Faringdon and Dickson should hope that the moribund National Bank of Turkey could be revivified to help BTC secure a trading hegemony with King George V's Mahommedan territories. By April 1919, BTC had acquired the National Bank, and the Treasury had agreed that it could resume business. Simultaneously, they bought the Levant Company Ltd, which aimed 'at reviving the commercial side of the...old Levant Company famous during the sixteenth and seventeenth centuries as the representative of British influence in the Near East', and which intended to concentrate on Mediterranean areas 'where hitherto Austrian and German interests had predominated'.[45] The wartime atmosphere of the arrangements was heightened by BTC's purchase of the mercantile firm of Whittall, with branches at Salonica and Constantinople, one of whose members was Edwin Whittall, the spy authorised by the British government in 1915 to offer the Turks £4,000,000 in return for peace.[46]

By this time, in the opinion of the Department of Overseas Trade, BTC were often 'apt rather inconveniently to insist' that they had a special claim on the government, having been created under official auspices.[47] In March 1919 they were appointed general agents for the sale of all surplus government stores in the Near East, and Severin de Bilinski, British delegate on the Inter-Allied Financial Commission in Greece and Turkey, was specially released from war work to become BTC's representative in the southern Balkans and Asia Minor.[48] They developed contacts with officials like Sir George Milne, Commander-in-Chief of the forces in Turkey, Sir Wilfrid Malleson, head of the British Military Mission to Turkestan, and Admirals Calthorpe and de Robeck, successive High Commissioners in

Constantinople. The most important consequence of this was BTC's involvement in high policy surrounding the British intervention in the Russian civil war in the Caucasus, Armenia, Georgia and Kurdistan.

The British had been involved, since 1917, in supporting anti-Bolshevik forces both in these huge Cossack territories, and in northern and far-eastern Russia. British policy was particularly concerned with these provinces around the Caspian and Black Seas, which trenched on to India, and the Persian and Mesopotamian oilfields. By November 1918, British forces were strongly committed to supporting the White Russians led by General Denikin, and in the following month, the British occupied the Black Sea port of Batum in Georgia, and took control of the Batum–Baku railway which traversed Transcaucasia, and reached to the Caspian coast. This was followed by a successful offensive by Denikin against the Bolsheviks from May to October 1919. At this stage, Lieutenant General Milne, commanding the Black Sea Army, formally asked BTC to open a banking branch in Batum, with Foreign Office cognisance. The branch opened in May 1919, with a manager named Oakshott, and acted as the state bank for Batum province. At the same time, Sir Oliver Wardrop, Chief British Commissioner in Georgia, Armenia and Azerbaijan, asked the BTC to open further branches at the Caspian port of Baku, at Tiflis and elsewhere in Transcaucasia. BTC had already appointed representatives at Baku and Tiflis, but had not opened branches, and before replying to Wardrop, they asked the Foreign Office what support would be given if Transcaucasia 'should be menaced by Bolshevist forces'.[49]

Possibly in response to Wardrop's request, BTC formed a subsidiary, the South Russia Banking Agency Ltd, in conjunction with three London joint-stock banks, to act as an adjunct to British policy in the area.[50] Initially, BTC's south Russian business was successful. Communications were bad, and the Georgian government proved very obstructive, but by late 1919, substantial Anglo-Georgian trade had been established especially in the export of manganese ore from Georgia. As Faringdon told Lord Curzon, the Foreign Secretary, 'The risks were evidently great, and the prospects of commercial profits exceedingly doubtful; but our action was guided by the belief that we were carrying out the objects for which the British Trade Corporation was created and received a Royal Charter.'[51] The policy was summarised by Winston Churchill when he told a War Office conference in July 1919, 'A great area had been won, and if it was to be held the population behind the line must be made more prosperous and in a more active condition than that on the other side... Millions of people to be held for generations to come, and the present was the time to act and gain the trade.'[52]

However, in November 1919, Denikin's fortunes changed, and from then until April 1920, when he resigned his command to Wrangel, he was in retreat. By July, Baku had been captured by the Bolsheviks, and BTC's representative, British Vice-Consul Hewelcke, imprisoned; British forces evacuated Batum on 10 July. Faringdon then determined to close the Batum branch, although as late as 12 August the Foreign Office (in a letter drafted in Lord Curzon's handwriting) asked BTC to re-open, and gave the guarantee of Lord Beatty, the First Sea Lord, that the Royal Navy would remain in the area.[53]

Another business proposal which was germane to the South Russia Banking Agency was a proposal by the Japanese government in August 1919 to form an international corporation of American, British and Japanese interests to undertake mining, railway and industrial development in Siberia. At that time, the White Russian Admiral Kolchak was Supreme Ruler of Siberia and far-eastern Russia, and British troops were occupying Vladivostock. The Japanese scheme was to develop Siberia under the auspices of the Kolchak regime, with some eighteen companies forming an industrial development group capitalised at 1 million yen. Japanese *zaibatsu* such as Mitsui and Mitsubishi were named, together with the BTC, MCWF and Lord Cowdray's group,[54] but the scheme foundered when Kolchak sustained a series of crushing reverses, and was murdered by the Bolshevists in February 1920.

Also in 1919, Lord Curzon, the Foreign Secretary, insisted that BTC, together with Rothschilds, be admitted as additional members of the English group of banks in the 'Four Power Consortium'. This Consortium had been formed in 1910 by bankers from Britain, France, Germany and the USA, supported by their respective governments, to regulate financial business with China. It aimed to prevent financiers outside the Consortium from making improvident loans which would increase the Chinese un-secured debt and add to the chaos of China's finances. In fact, the Consortium's own Reorganisation Loan of 1913, worth £25 million, proved to be the single most reckless of all foreign loans to China; whilst the controls claimed by the Consortium were increasingly resented by the Chinese. Until the mid-1920s the British and US governments continued to support the Consortium's financial monopoly; but in conditions of rising Chinese nationalism, this policy proved counter-productive. Although the Consortium out-lived BTC, it had long before lost its powers, and Faringdon never saw any material benefit from Curzon's gesture in 1919. The significance of the Chinese episode, with Curzon's pressure on BTC's behalf against the resistance of the existent five banks in the British group, is that it was the only example of the Foreign Office exerting itself in support of the new chartered bank: equally important, this lone case of preferential diplomatic treatment yielded no business to BTC.[55]

Their other trading activities in 1919–20 can be summarised swiftly. At Steel-Maitland's instigation,[56] they invested £100,000 in the Portuguese Trade Corporation, specially started to compete with German interests which had been active in pre-war Portugal. In conjunction with the London and Brazilian Bank, BTC formed the Anglo-Brazilian Commercial and Agency Co. Ltd to bring 'new capital and new blood' to 'cases where German commercial firms were monopolising the field of activities'. Docker's Belgian interests were reflected in the BTC's small investment in the Inter-Allied Trade and Banking Corporation Ltd, formed to promote Anglo-Belgian trade, and redolent by its very name of trade war.[57]

On the financial side, BTC formed the Trade Indemnity Co. Ltd, capitalised at £100,000, as a subsidiary to insure foreign trade credits; within a year, millions of pounds worth of goods had been exported by Britain backed by Trade Indemnity, although by 1925 the BCU was advocating a scheme of government reinsurance of commercial credit risks. The first industrial issue underwritten by BTC was for debentures of £500,000 issued by the Morgan Crucible company; and this reflected the apparent prosperity of the Corporation in 1919. Deposit accounts rose from £632,636 in 1918 to £1,673,440 in 1919; acceptances on account of customers rose from £212,181 at December 1918 to £1,147,385 in December 1919.[58] On an issued capital of £1 million, a dividend of $2\frac{1}{2}$ per cent was paid in 1918, and 4 per cent was paid for the two years to 1920.

However, in 1920 BTC's profits were squeezed, and the squeezing continued until the corporation was almost a husk in 1926. In the first case, the depression in the national economy reduced BTC's profit-earning capacity: during these adversities the hostility of the merchant banks and issuing houses in the City of London was especially injurious. Among the financial institutions, BTC was an isolated, hybrid and unwelcome interloper; and it is likely that City men went out of their way to keep business away from it. This was not balanced by favoured treatment from the government departments, despite the understanding which had been implicit in the charter of 1917. Indeed, where Whitehall did influence BTC's business growth, it was always fatal: BTC's enterprises selected in 1917–19 on strategic criteria were often unworkable on commercial criteria. BTC concentrated on areas of German commercial suzerainty, or tied itself to British imperial policy to safeguard India and oil supplies. The weakness of all this was that the BTC never defined its priorities: earning profits, or acting as an instrument of government overseas policy. The two were incompatible. Not surprisingly, after 1920 BTC paid no further dividends to its shareholders; authorised capital was reduced by £1 million in 1922; and by another £500,000 in 1923.

BTC's decline corresponded with the decline of the productioneers. Just as Docker withdrew from the FBI in 1920 in disgust, so shortly afterwards he left the Corporation. Although in BTC's official dealings, Faringdon and Dickson were more prominent than Docker, to the public in 1919–20 he ranked second in importance after the Governor in BTC. After his resignation, the government continued to renege on its implicit under-standing with Faringdon, who watched his new corporation decline just as the National Bank of Turkey had done before 1914. The latter sought 'to act as an agent of Empire' and 'had tried quite genuinely to follow its Government's wishes', but found Sir Edward Grey's Foreign Office 'was not over-interested in commercial activities in such imperial outposts' and was unwilling to jeopardise relations with its French partners in the Entente by supporting competition with the Paris-controlled Imperial Ottoman Bank.[59] Similarly, Lord Curzon's Foreign Office would not be fractious on BTC's behalf. The British attitude to such matters – the antithesis of the French and the undoing of BTC – is well summarised by the description in 1926 of Sir Edward Grey as 'not only a charming gentleman, but also a statesman utterly incapable of *trade diplomacy*, or of anything approaching a mean act'.[60] With these mores prevailing, BTC was futile, and it was foredoomed in a fiscal sense too. Faringdon, Docker and their associates had assumed in 1917 that some sort of imperial preference would be introduced in England, and indeed the principle seemed to be embodied in the Finance Act of 1919. But in fact, the British Free Trade Empire which had emerged around 1860 continued until 1931, when the crisis of world depression finally enabled the protectionists to impose their views. It is likely that if the British Empire had become an imperial *Zollverein* after the first world war, BTC would have become more useful to the government and more profitable to its investors.

Faringdon and Dickson laboured on until 1926. Faringdon might fulminate to the die-hard Lord Lloyd that the National Bank of Turkey, and by implication BTC, were 'more than ever desirable to keep the flag flying',[61] but in 1926 he agreed, after discussions with Sir Herbert Lawrence, that BTC should be absorbed by the Anglo-Austrian Bank. The scheme, whereby Anglo-Austrian acquired the BTC's undertakings and assets and became known as the Anglo-International Bank, almost failed at the last moment, for in October 1926, on the eve of the merger, and after months of rumours in Belgrade, it was discovered that over £100,000 had been misappropriated in BTC's Yugoslav operations.[62] It was with this ignominy that the trade bank which had been designed to smash the great German export banks ceased to exist. The Royal Charter of sixty years duration was surrendered after nine years; the Corporation itself entered voluntary liquidation; and the City, with economic historians ever since, forgot that it had ever existed.

The failure of BTC was more discreet than some other trading banks created by the productioneers. The British-Hungarian Bank formed in 1920 by the FBI activist, Godfrey Isaacs of Marconi Telegraph, sustained heavy losses through currency speculation; and George Manzi-Fé, whose testimony to the Balfour of Burleigh committee and lobbying of the FBI, resulted in the formation of the British-Italian Banking Corporation, was finally arrested at Le Touquet in 1929 after fraud and wild speculations had forced the Bank of England to intervene to prevent collapse. The FBI in 1920–1 also took an active part in trying to organise an Anglo-Chinese trading corporation: they collaborated with industrialists and the DOT, but the civil war in China and the industrial depression of 1921–2 in Britain robbed them of their impetus and no constructive arrangements were finalised.[63]

BTC was not the only institutional innovation with which Docker was connected which collided with the conservatism of the City establishment. He was also involved in BST Ltd, a company registered in December 1916, and whose initials signified the British Stockbrokers Trust. As an attempt to bring the trust movement to stockbroking and to attack the citadels of the City, it was immediately embattled with the Stock Exchange Committee. Docker's connection with the Trust is deduced from the fact that its leaders – Lord ffrench, Edgar Crammond, Sir Edmund Wyldbore-Smith, Sir Follett Holt and finally Sir Pierce Lacy – were all men who acted closely with Docker in the 1920s: indeed, in Wyldbore-Smith's case, it is doubtful whether he did anything without consulting Docker first. Further evidence that Docker was a grey eminence behind the Trust is that in 1922 he offered Lord Milner a seat on the board: he could not be in a position to do so unless he was also a major force in the Trust.[64]

When BST was launched, early in 1918, it was headlined in *The Economist* as 'The Country Broker's Revolt', and its early publicity was severely critical of the established institutions of the City of London. Although organisations such as the Investment Registry (formed 1903) and the British Trusts Association (formed 1917) had recently been created to act as issuing houses for domestic industry, and as incipient investment trusts, these were not yet prolific, or trusted, in the City. As one Milnerite complained in 1916, there was a 'peculiar lack of contact between the chief financial centre of the world and the industry of its own country': in contrast to the industrial securities market of New York or Berlin, 'London and the British investor who invests through London knows very little of British industries'. The pre-occupation of the City's investment bankers with foreign loans, coupled with commercial bankers' reluctance to lend on extended terms to domestic borrowers, left the English industrial capital market as prey for the more incompetent, greedy or crooked financiers.

Industrial issues, and particularly new schemes, were too often left to company promoters, who lost interest in the business once they had received their commission; the great issuing houses, which might have acted 'as a kind of general staff to industry', providing finance and sponsoring re-organisation, were instead 'more closely in touch with foreign countries than with British industries'.[65] BST was an attempt to remedy this situation, and to afford reliable and disinterested openings in industrial finance for the provincial investor. Some such guidance was certainly needed. The new issue business, which had only originated around 1860 and which only became common after 1919, 'was a haphazard and undisciplined process'. The Stock Exchange Committee's few formal requirements were framed to ensure that the security in question was large enough to justify an issue, and there was little attempt to establish the trustworthiness of applicants. Indeed, when BST was launched, the Stock Exchange Committee had no rules governing the advertisement of issues in newspapers, or the verification of claims made therein. Share pushers and bucket-shops 'preyed on gullible and unwary investors', while the financial press (excepting *The Economist*) were at best lazy and ignorant, or at worst venal and blackmailing, using extortion to get prospectus advertising. Other financial journalists were unwilling to criticise shaky ventures, lest in offending the issuing houses they lost lucrative prospectus advertising business.[66]

As BST's circular declared in 1918, country brokers were gravely unhappy before the war at the manner in which new capital issues were offered to them for subscription.

> The issuing houses, most of which are not of British origin, were in the habit of telegraphing to country brokers giving them a few hours to decide whether they would participate in any imminent issues. The country brokers had but small opportunity of investigating the inherent soundness of new issues thus offered for subscription. They were not given the chance. Anxiety for underwriting, fear of being excluded from future issues, doubt that a refusal might play into the hands of a rival, were all factors...which enabled the issuing houses to take this course.

BST's intention was to break the 'high-handed and overbearing attitude' of the London Stock Exchange, which it accused of being hostile to 'the interests of the investing public, the provincial brokers and the country generally'. The second aim of BST, which resounded with Docker's rhetoric, was to insist upon 'tied loans'. BST's circular described how most loans issued in London before the war had contained no stipulation that the proceeds should be spent on contracts placed in Britain.

> German manufacturers, being highly organised and supported by their

financial institutions, controlled many agencies for obtaining concessions and contracts, and took good care to see that the orders for materials were ear marked for themselves. Having secured the concession or contract it was quite simple to get it financed in London. Issuing houses of German origin commanded the situation... because they had channels of invest- ment... wh[ich] did not realise that they were being made the tools and servants of German economic penetration... at inflated prices, many British investors, who were themselves manufacturers, provided money for the development of German industries; and... gave their German rivals a powerful footing in... [overseas] market[s].

BST promised that it would fight to keep British capital applied to British industries, and to frustrate post-war German economic penetration. This xenophobia was not unwelcome among stockbrokers: in 1915 copies of newspapers which had criticised Kitchener were burnt on the floor of the Stock Exchange, and a left-wing stockbroker, Sir Richard Denman, MP, was hammered for his supposedly pacifist opinions.

BST emphasised that London stockbrokers were traditionally con- descending and indifferent towards provincial clients, even though 'the provincial centres are largely the wealth-producing areas', and they decided to kick against this domination. Indeed both the financial potential and the disabilities of provincial brokers had recently been personified by the Leicester stockbroker, Arthur Wheeler. He had compiled a mailing list said to include the names of half a million small investors which was at once envied and deplored by the London Stock Exchange Committee. His organisation made such an impact selling War Loan stock that he was created a baronet, but he was shunned by City orthodoxy as a provincial with unseemly competitive methods. When he became chairman of the Charterhouse Investment Trust in 1925, its brokers had permission to deal withheld by the Stock Exchange Committee until they had promised not to circularise clients except in the form of public offers of sale, and the prejudice against him was never eradicated. Similarly, in 1918, the London Stock Exchange Committee retaliated against BST by declaring with effect from 1 February that BST was 'a combination of stockbrokers' whose intended work was only appropriate to stockbrokers 'in their individual capacity'. For this reason, they declared that any country broker who was a shareholder in BST would forfeit his rights, under Rule 189 of the Stock Exchange, to have his orders executed by members of the London Stock Exchange at half the scales of brokerage charged to ordinary clients. This of course was a crushing blow, to which the country brokers had no answer except to abuse the London committee for 'unreasonableness and injustice'; and in mid-February, the country brokers were compelled to resign their shareholdings and active role in the Trust's management.

Although the ruthlessness of the London Stock Exchange's response was not universally approved, BST received a mixed press. *The Economist* judged that BST had fundamentally 'a strong case' about London's mistreatment of the provincial investor, and thought a new organisation of country brokers might be invaluable in 'the much-needed work of cleaning, improving and cheapening the machinery of industrial company pro-motion'. But they also felt that BST's anti-German sentiments 'smack[ed] of the parish pump', and that the proposal for tied loans would prove theoretically and practically unsound and lose Britain much financial business.[67]

BST's promoters were only momentarily downcast by this rebuff, and remained determined to force the City to recognise it as 'a feeder to, and not a competitor with, the London Stock Exchange'. Lord ffrench, formerly a railway contractor in China and Russia whom Docker had known since at least 1912,[68] was appointed chairman. Docker was also an admirer of BST's first managing director, Edgar Crammond, formerly Secretary of the Liverpool Stock Exchange. Indeed in 1921 he arranged through the BCU for a meeting of socialist, Tory, and Lloyd George Liberal MPs with the parliamentary chairman of the Asquith Liberals, at BTC's offices, to hear Crammond expound on the evils of the Budget.[69]

The parent BST company had on its board ffrench as chairman, Crammond as managing director, and two other directors, Wyldbore-Smith and a man called Chisholm. It spawned five subsidiaries during 1918–19: BST (Birmingham) Ltd in May 1918, the Mersey Investment Trust in July 1918, BST (North of England) Ltd in December 1918, BST (Edinburgh) in April 1919 and BST (Manchester) in August 1919. It was significant that the first branch was in Birmingham, where Docker was based, with his old friend Pierce Lacy (a future chairman of BST), for years chairman of the stock exchange there. The directors of these branches were ffrench, Crammond and Chisholm; from fear of further discrimination by the London Stock Exchange, the main movers and local supporters of BST hung back from the limelight. These five regional subsidiaries were intended to draw the potential investors in their catchment area, and to mobilise and unify the investment power of each region in a way that the London Stock Exchange could not afford to ignore. The parent BST topped the pyramid of these investment companies, and the structure recalled Docker's early idea of the FBI atop a pyramid of trade associations and of the contemporary organisation of the Whitley Councils.

A sixth subsidiary, BST (South America) Ltd was formed in November 1921, but remained a shell company until May 1924 when the whole group was re-organised. The South American company absorbed the others, changing its name to the British Shareholders Trust and raising its capital from £250,000 to £550,000. The change of name was significant, for the initials BST originally denoted 'British *Stockbrokers* Trust', and the substitution of the word 'shareholders' represented an attempt to quieten the antagonism of the City establishment aroused in 1918. In November 1924 Wyldbore-Smith replaced ffrench as chairman, although Crammond remained managing director. From this date BST began to lose its controversial reputation with orthodox stockbrokers, and soon settled into the comfortable rut of City institutions. The country brokers' revolt became a memory. It was at about the same time that a rapprochement began between British industry and the City, with merchant banks providing investment capital for home industries as opportunities for sound overseas investment vanished. More City bankers joined the boards of manu-facturing companies, financiers took a more responsible attitude to industrial flotations, and the old dichotomies were reduced. The story of the attempts after 1927 to rationalise the steel and cotton industries show that the City had grown more flexible and responsive, although as Steel-Maitland often complained, mutual jealousy and suspicion among bankers delayed progress. Nevertheless, as late as 1928, only two estab-lished London issuing houses. Higginson and Co., and J. H. Schröder, handled domestic industrial issues: the rest were still more concerned with exporting capital than making it available at home. In 1926 Wyldbore-Smith was succeeded as chairman by Sir Follett Holt, a man who had ordered much railway material from MCWF and Patent Shaft for South American lines before 1914, an activist in the BCU in the 1920s, who was, from 1927 onwards, Wyldbore-Smith's co-director of the Pullman company. In due course, Holt's successor was Sir Pierce Lacy. It is probable that Docker was the cord on which these pearls were strung.[70]

The similarities and lessons of BTC and BST transcend the nationalism of their names. Both were born out of the wartime corporatist movement, and met injurious opposition from the conservative pillars of the City of London who never forgave Docker for assaulting the status quo. Both companies were created in the height of war excitement, in the expectation that peace would bring 'a general scramble for the markets of the world, and a period of bitter international competition'. Germany's export expansion and industrial growth had 'excited the envy of every thoughtful British trader', as Docker wrote, 'conceived and carried out on lines never attempted in this country', with bankers, traders and government co-operating 'with the one object of developing foreign trade for the good of the whole German people'. But BTC in particular was never properly defined; it regarded itself as both an arm of government policy and as a profit-earning business, but these were irreconcilable and impossible functions without a government commitment to use and support its facilities. Docker had written that for the British Empire 'to regain commercial supremacy...there must be boldness of initiative and fearless rejection of obsolete methods'; 'if we are to succeed we must not pursue...the peddling and huckstering methods that found favour fifty years ago, but follow the larger view...and have no fear of greatness'. In the City he found little initiative, with still less rejection of past methods, and by the early 1920s it seemed to Docker that the last chance of retaining British supremacy had been squandered.[71]

8

Armaments, electricity and rolling-stock 1917–29

In all discussions between business men, politicians and economists during 1914 to 1918, the necessity of large-scale industrial amalgamations was repeatedly stressed. The constant re-iteration from productioneers, and others, was that Britain could only emerge from the period of reconstruction with its industrial hegemony unchallenged if mergers brought about economies of scale; but despite all the wartime rhetoric, positive action was slow to come. 'Mr Dudley Docker is the sole moving factor in this country at the present moment on that point', Sir Clarendon Hyde told Lord Faringdon in June 1917,[1] and his main achievement in this direction – the merger of British Westinghouse, MCWF and Vickers – is the subject of this chapter.

Some of the most striking pre-war vindications of German industrial methods had occurred in the electro-technological sector, led by AEG and Siemens. In contrast, no amount of special pleading 'could acquit British manufacturers of electrical equipment of the charge of ineptitude and indifference and...organisational chaos', and the 'agglomeration of firms producing unstandardised items' were an obvious target for reconstruction.[2] Indeed, Hugo Hirst wrote of the pre-war British electrical industry that 'its weakness, compared with the strength of the American or German electrical industry, has cast a reflection on the whole British industrial life'.[3] After considering these problems in 1917–18, Sir Charles Parson's committee on the electrical trades after the war[4] strongly urged that the British electrical manufacturers should amalgamate their companies, rationalise their activities and standardise their products; but it was left to Docker to give practical expression to these recommendations.

After the passing of the Trading with the Enemy Act (for which Docker had called) in 1916, the Public Trustee took over the Siemens electrical works at Stafford, along with other German-owned businesses. One of the pre-occupations of the Parsons committee was getting this factory, and the

American-owned Westinghouse works, into British hands to meet the challenge of post-war growth. According to one electrical manufacturer in October 1916, the Board of Trade wanted to solve the problem of Siemens' ownership by introducing 'a new strong manufacturing element...not previously...associated with the manufacture of electrical apparatus...who...have been in pre-war days coquetting with either American or German' companies. The Board of Trade, it seemed, were trying to interest 'the Dudley Docker crowd, and Sir Edward Holden' in Siemens, although it was known that Vickers were also anxious to buy the Stafford works and diversify into electrical engineering.[5]

The Board of Trade's moves in this direction had no positive results. Nevertheless, the emergence of the names of both Docker and Vickers as possible purchasers of Siemens, and the view that Westinghouse's Manchester factory should be got into British control, proved significant. Docker and Vickers were correct in appreciating that British electrical engineering had good medium-term prospects: although its output fell by 30 per cent in 1920–2, its share of British gross output rose from 1.9 per cent in 1924 to 3 per cent in 1935. Gross output in electrical engineering rose at an annual rate of 4.7 per cent during 1920 to 1938, and the sector provided jobs for 5 per cent of the manufacturing workforce in 1938 (compared with $2\frac{1}{2}$ per cent in 1920). By 1924, British electrical machinery exports out-stripped those of Germany, and were chasing the Americans; this progress was not checked by the depression of 1931–2. In the market for industrial electricity, the number of British factories using electrical power rose from 49 per cent in 1921 to 70 per cent in 1929, and 84 per cent in 1936.[6] In short, by 1918 the industry was primed for rapid acceleration.

British Westinghouse had been established by American interests in 1899, but achieved consistently disappointing results. Even during the Great War, when other electrical firms were profiting handsomely, Westinghouse wrote off £366,000 depreciation against net additions to plant and fixed assets of £102,000 – a deficit of £264,000. It also suffered from the wartime xenophobia, both because its managing director was German-born, and because it was American-controlled. It was on the latter ground that it was refused membership of the FBI in 1916, and this rebuff, together with the need to re-capitalise the company for post-war growth, led British Westinghouse to ask Docker to help transfer control to wholly British interests.[7]

Initially, in 1917, Docker approached Hirst about amalgamating GEC with British Westinghouse, but after this scheme was over-ruled by Hirst's co-directors, Docker approached the armament makers, Vickers. They were anxious to diversify into civilian lines in order to meet changed conditions, had been making electric motors and generators since at least 1905 and in 1915, as a trial of their capacity to adapt old skills to new technology, had supplied turbo-alternators to Philadelphia Power Station.[8] In the summer of 1917, British Westinghouse formed a committee to study the possibility of collaboration with Vickers, and after that committee had reported favourably in October, Docker and the Vickers representatives proceeded with a scheme to buy the electrical company. A new company, Electric Holdings Ltd, was jointly formed by Vickers and MCWF. Of its four directors, Sir Francis Barker was a Vickers director and FBI activist, whilst the other board members (Ludford Docker, Sir Ernest Hiley and Henry Walker) represented the rolling-stock interests. Then, later in 1918, Electric Holdings bought the Americans' controlling interest in British Westinghouse for £1.2 million. The terms of this transaction were singular, for Electric Holdings managed to avoid paying the Americans either in cash or immediately. Instead, they issued the Americans with £1,151,602 in 5 per cent debentures redeemable within ten years. The effect of this was that the Americans were paid off in instalments met annually out of the British company's profits: an arrangement which favoured the British and has the mark of Docker about it.

It was originally agreed that British Westinghouse would be re-named Vickers Electrical, but at the shareholders' meeting of August 1918, Docker instead secured the name of Metropolitan-Vickers Electrical Company (Metrovic). At this stage, Electric Holdings only controlled 50.6 per cent of the electrical company's 750,000 Ordinary shares and 610,000 Preference shares and in order to secure a majority holding of 75 per cent, Docker and his Vickers allies devised a new scheme which resulted in their controlling 76 per cent of Metrovic's voting stock. They subscribed for 110,000 new Preference shares at £2, and for 500,000 deferred shares at 1s each. These latter constituted a new class of capital, and despite their low value, bore the same voting rights as the £1 Ordinary shares and £2 Preference shares. The other shareholders were coaxed into accepting this arrangement on MCWF's undertaking to provide a further £750,000 for Metrovic, and there was subsequent resentment when this undertaking was broken. This anger increased in the summer of 1919 when the dividend fixed for the Preference shares was reduced from 15 per cent to 8 per cent, with the Preference shareholders being offered an option to convert into Ordinary shares in the two years to 1921. At the same time, in 1919, Metrovic's capital was further 'watered' by the issue of another million Ordinary shares, of which £100,000 was allocated for employees' possible subscription, and for which Electric Holdings subscribed

£900,000. Of this new capital, £700,000 was immediately loaned back to Vickers and MCWF (the owners of Electric Holdings), whilst the residue was lent to another recent acquisition of the rolling-stock company, Taylor Brothers, wheel and axle makers at Leeds. The sum of all these manoeuvres was that Metrovic's total capitalisation had risen from £1,395,000 in 1918 to £5,326,445 by the summer of 1919, and that Docker's new company, Electric Holdings, had jockeyed its way to control. Though Docker won admiration for his handling of this business, there is no doubt that it also made him enemies in the City.

Characteristically, Docker quickly filled the top echelons of Metrovic with his most trusted associates, such as Lincoln Chandler and Robert Hilton (who had acted with him on the Birmingham munitions committee in 1915). This led Sir Clarendon Hyde to observe to the Balfour of Burleigh committee, in June 1917, that Docker was replacing the old British Westinghouse management without sufficient thought of integrating Metrovic with MCWF. According to Hyde, 'One does not want to get rid of one series of controlling minds simply to place another series of controlling minds there.'[9] It was, indeed, a characteristic fault of the British merger movement that opportunities to integrate managerial functions (whether marketing, accounting or anything else) were neglected, and with the exception of his work at Saltley after 1902, Docker was surprisingly unresponsive to the possibilities of rationalisation in this respect.

MCWF's purchases of Taylor Brothers and Westinghouse coincided with the recruitment by Docker of several important new men to his companies. Two of these were former officials of the wartime Ministry of National Service, who had both trained as solicitors, Sir Ernest Hiley and Sir Philip Cunliffe-Lister. Hiley was 'a very able and quite admirable man' who had served as Town Clerk of Birmingham from 1908 until 1916. He had then followed Neville Chamberlain to the new National Service ministry, where he was implicated in the failure to organise manpower in 1917. He was afterwards hired by Docker and acted as his representative in both commercial and political matters until they quarrelled in 1921.[10] Another important figure, whom Docker recruited to his companies in 1919, was Sir Edmund Wyldbore-Smith, a former consular official, whose pre-war speciality had been trade fairs. He spent much of the war as senior British representative on the Commission Internationale de Revitaillement, an inter-Allied body which co-ordinated Allied purchases of munitions, food and other material. Wyldbore-Smith was also at the heart of plans for Belgian reconstruction, and his popularity in Belgian official circles promised to be useful to the Docker companies. Paradoxically, Wyldbore-

Smith had become unpopular with his Office colleagues: if Steel-Maitland is to be believed, other diplomats were jealous and resentful of the foreign decorations which Wyldbore-Smith received for his work on the Commission de Revitaillement[11], and his peacetime prospects in the government service were small. In the two decades before his death in 1938, Wyldbore-Smith served as the representative of Docker's interests in a multitude of companies, including the British Shareholders Trust, the International Sleeping Car Syndicate and Pullman. Two other associates in the period 1918–28 were George Taylor and his brother Tom, whose family business had been Patent Shaft's main competitor in the wheel and axle business for years, and was bought by MCWF at the end of the war.

Docker saw the purchase of Metrovic as the beginning of the British trust movement, and was so confident of the vindication of trusts that in January 1918, he privately urged the Minister of Reconstruction to appoint an investigative committee on trusts.[12] He must have felt himself to be a man whose moment had come, as on all sides his soldiers of corporatism began their march. The Metrovic merger was explicitly executed in the spirit of trade war. Vickers stated that the policy was for the new company to repeat 'the amazing growth of the Allgemeine Electrizitäts Gesellschaft' which commanded 'the strongest financial resources and widest ramifications',[13] and Docker shared this hope. Revealingly, a month after the Armistice, in December 1918, he wrote on behalf of Metrovic to Lord Robert Cecil of the Foreign Office:

> One of our people who had just returned from Germany tells me that the AEG's factory is full of motors complete except for the windings, which they are unable to carry out owing to shortage of copper...the longer supplies of copper are withheld from them, the better it will be for industry here, as...if they could obtain the necessary material they would...throw these motors...on the neutral or any other markets...Would it be possible for this to be borne in mind in...any Peace negotiations?[14]

Here were Docker's political and diplomatic, as well as business, priorities, implicit in his view that the fighting of 1914–18 had been an economic war largely caused by economic pressures.

Something must now be said of the armament company with which Docker had entered electro-technology, and to whose fortunes he was bound for another decade. Vickers had been among the leaders of the Sheffield steel industry by 1850, beginning its concerted assault on the armament market in 1888. In the next quarter century Colonel Tom Vickers (chairman of Vickers 1873–1909) and his brother Albert (chairman 1909–18) assembled an eclectic board of financial and scientific experts, merchant princes and retired officers. One gauge of their value is the amount of commission paid by Vickers to its directors in 1914–15: £88,285.[15] The board was distinguished by its 'capacity to meet pressures...not with the all too familiar policies of retrenchment, but with consistently bold strokes of innovation or diversification and, equally important, a consistent emphasis upon technical leadership of the market, whether it was civilian or military'. Market restraints were fought with product diversification and technical specialism and during their heyday of 1888–1914, 'the firm's reaction to external crisis or internal strain was...[to] respond aggressively; select related high technology markets; innovate in process, diversify in product'. Though they might be faulted for not trying to predict future growth beyond the medium term, the Vickers board conspicuously beat its competitors: the Armstrong directorate was divided in factions and dominated by a capricious and jealous autocrat; both Cammell Laird and Coventry Ordnance fell foul of the government, which halted orders until the boards were changed; whilst BSA and Hotchkiss Ordnance had weak or elderly directors.[16]

Douglas Vickers, who became chairman in 1918, presided over a board of directors who were 'personal types of industrialists; that is, they injected their personalities, their "genius", so to speak, as a subjective factor into their operations without the discipline of management by method and objective facts'.[17] The three most important members of the board were Sir Vincent Caillard (the finance director), Sir Francis Barker and Sir Trevor Dawson, all of whom, like Douglas Vickers himself, had been closely associated with Docker in the early development of the FBI and BCU. These men had what might be called the tycoon mentality: they believed that if only their board fought hard enough, always reacting boldly and decisively, promoting with more flair and pushing with more force, then sooner or later, they would surmount the obstacles which beat their competitors. As one sympathetic observer wrote in 1919, 'the Vickers system of business' was characterised by 'fearless exploration of untested lines of commerce and the cheerful acceptance of defeat should the eventuality happen to arise'.[18] The internal organisation of the head office was, however, riven with inefficiency. 'The Byzantine era in Vickers House', as one employee recalled Caillard and Barker's methods,

> had developed during the war and I was fortunate to see a little of the rich comedy on the sacred Second Floor where the two Caesars ruled an industrial world with Louis XVI offices, lying off a deeply carpeted corridor, with the private (male) secretaries in their offices opposite. An elaborate system of coloured lights, mirrors over the doors, bells and buzzers controlled the throngs of courtiers. It was a miniature Versailles of intrigue. The ambitious knew they must catch the eye of their

particular patron frequently – not only were there rich plums, rewarding missions and unlimited expense accounts – but failure to attend Court (unless abroad) meant exile on some remote and unfashionable corridor, in a small office receiving no In-coming mail, *then the inevitable end* of relegation to the Sheffield Works or worse, but it was agreed that there was nothing worse. You could – and I did – walk into a Director's office and come out a nominee director (with fat fees) on some big continental board.

Every morning queues assembled in the Corridor to chatter with a false amiability, keeping a sharp eye on the red lamp above Sir Francis Barker's door and peering up at the little mirror in the transom reflecting his desk – but he had a second desk out of sight – and interrogating his faithful shadow Mr Houchin, 'Any luck?' 'I'm afraid not, Mons. Venizelos is expected shortly, Mons. Loucheur at noon, and Mons. Edouard de Rothschild is calling before Lunch'.

Meantime the various directors had their own stratagems to effect escape, having inside doors to their colleagues' offices and thus a means of by-passing the followers who all unknowingly would continue to queue until Houchin or another secretary would take pity and remark, 'Are you expecting to see Sir Francis or Sir Vincent? But they went out an hour ago!'[19]

In 1917 Vickers faced huge strategy decisions at a time when they were already overworking to meet the demand for munitions. With their experience of the armaments downswing which had followed the Boer War, they recognised their bad peacetime prospects. These were made explicit by an official committee which reported to the Minister of Munitions in November 1918 'that the present outlay of the larger armament firms for armament production will be considerably reduced, and such manufacture will not improbably disappear as a speciality'. They predicted that

the country will insist on the production of all armaments being confined to Government factories; nor would the disappearance of the larger armaments firms materially handicap production in the event of a serious war, since during the present war a very large number of engineering firms have been educated in armament manufacture, and the basis for armament supply is so broad that specialising in the future on the part of a limited number of firms will probably not be necessary for the safety of the country.[20]

With these prospects, Vickers launched a hectic search for alternative growth areas, and under Docker's influence turned to electro-technology and rolling-stock.

Apart from market strategy, Vickers was also on the brink of a managerial revolution. In common with other industrial units of its size and generation, in 1918 Vickers was about to turn from, in Professor

A. D. Chandler's phraseology, an entrepreneurial firm, in which its top administration was dominated by its owners, to a managerial firm, in which senior management was undertaken by full-time salaried executives. Chandler's description of the methods of the founding entrepreneurs of American big business applies to Vickers in its Edwardian heyday.

> Where family members were no longer the chief executive or in other top management positions, close associates who had been personally selected by the family usually occupied these posts. The owner-managers prided themselves on their knowledge of a business they had done so much to build. They continued to be absorbed in the details of day-to-day operations. They personally reviewed the departmental reports and the statistical data. They had little or no staff to collect information... impressive, even brilliant business strategists... their moves were personal responses to new needs and opportunities. They did not plan systematically for the continuing growth... They rarely adopted formal capital appropriation procedures, rarely asked for budgets. In the more routine expansion of existing operations... they responded to ad hoc requests of middle managers.[21]

It was typical that Dawson, on becoming a managing director in 1906, had gone to pains to familiarise himself with every aspect of the Vickers business, and to master information about the daily running of every department.[22] Similarly, almost every important internal or external paper was marked 'Copy for Sir V.C.', but it was impossible for Caillard to monitor every development. The perils of this procedure emerged in a damaging lawsuit of 1920 between Vickers and the naval inventor, Admiral Sir Percy Scott. It transpired that Dawson and Caillard had kept incomplete records of their agreements with Scott to develop his ideas, and had only confused memories of the terms which had been settled. Vickers' subsidiaries were highly autonomous, and the degree of control exercised centrally from Vickers House, in London, was limited by inconsistent data-flow from the different works. With hindsight it seems that the group was too unsystematically organised for full consolidation of its facilities, depending on the ability of top management to absorb information about the various sections of the group. Such methods, of course, had worked adequately in the recent past, and seemed likely to maximise flexibility and to encourage initiative. If the practice of Vickers' more advanced German and American competitors was more exact, they were not behind contemporary British practice.

The foregoing picture of the Vickers owner-managers shows a group of men who had conducted brilliant business in the past, but who had deteriorated physically or mentally under wartime demands. At a moment when their reflexes were tired, and their statistical control never weaker, they had to reconvert to civilian markets and reform management procedures. Few of their heirs showed business aptitude: the new impetus had to be external: and Docker provided it. As soon as the Metrovic purchase had been settled, he started work on persuading Vickers to buy MCWF. In personal terms he was probably anxious to rid himself of the strain of the executive direction of such a big combine, for by 1918, his physical health was poor. The magnitude of the operations of a joint MCWF-Vickers trust must also have excited his imagination by its industrial grandeur: but he did not spoil the deal by impatience or soft-bargaining. In the discussions, he pitched his terms as uncompromisingly as when Mellon had wanted to buy MCWF for Standard Steel Car in 1913. At one stage in 1918, his negotiations with Vickers were abandoned because he would not accept auditors' examination of books as the method of establishing the relative values of MCWF and Vickers. He insisted that, apart from the fact that the companies' accounts worked on very different systems, anyway war conditions were no guide to values, and that pre-war conditions were no guide to Vickers' post-war prospects since their main business of armaments would have gone. MCWF's estimated market value in 1919 was £14.4 million.[23]

A particular trouble was that in the combined MCWF balance sheet, land, buildings and plant were shown at £1,690,000. But this figure was their value in 1902, all additions since having been written off to revenue; Docker argued that the figure was much too low. When discussions resumed, it was suggested that instead of auditors' examination of books, the future earning power of MCWF should be calculated from the wartime Excess Profit Duty's standards of profit. The EPD Standard of MCWF was £744,000, and this figure was used to value their works at £3,720,000. Caillard finally accepted the following figures as representing MCWF's asset value:

	£	£
fixed assets		3,720,000
investments		3,400,000
debtors	1,300,000	300,000
creditors	1,000,000	
stock (approx. pre-war value)		1,700,000
cash		2,100,000
		11,220,000

As to the fixed assets guessed to be worth about £3¼ million, Caillard wrote: 'The machinery is perhaps not the last word in up-to-date types, but the methods...are thoroughly efficient, and what impresses one in a visit is the... vim which prevails throughout.' This vague optimism was supported by the report of the auditor sent by Caillard to investigate MCWF:

> I was not able to verify the figures in any books, as they are not yet of course written up-to-date. I criticised their figures in every way I could, but they assured me they were satisfied as to their approximate correctness, and their knowledge of the results of this year's trading supported the larger increases shown. I have no reason to doubt their statements.[24]

MCWF had increased its capacity during the war by fully 50 per cent, and in recommending Vickers to buy the company, this point was seized by Caillard. He wrote, all too sanguinely:

> by working day and night shifts, the post-war output will be double the pre-war. In calculating the post-war revenue an increase of 75% will be assumed instead of 100%, in order to be on the safe side. This increased output will be achieved with scarcely any increase in overhead charges, as the increase of staff entailed would be negligible: thus the additional profit would be on a higher percentage on output than previously. There is no trouble whatever in securing orders, especially seeing the very large demands for rolling-stock, due to the cessation of production in all parts of the world during the war, for the next few years; and the very large and increasing demand for the products of Docker Brothers Ltd: the MCWF, we are told, literally commands the market.

Caillard went on to explain that

> The most attractive sides of the combination for Vickers Ltd lie in the acquisition at a reasonable price of a Great Standard Peace Industry, and the very considerable accretion of financial strength. Vickers Ltd is a great armament firm laid out before and during the war almost entirely for the production of materials of war. Even if Peace Industries had already been found on a sufficient scale to fill the Works which could be entirely detached from armament work – which is far from being the case – it would still take at least a year to get them into full swing, while no inconsiderable portion of the works must, at any rate for some time, be kept available for the production of war material, and this portion, until orders to occupy it come forward – a period impossible to forecast – will form a somewhat heavy unproductive charge on the Company's resources. The Metropolitan Company is in exactly the reverse position... The financial advantage is so great that it need not be dwelt upon.[25]

Caillard, though showing how Vickers had come to regret their near total commitment to armaments, certainly committed a solecism in expecting a 75–100 per cent growth in revenue from railway technology. In their eagerness to believe all this, the Vickers board exceeded the £11.2 million which Caillard calculated MCWF was worth, and paid altogether nearly £14 million.

This merger is a classic piece of over-capitalisation. It is doubtless significant that in March 1919, just after taking the further burden of the presidency of the FBI, Caillard broke down through overwork, and embarked on a rest-cure (which included a cruise on the Admiralty yacht as the First Lord's guest) until June.[26] Barker, who deputised for him, had also cracked under the recent strain, and was described by one friend as having become 'strange and not quite normal...forgetting entirely what he said...even a few minutes ago...[and] changing...conversation from business to any irrelevant thing'.[27] As it was, Vickers bought the Ordinary shares of MCWF 'at a premium of about 400 per cent',[28] and issued new capital amounting to £12,100,000. Vickers were not peculiarly reckless by the standards of 1919. One historian has described the capital market and merger booms of 1919–20 as being in a condition of 'meridian frenzy': the authorised capital of Lord Leverhulme's combine, Lever Brothers, mounted from £40,000,000 to £100,000,000 in 1919 alone, and in 1920, they signed an agreement to buy for more than £8,000,000 a company whose accounts they had not examined, and which transpired to be under immediate obligation to repay an overdraft of £2,000,000 to its bankers.[29]

There is no doubt whose influence pervaded the merger. Colonel Terence Maxwell, director of Vickers 1934–75, has described how the deal

> meant that Docker personally received a vast sum of money in preference shares which were almost as good as cash to him. Docker's personal profit from the deal must have been enormous...Docker was a man of great force of character...with cosmopolitan interests and with a position in the Midland Bank which enabled him to raise millions of money at very short notice. He also had about him a number of men that he backed and brought into high finance, and these men moved in advance of the main army, softening up the enemy positions...Douglas Vickers and the Board of Vickers had been dazzled by Docker's ability, high-level salesmanship, vision and reputation into paying more for the shares than they should have done...This rather ill-prepared dash into unfamiliar territory was the basis of all the troubles.[30]

It is certainly true that the Docker family received a large number of valuable cumulative Preference shares in Vickers which they gradually unloaded during the following twelve months. Dudley Docker sold 23,402 such shares between September 1919 and February 1920, holding 20,040 cumulative Preference shares in April 1920. His brother Ludford sold 28,139 of his 42,558 cumulative Preference shares in March and April 1920; while his son Bernard held 5,000 and his nephew John 1,000 such shares in the spring of 1920. Wyldbore-Smith and Hiley between them held an additional 7,000, and it is likely that they did so as nominees of DD.

Three supporters joined Docker on the Vickers board in May 1919, namely Edward Hickman, Chandler (who remained managing director of MCWF until December 1921) and Hiley. When Docker resigned with Hickman from the Vickers board in 1920, it was Hiley whom he nominated to succeed him on board committees (although they quarrelled in 1921, after which Hiley resigned from all the Docker companies and later became associated with Clarence Hatry, the fraudulent financier). Other Docker nominees were Wyldbore-Smith (who was a director of Vickers from June 1921 until May 1928), Bernard Docker, Henry Walker, Alexander Spencer, George Taylor and his brother Tom. Indeed, George Taylor was the first deputy-chairman of Vickers-Armstrongs, serving until December 1929, when he became head of the new combine which absorbed Vickers' steel interests, the English Steel Corporation. Also identifiable with Docker was General Sir Philip Nash, chairman of Metrovic, 1922–33, and a special director of Vickers, whose career as a railway engineer had culminated with his appointment as Director General of Transportation to the Army in France in 1917.[31]

Experience was to show that the combine was unmanageably diversified and over-extended. As Docker's own accountant was to write later, 'combinations or trusts can only be successful if confined to one trade or class of trade, that is to say one type of production or its subsidiaries'.[32] Caillard, Docker and Douglas Vickers created a huge diversified combine with vertical integrations in the hope that this would produce inherent financial strength. They discovered they were wrong. Their combine was not really vertical and 'contained a medley of unlikes' over which it was impossible to exert proper supervision. Their ambition might have been workable 'if productive and distributive efficiency could be obtained by every nice-looking mechanical scheme', but instead they found that components which appeared to fit together on paper, did not do so in real life.[33]

The productioneers at Vickers and MCWF were not the only industrialists to commit this error. John Brown's and Cammell Laird, for example, wrote off the armaments capacity of their joint subsidiary Coventry Ordnance Works, and merged it into the newly formed English Electric Company, whose other constituents included two firms previously associated with George Flett (Dick, Kerr and United Electric Car), together with the Siemens works at Stafford. John Brown's, too, bought in 1919 the Craven Railway Carriage and Wagon Company, of Sheffield, an 'old-fashioned company of excellent reputation',[34] as part of a diversification of their shipbuilding and armaments interests into rolling-stock. Both Brown's and Cammell Laird were a good deal disappointed in these acquisitions, as the world markets for rolling-stock shrank and British electrical components proved too divided and lacking in finance power.

One special characteristic of the Vickers–Docker policy emerged. Vickers' proudest boast since 1897, when they had bought the Maxim-Nordenfeld ordnance company and the naval yards at Barrow, had been that they were capable of creating from raw materials, without aid from any outside source, a battleship, with all its munitions.[35] This was first achieved with *Vengeance*, allocated to Barrow in 1897 as the first warship to be built there by Vickers, which on its completion in 1901 was the first ship of the Royal Navy ever built, engined, armoured and supplied with big guns by a single firm.[36] A measure of the technological virtuosity required is given by the Admiralty statement in 1936 'that the firms engaged in the different processes working up to the production of a warship would exceed one thousand spread all over the country'.[37] After 1918, when they tried to break into electro-technology, Vickers repeated the warship formula until they had the capacity to create, from raw material to finished product, without help from outside the Vickers group, a complete and finished electric power station, such as they built at Portishead, near Bristol.[38] According to Douglas Vickers in 1919, 'the changes brought about by the war' had created

> the necessity of doing business on a scale hitherto not reached by British manufacturers, but left to German and American competitors...in the past British manufacturers had been handicapped by making in too small units...the great American steel trust before the war had an output of steel greater than all the English firms combined. The two German electrical firms, their American rivals, and the American Machine Tool Works were all on a stupendous scale and commanded reserves un-approached in this country...organisations such as these had been able to initiate and follow well-defined and continuous policy individually, even if the total output was the same...the proposals...were...for...a combination of various allied industries, each supplementary to the other, using each other's products, and forming a complete organisation capable of handling within itself practically all the elements necessary...The Sheffield...parent works would feed the others producing the finished article.[39]

In 1919, Vickers therefore absorbed the machine manufacturers, Robert Boby, whose products included pneumatic plant for power stations and equipment for all classes of mills. Boby were intended to supply other parts of the Vickers combine in the same way that Sheffield fed steel, but instead, Boby were in constant financial difficulties, and heavily drained Vickers. Attempts to sell Boby in 1926 – 7, and again in 1935, led to the comment from Sir Pierce Lacy that it had become 'not a very saleable proposition'.[40]

Vickers started other, complementary electrical companies. The British Lighting and Ignition Company, later called the Vickers Train Lighting Company Ltd, was formed in 1917 but shut in 1925. The British Refrigerating Company Ltd was also formed by Vickers in 1917, but was soon wound up because of American competition. Vickers also held shares until 1925 in Compagnie Lorraine pour l'Éclairage des Wagons par l'Électricité, a company registered in 1914 to light trains under licence. Vickers also bought in 1919 W. T. Glover and Company Ltd, a cable-making company, whose value in December 1921 was put at £227,000: Vickers sold their entire holding in 1929 to Callendar's Cable and Construction Company.

Vickers found it impossible to get these electrical diversifications to pay, and failed to expand their management sufficiently to control these new acquisitions. A particular problem was that, because of wartime pressures, Vickers' Internal Audit Department had no accounts for 1914–20, and the whole accounting system, in the words of James Reid Young, who became their Chief Accountant in 1920, 'just went completely west during the war'. When Reid Young assumed responsibility, he found no previous balances to work on, and his first action was to sack about half of the accountancy staff, which then totalled between 150 and 200. According to Reid Young, 'it was a dreadful mess and...financially they did not know where on earth they were', and the delay in producing proper accounts led to a question in the House of Commons in July 1921.[41] The responsibility for this confusion nominally lay with Caillard, as finance director, although in truth, the problem of expanding the accountancy controls of an armament company in wartime was one that required superhuman capacities.

After launching their ambitious programme of diversification in 1918–19, Vickers found that they lacked the finance power to support it. Although issued capital rose by £13½ million in 1919–20, Vickers' cash needs were at least £8 million short by April 1920, and Caillard desperately cast about for external finance. Without telling Docker, he approached McKenna of the Midland Bank for a loan, but was turned down, and recommended to issue further debentures and sell investments for cash. Rothschilds suggested to Caillard that they might raise £4 million on the New York market, and Caillard himself drew up a complicated scheme to juggle further with the capital and mutual indebtedness of Vickers and Electric Holdings. Although these two devices might have brought temporary relief from the cash crisis, they would have further over-capitalised the group, and would probably have resulted in its bankruptcy by 1924. The decision of Caillard's co-directors to have nothing to do with either scheme showed good judgement.[42] The cause of this cash crisis was two-fold: the over-capitalisation of the MCWF merger and the disarray of Vickers' internal accounts and financial procedures. The result was to wreck the hopes of the new combine to repeat the pre-war successes of German and American trusts. As Douglas Vickers had said, such trusts 'commanded reserves unapproached in this country', and it became orthodoxy among most of his co-directors that their post-war strategy miscarried because British financial institutions were neither sufficiently powerful to get private savings into industrial investment, nor minded to provide the necessary financial power to create a giant industrial combine. Docker had previously arranged in December 1919 that MCWF would provide the Metropolitan Railway, of which he was a director, with the money for its post-war capital expenditure programme in return for orders worth not less than £1 million. Forty-two coaches worth £4,400 each and Metrovic electric engine equipment worth £153,094 were ordered in 1919, and further contracts followed; but although the manufacturers hoped this arrangement would secure them preferential treatment in future orders, it reduced their short-term liquidity.[43]

After Metrovic's formation, Vickers interested themselves in the Swiss electro-technical industry, the only one on the continent which had resisted German domination. They took interests in two Genevan firms, Secheron and Picard-Pictet,[44] and then approached the leading Swiss firm, Brown-Boveri, who were electrifying the Swiss railways, and owned subsidiaries in France, Italy, Norway, Germany and Austria. Barker went to Switzerland, and in the autumn of 1919, when Brown-Boveri increased its capitalisation from 36 to 48 million francs, Vickers took 7 million new shares, thus obtaining the single biggest holding, worth about £380,000. A loan was sought from a Swiss bank to carry out the purchase, and this caused Docker to complain:

> The terms demanded by the Swiss bank were not such as a firm of the standing of Vickers should entertain for a moment, involving as they did the payment of a minimum of 6% interest, plus a commission of $\frac{1}{4}$% quarterly, the issue of bills which might be put on circulation, a guarantee by Vickers and the deposit of security in the City of London. Such terms would have effectually prevented the raising of money in London at a reasonable rate and would not have been entertained at all if all negotiations with banks were left to one person who could form a judgement as to the effect that one operation would have on another.

This again indicates that Barker had lost his lucky touch although less onerous terms were eventually agreed.[45] The Brown-Boveri investment was not successful. The Swiss had only a limited home market in electro-technology because of the size of the country, and as their electrical supply was entirely derived from water-power, had no experience of steam turbines, large turbo-alternators, boiler plant and many other products. Given the large capital expenditure required for electrical development, the obvious alternatives for the Swiss manufacturers were either to combine into a single trust, or to develop powerful foreign outlets. Brown-Boveri had several Swiss competitors, including Oerlikon, Sulzer Frères, Secheron and Escher Wyss and these proved surprisingly resistant to combination; it was obliged to try 'to force a way into export markets even at the risk of unsound costing methods and at a heavy loss on contract prices'. This proved to be a disastrous strategy, and Brown-Boveri recorded a deficit of 25,570,000 francs in 1923, passing its dividend in that year and 1924.[46]

The incident of the Swiss bank loan led Docker to submit a long memorandum to the Vickers board in November 1919. He began with the ultimatum 'unless something in the nature of my recommendations be adopted...I could not in justice to myself, and to those who follow me, continue to remain a director'. He complained of general lack of co-ordination at board level, citing his embarrassment at having 'to plead complete ignorance' to McKenna after Caillard had asked the Midland Bank for a loan, and the fact that he had 'heard casually' from a co-director that the Vickers group were hoping to build a national arsenal in Poland without the policy of such operations being discussed by the board at all. He also complained that Vickers House were over-interfering in both the sales and production of Metrovic and MCWF, and warned 'Vickers ought not to run any sideshow'. He felt that the Vickers Sales Department, in particular, was 'antagonistic' towards representatives of its newly allied companies, especially Metrovic. The merging of agencies, at home and abroad, was being rushed: 'I know that it is argued that an amalgamated agency is less expensive than various units, but I am satisfied from experience that unless an amalgamation comes about naturally there is no saving in administration, but frequently the amalgamation is more costly than individual effort'. Docker's memorandum was a general assault on the conduct of business by Caillard, Barker and Dawson. Referring to the mushrooming of subsidiaries in sundry trades, he complained:

> there is an impression among the general public that Vickers are inclined 'to take up anything'. Whether or not this idea is correct is immaterial; there is no question that the public hold this view, and discuss it, especially in the City of London. The very suggestion that a Company is pursuing 'a hit or miss policy' is damaging to credit.
> During the last six months I have noticed that proposals are brought up to the Board which have been imperfectly examined, and in several

> instances I fancy negotiations have proceeded a certain distance before the matter has been mentioned to the Board at all. In my judgement all schemes should be first examined by one person, then investigated by the Chairman before being submitted to...the Board.

Clearly Docker not only found Vickers' way of business unsystematic, but also found it difficult to adjust to sitting on a board chaired by such a reticent personality as Douglas Vickers. He also criticised the proliferation of Vickers' subsidiaries:

> Some check must be made on the indiscriminate flotation of companies bearing Vickers' name. The constant announcement in the paper of a new Vickers company or the issue of a prospectus to which the public are invited to subscribe bearing the names of directors of Vickers or members of Vickers' staff causes comment in the City and has a bad effect on the public mind...I do not understand who authorises these companies...I regard it as fundamental that a complete and detailed financial statement should be prepared immediately setting out the assets and liabilities of Vickers Ltd and the associated and subsidiary companies.[47]

These criticisms of Vickers are identical to those levelled by Sloan against the owner-managers of General Motors: rapid expansion after 1918 without an explicit management policy to control the different subsidiaries; rapid diversification so that owner-managers lacked adequate knowledge or control of individual operating divisions; and a highly confused product line.[48]

In Docker's case, he could not get remedies implemented and a few months later, he determined to leave the Vickers board. The circumstances were telling. When the board met on 25 March 1920 to discuss the dividend to be declared for 1919, he proposed 10 per cent. That figure had been paid, free of tax, throughout 1908–12, and compared well with $12\frac{1}{2}$ per cent paid during 1913 to 1918. With one dissentient, the board agreed to his proposal. But only four days later, at a board meeting on 29 March, at which neither Docker nor Hickman were present, the board reversed this decision, and announced a dividend of $11\frac{1}{4}$ per cent, costing £1,292,431. Docker wrote to the chairman that this episode was

> most unsatisfactory, for it has defeated the object which we all had in view, namely, to fix the dividend at a sum which could be maintained steadily year by year. The impression now created is that the Board have been unable to maintain the $12\frac{1}{2}$ per cent and have strained to get as near to it as possible...The idea of an inauguration of a new conservative policy is not conveyed, while the same dislocation has been created on the share market as would have ensued if there had been a definite drop to 10 per cent...it will be impossible to drop the dividend again next year without creating a bad impression as to the profit-earning capacity of the

company – indeed the conservative policy which...we all accepted has been pushed on one side. The mischief is now done.[49]

The shareholders' meeting on 22 April confirmed, *inter alia*, the $11\frac{1}{4}$ per cent dividend and Docker's election as a director, but two days later, he wrote to Douglas Vickers resigning his seat on the board.[50] Nevertheless, four Docker nominees remained on the board, representing considerable holdings in the group. His criticisms were vindicated by events, for next year profits of £541,260 had to cover payment of £395,985 to Preference shareholders, and the dividend was nil to Ordinary shareholders.

The situation was primed for conflict between his nominees and the Edwardian armourers, the owner-managers whose responses had been shaped whilst 'The greatest development of private [armaments] manufacture took place in the long period of peace before the outbreak of war in 1914.'[51] The characteristics expected of Barker or Caillard are suggested by Churchill's remark of 1915: 'At the beginning of this war megalomania was the only form of sanity.'[52] Vickers were then admired for their 'fearless innovation' and 'cheerful acceptance of defeat'. But in 1918, the armament business faced a decade and a half of recession, and Vickers' touch was a jot less sure: praise of their fearlessness turned to complaint that they would 'take up anything'; instead of 'cheerful acceptance of defeat', their policy was called 'hit or miss'. What had been a reasonable business risk before 1914 was, after 1918, less reasonable; and the chief reason for this was the over-capitalisation of the Vickers group after the Docker mergers. Docker, although an acute judge of Vickers' internal weaknesses, helped to create the context which made them so perilous.

It is hard to define an over-capitalised company. A new company, either freshly floated or created by the merger of existing businesses, might earn higher profits after its formation so as to pay dividends which justified its capital structure. Alternately, a company which is reasonably capitalised in relation to assets may seem over-capitalised after several bad years' trading. 'The point to be emphasised is that over-capitalisation is *not* something quite definite, recognisable at any time, to which it is possible to attach a label, and...[find] a culprit...as over-capitalisation results from normal changes in value or in profits it is inherent in business and cannot be avoided.'[53] The results of over-capitalisation 'show themselves first on the minds and policy of the men who run the business', who 'have not freedom in making new departures, in taking risks, in undertaking business which will absorb further working capital...[and] have not the confident self-reliance which success brings'. Managers cannot mitigate the effects of a temporary falling-off in demand by such expedients as accumulating stock or overhauling plant; they cannot afford to try undercutting to stimulate demand; they cannot afford to spread overhead costs over a larger output; and 'it is not the least evil result of over-capitalisation that it tends to diminish the building up of reserves and so reduces the power of the Company to expand its business'.[54] This is just what happened to Vickers. In 1920 the amount required by Vickers to pay debenture interest, Preference dividend, Ordinary dividend at 10 per cent, and to cover Corporation Tax, without provision for reserves, was £2,521,000.[55] Reeling under the weight of such charges, the Vickers group failed to break into new and hostile markets.

Vickers' profit-earning capacity steadily receded over 1920–5. The results for 1924 (a profit of £1,909 after paying Preference shareholders £401,315) were the worst in the company's history, and as a result Docker was asked to help dismantle their over-extended range of subsidiaries. Perhaps with his Daimler experience in mind, he was authorised to explore the possibility of Vickers' Wolseley motors division uniting with the Austin and Morris companies. Wolseley had been formed by Vickers in 1901 with a view to the future potential of armoured fighting vehicles, and under the guidance of Albert and Douglas Vickers before 1914, 'had become the largest, if one of the most unprofitable, British car manufacturers'.[56] After the war, the company was chaired by Caillard, with Barker and Dawson as inactive directors, together with three ineffectual members of the Vickers family (Colonel Stuart Pleydell-Bouverie, Ward Grazebrook and Vincent Vickers) and the chairman's son, Bernard Caillard. In November 1919, Wolseley floated 6 per cent debentures to raise some £1,280,100 to finance post-war development, but these cost £140,250 to service annually,[57] and came on top of £300,000 in Preference shares paying 7 per cent (Vickers held all the Ordinary issued share capital of £1 million). Vickers' own liquidity crisis made it impossible to fund a proper programme at Wolseley, and the trade depression of 1920–1 proved an untimely blow to the company. Bernard Caillard, who was in charge of Wolseley at Vickers House, was 'quite incapable of running any business',[58] and two managing directors resigned between 1919 and 1923. The company completely failed to find a model for which a reasonable market existed, and their losses for 1923–5 totalled £841,000.

It was obvious that Vickers could not provide appropriate managerial supervision, or cash, or growth strategy, to turn the business into profit, so Docker was deputed to sell it. At meetings with Sir Herbert Austin and Sir William Morris in 1924, he urged that a merger of their three companies would create a combine better suited to rationalisation and mass production processes. Although this arrangement would have had benefits for Austin, who were also financially weak, it foundered on Morris' aversion to sharing his power, or compromising his independence, in any amalgamated company.[59] These were merger talks which Docker did not win, and from Morris' point of view, their failure was good business, for in 1926 he was able to buy Wolseley outright for £730,000 after it had failed to pay its debenture interest, and been put into the hands of the Receiver.

The losses at Wolseley were no worse than in some other divisions of the group, and in April 1925, Douglas Vickers summarised the position with this lament: 'When the manufacturer's costs are high he cannot quote low prices; when he cannot quote low prices he cannot fill his works; and when he cannot fill his works, his costs are higher; and so it goes from bad to worse.'[50] It became obvious that Vickers would soon be absolutely ruined, and in June 1925, an Advisory Committee was appointed (possibly at the instigation of the Midland Bank) to consider the crisis. This marked the public re-emergence of Docker in running the company. The committee members were himself, Sir William Plender, the accountant, and Reginald McKenna of the Midland Bank, who had dealt extensively with Vickers when he was First Lord of the Admiralty in 1908–11, and was a confrère of Docker. The trio did not make detailed examinations, but relied heavily on the analysis and drafting of an accountant named Mark Webster Jenkinson, who had been employed by Docker since 1921.

It is possible that Docker forced the appointment of this committee with the weight of shares which he had 'warehoused' in Vickers (i.e. held through nominees). Thus, in November 1925, Sir Basil Zaharoff wrote drily that 'DD, after studying the lists of shareholders, finds that the real large shareholding is in Birmingham – and not in Sheffield', and that DD was therefore seeking Douglas Vickers' resignation as chairman.[61] Another possibility is that Docker simply expressed City disquiet at the decline of Vickers to its directors, and the Advisory Committee was set up in response to this warning. Be that as it may, the Advisory Committee's effects were those of a coup by Docker against the owner-managers. Its report was an indictment of the administration and enterprise of 1920–5, and the ensuing re-organisation transformed Vickers. The report also revised the group's commercial targets: instead of a vertical combine of various supplementary allied industries, Vickers returned to concentrating on steel and ships. If the report underplayed the excessive amount paid (at Docker's instigation) for MCWF it was nevertheless an acute document. One employee who was dismissed in 'the inevitable day of the long axes' later recalled the tension as the ship heeled over and the order to the boats was imminent. Faithful old stalwarts, who had sold guns to the Tsar (but he had gone too) or destroyers to now vanished empires, hid in remote rooms. They called on each other to analyse the latest rumours and executions, and they would have done crosswords if they had been invented. A hush lay on the empty Directors' Corridor.[62]

The report was published on 10 December 1925, and its major recommendation was to write down the company's assets by £12,442,366. This was done, among other means, by reducing the issued Ordinary share capital from £12,315,483 to £4,105,161; whilst fixed assets were written down by £4,254,994 and the book value of subsidiaries by £5,488,316. Docker, McKenna and Plender wrote that Vickers' 'management had not the special experience required to direct and control so large and varied a body of industrial undertakings', such as had been accumulated in the diversification programme of 1918–20, 'particularly during a period of protracted and severe depression'. They urged that Vickers' future policy should

> concentrate on using to the best advantage its existing facilities, which are great, and under good management should be profitable; to dispense with all officials who have not justified their engagements; to cut down all salaries which are not fully merited; to eliminate waste in works management and production; to shut down plant and to wind up all...affiliated enterprises which...are...deadweight.[63]

A week later, an extraordinary meeting of shareholders met to approve the report. The meeting was turbulent, and it looked for one moment as if a resolution for its adjournment would be carried, but a clever speech by McKenna turned the meeting, which finally accepted the report with only five dissentients.[64]

It was not only Zaharoff who judged, 'If you were to leave what DD calls the Top Fancy Board as it is, the reduction of capital and re-organisation would come to nothing.'[65] The old board had lost their reputation for success, and it was essential that the new plans should be implemented by fresh names. In the major board re-shuffle that followed, the first-ranking change was the retirement of Douglas Vickers as chairman. He was given the honorific title of president of Vickers in 1926, but dropped even that in 1927, and for the last ten years of his life remained as a director only. The new chairman, General Sir Herbert Lawrence, was a former intelligence officer who became a partner in Glyn Mills, the bank which handled the accounts of both the Army and Vickers. Chief of General Staff to Haig in 1918, he returned to the City after the war and became a director of Vickers, by virtue of this bank's business with the firm, during the cash crisis of 1920. As an outside financier brought in after the MCWF merger, he was another reminder that the owner-managers could not keep control for ever; but he was not Docker's nominee.[66]

Seven other directors retired between December 1925 and June 1926. These included Lincoln Chandler, Lord Invernairn, Vincent Vickers, and several of the salaried managers associated with the unsuccessful post-war expansion, such as H. J. Morriss and Colonel W. C. Symon. Their successors included an old military colleague of General Lawrence, General Sir Noel Birch, the retiring Master General of Ordnance at the War Office, who had taken a dynamic lead in planning national policy on industrial mobilisation in the twenties. Another recruit was George Gall Sim who became secretary of Vickers in July 1926 and deputy-chairman of Vickers in 1929. Educated at Aberdeen and Oxford universities, Sim had entered the Indian Civil Service in 1901, working in its Finance Department, and culminating as Financial Commissioner of the Indian Railways, 1923–6. He had been the driving force behind early Indian railway electrification, and had probably impressed Docker and Vickers in that connection. Sim's dry humour delighted Lawrence, and he made great impact before his sudden death in 1930. Sim's low-key manner typified the approach which Lawrence brought to Vickers: if Albert Vickers had been a jovial predator, the quality that Lawrence admired in his executives was 'enthusiastic obstinacy to hedge around facts'.[67] This was the appeal of both James Reid-Young and Archibald Jamieson, the merchant banker who succeeded Wyldbore-Smith as a director of Vickers in 1928, and Lawrence as chairman of Vickers in 1937.

Two financial heavyweights who were Docker's associates joined the Vickers board in 1926. Sir David Yule, his co-director at the Midland Bank, was an East India merchant, almost the wealthiest man in Britain, who lived in complete absorption in business and almost hermit-like retirement. Yule gave considerable time to the reconstruction of Vickers in 1926, refusing to draw any fees until the company resumed payment of Ordinary dividend; but the closest financial direction came from Mark Webster Jenkinson. Jenkinson had served in the Ministry of Munitions, where his responsibilities included the Audit of all the National Factories and the design of their accounting systems, but in 1921 he was recruited by Docker as secretary of the Electric and Railway Finance Corporation, a private investment bank which Docker formed after his resignation from BTC. During the next five years he remained Docker's protégé.

From an early stage both Docker and Lawrence envisaged Jenkinson succeeding Caillard. Not only did Caillard bear some responsibility for the miscarriage of Vickers during 1918–25, but he was aged seventy and had been financial director for twenty years. He epitomised Vickers' owner-managers more than anyone else, and (unlike Dawson, who was ten years younger) no longer had the smell of success about him. It is remarkable that Caillard survived 1925–6 as financial director: Lawrence and Jenkinson both wanted to remove him. Finally, with Lawrence's approval, Jenkinson sought Zaharoff's help, explaining to him 'there is no-one better able to handle such a delicate matter, without hurting, as yourself'.[68] In August 1927 Caillard visited Paris, and over the course of several 'very painful' meetings,[69] was persuaded by Zaharoff to retire in return for £20,000 in cash, and £4,500 per annum for life.[70]

These changes at board level ushered in new policies at Vickers House. A new board structure, conceived by Jenkinson and adopted from the Advisory Committee's report, is shown diagramatically in figure 8.1.[71]

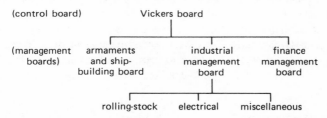

Figure 8.1 The re-organisation of the Vickers board structure 1925–6

Other economies were effected by disposing of the many subsidiary interests acquired during the peacetime diversification programme, but it is mistaken to treat Vickers' merger with Armstrongs (1927) as the main feature of the next fifteen years. It was in their concentration on becoming a leading steel combine, and their withdrawal from electro-technology and rolling-stock, that the most essential changes occurred.

The reconstruction of 1926 still left unanswered some profound questions about the future of the Vickers group. As posed by Sir George Buckham, Vickers' tank designer, the question was 'Are armaments dead?' Opinions differed as to the answer. Buckham himself believed 'if all we read is correct, then they are certainly dying, but...the only way to prevent war is to be ready for war, and if this is true, then armaments will always be required'. He doubted peace was yet 'so universal that Vickers-Armstrongs will be Industrialists instead of Armament makers', and expected 'much business will accrue from the mechanization of land armies'.[72] Buckham's colleague, Birch, the director in charge of land armaments, took an opposite view:

> that it will be impossible to pay a reasonable dividend to the shareholders if we continue to make armaments our principal source of revenue. Even

naval orders, owing to aircraft competition, may slacken. We should therefore aim at getting an increasing portion of our revenue from industrial and commercial sales, and should look to military armaments in the usual way only to cover working expenses; any exceptional receipts we may get owing to war or to the revision of military programmes should be looked upon as windfalls.[73]

The opinion of a Special Director at Sheffield was 'we must look less and less towards Guns and Armour as the main source of our profits, and turn our energies...towards commercial products, and preferably those requiring large quantities of steel...such as vessels required by the chemical industry, boiler drums, heavy forgings for marine work, etc.'.[74] Certainly, there was no quarrel that Vickers must never return to its Edwardian specialism: between 89 and 98 per cent of Sheffield profits in 1909–14, and 86 per cent of Barrow's turnover in 1908–12, came from armaments, whilst armaments turnover in 1930–4 had been reduced to an average of 46 per cent.[75] If Vickers recognised their duty to remain an armaments nucleus – 'the only organization of its kind in the British Empire',[76] as Lawrence told Hankey – they also sought steadier foundations.

At the end of 1927 Vickers had three strategic aims. The first was the disposal of Metrovic, which Lawrence's board thought it 'impossible' for them to run.[77] Though it had made a solid return of 8 per cent dividends throughout the twenties, managerial responsibility for it over-extended Vickers' organisation: it was an asset which they wanted to trade for cash. The second object was to limit the liability represented by Vickers' interest in rolling-stock; and the third was to lead the inevitable and long over-due reconstruction of the steel industry. All this was achieved in 1928.

To take Metrovic first, by the late twenties, British electro-technology had reached a critical juncture, as succinctly summarised in 1927 by the British Electrical and Allied Manufacturers Association, of which Docker was vice-president.

> The British electrical industry has two possible moves left – either to form closer associations with German and American manufacturing concerns, and so become absorbed in the international combine which may be formed ultimately, or to tighten up its own organisation, form a compact group of manufacturers with a common policy both in manufacturing (prices and orders) and in finance, and at the same time strengthen the central association. It cannot continue in the present system...and remain in existence...the industry has not more than two years in which to effect the necessary changes.[78]

Docker himself considered that 'co-operation with America was in fact forced upon [Metrovic]', because almost everywhere abroad, 'The Americans were first in the field.'[79]

By January 1928, Vickers had entered negotiations with Docker to sell control of Metrovic to American General Electric, headed by Gerard Swope.[80] Yule, Lawrence and Jenkinson handled negotiations, and from an early stage knew that Swope's plan was for American GEC also to take eventual control of British Thomson Houston, General Electric of Britain and English Electric. Lawrence adopted a characteristically ruthless position when he realised the magnitude of Swope's plans: he sought 'a definite undertaking' from Swope that Vickers would have an option to take up 500,000 shares in any new company formed after 'amalgamation... between the three firms we have in mind'.[81] On 13 February Docker accepted terms which Lawrence had offered on 1 February: £1,299,905 for 375,370 cumulative Preference shares, 265,300 Ordinary shares and 500,000 deferred shares. He added, 'As Mr Swope is anxious to get back to America, would it be troubling you to arrange for the transfer of the shares to be made out sometime tomorrow, leaving the Purchaser's name in blank and I will arrange to hand over the money in exchange for the completed transfers and share certificates.'[82] Swope also gave a written guarantee to Vickers of 'an option to purchase 500,000 shares on ground-floor terms in any new amalgamation',[83] although Vickers later accepted £25,000 instead of this option.[84] Vickers retained 100,000 Ordinary and 25,000 cumulative Preference shares in Metrovic, on which American GEC or its nominees had first option.[85] At this stage Docker also told Lawrence 'The deal has been arranged through me as intermediary but Messrs Vickers are not paying me any Commission nor am I their agent for the sale...the sale is now being effected at the net price to an independent purchaser.'[86] The subsequent conduct of Swope and Docker afforded Vickers considerable embarrassment, and the judgement of both Lawrence and Jenkinson turned against DD. Although, as we will see later, the possibility of Docker also taking MCWF off Vickers' hands was mooted in the same months of 1928, the sale of Metrovic proved to be the last intervention by Docker in Vickers' policy, and presaged the end of his influence.

In the month following Vickers' sale of shares to Swope, Lawrence was puzzled by continuing press reports that Docker had bought control of Metrovic,[87] and on 14 March he telegraphed to Swope 'may I assume that arrangement with you is unchanged?'.[88] Next day Swope replied, 'Control transferred to Docker with whom we are working in cordial co-operation to stabilize industry.'[89] At the same time Docker sent an enigmatic message to Lawrence 'that if he doubts any statements that he has seen I have made in the Papers, he might save himself expense and Mr Swope trouble by consulting the Register of the shareholders of Metropolitan-Vickers'.[90] This fiction was further supported by General Nash, Metrovic's chairman, in his speech to the AGM. He told shareholders that whilst GE of America had bought control of his company from Vickers, 'Dudley Docker came into the transaction and the control now lies in his hands.'[91] Lawrence can have believed none of this, and it may be imagined that he viewed Docker's behaviour with what one of his co-directors called 'his grim and icy disgust'.[92] George Taylor, now Lawrence's deputy-chairman, but once a close associate of Docker, held him responsible for 'the unfortunate state of affairs', and was particularly annoyed by Docker saying, 'Wyldbore-Smith was the only Vickers director who opposed the sale to Swope.' According to Taylor, 'Wyldbore-Smith strongly advocated the sale of Metropolitan-Vickers to Swope...and added that if it were not, "it would be a calamity"'.[93] It was not coincidental that a few weeks later both Wyldbore-Smith and Bernard Docker left the Vickers board.

The truth about the deal was certainly known to the government. Wilfrid Ashley, the Minister of Transport, wrote a paper on 'Electrical Development and American Capital' which was considered by the Cabinet on 13 March. He noted that in addition to Metrovic, Swope had recently bought electrical supply companies covering East Anglia, the south-east Midlands, and Wessex, and warned that a determined American assault was under way. The Cabinet referred the matter to the Committee of Civil Research, with Lord Weir and Sir Andrew Duncan of the Central Electricity Board seconded. Ashley emphasised the urgency, but characteristically little was done in the event.[94] Later in 1928, in one of the rare British mergers of the inter-war period which was aggressive rather than defensive in aim, Swope amalgamated Metrovic with British Thomson Houston,[95] and in December, Metrovic's name was altered to Associated Electrical Industries (AEI). The Americans, surprisingly, made no attempt to consolidate the facilities of the two companies, which continued to operate autonomously until the 1940s. Indeed, the new name of AEI did not catch on, and the use of 'Metrovic' persisted for several decades. (The seizure and show-trial in 1933 of several of their engineers posted to Russia made Metropolitan-Vickers a household name, and AEI was not popularised until after 1945.)[96] The American control of Metrovic was known to a limited circle only, and led to at least one incident which must have appealed to Docker's sense of irony. In 1928–9, Metrovic considered establishing a Hong Kong-registered company to buy the Shanghai Municipal Electric undertakings, which were then for sale, with a view to ensuring that future machinery orders were placed with Metrovic. In January 1929, Docker lunched with his friend Sir Victor Wellesley and another Foreign Office mandarin to discuss the Shanghai business. Ignorant of the fact that Docker was only providing a false Anglicised façade for Swope at Metrovic, they solemnly advised 'on general political grounds' that he should co-operate with American electrical interests in China. 'This seemed to be exactly what Mr Docker wanted to hear', the diplomats wrote in mystification afterwards.[97]

After the failure of an American attempt (1929–30) to get control of Hirst's GEC. Swope's high-handed scheming became increasingly erratic. In 1933 Jenkinson discussed with McKenna whether, with Hirst's co-operation, Swope could be persuaded to sell control of AEI. Jenkinson told Lawrence, 'McKenna thoroughly agrees with me that the control of the AEI in American hands is a menace to the electrical industry of this country.'[98] In April 1934 Docker inspired some untrue press reports that control of AEI was to be brought back to Britain in a £7 million deal arranged by the Tobacco Securities Trust headed by McKenna and Sir Hugo Cunliffe-Owen; but his motive in starting these rumours is unclear.[99] (Tobacco Securities had bought back control of Boots the chemists from the American druggists, Liggetts, in 1933, which was the inspiration for Docker's invention.) In September, when Swope sold control of AEI to a British group, Jenkinson told the new owners 'that we welcome the deal and that though we want to reduce our holding, we would do nothing for the present towards selling and interfering with their market'.[100]

The other parts of the Vickers group which were re-structured were not as easy to separate from the organisation as Metrovic. MCWF was even more associated with Docker than Metrovic, and was appreciably less profitable to Vickers. According to Jenkinson's calculations in 1928, the net purchase price of MCWF in 1919 worked out at £13,955,630, of which £5,199,387 represented the price of goodwill – the excess which Vickers paid for. Dividends received by Vickers from MCWF over 1919–27 totalled £4,010,153, averaging £456,390 per annum, or 3.54 per cent of the purchase price. Dividends paid by Vickers on the capital issued to buy MCWF shares totalled £5,434,697, representing on average £603,300 per annum, or 4.66 per cent of their purchase price. Jenkinson therefore submitted that the actual cost to Vickers of MCWF was the market value of the capital raised, plus expenses incurred, viz. £16,533,400.[101] As to MCWF's prospects in 1928, 'the construction and expansion of railways throughout the world (except in a few countries) has...passed the peak, and...the future...will be mainly concerned with the improvement of existing methods and equipment, possibly by electrification and standardisation'.[102] Lawrence had written as early as September 1927, 'I would prefer to get a good Carriage and W. merger thro' to the Armstrong deal',[103] and had asked Docker to seek this. It soon emerged that opportunities for the future of the rolling-stock group coincided with Vickers' needs in another direction.[104]

The group was painfully aware that their steel plant was inadequate, in comparison with their foreign competitors. George Vickers visited Bethlehem and other USA steel plants in 1926; and George Taylor toured the plant of German and Belgian competitors. Their reports were discouraging, and Taylor (who had been given overall responsibility for the Sheffield works) emerged as an opponent of Vickers' role as an armourer. When he took over at Sheffield, the works were mostly laid out for armaments production, and could only with difficulty be converted for commercial work. Their civilian lines (axles, tyres and springs; drop forgings for motor-car and aeroplane engines and special Duralumin forgings; special alloy steel for highspeed Twist drills and other tools; special Electric Steel castings: steel tubes, bars and billets; steel pressings and chassis frames; and magnets) did not carry the heavy on-costs. Taylor was convinced that unless heavy commercial work was introduced in large quantities, Vickers' River Don works would never be competitive or pay again. According to Taylor, Krupps and two Czech firms, Vítkovice and Skoda, could deliver marine engines at Barrow at two-thirds of Sheffield's cost price; whilst Bethlehem and Mid-Vale in America could cast ingots of 200 tons. Vickers' maximum weight of 160 tons could be achieved only with difficulty. He thought that the improvements necessary at the River Don works would cost £1,000,000 at least.[105] Buckham broadly agreed with Taylor. Discounting the importance of 'longer hours and lower wages' in other countries, he wrote:

> in America, Germany and other countries, before the War and since the War, much greater efforts have been made to develop and modernise their plants than have ever been attempted in this country...the main reason why we fail must be put down to inferior plant and inferior methods...the prices of our guns, mountings, etc., compare very unfavourably with either Schneider's, Skoda's, Bofors', Ansaldo's or Terni's, and something must be done...either a new or modernised factory is essential.[106]

It was against this background that Docker entered discussion, in 1927, with Cammell Laird, whose interests in shipbuilding, armaments, rolling-stock and electro-technology all competed with Vickers.

Vickers attached particular importance, initially, to reducing the role of MCWF. They wanted to release £5½ million in cash and securities which were tied up in it, to make their investments in trading assets more liquid, and to increase trading profits by amalgamation.[107] Early in February

1928, when Docker's negotiations over Metrovic were hanging fire, Vickers notified him that they would leave the Cammell Laird merger negotiations in his hands for another three months; but three weeks later, when the Metrovic deal had been concluded, McKenna approached Jenkinson with a remarkable proposal for Docker to buy Vickers' interests in MCWF.

> Mr McKenna pointed out that he was only interested himself in the matter as a friend of both parties, and with a desire to help Vickers ultimately to realise in cash the value at which our holding stood in our books, and he feared that should Mr Docker sever his connection with the control of the Metropolitan Company, the profits earned in the past would be seriously diminished.

McKenna's idea was that Vickers would receive £3,000,000 in cash, would be issued with bonds to the value of £4,000,000 and that a loan of £2,000,000 due by Vickers would be cancelled. McKenna suggested

> Vickers should sell to nominees of Mr Docker, whose interest in the matter would not be disclosed...under this scheme Mr Docker would not find any capital and if the business were successful, would acquire the shares without any payment...I suggested that if the shareholders were aware of this transaction they would criticise the Board, but his view is that the transaction, being carried out in the name of nominees, would never become public.[108]

McKenna explained 'my lever with F.D.D. would be his desire to help B.D. [Bernard Docker], whose ambition it is to make a success of the Wagon company'.[109] The piquancy of this suggestion is remarkable. Only nine years before Docker had made 'enormous' personal profit by Vickers' unwise purchase of MCWF.[110] Now a deal was proposed – surely with his tacit approval – in which he would take back that company on truly bargain terms. Unfortunately for him, the repercussions of his arrangement with Swope were just beginning to be felt at Vickers House, and on 8 March, Lawrence's board rejected McKenna's proposal.[111] A few days later George Taylor had an angry meeting with Docker, the upshot of which was that the latter 'decided not to take any steps to bring about the fusion between Metropolitan Carriage and Cammell Laird, and that Vickers could take any steps they liked, as [he] did not propose to take any further interest in the Company'.[112]

The main object of Vickers, in the negotiations which followed, was to obtain facilities to operate as industrial steel producers. George Taylor was convinced that Vickers were confronted by the choice 'of throwing our entire weight into the industrial arena, or going out of business entirely',[113] and thought both Vickers' steel plant, and Armstrongs' steel works at

Openshaw, Manchester, were 'very much out of date'.[114] Cammell Laird provided the remedy in an agreement with effect from 1 January 1929. The new English Steel Corporation (ESC) was formed, with Taylor in charge, to manufacture industrial steel at Sheffield, Manchester, Penistone and Elswick. The Metropolitan-Cammell Carriage, Wagon and Finance Company did wagon work at Birmingham, Nottingham and Leeds. Cammell Laird pursued shipbuilding and engineering at Birkenhead. Vickers-Armstrongs concentrated on naval shipbuilding and armaments; whilst Vickers remained a holding company. As *The Economist* commented, Cammell Laird and Vickers were overcoming the diffusion of managerial effort which was inevitable in vertical combines by splitting up their 'many-purposed businesses into single-purposed ones'.[115] Cammell Laird's accounts for 1927 and 1928 showed a loss of £112,046 and £80,694 respectively, and it needed strengthening no less than the rest of the steel industry: under this scheme its heterogeneous bulk was broken into three compact industries, two of which were strengthened by alliance with other factories doing like work.

No deal had such a profound meaning for Vickers since they had bought Maxim-Nordenfeld's Barrow yards in 1897, for the very reason that it reversed one of the primary points of the 1897 mergers. After the creation of ESC, the supply of raw material and forgings passed out of Vickers' immediate control, and they could no longer boast that they supplied armaments made from raw material to finished product 'without aid from any outside source'.[116] If, under George Taylor's leadership, ESC was beneficial to the rationalisation of industry, its inception had drawbacks for Vickers. Birch soon detected 'more than a tendency on the part of the English Steel Corporation to break away from the Vickers group', and claimed in 1929 'none of the Allied companies have any faith in the prices quoted by the English Steel Corporation, nor do they deal entirely with them, as they certainly should'.[117] It was a bitter irony that Taylor's new regime, with all its hopes of modernising capacity, coincided with the onset of the Depression in 1929. Business fell away, and Jenkinson wrote in 1930 that ESC's results 'have given me a nasty shock, for bad as I expected the figures to be. I did not anticipate anything quite so dreadful'.[118] Taylor's intention to finance renewals of plant through sales of obsolete and depreciated stock were dashed by the Depression, and two directors of Vickers-Armstrongs reported 'a considerable starving of maintenance, with lack of effective renewals' at ESC by 1931. 'There has been little development in Plant, and renewals have been carried out piecemeal and not in accordance with any general plan.'[119] As Birch wrote in the same month, 'There is something infernally wrong somewhere.'[120]

With effect from January 1932, ESC's capital was written down by £5,372,820 (which represented a capital loss to Vickers-Armstrongs of £2,830,000) and later in that year, Charles Craven went to Sheffield as managing director. Subsequently Craven supervised the expenditure of some £1,500,000 in renewals and modernisation of lay-out, so that if world conditions had made the early years of ESC disappointing to Vickers, its stabilisation was nevertheless a cause for satisfaction. An undoubted source of its strength was that Vickers-Armstrongs (unlike many of its competitors in steel) carried no debenture charges whatsoever. The policy of Lawrence and Jenkinson to put the group in a very strong cash position – it was the only large steel maker able to make a distribution to its Preference shareholders in 1931 – succeeded after 1933, and in the years before the outbreak of war ESC secured a notable reputation in its sector.[121]

Whilst George Taylor was responsible for ESC, his brother Tom became the first chairman of Metropolitan-Cammell. His task was more hopeless, for the group was saddled with over-capacity. Geoffrey Burton, its general manager, concluded in 1929 that, at best, their six factories would obtain orders for two-thirds of their capacity – say 600 coaches, 4,000 four-wheeled wagons and 3,000 bogie wagons – and that two factories should be sold.[122] This was duly done at Nottingham and Leeds, but rolling-stock so far from justified the optimistic forecasts of 1919, that in 1934 Metropolitan-Cammell's value was again written down, to only about £1,000,000. The contraction in rolling-stock business was world wide, and even Andrew Mellon's powerful Standard Steel Car Company, which had tried to buy MCWF in 1913, was sold in 1930 to the American Pullman interests to minimise the effects of over-capacity.[123]

So much for the purchase which Docker persuaded Caillard had 'financial advantages so great that it need not be dwelt upon'.[124] Certainly Vickers' association with Docker proved expensive, not just in £16½ million which Jenkinson calculated that MCWF had cost Vickers, but also in the cost of missed opportunity. If Vickers had combined after the Armistice with Cammell Laird, or a similar firm, and led the rationalisation of British steel manufacturing a decade earlier, not only Vickers' history, but the socio-economy of Britain might have been very different. The opportunities for an integrated steel firm, unhindered by debenture charges, were great in the twenties, and would unquestionably have changed the basis on which steel nationalisation was argued after 1945. The possibilities can be argued endlessly. What is more certain is the contrast between Vickers in the last years of the owner-managers, and the reconstructed Vickers of Lawrence and Jenkinson. In the first period, entrepreneurs who sensed that their role as national armourers was defunct, launched a hectic post-war expansion, lacking either explicit management policy or sufficient financial data to control each specific division. Without adequate centralised pooling of information, it was impossible to control individual operations. Although the Depression that began in 1920 demanded the highest managerial co-ordination, the owner-managers could only offer the intuitive judgements which had worked so well before 1914. They still sought to master every operating division among themselves, but vague demarcation of responsibilities led to inconsistent allocation of resources, and an increasingly confused and unprofitable product line. Vickers became a rather formless aggregation, a sort of general engineering stores, always chronically short of cash to cover operating needs. The later Vickers, with its Scots and ex-Servicemen and systematised data, was a very different enterprise. Vickers House knew how much was being contributed to profitability by each division of the group, and with these aids to review and control efficiency, the prosecution of each of the group's operations might safely be left to management *in situ*. The medium for these changes was Docker. Whatever mergers Vickers had made in 1919, the addition of civilian industry would have introduced outside financiers and professional managers to supersede the owners, but Docker brought particular influences to bear and the course of events bore his mark. His powerful personality, and his reputation for business invincibility, contributed to Vickers' inaccurate self-assessment after the war. Some members of the board – possibly Douglas Vickers himself – apparently felt 'they could go to sleep on their shares so long as Mr Docker was at the head'. As a result, systematic reform of management and marketing strategy was too long delayed, and warning signs passed unheeded. His reputation as an industrial titan and financial wizard proved to be a self-defeating exaggeration, especially as in the 1920s he refused to exert himself for long in any cause. His conduct towards Vickers showed the extent to which he used manufacturing industry as a field for sharp financial operations. Although in 1920, and again in 1925–6, he proved that he had the capacity to make shrewd and acute criticisms of industrial policy, he was unwilling to apply himself to the slow and tedious business of constructive reform. He sent Webster Jenkinson into Vickers to do that for him, and withdrew from active involvement until the chance of more financial wheeling emerged in 1928. Docker came to Vickers in his cynical old age, and his dealings with them show him at his worst.

9

Inter-war politics 1922–39

Docker's dislike of the financial and industrial policies of the Lloyd George coalition have been mentioned before, and there is no doubt that he welcomed its fall in 1922, even though he was one of the men consulted in the autumn of 1921 when Lloyd George was planning the Gairloch programme to reduce unemployment.[1] He became president of the BCU in January 1922, belatedly formal recognition of the importance he had long held in the organisation, and spear-headed an appeal for funds.[2] By that time, however, Docker already despaired of politics in industrial society. The welter of reconstruction plans with which he had been associated, covering the Foreign Office, FBI, electro-technology, railway operations and export finance, had all failed, and in his judgement, the last chance of British industrial hegemony had been missed. He had no hope of shaking out the country's political and administrative mandarindom, which he felt had sold the pass; and he could no longer pretend that protection, amalgamations or Germanophobia were panaceas.

The general election called by Baldwin in 1923 on the cause of tariff reform showed Docker's disillusion clearly. He himself 'was very doubtful of the wisdom of forcing a General Election, with its concomitant... dislocation of industry'. Measures to combat unemployment in the coming winter were far more urgent than 'projects for the protection of home markets in the more or less distant future', Docker felt; the impetuosity with which Baldwin's 'comparatively unknown' government had embraced protection could only 'create distrust, suspicion and uncertainty among the industrial community', and its effects were likely to be nugatory.[3] As far as Docker was concerned, the government's unconvincing conversion to protection was ten or fifteen years too late, and tariffs were no longer the panacea that they would have been at the state of British industrial evolution reached during and immediately before the first world war. Nevertheless, as president of the BCU, he addressed an appeal to member companies in November 1923 for funds to help return eighty members of the Industrial Group, explaining that 'Labour and Liberal policies will spell the destruction of...fundamental British industries'.[4] If Docker doubted the relevance of the tariff election, another power in the BCU, Sir Allan Smith of the Engineering Employers Federation, who had a strong antipathy to Baldwin, was utterly opposed. He had been BCU sponsored MP for Croydon since 1919, but in November 1923 preferred to contest a Glasgow constituency as an Unionist Free Trader. The BCU was an ostensibly protectionist pressure-group – originally called the London Imperialists, after all – and Smith's defection was an irreparable blow. In a wider sense, too, Baldwin's defeat was fatal to the BCU's vitality as a protectionist lobby-group. By the end of the following year, its most successful member, Cunliffe-Lister, was saying that he would prefer Anglo-German treaties and steel cartels to the introduction of Safeguarding of Industry legislation, and by 1927 Amery was writing in exasperation of him that although he understood finance and imperial development, he 'had all the enthusiasm and guts knocked out of him in 1923, and is now too opulent to recover them'.[5] The diminution of Cunliffe-Lister's commitment was similar to that of other BCU leaders, whose high-pitch of wartime imperialism wound down after 1918, and almost disappeared after 1923 under the emollience of the second Baldwin government.

The other obsession of the BCU's productioneers – that of breaking German industrial power – also became irrelevant in the early 1920s. The imbroglio of Germany's reparations payments, including the French occupation of the Ruhr in 1923, inflated the cost of raw materials to British industry and disturbed Britain's overseas markets; and within five years of the Armistice, British manufacturers longed for German stabilisation. Docker had first-hand experience of all these developments. A deal between the Metropolitan Railway and AEG, which he set up in 1920–1, collapsed because of the provisions of the Reparations Recovery Act passed by the Lloyd George government later in 1921. MCWF and Vickers suffered greatly from the dislocation of markets and rising costs caused by the Ruhr crisis of 1923. Moreover, the Midland Bank handled the British business of the Reichsbank (Germany's central bank), and its directors were all too aware of the frightening instability caused by Germany's high inflation and industrial disorder. By 1921, when sanctions were in force, the Midland Bank's direct business with Germany 'had absolutely come to an end', although a few enquiries were received for German business through neutrals. The Midland directors feared that the threatened imposition of a tariff premium on German goods as a punishment for reparations defaults would force Germany to attack neutral markets and 'completely cut [Britain] out in North America, South America, China [and] Scandinavia'.[6] In such conditions the rhetorical anxiety of pre-war financiers and manufacturers about German business rivalry was obsolete. There is a sense in which these post-war problems were of the business men's own making. Their harping during 1915 to 1918 on the unassailable German economic strength which Britain would have to fight when peace came, their insistence on the unfair and insidious method of Hun competition, greatly affected public opinion and government policy. It forced Lloyd George to seek more punitive peace terms with Germany than would otherwise have been the case: the telegram of April 1919 supported by 279 Unionist MPs, led by the journalist-businessman Kennedy Jones, expostulating with him for not treating Germany implacably, was an example of the effects of the wartime rhetoric which drove Britain to make its Carthagenian peace. Yet ironically it was these peace terms that destabilised the German economy, dislocated European trade and brought attendant calamities onto British industry.

The BCU survived until 1925, but both morale and organisation declined after 1923. With the Industrial Group firmly established in the House of Commons under an independent administrative apparatus, and with alarmism about Bolshevik shop-stewards diminished, the BCU had little *raison d'être*, and Docker's dream of a manufacturers' party was hopeless. Once the Lloyd George coalition had fallen, the Conservative party resolved to obliterate all vestiges of Lloyd George's corruption by returning to the bi-partisan battles on which professional politicians thrived. This was a Conservative party, as an informant told Bonar Law, which admired Austen Chamberlain as 'excellent because he was supremely commonplace and as he lacks inspiration...therefore offended no-one'.[7] To Conservative orthodoxy, the coalition of 1916–22 became the time when 'The crooks [were] on top',[8] and its political culture was utterly repudiated. Even a productioneer like Steel-Maitland judged 'it really providential that Baldwin was made Prime Minister' because he was such 'a very attractive simple fellow' who had no claim to brilliance.[9] In this atmosphere, capitalist leaders were expected to keep a lower profile, and political militancy among business men became a grave solecism. There was no place for the BCU or for Docker's politics in the atmosphere of the 1920s.

The relaxation after 1923 was epitomised by the way in which the general organisation of the BCU was taken from the hands of Sir Allan Smith, a cold, ruthless and refractory autocrat, and placed in those of Willey, 'a nice, get-together sort of chap, without much political sense'.[10] Increasingly, its main activity was the demoralising business of fighting an extortionary lawsuit brought against it by a man whom Docker had

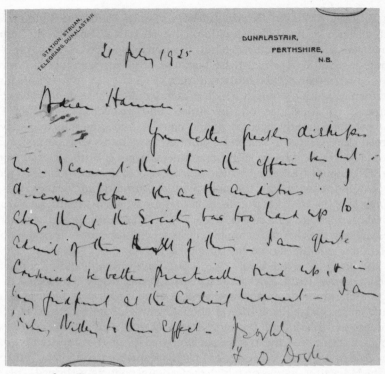

My dear Hannon,
   Your letter greatly distresses me. I cannot think how the affair was not discovered before – who are the auditors? I always thought the Society was too hard up to admit of this sort of thing. I am quite convinced we [had] better practically wind up, and in my judgment at the earliest moment. I am writing [to] Willey to this effect.
   Yrs vy truly
   F. D. Docker

Ill. 8 Docker's letter to Hannon, 21 July 1925

investigated by private detectives, and called 'a blackguard [who] ought to be in jail'.[11] Harold Duncan pursued an absurd claim against Sir Allan Smith, Steel-Maitland and Cunliffe-Lister in the hope that the two Cabinet Ministers' embarrassment at being defendants would lead to a settlement. Docker was furiously opposed to this blackmail, and the suit was defended at every stage; but it was exceedingly vexatious to everyone concerned.[12] Another piece of misbehaviour delivered the BCU's deathblow. In 1922

Docker's former personal secretary was taken on to the BCU's administrative staff. He was clearly in financial trouble by 1924 ('this being quarter day I am very much pressed for ready money'), and in July 1925, it was discovered that he had embezzled £544 from the Union. Docker was informed by Hannon whilst shooting in Scotland, and within two months had arranged for the BCU to shut.[13] (His death warrant for the Union is illustrated above.) Its few remaining activities were absorbed by the Empire Industries Association, a minor body then associated with Caillard, Hirst and Hewins, which gained importance after 1945 as the organisation through which Leo Amery led opposition to the Washington Loan Agreements and to the General Agreement on Tariffs and Trade (GATT).[14]

The decline and death of the BCU were part of the wider complacence about industrial policy which characterised Britain in the 1920s. The greatest industrial question towards the end of that decade, upon which national defence and many thousands of jobs depended, was the rationalisation and modernisation of the steel industry. It is upon this practical case that the industrial policies of the Baldwin government and the political efficacy of the 'governing institutions' deserve to be judged. In the event, Steel-Maitland battled almost alone in the Cabinet for constructive and systematic policy on a subject on which MPs 'through no fault of their own, are almost entirely lacking in reliable information'.[15] As one steel manufacturer, Hichens of Cammell Laird, who urgently wanted rationalisation, complained in 1928, 'there is nobody whom he can get at who will decide to do anything. In Lloyd George's day when there was industrial difficulty he would get half a dozen big employers together, snatch at a plan suggested by one of them and carry it out...Now nobody has the courage to do anything.'[16] Docker deplored this feckless attitude of the Baldwin government and held it responsible for the 'perilous position of the country' in the early 1930s.[17]

Docker's influence on industrial policy and economic controversies is hard to trace because of his increasing taste for anonymity, manifest by 1921 when he donated £300 to the Tariff Commission, but had the money put down in Caillard's name because he was 'particularly anxious' that his own name should not appear. Nevertheless, as late as December 1930, he was entangled in political negotiation together with Nugent of the FBI, Hewins of the Tariff Commission, and Colonel John Gretton, the multi-millionaire brewer who led the die-hard group of Conservative backbenchers.[18] In the same year, however, he declined to contribute to the fighting fund of Beaverbrook's Empire Crusade, explaining in disillusion, 'if I knew who was going to lead the side and where he was going to lead us to, I should be only too pleased to help...[but] in the meantime, as I have had such an unfortunate experience in supporting so many sides, which have led us into disaster, please excuse me'.[19] In the mid-1930s, too, through the good offices of Guy Locock, he was re-elevated 'as a kind of elder statesman of the FBI', and in 1934, during the FBI presidency of Rolls Royce's Lord Herbert Montagu-Douglas-Scott ('a most charming person, but...not one of the leading industrialists in this country'), was perhaps as instrumental as Scott in arranging the FBI's Mission to Japan and Manchuria led by Lord Barnby.[20]

There were, however, three areas of policy-making in which Docker did intervene in the age of Baldwin: railways, labour and foreign affairs. As a director of London's Metropolitan Railway from 1915, he was appointed in 1927 to its sub-committee on political developments in transport policy and to a successor committee of 1931–3 on the proposed nationalisation of London Transport. During 1932 to 1933 he led the Metropolitan board in their resistance to inclusion in the London Transport Passenger Board (LTPB), and in their negotiations for generous financial compensation. Manville, Wyldbore-Smith and Bernard Docker all joined the railway's board after 1926, and there was a solid Docker cadre in its direction. DD organised a characteristically stubborn and ingenious rearguard defence of Metropolitan, which was, however, absorbed by LTPB with effect from June 1933. As London Transport's historians conclude, 'The Metropolitan's long fight did credit to the pugnacious spirit of a proud and well-run railway', but their 'dogged action...had little chance of success.'[21]

Steel-Maitland was Minister of Labour during 1924 to 1929, and turned to Docker for guidance on several occasions. In 1925, Steel-Maitland and Baldwin tried to obtain what they both called 'a Peace Treaty for a limited time' in industrial relations. The idea was to elicit compromises and concessions from both employers and trade unionists, and then to weld a binding industrial concordat between them. When Docker met Steel-Maitland on 31 March to discuss the Peace Treaty scheme, he 'heartily agreed' with it, and undertook to sound out the engineering employers about the main points which they would like embodied in the treaty. The idea of 'peace negotiations' was especially attractive to Docker. He had always urged that class tensions in industry would dissolve whenever representatives of the different sides became personally acquainted through frank discussions. The 'psychological' obstacle in industrial relations would be surmounted by this device of regular meetings. Moreover the groundwork for establishing the concordat required skills which he admired in others and in which he excelled – discretion and bargaining finesse. Steel-Maitland's Peace Treaty scheme reflected the view common among the Birmingham business men that most matters could be fixed by knowing the top people personally. At this meeting with Steel-Maitland in March 1925 Docker also urged 'a point more fundamental still', that many British industries 'were right behind in equipment', and that 'it would be a great inducement to employers to join in heartily' in the Peace Treaty if the next Budget included an income tax allowance for manufacturers re-equipping with modern machinery. As one example of British desuetude, he claimed that Indian coal mining was technically ahead of the mother country's, and urged government action to help to arrest this decline.[22]

The crisis in the coal industry soon overwhelmed the idea of a Peace Treaty, but Docker was equally ready to advise on the General Strike of 1926. He greeted the Strike as a heaven-sent chance to revise industrial relations law to the employers' advantage by curtailing the right to picket, and urged this on Steel-Maitland.[23] It typified Docker's individuality that whereas most of his contemporaries looked on the General Strike as a setback to industrial peace which jeopardised national stability, his pre-occupation lay with the positive use to which it could be put. There were few situations, indeed, in which Docker could not see productive possibilities which less flexible minds overlooked.

In the aftermath of the General Strike, Steel-Maitland returned to his hopes of 1925 that an 'industrial concordat' could be attained between labour and employers. In October 1926, he recommended to Baldwin a scheme whereby a few of the more enlightened leaders of both sides of industry would be got together for frank discussions, rather as had been tried in the National Industrial Conference of 1919. Steel-Maitland envisaged labour being represented by Philip Snowden, Arthur Pugh of the Iron and Steel Trades Federation, and Ernest Bevin of the Transport and General Workers Union. He wrote:

> On the Employers' side, one of the chief difficulties will be to get the admission that they too have shortcomings which they ought...to tackle. When speaking of individual industries they will admit as much. But when speaking for industry as a whole they always talk as if the mote and the beam were in the eye of the employee. For this reason Montagu Norman [Governor of the Bank of England] should be a good ally. The Chairmen of the Big Banks know the truth as well as he, but mutual jealousies prevent their being helpful.

He also nominated, together with Norman, Lord Weir of the National Confederation of Employers Organisations, adding regretfully, 'Dudley Docker would probably be the best, if he would give time and trouble to the business, but I am afraid he would not do so'.[24] Docker was unwilling to tire himself trying to shore up a structure which he had himself condemned as unsound for almost twenty years. His disenchantment at

the waste of Britain's wartime reconstruction opportunities was over-
whelming: his faith in the possibility of effective reforms was fitful. He
would probably have agreed with Ramsay MacDonald, who wrote after
becoming Prime Minister in 1929:

> British manufacturers are not facing up to their problems with live minds
> and with a knowledge of world conditions...the British manufacturer is
> out-of-date in his methods and...his own incompetence is one of the
> largest factors in [trade] prospects...His industry is over-capitalised, his
> machinery is out-of-date, his organisation is of the most primitive kind
> and he will either not take the trouble or he has not the vision to take
> advantage of...opportunities.[25]

One remaining area of Docker's intervention was Foreign Office organisation. Late in 1930, Docker was in contact with his wartime colleague
on the Faringdon committee on commercial intelligence, Sir Victor
Wellesley, who was Deputy Under Secretary at the Foreign Office in charge
of the Western Department. Wellesley was dissatisfied with the Office's
contribution to the new Labour government's discussion of the tariff
question, and feared that diplomats were not putting the arguments
against protection coherently. The fear developing among diplomats like
Wellesley was that 'a high protective tariff, combined with Empire
preference, implies a measure of dissociation from Europe, a corresponding
diminution of our influence over European affairs, and possibly a growth
of economic antagonism';[26] and Docker, for reasons shown in chapter 10,
had moved from the economic colonialism of his middle-age to a more
geo-political belief that Britain's industrial future probably lay as part of
a larger European or continental economic organisation. Docker and
Wellesley agreed that the deteriorating world economic position made it
urgent for the Foreign Office to have proper machinery to monitor 'the
intimate connexion between modern industrial developments and foreign
affairs', and both men perhaps shared the view that the recent Hawley-
Smoot tariff act in the United States was 'a virtual declaration of economic
war on the rest of the world'.[27] Wellesley, moreover, had 'never understood
why the Department of Overseas Trade was created an *economic* intelligence
Department' and wanted to stop 'Commercial Secretaries from trenching
on the ground of the political staff'. For Wellesley the DOT 'was primarily
set up for the use of the public and the public does not require economic
but *commercial* intelligence'; he felt the Foreign Office must re-assert its
control over economic intelligence.[28] On the basis of their discussions,
Wellesley prepared a long and emphatically argued memorandum for
circulation in the Foreign Office, urging a new department there; and
Docker had interviews with several politicians to explain the views of

Wellesley and himself. In January 1931, he lunched with Ramsay MacDonald, the Prime Minister, in order to discuss the matter; and in February, he saw Arthur Henderson, the Foreign Secretary, and J. H. Thomas, the Lord Privy Seal.

The fundamental proposition of Wellesley's memorandum was that 'the political importance of the economic factor in international relations will become more and more the dominant consideration upon which diplomacy will have to concentrate...The political problems of the future will be essentially economic problems...what is purely commercial and technical in detail becomes in the aggregate highly political.' It seemed to Wellesley and Docker that because 'the more perfect the process of industrial integration becomes, the more nearly it approaches the condition of a State trading as a single organism', so the importance of economics would become increasingly predominant. 'The rational goal of modern economic society, so far as political forces do not operate to deflect its course, is to become a world society'. According to Wellesley, Britain in 1931 should

> not let the fear of...military danger blind us to the much greater and more immediate danger that is developing at a stupendous rate under our very eyes, namely, the clash between highly perfected economic systems, the results of which may be as disastrous to the world...as military war in the old sense. Powerful States are busily perfecting their economic machines, not necessarily with the express object of waging economic war on any particular country, but, just as before 1914 nations perfected their military machine in order to play a dominant role in world affairs, so now they perfect their economic machine for the same purpose. This may result in Great Britain being reduced to the position of a poor second-rate Power with a low standard of living before we quite realise what is happening. The immediate danger of threatening Great Britain is not... another war, but that she may be crushed between the economic hegemonies of Germany and America.

Wellesley's memorandum represented Docker's view, and it is interesting to find that DD, who had thought Britain at its industrial turning-point in 1918, thought in 1931, after the wasted 1920s, that Britain was in imminent danger of decline into an industrially backward and politically minor power. The onset of rearmament in 1936, and the economic repercussions of the war, prevented the fulfilment of this prediction in his lifetime; but twenty years after his death, it was an established fact.

The new department proposed by Docker and Wellesley had a sticky reception. Ramsay MacDonald told Docker that although he found the idea acceptable, he had not the time to get involved himself, and that it would have to be settled by the Foreign Office internally.[29] Inside the Office, 'Wellesley was widely regarded as an eccentric, whose over-categorical arguments might be...dismissed as springing from an *idée fixe*'.[30] He was opposed by various colleagues who felt that he was seeking to engross larger areas of foreign policy making, or who were unsympathetic to his profoundly materialist and pre-determinist view of diplomacy. Wellesley was helped by the increasing discussion of tariffs which culminated in the introduction of a 10 per cent general tariff in February 1932; and by an informal arrangement of December 1931, Wellesley was authorised to re-arrange the work of his Western Department so that one official would be responsible for all tariff work. The official concerned was F. T. A. Ashton-Gwatkin,[31] who until January 1933 had only one assistant, Walford Selby. In view of the fact that the World Economic Conference opened in June 1933, this arrangement was pitiable.

The opponents of Wellesley's scheme were not confined to diplomats jealous of their departmental prerogatives. Sir Warren Fisher, head of the Treasury and of the Civil Service Department, recognised that Wellesley's proposals were intended to reduce the Foreign Office's dependence on his ministry and his first reaction to Wellesley's 'impertinent' proposal, 'Sock him on the jaw', has been famous in Whitehall ever since. Docker had never admired Treasury methods, and was a proponent of Foreign Office supremacy; but Wellesley's antagonism of Fisher was fatal to his hopes of getting a full-blooded economic department. Even when a bromide version of the scheme was launched under Ashton-Gwatkin in 1934, the Treasury continued to raise obstacles which frustrated activities. The remittal of information from foreign Missions to Ashton-Gwatkin's department remained inconsistent, and his London colleagues were jealous and fearful that he would supplant them. Their attitude can be imagined from the nickname which Sir Robert Vansittart, head of the Foreign Office, invented: he joked that Ashton-Gwatkin had the Cuckoo's Department which would soon oust all others from the nest.[32] Altogether, the Economic Relations Section was a mouse, not the tiger of wrath which Docker wanted, nor the horse of instruction conceived by Wellesley. The wrangling and empire-building which wasted this potentially valuable idea resembled some of the frustrations which Steel-Maitland had met at the Department of Overseas Trade in 1917–19. In both cases, the Foreign Office resisted new administrative machinery because of ignorance and laziness; whilst other ministries, responsible for trade and finance, refused to consider any object but the maintenance of their own powers. As Docker and Wellesley both themselves realised, this was a product of British traditions of individualism and of the extent to which many national institutions were so long established that it would need a revolution to overthrow old practices.

Co-operation between the British diplomatic and business communities had improved since 1918, but it remained injurious to a diplomat's career to become overly identified with commercial enthusiasm. One of Docker's acquaintances was Sir Malcolm Robertson, British Ambassador in Argentina, who wrote from Buenos Aires in 1929 that his 'campaign about British trade in Argentina' had attracted 'more publicity than is good for a diplomat's career'. After 'an enthralling three years here, dealing with practically nothing but trade, and thinking of little else', he found that the Foreign Office could offer no prospect of further employment; and his fate was both a caution to fellow diplomats who might otherwise have engaged in the export struggle and a pointer to the resistance which the Economic Relations Section was bound to meet.[33]

Docker was also an intermediary in the honours lists, seeking for various acquaintances peerages, knighthoods and even ecclesiastical preferment.[34] His own career was almost recognised by the Baldwin government with a barony. Early in 1929, Steel-Maitland was asked by the Conservative Central Office to enquire if Docker would accept a peerage, for which he had never asked. On receiving an affirmative answer, the Conservative party chairman, J. C. C. Davidson, wrote to Cunliffe-Lister in February asking him to recommend the idea to Baldwin as 'it might be useful in the Midlands' in election year. Sir Robert Vansittart, the Prime Minister's Principal Private Secretary, knew of the idea, and approved; and Davidson was optimistic that Neville Chamberlain would also support it.[35] Other business men who were nominated for baronies at this time were Jesse Boot the retail chemist, Sir William Berry the newspaper proprietor, a chemical manufacturer called Brotherton and an American financier named Urban Broughton: Docker's contribution to British public life far surpassed any of them. The peerage was, if anything, overdue. However, at a late stage in May 1929, Docker was excised from the forthcoming list because of objections that 'his career had unfitted him for an honour'. This 'puzzled and astonished' Steel-Maitland, who had been asked to make the original approach, and he wrote a long remonstrance to Vansittart to the effect that the City establishment were 'unfair [to Docker] in their judgements partly from jealousy, partly because life had been made easy for them...I have no doubt Docker has made enemies and people put a worse construction on what is done by a person who has trod on their toes than on the same act...[by] some hail fellow, well met.' Steel-Maitland asked Vansittart to consult Cunliffe-Lister, who knew Docker 'better than anyone', and himself made appointments with Sir Edward Peacock of Barings and with Lord Weir to get their view of Docker's business reputation.[36] It was Steel-Maitland's view that after consulting all this evidence, Baldwin should personally satisfy himself that Docker merited his barony.[37] As it was, Baldwin lost the election in May 1929, and with it, any opportunity to redress the slight to Docker. Docker had several admirers in the Cabinet of 1924–9, notably Churchill, Cunliffe-Lister and Steel-Maitland, and working acquaintance with the Chamberlain brothers, but he also had at least one opponent. Wilfrid Ashley, the Minister of Transport, who deplored the Docker–Swope deal over Metrovic in 1928. It may well have been this transaction which provoked Docker's City critics to block his peerage. The position of his supporters was perhaps weakened by the fact that he 'never subscribed' any money to Conservative Central Office at any time, although of course he had privately financed many parliamentary candidatures. This would certainly have placed him at a disadvantage to men like Urban Broughton who paid for their titles in cash.[38]

Whatever Steel-Maitland's fears for Docker's feelings ('though he is a strange fellow, I like him', he told Vansittart), it is unlikely that DD felt hurt by the episode; and it may have been a consolation when Bernard Docker was knighted for his work for medical charities in 1939. (Bernard though was less satisfied, and in 1941–2, made a concerted effort, through Hannon, to obtain a baronetcy.)[39] It was perhaps appropriate that someone who, like Dudley Docker, spent so much of his life attacking the political establishment and disturbing conventions, should have been rebuffed in such a peculiar fashion. He may even have derived obscure satisfaction at finding his poor view of the world confirmed by this incident. As it was, he remained a sufficiently proud son of Birmingham Unionism to donate a portrait of Neville Chamberlain by James Gunn to the Carlton Club in 1938.

10

International electrical and railway trusts
1914–44

By 1920, as we have seen, Docker felt bitterly disillusioned with post-war reconstruction, and had withdrawn, partially if not completely, from the FBI, BTC and Vickers. For the next twenty years, his industrial imagination and financial ingenuity turned from the national confines of British business to the world domains of multi-nationals, and he became an adept in the diplomacy of international trusts in railways and electricity. In financial terms, he could make a fortune in commissions, acting as an intermediary in dealings between the trusts, whilst personally, he relished the role of go-between and enjoyed the excitement of planning and executing immense deals. Politically, it is possible that he was influenced, at second-hand, by the arguments of Sir Halford Mackinder's *Democratic Ideals and Reality* published in 1919. Mackinder was a geographer and politician who had succeeded Hewins as Director of the London School of Economics and carried weight with some productioneers. He argued that existing individual nations had no economic future except as part of consolidated groupings based on the continental land masses. He identified a combination of Russia and Germany as the greatest potential menace to Britain, instancing Russian raw materials and German technical organisation as natural collaborators, and he concluded that Britain's geographically dispersed Empire was an unrealistic means to industrial hegemony. Docker apparently absorbed these views, or reached similar ones by a less academic method, and from the early 1920s developed Belgium as a base for his operations on the European continent. Many of Docker's activities, moreover, were in concert with Belgian and French electrical financiers who were prominent in the Pan-European movement led by Count Richard Coudenhove-Kalergi, which sought European political union, using arguments which had some resemblance to Mackinder's. It is unlikely that a full account of his international activities in 1920–44 will ever be known, but the following chapter will show some highlights.

199

British electro-technology, headed by Hirst's General Electric Company, with Metrovic and English Electric (EEC) close behind, found itself badly placed in 1919–21. Metrovic's prices for converting electric locomotives in August 1921 were 25 per cent higher than the Germans', for example.[1] By February 1921 Hirst was warning privately, 'if the sluices of importation are not closed only one of two things can happen – we shall be ruined, or in self-defence we must make an agreement with our foreign competitors asking them to please let us live... in England and they may have the rest of the world'.[2] Docker, with his knowledge of Metrovic's experiences in 1919–20, reached a similar conclusion, and in the early months of 1921, Hirst, Docker and McKenna were in negotiations with AEG about a possible agreement to keep the German electro-technology out of the British domestic market, and to divide overseas markets by formal agreement.[3] Hirst had visited Germany in July 1920, and had been told by the leaders of AEG that 'they were not yet out for a world policy' again, because they needed time to recover their credit and develop hydro-electricity to counteract the post-war German coal shortage. The Germans had therefore concluded they must reach accommodation with either their British or American competitors. In Hirst's words,

> We are nearer, more convenient, they see greater advantage to themselves with us. That is the *bona fide* feeling which exists in Germany and we ought to take advantage of it... The Germans want relations with England so as to secure their raw materials and credit. Above all there is one great danger to the Germans, the danger of socialism; that is why they want to have English partners and shareholders. They feel that the more they are mixed up with us, the safer they are.[4]

Exact details of the agreement reached by Docker and Hirst with AEG are unknown, but certainly included arrangements for Anglo-German co-operation in Russian business. Each side needed the other to make progress in Russia, with the Germans providing knowledge of the market and cheap productive capacity, whilst the British could finance the transactions and provide diplomatic and political support. A joint Anglo-German initiative had been made by June 1921,[5] but its achievements were apparently minimal.

Docker was also in contact with Metrovic's American competitors at this time. In January 1921 he told Hannon, over lunch at the Savoy, of his 'plans for bringing American and British finance into closer relationship',[6] and in November, he had talks with Hirst, McKenna and Swope (of General Electric of America) about the possibility of merging British GEC with the American-owned British Thomson Houston company.[7] This would have been only the first stage of a larger unification of the British electro-technology manufacturers, for Hirst had long hoped that GEC could combine with Metrovic,[8] and EEC was also mentioned in the discussions. No agreement could be reached, however, and in May 1922, Hirst formally declined the American overtures.

The Americans and Germans were not the only people with whom Docker was involved. At some date before 1914, Docker had encountered in Belgium a young Jewish electrical engineer named Dannie Heineman. Born in North Carolina in 1872, Heineman had been partially educated in Germany (and was a class-mate and life-long friend of Konrad Adenaeur, German Chancellor of 1949–63), qualifying as an electrical engineer at Hanover in 1895. He spent the following ten years working in Belgium, Germany and Italy on tramway electrification, power-station building and the development of electricity distribution services. In 1905, he took over a Brussels-based company Société Financière de Transports et d'Entreprises Industrielles, known as Sofina, with a staff of two men, to exploit his knowledge, and Sofina's meteoric rise (it had staff of 40,000 by 1939) was one of the glories of Belgian economic history. Docker invested in Sofina some time before the German invasion of Belgium, and in the pressure of the times almost forgot about it. Before and during the first world war, Sofina was considered 'German to the core', and this caused alarm when, in 1914, it organised an English syndicate to absorb the principal tramway and lighting concerns in India. The syndicate was poised to take over the services at Calcutta, Madras and Bombay when war began and the scheme had to be abandoned: it is unknown whether Docker was party to it. Sofina naturally suffered severely during the German occupation, but Heineman himself did superb work in preventing mass Belgian starvation, and was Herbert Hoover's assistant in the work of the Commission of Belgian Relief. Though Heineman shunned personal publicity as much as Docker, his wartime work earned him the gratitude of Belgium, and entry into the highest official circles. From about 1927 he was leader of the Pan-European Union in Belgium, and the work of Heineman and some of his Sofina associates led Coudenhove-Kalergi to write that the leaders of the European electrical industry 'were generally more broad-minded than most of their colleagues in other production branches'. He became a close friend of King Albert of Belgium, and after the latter's death in 1934, was equally admired by King Leopold, for whose speeches on economic subjects he was often responsible. After the Armistice, Heineman turned Sofina into one of the world's most successful public utility, engineering, management and holding companies, and Docker woke up to find that his casual pre-war investment had enormously appreciated in value. DD found in Heineman a man of terrific energy and organisational talents, and he soon became

Sofina's senior British contact and aide. Docker's admiration for Belgian business methods strengthened in the inter-war period.[9]

Belgium had been the most highly industrialised European nation as early as 1870, with 40 per cent of its labour force then in mining, manufacturing or construction. It had a well-developed banking structure, and the Société Générale de Belgique, chartered in 1822 by the government, had been the first joint-stock bank in the world for promoting industrial development. There had been cartels in Belgium since the 1850s, and successive Kings of Belgium took a keen interest in industrial development, as witnessed by the Superior Council of Commerce and Industry, upon which Docker based his concept of the FBI. Electricity was a great stimulus to Belgian development, and according to the historian of the Société Générale de Belgique, 'it was the Belgian-built tram which popularised the country's industrial image across the world'.[10]

Belgian industry was laid waste in 1914–18, and a great effort was made at post-war reconstruction. One of the leading figures, until recruited to private industry by Dudley Docker in 1919, was Sir Edmund Wyldbore-Smith, Board of Trade representative on the Anglo-Belgian Trade Committee, and British representative on the Inter-Allied Commission on Belgian reconstruction. Belgian industrial rationalisation was attributable to the intervention of both banks and government. Trade associations were created to encourage and organise exports, superseding individual manufacturers; the Belgian Overseas Trade Department was re-organised; the iron and steel industry formed a unified purchasing and selling agency, Socobel, in 1924; and private bankers were encouraged to specialise in supporting particular industrial combines. Moreover, as there was no metallic backing to the Belgian franc, most Belgian business men bought British and American currency to invest in Britain or America, where they expected better security, with the result that Belgium's foreign investments became increasingly pervasive. In the boom that followed, export credit guarantees rose from 18 million francs in 1922 to 211 million francs in 1928.[11] Much of this Belgian revitalisation was along lines for which British productioneers like Docker had called in 1915–19; it is significant of the special empathy which British trade warriors felt for Belgium at this time that in May 1919 Steel-Maitland proposed to the Cabinet that Belgium should be included in any future imperial preferential scheme.[12]

One of the features of Belgian success, from about 1921, was the rise of Brussels as an international finance centre for electric power schemes. Many electrical supply undertakings which had previously been controlled by Germans or Swiss were acquired by Belgian trusts, such as Charleroi, the Société d'Électricité et de Mécanique (SEM), Constructions Électriques

de Belgique (CEB) and Sofina. Belgian capital penetration by these multi-
nationals was facilitated by elastic company legislation, notably by the
Belgian practice of creating special founders' shares of limited value whose
voting rights permanently outweighed other forms of capital. Of the four
Belgian financial trusts, Sofina stood apart from the others, both by having
a large number of its voting shares for sale publicly, and by not being
closely allied with a specific electrical manufacturing group. Charleroi, for
example, which was the strongest of the trusts, controlling most of the
Belgian trams and electrical supply companies, was identified with the
Jeumont group of France and with International Telegraph and Telephone
of the USA. SEM, which had many contacts with Belgian metallurgy, was
indirectly a subsidiary of General Electric of America; whilst the weaker
CEB was controlled by an Anglo-French group. Sofina was exceptional in
not having such close manufacturing allegiances,[13] and its free-wheeling
position was doubtless one of its attractions to Docker. It meant that
whenever he was able to arrange British financial participation in one of
Sofina's overseas schemes, this would be conditional on part of the
contracts for the work being placed in Britain with, say, MCWF and
Metrovic.[14] On top of this, Sofina's role as an electrical consultant to large
electrical supply companies, and to railways such as the Metropolitan,
meant that it had great influence on the dispersal of orders.

Docker himself never sat on the Sofina board, but its three British
directors in the twenties were men associated with him: Wyldbore-Smith,
Reginald McKenna and Sir Pierce Lacy. In addition, when Sir Philip
Cunliffe-Lister lost office on the formation of the first Labour government
in January 1924, he joined the boards of several Sofina subsidiaries, such
as the Compania Hispano-Americana de Electricidad (Chade) and the
Société Internationale d'Énergie Hydro-Électrique (Sidro), which controlled
interests in Mexico and Spain, and toured Argentina to inspect their
operations there. When he returned to the Cabinet, in Baldwin's second
administration of November 1924, Heineman promised that he could
resume his Sofina directorships if he again left the Presidency of the Board
of Trade, as indeed occurred during Cunliffe-Lister's next spell of opposition
in 1929–31. This led to some questionable dealings when, in 1927,
Cunliffe-Lister put heavy pressure on the Foreign Office to afford diplomatic
support to Sofina's subsidiary, Anglo-Argentine Tramways. Diplomats were
startled to find that no Board of Trade officials 'knew anything about the
matter', and that its President was acting unilaterally; as late as 1929, Sir
Miles Lampson held an 'uneasy suspicion' that Cunliffe-Lister's relations
with Sofina were the root of the undue partiality which the Board of Trade
and DOT showed for Anglo-Argentine. Lister's conduct was certainly

surprising in a man who had offered to resign from the Board of Trade during the coal crisis of 1925 simply because his wife was a colliery owner and there might be a conflict of interest ('the best thing in British public life is the standard it exacts', he sententiously told Baldwin at the time).[15]

Sofina's other ramifications were considerable, and included the business empire of Docker's counterpart in the history of French electro-technology, Louis Loucheur. Loucheur was born in 1872, and after working as an engineer with the Chemin de fer du Nord from 1893, formed his own company, Girolou, at the turn of the century, in partnership with a schoolfriend called Alexandre Giros. This enjoyed considerable success in railway electrification and hydro-electric development, both in France and overseas, and in 1908, the two partners floated a new company, the Société Générale d'Entreprises (SGE). This became not only a great force in French electro-technology and electrical services, but also established subsidiaries in Ottoman Turkey (1909–10), Morocco (1911), Russia (1912) and elsewhere. The wartime mobilisation of French industry entangled Loucheur in government, as Under Secretary and later Minister for Armaments, and as Minister of Reconstruction in the critical period, 1917–20. On six occasions between 1921 and 1931 he was appointed to senior portfolios, such as Commerce or Finance, in short-lived French governments; and much of the responsibility for running SGE devolved upon his partner, Giros. Sofina had a holding in SGE, and in many of its electrical, tramway and other subsidiaries in France, Turkey and north Africa; Giros himself was a director of Sofina.[16] As Cunliffe-Lister informed Bonar Law, Heineman 'always [kept] in the closest touch with Loucheur' on business and political matters.[17] Loucheur was a vigorous and dictatorial man, intelligent but unscrupulous, notoriously corrupt, who led the French branch of the Pan-European Union, and was distrusted in official British circles as 'a Cartel Diplomatist' seeking French hegemony of Europe with the help of German industrialists. His proposal for a supernational institution to assure democratic control of the continent's cartels and trusts was ruined by the onset of economic depression in 1930, but enjoyed the support of Heineman and other electrical magnates.[18]

In Italy, Sofina was associated with Giuseppe Volpi who in 1905 had formed the Società Adriatica di Elettricita which later gained control of the electric grid of fifteen Italian provinces. A powerful financier, Volpi had held a Montenegrin tobacco monopoly and numerous other business interests in the Balkans and Asia Minor. He was also responsible for building a new industrial harbour at his birthplace of Venice, and in the 1920s gained effective control of the Banca Commerciale, 'a cannibal octopus' of Italian industrial finance. A member of the Fascist party from

1923, Volpi was Governor of Tripolitania (Libya) in 1921–5 and Italian Minister of Finance 1925–8, from which post he was forced to resign by ubiquitous stories of his corruption. He had diplomatic experience, signing the Ouchy peace treaty with Turkey on Italy's behalf in 1913, and leading a secret mission to Belgrade which resulted in the settlement of the Adriatic Question at Rapallo (1922). Volpi was, like Loucheur, a shrewd and untrustworthy financier, with high intelligence, organising power and force of personality. A self-made man, who was made Count of Misurata in 1925, Volpi had an imposing and self-satisfied manner with traces of pomposity which were uneffaced by his reputation for financial skulduggery.[19]

Sofina's leaders were almost a roll-call of the successful trade and finance ministers of western Europe in the twenties. The president of its Spanish subsidiary, Chade, was Francisco Cambó y Battle, a lawyer and Catalan nationalist, who, after serving as Spanish Minister of Public Works, reformed many administrative abuses whilst Minister of Finance in 1921–2. Cambó, 'the greatest industrialist of Barcelona and probably the richest man in Spain' by 1936,[20] had a persistently pro-German reputation, and in 1920 acted with Heineman in acquiring German electrical interests in Brazil. He had long urged a scheme whereby the many Spaniards who invested abroad in foreign banks and received relatively low interest instead combined their funds in Spanish investment trusts, which would then participate in foreign industrial enterprises. Cambó argued that this would both secure a better return for Spanish investors, and result in Spanish-nominated directors joining the boards of the foreign companies selected. Clearly, as Sofina's growth was partly induced by Belgian investors' fears that the Belgian franc would depreciate, so similar apprehensions about the Spanish currency and political stability were behind Cambó's interest in Sofina.[21] Sofina's prize Spanish property, the Barcelona Traction, Light and Power Company, was owned by Sidro, which Sofina bought in 1924. Under the direction of Heineman and Cambó, Sidro proved a solidly profitable holding company, whose hydro-electric subsidiaries were British or Belgian managed 'venture[s] in economic colonialism'.[22] Cambó himself became *persona non grata* with Miguel Primo de Rivera, Spanish dictator in 1923–30,[23] and his political career ultimately proved to be Sofina's undoing in Spain. Whilst Minister of Finance, Cambó had denounced the tobacco-smuggling millionaire Juan March, and initiated legal investigations which dogged March for years. The two men became implacably opposed, and in 1947, by legal juggling, March had Barcelona Traction falsely declared bankrupt and handed over to him. The affair was a grotesque reflection on Spanish judicial procedure, and led to litigation between the governments of Belgium and Spain in the International Court of Justice from 1958 until 1970.[24]

It was against this background of international negotiations, and strategic re-grouping, that in December 1921 Docker registered a new private company, the Electric and Railway Finance Corporation (Elrafin), with issued capital of £500.000 (of which part was held by Sofina). His co-directors were Bernard Docker, Heineman, and Lord Cowdray's brother, Sir Edward Pearson, representing the electrical and railway interests of the Whitehall Securities group run by Cowdray. (After Pearson's death in 1925, Cowdray's legal partner, Docker's co-director at the Metropolitan Railway, Sir Clarendon Hyde, joined Elrafin's board.) Docker recruited as secretary of Elrafin an accountant named Mark Webster Jenkinson, encountered in chapter 8 helping Docker to re-construct Vickers in 1925–6; it is likely that the two men had become acquainted when Jenkinson was Chief Liquidator of Contracts at the Ministry of Munitions, and Docker a member of the Ministry's Advisory Council on Liquidations, in 1919–20.[25] With this personnel, and from adjacent offices to Metrovic at 4 Central Buildings, Westminster, Docker began to run his private industrial bank. In the expert judgement of the British Electrical and Allied Manufacturers Association in the 1920s, British finance corporations were useless to British electrical manufacturers unless the latter formed 'an International Electrical Manufacturing Cartel'. BEAMA believed that 'an effort should be made to develop large-scale power finance groups capable of dealing with super-power schemes in any market', for otherwise the 'only alternative... lies in closer association between British manufacturers and the powerful organisations already operating in Belgium and possibly in the United States'.[26] Elrafin reflected this view, and was the medium for British industrial and financial interests to participate with Sofina and other trusts in super-power schemes throughout the world. British electro-technology was demonstrably too weak to enter such schemes except with foreign collaborators.

Britain's electrical competitors were delineated distinctly. The Americans were the main rivals in the British dominions, Japan, China, Argentina, Brazil and Chile, although the Germans also had a foothold in the five latter markets. Other competition came from Belgians, Dutch, French, Japanese and Swiss, whilst British manufacturers found that high tariffs prevented any penetration of European markets.[27] Initially Docker failed to lure Sofina's order to Britain. He recounted in 1927 how he had tried for the past ten or twelve years to induce Heineman to place business in Britain. The latter originally replied that British electro-technology 'lagged behind' too much to be useful, and did not think Britain had caught up until the mid-twenties: but thereafter, according to Docker, Sofina 'promised upon all occasions to give the English firms an opportunity to take the business'.[28] In 1927, orders recently placed by Sofina in Britain totalled about £1,000,000, of which the biggest was a Metrovic contract for Chade. Another large order went to Babcock and Wilcox, 110 omnibuses had been ordered from Daimler for Buenos Aires, and Docker Brothers were among the firms which received smaller contracts.[29] Heineman's volte-face on placing orders in Britain was apparently hastened by the Foreign Office's reluctance in 1924–7 to support Anglo-Argentine Tramways, a company which controlled about 60 per cent of the public transport in Buenos Aires. Most of the debentures of £11 million were British owned, but the Ordinary share capital, carrying the voting rights, was Belgian controlled, and few orders for material were placed in Britain. Heineman had counted on British diplomatic intervention to win an underground railway concession, and it was partly Whitehall's refusal to back a Belgian-managed company that forced Heineman to begin directing more business to Britain.[30]

Elrafin also had a role in the capital reconstruction of Sofina in 1928–9. At that time, the market value of the various enterprises managed by Sofina was approximately £170 million, and the trust raised about £10 million by issuing new Ordinary shares. The capital was overhauled, with shareholders receiving one new share for every old one surrendered, plus the right to take up $1\frac{1}{2}$ new shares at over £47 each; whilst new capital was raised through sixty-two institutions in Amsterdam, Brussels, Berlin, Hamburg, London, New York, Madrid and Zurich. Apart from raising cash, one aim of the operation was to have Sofina shares dealt not only on the Brussels Bourse, but also in London, Zurich, Amsterdam and Berlin. Some 29,593 shares were issued to the various founders of the new Sofina, and these founders' shares, of course, under Belgian law enjoyed exceptionally privileged voting rights. British founder-shareholders included the Midland Bank, Vickers, Elrafin and Docker, in his personal capacity. In London, early in 1929, 3,750 shares in Sofina were offered on the London market at just over £200 each, underwritten by Elrafin in conjunction with BST.[31]

The climax of Docker's involvement with Sofina appears to have come in the autumn of 1929. By that date, Vickers wished to sell the holdings in Sofina of their subsidiary, MCWF, which was about to merge with the rolling-stock interests of Cammell Laird. On 20 September, Webster Jenkinson complained privately that Docker had been working against such a sale, as he hoped to achieve a controlling interest in Sofina.[32] A full account of DD's plot has not been traced, but it is perhaps not coincidental that it occurred at a time when his interests had just emerged in their full power in the running of another Belgian-based trust, Compagnie

Internationale des Wagons-Lits, as described later. A merger between Sofina and CIWL would have created an international services trust of a magnitude to satisfy even Docker's ambitions. If Docker's coup at Sofina was ever launched, it did not succeed, and Heineman was not dislodged until he retired to the USA after the second world war.

The most ambitious schemes which Docker fronted for Sofina were in Egypt. In the mid-1920s Elrafin produced a hydro-electric scheme to heighten the Aswan dam, to create a new reservoir at Djebel Awlia, and to irrigate some 800,000 hectares. Docker interested Heineman in the scheme, and they determined to constitute an Egyptian company to hold and work the hydro-electric concessions, which would have required tens of millions of capital. During 1927, Heineman and Wyldbore-Smith (also a director of the Suez Canal Company) had long and promising conversations with the King of Egypt and his Prime Minister about the scheme, whilst Docker remained in 'very close touch' with Lord Lloyd, the British High Commissioner for Egypt and the Sudan, whom he had known for some twenty years. The British government were also kept informed by Sir George Grahame, their Ambassador in Brussels, who had a high opinion of Heineman, and had been told by Sofina that the bulk of machinery orders for the Aswan scheme would be placed in Britain.[33] The heightening of the dam was heavy with political implications. In 1924 the British Governor General of the Sudan had been murdered in Cairo, and Lord Allenby, then British High Commissioner for Egypt and the Sudan, had rashly threatened Egypt's supply of the waters of the White Nile in revenge. Fear of this punitive menace in the future led Egyptian leaders to wish to heighten the Aswan dam, enlarge the reservoir and store more Egyptian water on Egyptian territory. Docker's proposals therefore had an important political complexion. It was also evident that great business jealousies, as well as political repercussions, would be excited by such an immense piece of public contracting, and early in 1928, Docker took steps to secure his interests in the anticipated propaganda war. He joined a syndicate with Sir Harold Snagge, a director of Barclays Bank who had once sat on BTC's board, and Sir Warden Chilcott, a flamboyant but corrupt Conservative MP,[34] to buy the *Egyptian Gazette*, described by Lord Lloyd as 'the most widely read organ in the British community in Egypt'.[35] Docker apparently already had a financial interest in another Egyptian newspaper, the *Kashaf*, founded in 1926 by his business agent in Egypt, Ahmed Aboud, and his avowed aim in buying the *Gazette* was to further his commercial interests. Later in 1928, he seems to have fallen out with Chilcott,[36] and finally to have acquired control of the *Gazette* by himself.

Docker himself called at the Foreign Office to explain his Aswan project in April 1929. He estimated that it would require capital of about £30 million, and said that Elrafin's principal backers would be McKenna of the Midland Bank, Goodenough of Barclays Bank, Lord Cowdray's group and Sofina. The finance, although 'largely cosmopolitan', would be raised on the British capital market, and machinery orders worth £6 million would be placed in Britain. Italian or Swiss engineers would have to be employed, as there were no British specialists with the necessary technical experience.[37] Once again the Foreign Office were chary of Elrafin. Just as, in 1927, the Department of Overseas Trade had judged that 'the interests of the Dudley Docker group are extremely mixed',[38] so in 1929, the Foreign Office felt alarmed by the cosmopolitan financiers behind DD. Instead, they inclined to back a rival group comprising EEC, Callendars, the cable makers and the constructional engineers, Dorman Long. In retrospect, it is clear that this second group would have been stretched to meet the financial requirements of the scheme; and that Docker was correct in his conclusion that Britain possessed neither the financial nor the technical expertise to manage the whole project. At the time, though, some people who lacked Docker's percipience considered him unpatriotic for his involvement with multi-nationals.

Whilst these preliminaries to the hydro-electricity scheme were being undertaken, Docker and Heineman also tried to develop Egyptian business in another direction. The Egyptian government had a scheme to electrify the railway from Cairo to Helouan, and in 1928 appointed as its technical consultant for this work Sir Philip Dawson, the electrical engineer who was Sir Edward Manville's partner. It was Lord Lloyd's view that railway electrification was an unnecessary extravagance in a country where there was no congested suburban traffic to justify it, and that Egyptian surpluses would be better spent on the people; but to electro-technologists, the attraction of harnessing Egypt's hydro-electric potential to its railway system was immense.[39] Sofina, Elrafin and Metrovic combined to chase this piece of business, with Heineman subordinating himself to Docker, who organised a formidable negotiating team of himself, his Egyptian agent, Aboud, and the Duke of Atholl. Aboud was a wily adventurer gifted at intrigue. The Ottoman government had paid for him to study engineering at Glasgow University in 1906 (where he married a Scotswoman), before placing him in the Turkish public service. During the war, he worked for the Turkish forces at Bagdad and Damascus, before becoming an Army and railway contractor in Palestine who was notorious for peculation. He returned to Egypt in 1920, where he entered Parliament in 1925 to pursue an erratic course which was deplored by Lord Lloyd. He was the largest shareholder in the British-controlled Egyptian General Omnibus Company, as well as proprietor of the *Kashaf* newspaper, and Egyptian agent for more than twenty important British firms. Aboud also had extensive shipping interests, built the repair yards at Alexandria harbour, owned a larger palace than the King of Egypt and by his domination of the country's sugar industry was a force in the world sugar market. According to an official comment of 1930, 'shrewd, ambitious and unscrupulous...his enterprise and initiative have singularly benefited United Kingdom manufacturers'.[40] One can hardly find a man more dissimilar than the Duke of Atholl, a Scottish territorial magnate, whose attempt to alleviate the Scottish housing problem in conjunction with the Beardmore naval works with the Atholl Steel Houses scheme of 1925–6 had been a well-intentioned failure. He had first visited Egypt as a soldier in 1897, serving under Cromer and Kitchener, and fighting beside Winston Churchill at the battle of Omdurman: subsequently, in 1921, he had declined the throne of Albania.[41] The main rival to Docker's group was EEC, whose managing director made a sensationally ill-judged attempt to bribe Sir Philip Dawson, then had an attack of nerves, and tried to explain away his remarks about 'practical suggestions...to our mutual advantage' in a fashion which was undignified and implausible.[42] Metrovic soon found out about this, and by April, when Atholl was in Cairo, he was able to give photographic copies of the correspondence with Dawson to Lord Lloyd. Aboud (who was made a pasha in 1931) orchestrated a furious press campaign against EEC, at which they retaliated, with the upshot that in May 1929 the Higher Council, 'which is the most unsuitable name given to a very corrupt body of advisers at the Ministry of Communications', decided not to electrify the railway until the larger Aswan proposals had been settled (although Dawson had found in favour of Docker and Metrovic).[43] The bitterness of the quarrels between the two British companies was one cause of the Egyptian decision not to proceed, and Docker must have been embittered that the large orders involved were lost to Britain. This wasteful affair was a perfect illustration of what the productioneers had warned over ten years before: 'that the only chance for the future of British overseas trade lay in combined trading rather than trading by units'.[44]

According to Atholl, his Aswan proposals 'were very near being signed and really agreed upon' when, in June 1929, a Labour government was elected in Britain. Arthur Henderson, the new Foreign Secretary, dismissed Lord Lloyd in July, and in the same month, launched negotiations for an Anglo-Egyptian treaty. He hoped to renounce British control of Egyptian internal affairs, and withdraw our troops from the canal zone, but his discussions, being ill-timed and ill-advised, soon collapsed. Atholl complained in the House of Lords in December 1929 that immediately after the Labour government entered power, 'Egypt ceased to go on with this [Aswan] proposal', and said that Labour's wish to withdraw the British military presence had 'done incalculable harm'. The Docker group had been intending to spend about £26,000,000 in Egypt, with orders of £20,000,000 for Britain, but 'nobody', said Atholl, 'is likely to put a sum of that sort into Egypt if there is not going to be any protection of foreigners or their trade'.[45] Later, in 1931, Docker revived his proposals in more detailed form, which he again pressed on the Foreign Office. Sir Lancelot Oliphant, the Assistant Under Secretary, warned that such 'super schemes for electric power development are so gigantic that we must walk delicately',[46] although the Board of Trade assured the Foreign Office in 1932 that 'the Docker group are sufficiently powerful to be their own pioneers'.[47] Bernard Docker arrived in Cairo on 31 March, and by 7 May, Sir Percy Loraine, Lloyd's successor as High Commissioner, was reporting that Bernard 'had already nobbled the principal potential customers of [electric] current', and was trying 'to absorb the existing concessionary companies'.[48] But the larger Aswan scheme proved too ambitious and costly in Docker's lifetime.

Sofina was not Docker's only Belgian interest, for in the mid-twenties he became involved with another international trust, Sir Davison Dalziel's International Sleeping Car Syndicate. Dalziel had known Docker since placing Pullman orders with MCWF in 1908, although they were afterwards said to be on bad terms. Around the turn of the century Dalziel emerged as the chief English participant in the Compagnie Internationale des Wagons-Lits which had been registered at Brussels in 1876, with King Leopold of the Belgians heading the share subscription list. Although its operational headquarters were at Paris, CIWL's subsequent success typified Belgium's economic growth; by the turn of the century, its ramifications extended over all of Europe and part of Asia. The luxury and reliability of their international sleeping car routes were legendary before 1914, and indeed services like the Orient Express (which ran from 1883 until 1977) created a unique culture. CIWL never operated in Britain on the continental scale, but Dalziel joined the group in 1902 with the aim of attracting more British travellers onto the continental system. In 1919, Dalziel became chairman of the CIWL board and president of the Managing Committee, and during the following decade, he tightened his grip on control.[49] With Dalziel leading both Pullman in Britain and CIWL on the continent, he naturally brought them into closer co-operation, and the Belgian trust took a sizeable holding in Pullman. From then until 1939, they operated in tandem, although CIWL dwarfed Pullman in size and prosperity: in December 1932, it owned 2,278 sleeping cars, whilst Pullman had only

233 cars in 1934. Under these arrangements, Dalziel introduced Pullman Cars to service on the continent, and this move was of material importance to Docker, because the two manufacturers of the cars after 1926 were MCWF and the Birmingham Railway Carriage Works, of which Bernard Docker became a director in 1928, and later chairman. This unification of Dalziel's interests widened British rolling-stock makers' access to continental markets at a time when foreign orders were urgently sought.

The Pullman alliance was only the first stage of Dalziel's strategy for CIWL. Their greatest competitor as a travel agency was Thomas Cook's, and around 1927, the Belgian trust bought complete control of the old British firm. Docker was reputedly behind the amalgamation, for which BST provided finance,[50] and certainly his associates soon came to dominate the British management of CIWL. Dalziel had no immediate heirs, and he provided for the succession by forming the International Sleeping Car Share Trust, capitalised at £5¼ million, in November 1927, which owned 30,000 out of 150,000 Preference shares in CIWL, and 495,000 out of 4,450,000 Ordinary shares. Dalziel became ill only a month later, in December 1927, and after his death in April 1928, was succeeded by some familiar names. At Pullman, four new directors had been appointed in 1927: Lord Ashfield, Stanley Adams, Sir Edmund Wyldbore-Smith and Sir Follett Holt, an old contact of Docker's in South American railway business and at the BCU and then chairman of BST. Wyldbore-Smith as usual was acting as Docker's nominee, and after his death in 1938, was succeeded by a young baronet called Sir Basil Goulding, step-son of Stanley Adams, son of a former Metrovic director Sir Lingard Goulding, and great-nephew of Lord Wargrave, the MCWF director. On the CIWL board, too, Wyldbore-Smith succeeded Dalziel as British vice-president.

CIWL, Pullman and Thomas Cook were all thus partly directed in 1927–39 by Englishmen clustered around the Docker companies, and it may well be that Docker hoped in 1929–30 to merge them with Sofina, but was foiled by the international financial dislocation of the Depression. He remained in almost daily touch with Belgium until its invasion, and indeed in the phoney war of 1939–40 the Foreign Office opened a file on his complaints to them that he could not make telephonic contact with Brussels. Docker and Wyldbore-Smith successfully approached the Midland Bank in 1931 for five months' loan to CIWL of £250,000 to service their sterling obligations, interest and sinking fund, and close connections continued between the Bank and the trust.[51] It was therefore not surprising that after the British government appropriated Thomas Cook's from its Belgian-registered owners, on the grounds that Belgium and France were under German occupation, the travel agency passed into the ownership of Docker's Midland Bank.

His involvement in these European railway and power companies outlasted his period as an English railway director, and demonstrated that his interests increasingly took a continental, rather than merely a national, aspect. There were two certain reasons for this. He believed that the rational tendency in modern business was continental or global; but, at least equally important, he was tired and bored with running factories in England under adverse economic conditions and an unsympathetic social climate. He discovered that international finance was less work and less worrying, but more enriching, more creative and more amusing. There is a third possible reason, of which one can be less sure. Docker's business mind was always responsive to the national mood, which in the inter-war period was increasingly pessimistic and defensive. At home in the 1930s there was a great spreading of domestic price-fixing arrangements and other restrictive measures which aimed at reducing competition: overall the industrial economy grew less dynamic or adaptable. Abroad there was an increasing loss of nerve about British capacity: one British diplomat, in 1929, commented that while Britain had won the war, Germany was winning the peace: 'We...glory in our past, but by continually pleading poverty and war exhaustion we not only damage our prestige abroad but we risk being relegated to a second place in the sun and allowing ourselves to be ousted by Powers having far smaller resources.'[52] It is possible that Docker's continental business operations were a reaction to the fatalist, enervate and backward-thinking tendencies in Britain, epitomised by Victor Wellesley's famous refrain 'the position is hopeless, and we are helpless'. British society, he may have concluded, was not favourable to his brand of enterprise: Belgium was. Although the world war cut him off from the Belgian trusts, and his health weakened after 1938, his questing business acuity was undiminished; *faute de mieux*, he had to find outlets in Britain. As the next chapter recounts, he re-exerted his influence in BSA where he took a decisive part until his death in 1944.

11

Birmingham Small Arms 1918–44

Although Docker retired as deputy-chairman of BSA in 1912, he remained deeply involved in its management for another thirty years. Several of its most important directors were men at least partly obliged to him for their positions; but he was also a shareholder, and dominated the Birmingham Advisory Committee of BSA's bank, the Midland, which approved and controlled loans to industry in the Birmingham area from 1923. During the first war, he was solicitous for BSA's interests in his work for the Birmingham munitions organisation; it was also his intervention that secured the doubling of the BSA and Daimler's directors' fees, free of tax, in 1917.[1]

A former Financial Controller of British Leyland wrote in 1978 that in the period after 1945, 'the BSA Group was subjected for some twenty-five years to a whole series of irrelevant structural re-organisations, top management reshuffles and abortive attempts at new product development'.[2] This description could in fact have been applied with almost equal fairness to BSA back to 1918. As described in chapter 3, BSA was never happy in the armaments business, and had an arduous time trying to manage the diversification programme between 1897 and 1914. These traditional difficulties became even more acute after the Armistice, and the collapse of BSA in 1973, followed by the formation of the Meriden Co-operative, had been foreshadowed by seventy years of managerial trouble. The history of BSA was, in fact, an extraordinarily repetitive story: for three-quarters of a century, its directorate was regularly rent by crises of personality and strategy which progressively weakened the group.

Certainly, in Docker's lifetime, many of the directors installed at BSA were unimpressive men. His own successor as deputy-chairman, Neville Chamberlain, was an indifferent business man, who was judged a feeble planner by most colleagues.[3] Neville Chamberlain's life-long friend, Arthur Wood, who was a director of BSA from 1907 until his death in 1934, was

214

equally feckless. Sir Hallewell Rogers, chairman of BSA in 1906–28, was 'a most loyal and sincere friend and a great gentleman' but not a dynamic entrepreneur; T. F. Walker, who sat on the board from 1887 until 1919, and was Rogers' immediate predecessor as chairman, had another timid and inhibiting spirit.[4] Whereas Vickers, when they had wanted to recruit an artillery expert from the government service, had found, in Lord Fisher's phrase to Churchill, 'a pusher like [Sir Trevor] Dawson who will go everywhere and buy everything',[5] BSA only managed to find Sir Capel Holden, Superintendent of the Royal Gun and Carriage Factory at Woolwich, 'a man of simple life and blameless morals',[6] and a pioneer motorist, but worse than mediocre in business.

One of the most deleterious influences on British industry in the twentieth century has been the insularity of its professional engineers. Docker's own view that British industry needed, above all, 'an outlay of Brains' to improve its flexibility has been described in chapter 3. The baneful consequences of narrow British engineering practices were forcibly illustrated by BSA, which consistently failed to co-ordinate the productive and marketing elements of their business, generally because their engineers' pride in their products was too unrelenting to allow modifications which would take account of costings or market taste. British engineers tended to make the technical integrity of their product paramount over commercial considerations, and to evince uncomprehending hostility towards the financial and marketing sides of business. Certainly the history of BSA included some appalling commercial decisions taken by trained engineers which confirm the epigram coined by a nineteenth-century Rothschild: 'There are three ways to ruin: gambling, women, and engineers. The first two are more agreeable – but the last is more certain.'[7] The incubus eventually infected the group's managing director, Percy Martin, despite his continental training; and after twenty years of work in the Black Country, no man better epitomised the entrepreneurial weaknesses of the British engineer.

Like Vickers, BSA expected the armaments business to disappear after the Armistice, and swung into a policy of peacetime diversification. They bought two Sheffield steel firms, William Jessop (costing £1,400,000 and with share capital of £407,480) and Burton-Griffiths. BSA intended to expand their production of bicycles, motor-cycles and machine-tools, whilst retaining an organisation which could respond at any moment to a call for arms should the government again have need of supplies.[8] As Rogers explained, BSA's 'five years' war production of Lewis guns and military rifles gave us an exceptional experience in the obvious methods of reducing costs', and their policy was framed in 1919 'to make the smallest possible range of products on the largest possible scale'.[9] Their diversification yielded great trouble. In 1919 they established the Daimler Hire Car Company with about 250 cars, and as a complement to this, later agreed to buy the bubble Air Transport and Travel Company (Airco) from its promotor, George Holt-Thomas. He was a publicist and magazine journalist with more ingenuity than scruples, who during the war became 'something of a Napoleon in business, conceiving and carrying out great financial schemes to complete a chain that would circle the whole industry of aviation'.[10] BSA's intention was to develop Airco's charter business parallel to the Daimler Hire organisation, but their arithmetic was absolutely inadequate.

Whatever Holt-Thomas' personal shortcomings, Airco had an extremely distinguished place in the history of civil aviation. The company's chief pilot and aerodrome manager, Captain Jerry Shaw, made the first commercial charter flight in the world from Hendon to Le Bourget on 15 July 1919,[11] and Holt-Thomas introduced a much-publicised Cross-Channel service (with the incongruous gimmick of free trips for Labour MPs).[12] The London–Paris Air Mail Service was also started by Airco pilots, and ran as Britain's first aerial mail service, under BSA auspices, in 1920.[13] Airco's chief designer, a young man called Geoffrey de Havilland, had brilliant talents which were later world-famous. One aviation authority, writing in 1930, recalled that Airco's 'pilots were the finest in the World, they ploughed through weather, in their effort to prove the value of air transport, which would shake the pilots of today [and the passengers too] – and they had no luxuries such as radio telephones and turn indicators'.[14]

Holt-Thomas owned the entire Ordinary share capital of Airco, which was never publicly issued; although during the wartime expansion, £350,000 Preference shares and £250,000 7 per cent Notes had been taken by the public, these did not carry voting rights. At the end of 1918, Holt-Thomas approached BSA with a proposal to sell Airco for a price based on the value of the assets plus payment for goodwill up to £800,000. BSA decided in early 1919 that Holt-Thomas' price was too high, 'and the matter went to sleep' until the end of the year, when Holt-Thomas managed to hustle BSA into an agreement. He went to Martin with a story that Airco were on the point of signing a contract with a financial house to make yet another capital issue to the public. In Martin's own words, Holt-Thomas warned that if this new capital was issued in Ordinary shares,

> he would be in a position of a minority instead of a majority shareholder and would not thereafter be able to negotiate with the BSA with a free hand...when Mr Holt-Thomas came to me he was in a position of having

to decide immediately whether...he would go on with his proposed public issue and I had to take some definite step at once...[otherwise] our chances of purchase would for all practical purposes have gone forever.

I thought the proposal was sufficiently favourable for us to justify me in requesting him to break off his negotiations and stop his public issue.

We are therefore under moral obligations to Mr Holt-Thomas to proceed with the present deal because...my action interfered materially as between him and his financial house.

In other words, Holt-Thomas panicked the gullible Martin into a commitment which BSA felt obliged to keep. Martin's enthusiasm for the deal was only equal to the superficiality with which he understood it. 'I do not propose in this short report to trouble you with the details of the share capital of the other subsidiary companies', he airily told his BSA co-directors; the Preference shareholders would have to be deprived of their participating rights, but 'I am advised there is no insuperable difficulty to this being done when the appropriate time comes'.[15] As far as he was concerned, Airco's factory at Hendon could be used for making motor-bodies, and their factory at Walthamstow for making engines, whilst there was also a possibility of claiming £350,000 in back royalties from the government. All this delectable fruit was promised by Holt-Thomas, and Martin swallowed it in a trice.

Martin's remark that the BSA board need not trouble with details of the subsidiaries' share capital recalls Caillard's remark a year before to Vickers' directors that the financial advantage of the MCWF merger was 'so great that it need not be dwelt upon'. Such insouciance was equally misplaced. BSA absorbed Airco, and for a moment Holt-Thomas even sat on the BSA board, but this amity did not last. He himself wrote in 1926 of 'my lamentable amalgamation with the BSA (in which they scandalously cut off the Aircraft within a week of amalgamation, and on which my resignation naturally followed)',[16] and BSA ultimately found that, including the bank overdraft of £660,000 which fell due in March 1920, their Airco liabilities exceeded £1.3 million.[17] Sir William Peat was appointed Liquidator of Airco, BSA passed its dividends throughout 1921–4, and Docker told shareholders in 1922: 'I know something of this board and of this business, and...[although] It is not satisfactory to know you don't get a dividend...it was impossible to earn it.'[18] It is improbable that he was consulted about the Airco deal, for he would never have succumbed to Holt-Thomas' ploy.

As shown in table 11.1, the Airco mis-investment weighed as heavily on BSA's profits during the twenties as Vickers' *mésalliance* with MCWF: however, unlike Vickers, managerial practice and board membership were not reformed effectively. Though Chamberlain left the directorate to

Table 11.1 *The fortunes of BSA 1914–32*

Year	Net profit (£)	Rate of dividend (per cent)
1914	190,429	15
1915	408,455	20
1917[a]	427,976	20
1918	435,207	20
1919	373,091	10
1920–1[b]	566,881	5
1921–2	−469,168[c]	nil
1922–3	−166,671	nil
1923–4	125,060	nil
1924–5	179,382	5
1925–6	184,885	6
1926–7	111,883	nil
1927–8	72,063	nil
1928–9	216,188	3
1929	168,188[d]	6
1930	148,026	5
1931	−204,194	nil
1932	−797,928	nil

Notes: a. No data for 1916. b. For eighteen months ending 31 January 1921.
c. Figures underlined indicate deficit. d. For six months ending 31 July instead of
31 January.

Source: Economist.

become Postmaster General in 1922, other defectives such as Wood and
Holden remained. Of the two Sheffield men who became directors when
their businesses were bought in 1919, E. M. Griffiths resigned in 1921 and
Sir Albert Hobson, the chairman of Jessups, died in 1923. New directors
in the 1920s made no inroads into the board's narrow base. It was joined
in 1923 by Arthur Hungerford Pollen, a naval propagandist and inventor
of a brilliant system of long-range naval fire control. He had collaborated
in writing the BCU's anti-Bolshevik propaganda of the early 1920s with
the next recruit to the BSA directorate, Patrick Hannon, who joined in
1924. Hannon had succeeded Rogers, the BSA chairman, as MP for the
Moseley division of Birmingham in 1921, and in the period after 1924,
was responsible for BSA's liaison with Whitehall and with foreign governments. Hannon, like Pollen, was a blusterer who fancied himself a business

man of modern outlook, but neither of them made any impact on the effete regime of Rogers and Manville.

Having passed Ordinary dividends in 1921–4 in the wake of the Airco losses, BSA also passed payment in 1926–8 as their other diversifications failed to bring returns. Docker would have known the inside story of all this, not only because such an indiscreet participant as Hannon would have burst to tell him, but because of his position at the Midland Bank. In January 1923, the Bank had appointed a Birmingham Advisory Committee, on which Dudley Docker was by far the strongest power. Bernard Docker was appointed a member in June 1925, and there was no countervailing force among its other one or two members. The main responsibility with which the board was charged was to scrutinise all applications and renewals for overdrafts and loans in the Birmingham area of £5,000 or more, or £10,000 at a few big branches. The aim was to de-centralise some of the power which had accumulated during Sir Edward Holden's chairmanship, but it immensely enhanced Docker's power in the Midlands.[19] The size of BSA and Daimler's borrowing from the Midland Bank in the twenties and thirties is no longer recorded, but must have been considerable: in 1932, they had a combined overdraft limit of £250,000.[20]

The rifle side of BSA's business fluctuated wildly, and although its ratio of profits to sales was sometimes almost four-fold higher than the bicycles department, it was not a reliable component in the group. Although their weekly output capacity reached 8,000 Lewis rifles and 2,000 Lewis guns by the end of 1918, they had no British government orders in the 1920s and were left with an immense post-war surplus capacity. Much of this was scrapped by 1921, but other machinery was retained. Their only foreign orders seem to have been 10,000 Short rifles for Siam in 1919, and 346 Lewis guns for Japan during 1921 and 1923. In 1923 hopes were raised that the War Office would sell 300,000 of its stock of American-made rifles of 1914 pattern to Serbia and that the proceeds would be spent on ordering at least 150,000 new rifles from BSA. This proposition seems to have been brought to the War Office by BSA themselves, who quoted a figure of £4 14s 4d per rifle to the Serbs and were apparently willing to manufacture at cost price for the British, but the deal eventually collapsed through the Serbs' shortage of money.[21]

Led by Hannon, BSA tried to obtain other foreign armament orders, either for new material or for second-hand War Office stocks whose proceeds could be spent on new rifles or guns. As BSA told Cunliffe-Lister in 1925, an order for 100,000 rifles would employ at least 1,125 men for two years at total annual wages of nearly £169,000 while an order for 1,200 Lewis guns would employ at least 170 men for nine months at total wages of £19,000.[22] Hannon spear-headed an energetic sales drive in the Baltic, where the Esthonian Finance Minister told him governments wanted close business contacts with Britain 'because we feel these business relations to be genuine business relations without any aim of political, intellectual or national hegemony which has almost been the *leit-motiv* of German economic penetration to the East'. He added, however, that the Esthonian experience had been that 'British business interests are too big and too world-wide...to concentrate themselves for the more close study of the small and at present not very important' Baltic market.[23] In the event, 1,500 Lewis gun barrels were sold to Latvia in 1924–5. Another market which Hannon explored at this time was Greece.[24]

Still no orders eventuated, and in March 1925 Hannon issued an ultimatum on BSA's behalf to the Secretary for War, Docker's old acquaintance Sir Laming Worthington-Evans. 'You, as a business man, will understand that we have shareholders', he wrote, 'we hold our Annual Meeting very shortly: and we must in some way justify the continued maintenance of a highly expensive enterprise which not only brings us no return at all but imposes upon our profitable undertakings a very heavy charge.'[25] In a formal meeting at the House of Commons, Hannon warned Worthington-Evans that BSA would have to convert its idle plant to civilian production unless government assistance was received. The first possibility was a government subsidy, but Hannon regarded this as a waste of money which would not ensure that the specialist BSA staff was kept together. The second possibility was orders for new rifles, but Hannon said that BSA would need British government orders for 40,000 rifles a year worth £200,000 to keep going; and Worthington-Evans replied that neither Parliament nor the Treasury would sanction such expenditure. Hannon added that BSA 'would not search for or take orders for the manufacture of new rifles for foreign customers', because they had concluded from recent experience in the Balkans and Baltic that 'the financial outlook for business of this sort was not good enough'. The third alternative was adopted: BSA was confirmed as sole agent to sell War Office surplus weaponry and in return maintained plant capable of producing 500 rifles per week at the commencement of an order rising to 1,000 per week in three months or 2,000 in a national emergency. Worthington-Evans impressed on the Director of Army Contracts 'the necessity for both sides not to let small points stand in the way'.[26] To underline the urgency, another BSA director, R. A. Rotherham, repeated to Worthington-Evans on 23 April the warning that 'the time has come when we must contemplate definitely and once and for all diverting our capacity for the production of military small arms into other channels which will give more regular employment'.[27]

The War Office recognised the advantage of putting its sales of surplus arms through a company like BSA. 'I am for making money where and how we can', minuted the Master General of Ordnance, Sir Noel Birch (later director of Vickers), 'goodness knows the country wants it.'[28] As the War Office told the Treasury, it was 'impossible' for them to sell their surplus weaponry 'except through private firms' because of the 'pernicious system of "commission"...inseparable from these deals' in which a government department could not be directly involved;[29] and according to Henry Tarrant of BSA, '"local" payments of say 3s 6d per stand of arms would possibly have to be made and a commission of $2\frac{1}{2}$ per cent to their local agents'.[30] Almost immediately after settling this arrangement with the War Office, BSA sub-contracted their agency to an arms dealer called Soley, 'a sanguine and adventurous man probably without much to lose'.[31] The latter was subsequently succeeded as head of the Soley Armaments Company by another adventurer, Captain John Ball, later condemned by the Royal Commission on the Private Manufacture of Arms as irresponsible and swashbuckling, who continued to act for BSA until 1935.[32]

Having delivered some 1,601,600 rifles during the Great War, BSA had no further British government orders for Lee Mk I and III rifles for seventeen years. With the onset of rearmament in 1936, 10,900 rifles were ordered, rising to 18,400 in 1938, 41,900 in 1939 and 68,200 in 1940.[33] It is true that in 1927–34 BSA supplied 7,854 Short rifles for use in India, Egypt, Iraq and by the Crown Agents, but these orders did not pass through the War Office whom BSA was ostensibly serving. Southern Rhodesia and South Africa also gave small annual orders for Lewis guns or Short rifles, totalling under 40,000 in 1921–35. Other foreign orders totalling 4,664 guns and rifles in 1926–34 went to Argentina, Japan, Portugal and Persia.[34] Larger orders to Russia in 1924 and to China in 1929–30 were lost owing to British government prohibition of armaments exports to those countries.[35]

In these conditions of disarmament from 1918 to 1936, BSA concentrated on bicycles, motor-cycles, machine-tools and Daimler motor-cars, and as shown in table 11.2 armaments never accounted for more than 9 per cent of the group's turnover during the seventeen years of disarmament. The relative value of rifle and cycle sales, and the ratio of profits to sales in the different divisions, are shown in figures 11.1, 11.2 and 11.3, and demonstrate the predominance of civilian over armaments production. Though less money was made from civil products, they did not inflict the same uncertainties on the group as rifles.

'When I was a boy, negroes did not ride bicycles', Philip Snowden the Chancellor of the Exchequer told his Cabinet colleagues in 1930, 'now they do ride bicycles, and workers are employed in Coventry to make those

Table 11.2 *The proportion of BSA turnover attributable to armaments, and BSA profits and losses on armaments and total business 1930–4*

Year	Proportion of BSA turnover attributable to armaments (per cent)	BSA profit/loss on armaments (£)	BSA total profit/loss (£)
1930	6.2	+10,365	+242,276
1931	8.9	−2,061	−112,944
1932	5.1	−15,970	−688,647
1933	8.0	+46,543	+245,532
1934	3.0	−8,035	+127,500
Average	6.2	+6,168	−37,257

Source: Royal Commission on Private Manufacture of Armaments (1936), p. 492.

bicycles.'[36] Trading profits on bicycles had been £63,348 in 1913, and reached £188,239 in the peace boom year of 1919; but by 1924 they settled at about £167,000 and almost £170,000 was recorded for 1930. Then, with the onset of world depression and BSA's own financial crisis, bicycle trading profits collapsed to £3,507 in 1931 and did not regain six figures until £113,981 was earned in 1936. Clearly not enough negroes were riding BSA bicycles in the thirties – perhaps because they were sold at the higher end of the market – but the real cause of this uneven performance was that the financial and managerial ills of BSA's motor division were contaminating the whole group.

After the war Daimler models appealed to a small and diminishing class of customer. 'Want of purpose and division of ideas were always the twin evil spirits of the Daimler Company...[which] wasted too much of their strength on making an uneconomically large variety of models, and in pursuing a number of rather grandiose schemes which diverted their Designers...from rationalising production', conclude two motoring historians. 'Although not all of their models were ponderous or sluggish, their public image in the twenties was one of slow-moving Royal cars of prodigious size, funerals, and old ladies in Kensingtonian hats, hidden from the view of the cars behind by the haze of oily exhaust smoke emitted by the Silent Knight engines.' Their attitude is well conveyed by Pollen's memorandum on marketing strategy for the USA: 'the aim must be to commend [Daimler] to the old rich, and therefore the more fashionable and well-bred class, the less to the new and vulgar. The *nouveaux* should be kept at a distance but not refused.'[37] Daimler's adherence to the Silent Knight

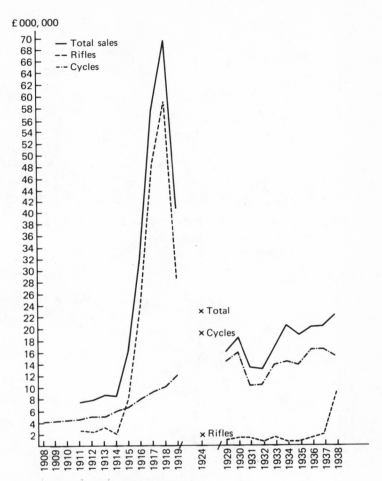

£ 000, 000

Figure 11.1 BSA's sales 1908–38
Note: No data available 1920–3 and 1925–8.
Source: BSA papers.

engine typified the faults of their higher management. Manville and Martin had bought the rights of this double sleeve valve engine in 1908 to compete with the reputation for silence of the Rolls Royce Silver Ghost engine. It took much work and expense for Daimler to make a commercial success of the Silent Knight, which in many respects was an admirable engineering

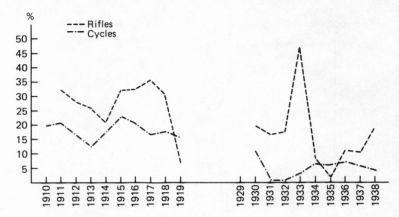

Figure 11.2 BSA's ratio of profits to sales 1910–38

Note: No data available 1919–29.
Source: BSA papers.

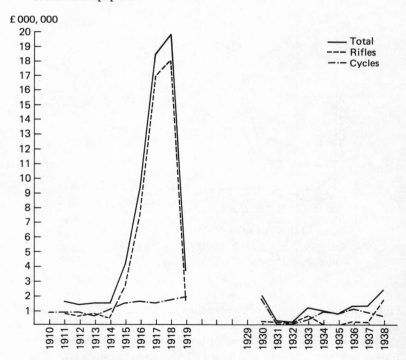

Figure 11.3 BSA's profits 1910–38

Note: No data available 1919–29.
Source: BSA papers.

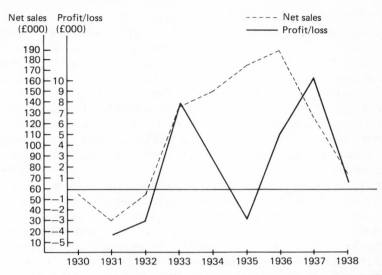

Figure 11.4 Sales, profits and losses in the Daimler motor-car business 1930–8

Source: BSA papers.

development. But silent though it was, its oily exhaust fumes were unpopular, and whether for reasons of sentiment or conservatism, Manville and Martin delayed replacing it until 1933. Part of the trouble was that Daimler suffered from insufficient capital investment during BSA's cash shortage in the 1920s, and felt obliged to postpone the outlay in plant and tools which large-scale production of a new engine would have required. As shown in figure 11.4, Daimler's performance remained unsatisfactory even after 1928, when its chairman Manville replaced Hallewell Rogers as chairman of the BSA group. The productive inefficiency caused by insufficient capital investment and by unimaginative management was one reason why the company could sustain a loss of £2,864 when the value of Daimler sales peaked at £176,031 in 1935.

Daimler must be excepted from the recent conclusion of two historians of the British motor-car industry between the world wars that 'the most impressive feature is the resilience of the industry despite major disabilities imposed by the weakness of the British economy as a whole'.[38] The fact is that Rogers, Manville and their colleagues woefully lacked strategy or controls. 'The old style Board of Directors is out of date; it has had its trial since the war and has been found wanting', E. M. Griffiths told Martin. 'The unfortunate system of appointing Directors having no knowledge of the business has been tolerated too long in this country, and Directors serving on multiple companies are a great source of weakness.'[39] Daimler's marketing policy was an extreme case of British motor manufacturers' arrogant inflexibility which weakened Britain's hold on world markets. The 'Americans for example have a motor monopoly in the Argentine simply because they build what is wanted', Robert Vansittart wrote in 1927 with Sir Victor Wellesley's concurrence, 'The British firms go on building not what is wanted but what they think *ought* to be wanted, *i.e.* what they have always made.' In Argentina the rough roads required ordinary cars to have a higher clearance and higher horsepower, yet Morris alone 'had the enterprise to raise his 11.9 hp to 15.9 and has got an immediate footing, for the Argentines would always sooner buy from us, even if they pay a bit more'.[40] It is true that British manufacturers of popular cars claimed to find it impossible to sell abroad in an equal market because of the high horsepower tax imposed by the Treasury; but this excuse did not apply to Daimler at the top end of the market. The extraordinarily unenterprising marketing of prestige British motor-cars continued until at least the 1970s: companies like Rolls Royce, Jaguar, Daimler, Alvis or Aston Martin were proud to boast that they had waiting lists for their products running into years, without apparently contemplating an increase in capacity to meet customers' demand. The pretence that a long waiting list enhanced the product's reputation was belied by Germany manufacturers, such as Mercedes.[41]

In a desperate attempt to widen Daimler's market appeal, BSA bought Lanchester Motors for £26,000 in 1931. They had employed Frederick Lanchester as a full-time technical consultant until he differed once too often with Martin in 1929, and desiring 'to expunge the rather unfair impression that their cars were only suited to the dowagers or the dead', they bought his company in the hope that Lanchester models would move Daimler Motors into a more popular market. The whole deal was rushed through in a fortnight after Lanchester's bankers suddenly demanded repayment of an overdraft of £38,000 and the company was confronted with the options of amalgamation or bankruptcy. 'With bewildering speed...the transaction was put in hand; like rabbits hypnotized by bright lights, the Lanchester board agreed to terms which left it entirely to Daimlers to decide what kind of motor-car should bear the name of Lanchester.' There must be suspicion that the extensive influence of BSA directors was behind the bank's arbitrary decision to re-call the loan and trigger the Lanchester cash crisis which forced them into BSA's clutches: but nothing definite is known. As it was this hasty Lanchester deal soon soured like the Airco *mésalliance* eleven years before. BSA transferred the Lanchester stock and plant to the Daimler works at Coventry, sacked most of the Lanchester staff and converted the old Lanchester Works to machine-tool production; 'Lanchester was to be used primarily as a convenient name of great reputation with which to launch a new range of smaller Daimler models designed to attract the middle-class market.'[42]

There is no evidence that this new policy had been considered in detail within BSA, and like the Airco deal, it came at a critical financial time. They sustained a net loss of £204,194 in 1931, and could ill afford either the Lanchester purchase or the necessary expenditure to make it a success. Manville used the pretext of the 1931 crisis to obtain the retirement as BSA directors of the otiose Holden and Rogers – the latter was very depressed by his forced retirement and died soon afterwards.[43] At the same time Commander Godfrey Herbert, DSO, managing director of BSA Cycles since 1921, was appointed to the BSA board. Herbert, who came from a Kenilworth family, became a particularly trusted lieutenant of Docker in the crisis that followed. One of the first submarine officers of 1905, he had shown outstanding bravery during the early days of submarines, and narrowly escaped death several times. As commander of the decoy merchantman *Baralong* in 1915, his sinking of U-boats 'was one of the most famous incidents of the 1914–18 War, chiefly because his failure to take any...crew [as] prisoners led to German demands for his trial and to a price being put on his head'.[44] But these board changes proved largely cosmetic, and BSA could devise no measures to improve their position. By the summer of 1932 they were faced with a net trading loss of £797,928 and Docker was consulted. He arranged for Sir Mark Webster Jenkinson to report on the group's strategy and structure, and as the accountant who had masterminded Vickers' recovery, Jenkinson recommended that BSA's capital should be reduced, and that their subsidiaries should be amalgamated and simplified. Docker discussed Jenkinson's report fully with Manville, Martin and other BSA officials, as well as with management at the Midland Bank. He considered Pollen 'the strongest Director on the Board', whose previous success with the Linotype Company suggested that he could 'pull the business round if anyone can'.[45] On 3 July Docker finalised an agreement with Martin and other directors whereby Pollen became the new chairman, and all the present directors gave Pollen a letter of resignation for use if and when he saw fit.[46] Pollen was initially reluctant to accept this chair, as he had to relinquish the Linotype chairmanship, which provided a company house as well as a salary of £6,000 per annum;[47] but Docker persuaded him to accept. Pollen attacked his new responsibilities with the massive unfocused vehemence that characterised him, and it soon proved a mistake for Docker to have catapulted BSA into 'baffling negotiations with [such] an impossible personality'.[48]

Docker was originally convinced in July 1932 that Manville must retire not only as chairman, but as director of BSA, but later concluded that this was undesirable because 'Manville has other interests with [the Midland] Bank and if he were turned off without the option of continuing he might think it was due to the Bank's action', and withdraw his other accounts.[49] This was the first good resolve to be discarded. Pollen and Docker had also agreed that Martin should lose his board status, and concentrate on his work as general manager of Daimler, and it did seem that Martin had accepted this in principle, too.[50] Indeed, Pollen also wanted to remove the other executive directors, R. A. Rotherham and W. L. Bayley, but again, time was lost. Meanwhile, under the conditions of the Depression, BSA was rapidly weakening. The group's output of motor-cycles and cycles was down by 24 per cent in 1932 as compared with 1931; whilst steel output, and the output of machinery and small-tools, fell by 40 per cent and 50 per cent respectively.[51]

By October 1932, Hannon was predicting that Pollen's 'impulsive and dictatorial methods' of re-organisation would end in a collision with Martin; and the level of aggression can be gauged from the fact that Manville was left in tears after one board meeting.[52] By the beginning of December, Pollen had isolated himself so completely that Martin felt strong enough to announce that he would no longer co-operate with Pollen as chairman. After Martin had declared himself at the board meeting of 6 December, a highly critical resolution was passed, the wording of which has not survived, as Pollen's eventual resignation was conditional upon it not being entered in the BSA minute books.[53] Pollen was absent from the meeting, and when he spoke next day to Hannon, he was 'terribly overwrought and...incoherent', but complained that he was being ruined by a 'pack of lies'.[54] Hannon delighted in his role as intermediary between Pollen and the other directors,[55] and certainly kept his mentor, Docker, informed.

Docker was decisive in obtaining the appointment, later in December 1932, of Pollen's successor as chairman, Sir Alexander Roger, who became BSA's fourth chairman within five years. Roger was an Aberdonian who, as a young man before the first war, had been a junior partner of Lord St Davids in the investment trusts sited at 117 Old Broad Street in the City of London. Early in the war he organised the Red Cross Motor Ambulance Services, before going to the Ministry of Munitions as Director General of Trench Warfare Supplies. At Munitions he enjoyed a golden reputation with ministers like Lloyd George and Addison, and in October 1917, he was put in charge of planning financial facilities for the post-war transition period at the new Ministry of Reconstruction.[56] After the war, he became Docker's co-director at the Midland Bank, and his appointment to BSA was a clear sign that the Bank was intervening to ensure stable management of one of its biggest and oldest clients. On the debit side, his previous work as a City financier had given him little experience of industrial management, and his undoubted qualities were not those best suited to solving the personal contumely and managerial disorganisation which posed BSA's main problems in 1932.

On 13 December, Roger listed the terms on which he accepted the job, to which Martin agreed next day.[57] He was well aware that the trouble between Pollen and Martin, and indeed between the various operating divisions of the company, came from bad demarcation and vague job definition. Roger therefore insisted that all important duties and responsibilities must be defined in writing, and that the distinction between the responsibilities of the managing director, two general managers, engineers and designers must be delineated. He also instituted a new Intelligence Committee, comprising departmental heads and any directors who wished to attend, to meet weekly to co-ordinate business. All salaries and expenses were also reviewed; all capital expenditure above £500 would have to be submitted in future, with detailed costings, for approval by board committees; and a 'bold new policy' would be launched in motor-car sales.

In the spring of 1933, Roger's new regime encouraged confidence,[58] but by the autumn, the position had deteriorated. Martin remained troublesome. One director admitted in October that 'for some time' he had 'not liked the way Martin has behaved',[59] and Hannon described the board meetings as 'lop-sided and ill-balanced' and devoid of any 'feeling of mutual confidence and accommodation' between the directors. The clash of personalities was chiefly between Roger and Martin, but Martin had also come to resent the two new general managers. Herbert and Turrell. He manifested this resentment by ignoring all communications from Roger, or else handing them over to someone else,[60] complaining that since becoming chairman, Roger had entered 'continuous communication' with Turrell and Herbert, which had excluded him from much policy-making, and had made his position 'practically impossible'. Under Roger's regime, his authority and experience had been ignored; and he particularly resented 'the placing [of] highly skilled engineers responsible for motor-car production under the control of an officer whose acquaintance with that branch of engineering is very limited'. The resentment by British engineers of financial supervision, or marketing pressures, on design and production methods was smouldering inside Martin.

In mid-December 1933, a new re-organisation, designed by Docker,[61] was made. Martin retired from all executive responsibilities within the BSA/Daimler group, and a new co-ordinating sub-committee was set up under Roger to remedy the laxities in the sales organisation. Martin's successor as managing director, Captain Geoffrey Burton, had been a notably successful general manager at MCWF in 1927–30, and owed this BSA appointment to Docker. Other appointments of Docker men to the BSA board followed later in the 1930s. Noel Docker, the younger son of DD's elder brother Edwin, and previously an Elrafin employee, became a director of BSA in 1937, and another director who owed his position to Docker was Bernard (afterwards Lord) Freyberg, VC. Freyberg's wife, previously the widow of Francis McLaren (whom Docker had succeeded as a director of the Metropolitan Railway in 1915), was sister-in-law of Docker's friend, McKenna; the job seems to have been settled through this connection after Freyberg was invalided out of the army. Most important of all, when Sir Alexander Roger was made Chairman of the Tank Board in 1940, Bernard Docker succeeded him as chairman of BSA, whilst also acting as managing director during Burton's secondment to the Ministry of Supply. Dudley Docker took a leading part on BSA's behalf during 1940 in obtaining finance from the Midland Bank for wartime capital expenditure,[62] and despite his preference to act through nominees, he himself joined the BSA board in 1940 and sought to secure his son's industrial future. This proved to be his Parthian shot at BSA's strategy, but no less fateful or unlucky than the others. On three occasions the company had bought other businesses (Daimler, Airco and Lanchester) on financial terms that had proved all but ruinous; and it elected a succession of chairmen who lacked variously the energy, imagination or experience to grapple with its organisational failings. Docker held almost sole responsibility for the financial incubus of the Daimler merger, and his subsequent interventions, though decisive, were too spasmodic to succeed. Although he perceived the weaknesses of BSA at least as clearly as anyone else involved, he approached it as a financier dealing with an industrial investment, applying concentrated bursts of attention at moments of particular crisis, but neglect in the long intervals between. The appointment of Sir Alexander Roger epitomised his failing; while he recognised the need of strong leadership at BSA, his support for combative but muddle-headed men like Herbert or Pollen was no cure. He did not give enough thought to BSA, and nor did anyone else whose thoughts were worth having.

As it was, this indulgent but changeful father, as A. L. Smith had described him, set his heart on founding an industrial dynasty. In June 1944, as Hannon recorded a few days before the elder Docker's death, Burton was dismissed from BSA. In telling Hannon the story, Burton 'spoke bitterly about D.D.' and conveyed a great sense of grievance. He had been summoned to spend two nights at Amersham with D.D. and was told quite plainly that he had to go. Only reason given was Bernard should be Managing Director of entire group...Have agreed that no animus or ill-feeling should be shown towards the Docker family.

[Burton] Asked me definitely whether he could trust Bernard, and I said 'Yes'.[63]

Whether this insinuation of DD's untrustworthiness is fair or not, his success in arranging, in the last weeks of his life, that his son would be managing director, as well as chairman, of BSA was destructive in the long run. Bernard Docker, who had been pitchforked to industrial responsibility at an unfairly young age, and who had spent over twenty-five years of business life in his father's shadow, was transformed after his parents' death (Lucy Docker died at Monte Carlo in February 1947). In 1949 he married a second time: his new wife, Norah, was the widow of Sir William Collins, the head of Fortnum and Masons and of Cerebos Salt, whom she had self-avowedly married for his money in 1946.[64] She had previously been the widow of Clement Callingham, the chairman of Henekeys, wine and spirit merchants. Lady Docker had suffered a hard life, her father having thrown himself off the Holyhead to Dublin ferry when she was sixteen in 1922, and had made her own way in an unfriendly world. As a young woman, she was a dance hostess at the Embassy Club and her protectors included Cecil Whiteley (Common Serjeant of the City of London), the ninth Duke of Marlborough and, for years before their marriage, Clement Callingham. These early adversities made her sensitive to insult.

This marriage altered Bernard Docker, and he became increasingly erratic. He and his wife were hard drinkers, and in 1949–56, they became famous for the furious whirl of their social life. Their yacht *Shemara* (built by Thornycrofts to Bernard Docker's specification for £100,000 in 1938) was constantly photographed in the popular press, but was only one of their dramatic means of transport. 'The large sum in excess of £100,000 per annum which Daimler spend on advertising could be a dead loss if one of the distinguished directors of BSA went about in a cheap car', Bernard Docker opined in 1949;[65] and the board enjoyed a fleet of Daimler limousines, of which the most famous (gold-plated with zebra-skin seats) carried Lady Docker about as an advertisement for her husband's company's wares. Altogether five Daimlers were made to his special instructions (The Gold Car; Blue Clover; Silver Flash; Star Dust; and Golden Zebra) to exhibit his wife: and he seems sincerely to have believed that it was a good advertisement for the company to fly Star Dust and Golden Zebra to Monaco in 1956, at a cost of £2,140, when his wife joined the celebrations of Grace Kelly's wedding to the Prince of Monaco. At the same time, Sir Bernard took to charging her gems and clothes to the company on the pretext that his wife's glamorous reputation was a major asset to the BSA group. He also presided over a series of ill-considered mergers with bicycle and other companies.

His mountingly imperious conduct culminated in a board meeting of May 1956 when, after his proposal to make his wife's brother-in-law (R. E. Smith) a director of BSA was defeated by five votes to four, he declared it passed by his casting vote, and abused the directors who voted against him. His subsequent sacking from the board by his co-directors with the support of institutional shareholders like Prudential Assurance, and very unfavourable publicity which continued until 1958, ruined the Docker reputation, and must have made DD revolve in his grave in Coleshill churchyard. Bernard Docker buying advertising time on commercial television to appeal for 'fair play' in the battle to control BSA; Norah Docker circularising shareholders with an appeal to support her husband and enclosing a signed photograph of herself for 'you or your children'; or the semi-hysterical newsletter called *The Docker Digest* – all would have been anathema to DD, who believed that power struggles should be conducted in low voices behind closed doors, or in a relaxed murmur over lunch at the Ritz or Savoy.[66] And yet for old BSA hands like Hannon the rows of 1956–8 must have been uncannily like those surrounding Percy Martin in 1931–4.

It was not only at BSA that Bernard was unstuck. In 1953 he resigned from the Midland Bank after his co-directors had indicated their intention to propose his dismissal at the next meeting of shareholders. His appearance in the gossip columns had proved uncongenial to the Bank: their excuse for removing him was a prosecution then contemplated for breaches of currency control regulations which had occurred whilst *Shemara* was on a foreign cruise.[67] Other Docker companies underwent a decline. Elrafin suffered when the Peron junta nationalised railway and other foreign holdings in Argentina in 1947–8, and was hit by Juan March's seizure of Sofina's prize asset in Fascist Spain in 1947. Certainly, by 1960, shares in Elrafin nominally worth £1 were given a market value of 3s and the corporation was semi-dormant.[68] Birmingham Railway Carriage and Wagon Company, having celebrated its centenary in 1954, also declined, and in the 1960s was reconstructed into the First National Finance Corporation, a speculative secondary bank led by Pat Matthews, which came to grief in the financial crisis of 1975. The *Shemara* was sold to Harry Hyams, a London property dealer, and in 1966 Bernard Docker sold his estate at Stockbridge in Hampshire for £400,000 and went into tax exile in Jersey. The quiet of his retirement occasionally punctuated by the excitement of his wife giving press interviews, he died in May 1978 after a stroke. His widow survived in reduced circumstances until 1983: by then Dudley Docker's rich prizes were lost, all his great schemes vulgarised and his powers long scattered.

12

Conclusion

Dudley Docker did not live to see this morality tale unfold. Just after forcing Burton to retire in June 1944, he contracted tonsillitis: with the auricular fibrillation which had affected his heart since about 1938, this was a serious condition: a further complication, Ludwigs angina, for which there was no treatment, set in: he drifted into unconsciousness and on 8 July 1944, at his house outside Amersham, Dudley Docker ended almost eighty-two years of life.

Unlike his brother Edwin, whose sole executor had been DD, and whose will had been unsuccessfully contested in O'Dare *versus* Docker in 1926–7, DD left his affairs in order. The estate was valued at £887,692 gross. He was one of twenty-one men who died in 1944 leaving estates worth between £500,000 and £1 million, and there were fourteen men who left over £1 million in 1944. Of the fourteen millionaires, three each were landowners, bankers, brewers or distillers, and retailers, while only two were manufacturers (of Celanese and tobacco).[1] Docker would have found this conclusive proof of the neglect which British manufacturing had suffered. The fact that he himself did not leave over £1 million reflects the precautions he had taken to avoid death duties, and the depreciation during the war of his overseas electrical investments.

Dudley Docker was in business for sixty-three years, a Victorian from Birmingham who started under two railway arches and died with the giant factories of BSA and Daimler working day and night in war production. He presided over the swansong of the British rolling-stock industry and after his retirement watched it shrivel; he helped to float the British motor-car industry; in a century of war he transformed two of Britain's largest armament companies. He was, with Hugo Hirst, the foremost Briton participating in the world's electrical trusts, and was feared from Buenos Aires to Shanghai. For over thirty years he was a stalwart of the Midland Bank, holding immeasurable power over all its industrial lending in the Birmingham region. His life in turn reflected the economic anxiety, political

234

bitterness and social unrest of the Edwardians; the hyper-nationalism and
deformed ideals of the Great War; and the sedentary decline of the age of
Baldwin. He would have regarded his career as a response to Britain's
industrial self-enfeeblement, and would not have been surprised by the
irreversible loss of territory and wealth that occurred in his son's life.

In peace or war, boom or slump, national ascendancy or imperial decline,
Docker's acquisitiveness was compulsive, single-minded and repetitive. He
did not know what else to be. Docker would have dismissed with a
contemptuous grunt the cavilling of R. H. Tawney in *The Acquisitive Society*
of 1921. 'To those who clamour, as many now do, "Produce! Produce!"
one simple question may be addressed: "Produce What?"'...What can be
more childish than to urge the necessity that productive power should be
increased, if part of the productive power which exists already is
misapplied?'[2] To Docker, Tawney's questions would have been unrealistic,
meaningless, crankish, incomprehensible; yet the answers make a mockery
of his life.

Judged by his own values, Docker's achievements are mixed. He foresaw,
but also exemplified, British decline. If increased production was a socially
desirable goal for the country, many of his views were good prescriptions
for that end, but some of his actions were not. In business his talents lay
in finance and dealing. After about 1906 one looks in vain for signs that
he thought carefully about long-term investment, efficient use of resources
or balanced labour relations in his companies. He avowedly treated
industry as a vehicle for financiers to make money from, and lacked
patience for methodical consolidation of his deals. He betrayed no interest
in salesmanship, and had little ability at it except in cases where the terms
of payment were deferred or complicated in other respects. With the
exception of rolling-stock in 1902, none of his great mergers were good
for business or for the social and political economy of Britain. Though he
was tenacious and stubborn, he was too restless and impatient to apply
himself consistently to his responsibilities. His reliance on his personality
in all his dealings, and his view that most matters can be fixed by knowing
top people personally, ran as a strange counter to his love of anonymity,
and explains his frustration with politics where matters cannot always be
'fixed'. As a leader of the Birmingham manufacturers, and their contact
with the Milnerites, he was an enemy of the party system and parliamentary
government, with life-long loathing of the subtle dialectics and periphrasis
of Whitehall and Westminster; his vision of a corporatist state, though it
seems naive, carried real power for a time. If any system of government
or set of attitudes could have maintained British export hegemony, which
is doubtful, it would have been Docker's.

Docker considered himself above all as a realist: as a business man unfettered by sentiment, aesthetics or idealism who owed his success to his perfectly honed sense of reality. In fact his power, and his historic interest, came from his sense of possibility. Throughout his life, he saw positive possibilities in situations which contemporaries regarded with despair: his ingenuity was so complex and so wakeful that even the business depression after the Boer war, the slaughter of 1914–18 or the General Strike excited him with their creative possibility. Docker was a man 'with the cynic devil in his blood', in Kipling's words,

> That bids him flout the law he makes,
> That bids him make the law he flouts.

He was not an opportunist, but a man who created possibilities. It was this that made him a distinctive figure of his times. As Robert Musil observed in his novel *The Man without Qualities*, the consequences of such a disposition 'make the things that other people admire appear wrong and the things that other people prohibit permissible, or even make both appear as a matter of indifference'.[3] Such a man was Dudley Docker.

Notes

The following abbreviations are used in the notes.

Adm.	Admiralty papers
ASM	Sir Arthur Steel-Maitland papers
BEAMA	British Electrical and Allied Manufacturers Association
BCU	British Commonwealth Union
BL	Bonar Law papers
BM	British Museum
BSA	Birmingham Small Arms
BST	British Stockbrokers Trust
BT	Board of Trade papers
BTC	British Trade Corporation
Cab.	Cabinet Office papers
CP	Cabinet paper
DBB	*Dictionary of Business Biography*
Elrafin	Electric and Railway Finance Corporation
EPA	Employers Parliamentary Association
FBI	Federation of British Industries
FO	Foreign Office papers
H	Hannon papers
LG	Lloyd George papers
M	Maxse papers
MBA	Midland Bank Archives
MCWF	Metropolitan Carriage Wagon and Finance Company
Metro.	Metropolitan Railway
MR	Metropolitan Railway papers
MT	Ministry of Transport papers
Mun.	Ministry of Munitions papers
PSO	Principal Supply Officers
Reco.	Ministry of Reconstruction papers
SMT	Securities Management Trust
Swin.	Lord Swinton papers
TC	Tariff Commission
WO	War Office

1. Dudley Docker and his world

1 H. G. Wells, *An Experiment in Autobiography* (1934), p. 759.
2 Steel-Maitland to Bonar Law, letter of May 1916, Steel-Maitland papers (hereafter ASM) 170/1/366.
3 Quoted in L. Urwick and E. F. L. Brech, *The Making of Scientific Management* (1949), p. 83.
4 Docker, speech at Wednesbury Town Hall, quoted *Midland Advertiser*, 21 December 1918.
5 Docker, 'The Industrial Problem', *National Review*, 72 (1918), p. 306.
6 Eric J. Hobsbawm, *Industry and Empire* (Penguin, 1970 edn), p. 178.
7 Docker, essay in Sydney Chapman (ed.), *Labour and Capital after the War* (1918), p. 129.
8 Steel-Maitland to Lord Milner, 19 February 1910, ASM 147/1/12. On the representation of business interests in Birmingham civic life, see H. J. Dyos, *The Study of Urban History* (1968), pp. 320–7; E. P. Hennock, *Fit and Proper Persons* (1973), pp. 46–54. The most pertinent study of the business efficiency movement in the Midlands is Linda Jones. 'Public Pursuit of Private Profit? Liberal Businessmen and Municipal Politics in Birmingham 1865–1900', *Business History*, 25 (1983).
9 Moisei Ostrogorski, *Democracy and the Organisation of Political Parties* (1902), pp. 168–9.
10 Docker, speech of 30 May 1918, reported *Economist*, 1 June 1918.
11 Stephen Blank, *Industry and Government in Britain* (Farnborough, 1973), pp. 13–14.
12 For Docker's offer of a directorship of the British Stockbrokers Trust to Lord Milner, see Steel-Maitland to Docker, 20 December 1920, ASM 193/184/519. For offers to Steel-Maitland, see Docker to Steel-Maitland, 24 October 1911 (ASM 153/4/57), 30 November 1911 (ASM 153/4/68) and 17 May 1915 (ASM 165/1/543). Docker welcomed Milner's appointment as Secretary of War *vice* Lord Derby: Docker to Maxse, 20 April 1918, M 474/78.
13 Leopold C. M. S. Amery, *Diaries 1869–1929*, vol. 1 (1980), p. 44; Sir Clinton Dawkins to Lord Milner, 17 November 1901, Milner papers 3; Leopold J. Maxse, *Germany on the Brain* (1915), p. 75; G. E. Morrison to Heinrich Cordes, 13 January 1910, Morrison papers 55; and see generally Geoffrey R. Searle, *The Quest for National Efficiency* (Oxford, 1971), pp. 55–7.
14 Docker, quoted *Economist*, 29 May 1915 and 2 March 1917.
15 Hugo Hirst, 'The Higher Aspect of Business', lecture at Christ's College, Cambridge, 30 January 1914. This lecture was issued as a pamphlet, one copy of which is in the papers of the Parsons committee on the electrical industry after the war in BT 55/21. See also my entry on Hirst in *DBB*.
16 Philip Lyttelton Gell to Milner, 2 February 1900, Milner papers 5.
17 Gell to Milner, 12 April 1900, Milner papers 5. For a more detailed discussion of this view, see Searle, *Quest for National Efficiency*, pp. 34–53 and *passim*; Arnold White. *Efficiency and Empire* (1901), pp. 17–18, 28–30 and *passim*.
18 Diary of Christopher Addison, 12 October 1915.
19 On Girouard, see Addison diary, 27 May and 16 July 1915; on Geddes, *ibid.*, 23 December 1915; on Stevenson, 12 October 1915. Cf. my entries on Geddes

and Girouard in *DBB*; and Christopher Wrigley, 'The Ministry of Munitions', in Kathleen Burk (ed.), *War and the State* (1982), pp. 41, 44 and 54.

20 G. E. Morrison, *Correspondence*, vol. 2 (1978), p. 625.
21 Edgar R. Jones, MP, of Ministry of Munitions Priority Dept, to Addison, 8 May 1917, Addison box 23.
22 Sir Keith Joseph, *New Statesman*, 18 April 1975.
23 Martin J. Weiner, 'Some Leaders of Opinion and Economic Growth in Britain 1918–74', *Journal of Contemporary History*, 14 (1979), p. 354.
24 Lionel Hichens, *Some Problems of Modern Industry* (Watt lecture, 1918), p. 57. See my entry on Hichens in *DBB*.
25 David Landes, *Unbound Prometheus* (1969), p. 293.
26 Charles S. Maier, *Recasting Bourgeois Europe* (1975), pp. 73–6, 142. Von Moellendorff had followed Rathenau from AEG to the Raw Materials Division of the War Ministry, and later served as State Secretary at the Economics Ministry.
27 Hugo Hirst, *The Higher Aspect of Business* (1914), in BT 55/21.
28 Docker to Steel-Maitland, 25 May 1912, ASM 156/314.
29 Charles Packe to Steel-Maitland, 3 July 1914, ASM 164/1/101.
30 Docker to Steel-Maitland, 29 July 1915, ASM 165/1/179.
31 Docker to Steel-Maitland, 12 January 1916, ASM 170/1/154.
32 Docker to Sir Peter Rylands, 10 August 1916, FBI C/3.
33 Rylands to H. G. Tetley of Courtaulds, 19 March 1920, Nugent papers.
34 Sir Vincent Caillard to D. Lloyd George, 18 October 1918, LG F6/1/24. Apart from his colds and gastritis, the only other serious illness mentioned by Docker was a severe attack of measles in the early summer of 1926.
35 Docker to Maxse, 20 April 1918, M 474/78–9.
36 Sir John Elliott, 'Early Days of the Southern Railway', *Journal of Transport History*, 4 (1960), p. 203.
37 Sir Charles Tennyson, *Stars and Markets* (1957), p. 146; Docker to Maxse, 12 October 1922, M 342/440; information from John Docker.
38 Hickman in *Economist*, 9 June 1917; Aston (possibly a relation of Docker's wife), *Economist*, 3 June 1911.

2. Domestic life and early career

1 *Birmingham Gazette*, 11 November 1887 and 10 June 1907.
2 Other biographical information on Ralph Docker is contained in *Birmingham Daily Post*, 11 November 1887; *Smethwick Telephone*, 26 November 1887; F. W. Hackwood, *Some Records of Smethwick* (1896); Birmingham Poll Book for 1837.
3 Lord Dalhousie, quoted *Spectator*, 17 June 1882; Kenneth Rose, *The Later Cecils* (1975), pp. 232, 234–6; Sir Philip Magnus, *King Edward the Seventh* (1964), pp. 80 and 163. Ralph Docker's brother Henry lived at Boulogne, and the marriage may have been contracted there.
4 John Dale (ed.), *Warwickshire: Historical, Descriptive and Biographical in the Reign of King Edward VII* (nd ?1910), p. 105.
5 T. W. Hutton, *King Edward's School, Birmingham 1552–1952* (Oxford, 1952), p. 51.

6 *Midland Advertiser,* 29 May 1909.
7 *Birmingham Post,* 10 July 1944; Docker to Steel-Maitland, 15 June 1916, ASM 170/1/71.
8 Docker, speech to Wednesbury Business League, 2 May 1910, in *Midland Advertiser,* 7 May 1910.
9 Gell to Lord Milner, 22 March 1901, Milner papers 5.
10 G. N. Hill, 'The Varnish and Lacquer Industry', *Royal Institute of Chemistry Journal* (1940), p. 198. Gerald P. Mander and Sir Geoffrey Le M. Mander, *The History of Mander Brothers 1773–1955* (nd ?1956); P. W. Gibbs, 'Historical Survey of the Japanning Trade', pt 4. *Annals of Science, 7* (1951), p. 216; Francis White, *History, Gazetteer and Directory of Warwickshire* (Sheffield, 1850); William West, *History, Topography and Directory of Warwickshire* (Birmingham, 1830), p. 328.
11 Docker, speech of 22 February 1909 to Wednesbury Municipal Technical School, quoted *Midland Advertiser,* 27 February 1909.
12 An interesting study of Birmingham life and attitudes at this date is John MacDonald, 'Birmingham', *Nineteenth Century, 20* (1886), pp. 234–54.
13 *Wisdens* (1882), p. 203 (1883), p. 206 (1885), p. 232 (1886), p. 325 (1941), p. 395; T. W. Hutton, *King Edward's School, Birmingham,* p. 170; F. W. Hackwood, *Some Records of Smethwick* (1896), p. 116; *Victoria County History of Warwickshire,* vol. 2 (1908), pp. 396–7, 404; *Birmingham Express and Gazette,* 10 June 1907.
14 Leslie Duckworth, *The Story of Warwickshire Cricket* (1974), pp. 16 and 22; *Wisdens* (1887), pp. 257–8; *Birmingham Mail,* 10 July 1944.
15 *Birmingham Express and Gazette,* 10 June 1907.
16 Duckworth, *Story of Warwickshire Cricket,* pp. 37–9.
17 The preceding five paragraphs are based upon *Birmingham Gazette,* 28 December 1887; *Birmingham Daily Post,* 29 December 1887; Lucy Docker's will dated 1946; Conrad Gill, *History of Birmingham,* vol. 1 (1952), p. 218.
18 *Country Life,* 9 November 1978, Supplement, p. 31.
19 A. L. Smith to Steel-Maitland, 10 October 1915, ASM 165/2/347. See also Steel-Maitland to Docker, 12 October 1915; Docker to Steel-Maitland, 19 October 1915, ASM 165/2/127 and 128.
20 Information from Mr S. W. Alexander, financial editor of the *Daily Express* and other Beaverbrook newspapers 1923–46, who knew both Bernard and Dudley Docker personally.
21 *Times,* 20 June 1934; information from Mr George Docker, 1980.
22 *Birmingham Daily Post,* 28 June 1906. The firm of Ash and Lacy, with a workforce of 704 employees, became prosperous steel products makers in the West Midlands, with sales and profits in 1980–1 worth £27.86 million and £2.64 million respectively.
23 Diary of Sir Edward Holden, 25 May 1900, MBA.
24 *Birmingham Daily Post,* 28 June 1906.
25 John F. Ede, *History of Wednesbury* (Wednesbury, 1962), pp. 243–5 and 282; *Midland Advertiser,* 15 November 1902; evidence of J. F. Cay to the Tariff Commission, 24 November 1904. TC 35.

3. Birmingham's industrial titan 1902–14

1   *Financial Times*, 20 March 1930. The Metropolitan Carriage and Wagon Company, with which this chapter is mainly concerned, was wound up in October 1934 and is distinct from the extant Metropolitan-Cammell Co., to which no reference is intended.
2   Quoted D. L. Burn, *The Economic History of Steel-Making* (1940), p. 304; Leslie Hannah, *The Rise of the Corporate Economy in Britain* (1976), pp. 17, 24 and *passim*; J. S. Jeans, *Trusts, Pools and Corners* (1894).
3   *Birmingham Daily Gazette*, 2 November 1911.
4   *Birmingham Express and Gazette*, 10 June 1907.
5   Docker to Steel-Maitland, 25 October 1915, ASM 164/3/14/141. For a more detailed survey of the past history of the five rolling-stock companies, see J. H. Price, *Tramcar, Carriage and Wagon Builders of Birmingham* (Hartley, Kent, 1982), pp. 5–31.
6   Quoted Searle, *Quest for National Efficiency*, p. 1.
7   *Statist*, 5 April 1902; *Midland Advertiser*, 15 November 1907.
8   *Economist*, 5 April 1902; *Times*, 31 May 1907.
9   *Midland Advertiser*, 31 May 1902.
10 *Times*, 31 May and 3 June 1907.
11 Diary of Sir Edward Holden, 31 October 1906, MBA.
12 G. C. Allen, *The Industrial Development of Birmingham and the Black Country* (1927), pp. 357–8. For example, in 1903 Mulliner Wrigley, the Coventry coachmakers, merged with the newly formed armaments and shipbuilding company, Cammell Laird of Birkenhead.
13 *Times*, 3 June 1907.
14 S. B. Saul, 'Mechanical Engineering Industries 1860–1914', in B. E. Supple (ed.), *Essays in British Business History* (Oxford, 1977), p. 36. For an invaluable study of a French rolling-stock maker, the Fives-Lille company, see François Crouzet, 'When the Railways were Built', in Sheila Marriner (ed.), *Business and Businessmen* (Liverpool, 1978).
15 Steel-Maitland, memorandum of conversation with R. A. Pinsent, 29 April 1915, ASM 165/1/544.
16 The Metropolitan Amalgamated Carriage board in 1902 comprised F. D. Docker (chairman), Sir George Scott Robertson (deputy-chairman), W. Charlton,   G. D. Churchward,   Ludford   Docker,   C. W. Hazlehurst, W. L. Hodgkinson, J. Kershaw, J. P. Lacy, W. L. Mathews, W. O. Roper, J. T. Sanderson, A. L. Shackleford, W. C. Shackleford, H. Wheeler and P. Wheeler. On Scott Robertson, see Robert A. Huttenback, 'The Siege of Chitral and the Breach of Faith Controversy', *Journal of British Studies*, 10 (1970), pp. 126–144.
17 *Midland Advertiser*, 21 December 1918.
18 Docker to R. H. Selbie, 28 April 1924, MR 10/833. Emphasis in original. See also Hannah, *Rise of Corporate Economy*, pp. 25–6, 78–9.
19 Saul, 'Mechanical Engineering Industries', p. 46.
20 Evidence of W. C. Shackleford and J. F. Cay of Metropolitan Carriage to Tariff Commission, 7 November 1905, TC 52. As one example, the civil engineer appointed in 1909 as the new general manager at Wednesbury had previously

been manager and assistant mechanical engineer at the Harwich works of the Lancashire and Yorkshire Railway (*Birmingham Gazette*, 21 May 1909).

21 Christine Shaw, 'The Largest Manufacturing Employers of 1907', *Business History*, 25 (1983), pp. 42–60.

22 Diary of Sir Edward Holden, 17 and 24 January, 29 March 1905, MBA.

23 *Times*, 25 March 1919; this was not a new lesson for British industry: the investments of a textile firm like Black Dyke Mills had risen from £4,860 in 1853 to £349,736 by 1862 and £696,176 in 1867. This figure only included stocks and bonds, but excluded landed estates, bought from the firm's resources as personal assets for individual partners and debited against their accounts, worth some £709,700 (1860–73); nevertheless it shows the part the London money market and Stock Exchange could play in the fortunes of a textile manufacturing concern. See Eric Sigsworth, *Black Dyke Mills* (Liverpool, 1958), pp. 224–33.

24 Sir John Aspinall, memorandum of 9 January 1919, in MT 6/3063.

25 Diary of J. M. Madders, 9 November 1910, MBA; *Statist*, 21 October 1911.

26 Docker, speech of 27 May 1909, in *Midland Advertiser*, 29 May 1909.

27 *Times*, 31 May 1907.

28 Docker, speech of 1 June 1904, in *Midland Advertiser*, 4 June 1904; Ede, *History of Wednesbury*, p. 283; *Times*, 29 May 1907.

29 Sir Vincent Caillard, memorandum on merger between Vickers and Metropolitan Carriage, dated January 1919. Vickers microfilm R 325. On the Kylsant case generally, see Edwin Green and Michael Moss, *A Business of National Importance: the Royal Mail Shipping Group 1902–37* (1982). The accountancy consequences of the Kylsant case are treated in J. R. Edwards, 'The Accounting Profession and Disclosure in Published Reports 1925–35', in T. A. Lee and R. H. Parker (eds.), *The Evolution of Corporate Financial Reporting* (1979), pp. 282–95; Edgar Jones, *Accountancy and the British Economy 1840–1980* (1981), pp. 150–2.

30 Diary of Sir Edward Holden, 2 November 1903 and 31 October 1906, MBA.

31 Tennyson, *Stars and Markets*, p. 125.

32 Diary of Sir Edward Holden, 27 May 1913, MBA.

33 *Ibid.*, 9 June 1902.

34 Diary of H. A. Astbury, 20 January and 6 April 1937, MBA.

35 Docker, speech of 23 February 1916, in *Globe*, 24 February 1916.

36 Harvey O'Connor, *Mellon's Millions* (1933), p. 60.

37 Docker, letter in *Economist*, 7 February 1914.

38 Docker, speech of 30 May 1907, in *Midland Advertiser*, 1 June 1907.

39 Ludford Docker to Bonar Law, 14 March 1914, BL 31/4/28.

40 Evidence of Sir Clarendon Hyde to Balfour of Burleigh committee, 14 June 1917, BT 55/11. For the effects on a Serbian railway and armaments loan, see Sir Vincent Caillard of Vickers to Sir Francis Bertie, 10 January 1910; Sir James Whitehead (Belgrade) to Foreign Office, telegram 10 January 1910, FO 371/982; diary of J. M. Madders, 15 November 1909, MBA. It should be added that the French system, with the discretion it left with the Finance Ministry, gave scope for venality: the 'notoriously corrupt' Finance Minister, Caillaux, thus profited from a Serbian loan of 1914, according to Baron Emile de Cartier de Marchienne, successively Belgian Minister to Peking, and Ambassador in Washington and London, quoted diary of G. E. Morrison, 9

January 1914. On the placing of orders for electrical machinery for the Rand mines in Germany for want of tied loans, see Morrison diary, 11 January 1911, and Renfrew Christie, 'The Electrification of South Africa 1905–75', Oxford D. Phil, 1978.

41 *Economist*, 7 February 1914.

42 J. O. P. Bland to Sir Valentine Chirol, 12 January 1912, Bland papers vol. 6, emphasis in original; Sir Edward Grey, minute of (4 or 5) October 1913, FO 371/1826.

43 Caillard to H. A. Gwynne of the *Morning Post*, 21 July 1914, Gwynne papers, box 17.

44 Docker, 'The Industrial Problem', pp. 305–6.

45 *Times*, 30 May 1914; *New York Times*, 21 June 1914.

46 Docker, 'Causes of Industrial Unrest', *Sunday Times*, 2 September 1917.

47 *Times*, 29 May 1907.

48 *Midland Advertiser*, 19 November 1904; *Birmingham Daily Post*, 24 November 1904.

49 *Midland Advertiser*, 1, 15, 22 and 29 August 1908.

50 Steel-Maitland, memorandum of conversation with Docker at Saltley on 4 February 1909, dated 8 February 1909, ASM 193/94/2.

51 *Birmingham Daily Mail*, 1 July 1913; Richard Hyman, *The Workers Union* (1971), pp. 51–60.

52 For the 'very well-marked confidence' of the Workers Union in the Midlands Employers Federation, see Lord Askwith, Memorandum on employers associations, 30 August 1917, in Reco. 1/376; Hyman, *Workers Union*, pp. 56–7.

53 Docker, 'The Industrial Problem', p. 301.

54 Docker, in *Daily Mail*, 8 June 1912.

55 Docker, *Sunday Times*, 2 September 1917; Docker, 'The Industrial Problem', pp. 308–9.

56 H. G. Wells, *An Experiment in Autobiography* (1934), p. 766.

57 *Midland Advertiser*, 4 January 1908, 23 April 1910, 10 October 1914; William Parsons to Steel-Maitland, 8 March 1910, ASM 147/3/39; A. J. Marder, *British Naval Policy 1880–1914* (1941), p. 77; Paul Kennedy, *The Rise of Anglo-German Antagonism 1870–1914* (1980), pp. 381–2.

58 *Economist*, 29 May 1915.

59 TC 32.

60 Docker, speech of 27 May 1909, in *Midland Advertiser*, 29 May 1909; A. E. Dingle, '"The Monster Nuisance of All": Landowners, Alkali Manufacturers and Air Pollution 1828–64', *Economic History Review*, 35 (1982), pp. 529–48.

61 D. L. Burn, *The Economic History of Steel-Making* (1940), p. 225.

62 Docker, speech to banquet of Walsall Chamber of Commerce, 25 January 1913, in *Midland Advertiser*, 1 February 1913. But see the conclusion of Keith Sinclair, 'Hobson and Lenin in Johore: Colonial Office Policy towards British Concessionaires and Inventors 1878–1907', *Modern Asia Studies*, 1, pt 4 (1967), p. 352: 'The Colonial Office, far from being manipulated by investors, was unresponsive to their needs, and treated them with a coolness which did not always stop short of contempt.'

63 J. A. Hobson, *Imperialism* (1902), p. 91.

64 *Midland Advertiser*, 1 June 1907 and 29 May 1909.
65 TC 35; Docker, speech of 30 May 1907, in *Midland Advertiser*, 1 June 1907; evidence of I.G.A.P.C.E. Manzi-Fé of Credito Italiano to Balfour of Burleigh committee, 17 May 1917, BT 55/11; Albert Ball, 'German Methods in Italy', *Quarterly Review*, 224 (1915), pp. 136–49.
66 R. K. Middlemas, *The Master Builders* (1963), p. 271; *Midland Advertiser*, 12 March 1910. The presidential carriage was 78 feet long, 10½ feet wide, and 14 feet high from rail to roof. The drawing room was furnished in the style of Louis XVI, panelled in green silk, with a full-size ornamental chimney and grate; and there were also attached three bedrooms, three luxurious bathrooms, a study and servants' quarters. There were electric light fittings throughout, and the steel exterior was painted ivory, with blue and gold decorations.
67 Ludford Docker to Steel-Maitland, 16 April 1910; Dudley Docker to Steel-Maitland, 14 April 1910, ASM 146/4/51 and 63.
68 Madders diary, 8 January and 18 March 1910, MBA.
69 Middlemas, *Master Builders*, pp. 254–8.
70 A photograph of the Chinese visitors with the Metropolitan directors at Saltley in May 1906 is in Sir Benjamin Stone's collection in Birmingham Reference Library. See Dorothy McCulla, *Victorian and Edwardian Birmingham from Old Photographs* (1973), plate 73, in which Docker is 8th from the right. On Prince Carol's visit, see F. B. Eliot to Steel-Maitland, 15 August 1911, ASM 153/5/3.
71 *Times*, 2 June, 5 July and 9 July 1911; *Contractors' Chronicle*, 17 (July 1911). See also R. T. Naylor, *History of Canadian Business 1867–1914* (1974), pp. 260–93 and *passim*; Sir Percy Girouard, memorandum on Canadian business, 10 October 1912, Armstrong papers 164.
72 Docker to Steel-Maitland, 6 June and 17 June 1911, ASM 150/4/83 and 4.
73 *Midland Advertiser*, 4 June 1904; cf. Amery to Milner, 20 June 1903, in Amery, *Diaries*, vol. 1, p. 47.
74 Searle, *Quest for National Efficiency*, pp. 57–9; Lord Balfour of Burleigh in discussion of 7 June 1917 on fiscal policy, BT 55/13. Apart from China and Japan, MCWF also supplied rolling-stock to Siam.
75 Diary of Sir Edward Holden, 25 August 1913, MBA.
76 R. C. Trebilcock, *Vickers Brothers* (1977), pp. 135–9; O'Connor, *Mellon's Millions*, p. 282.
77 Steel-Maitland, memorandum of conversation with R. A. Pinsent, 29 April 1915, ASM 165/1/544. Arthur Keen junior fell into a depressive anxiety after succeeding to his father's responsibilities, and committed suicide in June 1918.
78 Sir Patrick Hannon to Sir Bernard Docker, 21 May 1951, H 33/4.
79 Holden diary, 7 October 1908, MBA.
80 *Arms and Explosives*, April 1906, p. 43.
81 BSA 3/3/2; *Arms and Explosives*, April 1906, pp. 43, 69; David French, *British Economic and Strategic Planning 1905–1915* (1982), p. 45.
82 BSA to War Office, 1 February 1908; Kenneth R. Davies to Henry de la Bere, 31 April 1909, BSA 3/3/9 and 10.
83 Baguley's report to the directors of 20 October 1909, BSA 1/2/5.
84 Report of BSA Motor Committee, 22 June 1910, BSA 1/2/17.
85 S. B. Saul, 'Motor Industry in Britain to 1914', *Business History*, 5 (1962),

pp. 23–5 and 39; article on Manville in *Birmingham Gazette*, 11 December 1907.
86 Mun. 5/149; Christopher Addison, *Four and a Half Years* (1934), p. 286; Ian Lloyd, *Rolls Royce*, vol. 1 (1978), pp. 77, 78, 80, 117.
87 R. A. Church, *Herbert Austin*, p. 172.
88 *Times*, 28 and 30 July 1910.
89 Lloyd, *Rolls Royce*, vol. 1, p. 17.
90 *Economist*, 1 October 1910; *Financial Times*, 27 September 1910.
91 Madders diary, 22 February, 25 July and 7 November 1912, MBA.
92 *Ibid.*, 11 September 1913.
93 Anthony Bird and Francis Hutton-Stott, *Lanchester Motor Cars* (1965), p. 132.
94 Saul, 'Motor Industry in Britain to 1914', pp. 41–2.
95 Dudley Docker, 'The Large View in Business', *Ways and Means*, 2, 27 September 1919, p. 300.
96 Holden diary, 20 November 1913, MBA.
97 Holden diary, 27 November and 2 December 1912, MBA; James Devonshire before the Parsons committee on the electrical industry, 19 October 1916, BT 55/20.
98 Ian D. Colvin, 'A National Policy', *National Review*, 66 (February 1916), pp. 866–7.
99 Sir Joseph Lawrence to Walter Runciman, 12 January 1916, TC 22.

4. Business Leagues and Business Newspapers 1905–14

1 Ferdinand Lundberg, *The Rich and the Super Rich* (New York, 1968), p. 66.
2 Dudley Docker, speech of 26 February 1910, in *Midland Advertiser*, 5 March 1910. For background to this chapter, see Geoffrey R. Searle, 'Critics of Edwardian Society: The Case of the Radical Right', in Alan O'Day (ed.), *The Edwardian Age* (1981), pp. 79–96; Geoffrey R. Searle, 'The Revolt from the Right in Edwardian Britain', in Paul Kennedy and Anthony Nicholls (eds.), *Nationalist and Racialist Movements in Britain and Germany before 1914* (1981), pp. 21–39; Gregory D. Phillips, 'Lord Willoughby de Broke and the Politics of Radical Toryism 1909–1914', *Journal of British Studies*, 20 (1980), pp. 205–24. Willoughby de Broke was an acquaintance of Dudley Docker, and his papers contain extensive correspondence with Ludford Docker.
3 Docker to Steel-Maitland, 10 March 1906, ASM 128/K–L/46. For a similar view, see Amery, *Diaries*, vol. 1, pp. 72–4. On the attitude of the business efficiency movement to Balfour, see Searle, *Quest for National Efficiency*, pp. 143–4.
4 Docker to Steel-Maitland, 3 January 1906, ASM 128/K–L/26 and *passim*.
5 Docker to Steel-Maitland, 2 April 1906, ASM 128/K–L/59.
6 Steel-Maitland to A. L. Smith, 11 April 1918, ASM 181/632; Steel-Maitland to W. L. Grant, 3 September 1910, ASM 148/7/25.
7 *Economist*, 5 April 1902.
8 George Flett to W. A. S. Hewins, letter 2 November 1904; Hewins to Flett, 24 August 1905, TC 3. See also A. J. Marrison, 'Businessmen, Industries and Tariff Reform in Great Britain 1903–1930', *Business History*, 25 (1983).
9 *Midland Advertiser*, 31 May 1902.
10 Dudley Docker, speech of 1 June 1904, in *Midland Advertiser*, 4 June 1904.

Lord Rosebery made a similar call at this time: see Searle, *Quest for National Efficiency*, p. 146.

11 See, for example, Lord Faringdon's comments in the discussion of fiscal policy between the members of the Balfour of Burleigh committee, 7 June 1917, BT 55/13.

12 Evidence of J. F. Cay, 24 November 1904, TC 35. Evidence of Cay and William Shackleford, 7 November 1905, TC 52.

13 Docker, letter in *Economist*, 7 February 1914.

14 Quoted Zara Steiner, *Britain and the origins of the First World War* (1977), p. 60. For begrudging admiration by a Milnerite of Hamburg-Amerika methods, see Morrison diaries, 12 June and 14 December 1901.

15 Docker to Steel-Maitland, 2 April 1906, ASM 128/K–L/59.

16 Docker to Steel-Maitland, 10 March 1906, ASM 128/K–L/46.

17 Henry Walker to Norris T. Foster, 26 November 1907; Foster to Walker, 28 November 1907, ASM 94/2.

18 Steel-Maitland, note of conversation with Docker at Saltley on 4 February 1909, dated 8 February 1909, ASM 94/2.

19 Amery, *Diaries*, vol. 1, pp. 67–8; *Times*, 18 July 1936.

20 Steel-Maitland, note of conversation on 25 February 1909 with Dr H. W. Pooler, ASM 94/2.

21 *Birmingham Gazette*, 11 January 1909.

22 Edwin H. Sutherland, *Sutherland Papers* (Bloomington, Indiana, 1956), pp. 92–3.

23 Steel-Maitland to Docker, 2 January 1914, ASM 162/26.

24 Steel-Maitland to Docker, 10 January 1916, ASM 172/1/3.

25 Papers covering this episode are ASM 165/1/535–44.

26 Steel-Maitland to Sir Basil Zaharoff, nd (December 1919), ASM 252/708.

27 Docker to Sir Patrick Hannon, 3 March 1920, H 12/1.

28 *Times*, 26 October 1908; even such a dilettante business man as Meade Falkner of Armstrong Whitworth felt this: see Falkner to Lord Rendel, 4 August 1904, Rendel papers, box 170.

29 *Globe*, 15 June 1914.

30 Middlemas, *Master Builders*, pp. 254–8, 271. See my entry on Norton-Griffiths in *DBB*.

31 Baldwin papers 164; a first-rate account of Worthington-Evans by Winston Churchill, first published as an obituary tribute in the *Times* of 16 February 1931, is reprinted in Martin Gilbert, (ed.) *Winston S. Churchill*, companion vol. V, pt 2 (1918), pp. 271–3.

32 *Midland Advertiser*, 10 April and 25 December 1909; 8 January 1910.

33 Hobson, *Imperialism*, pp. 107, 111.

34 Madders diary, 14 June 1910, MBA.

35 Diary of Sir Maurice Hankey, 15 August 1917, quoted S. W. Roskill, *Hankey, Man of Secrets*, vol. 1 (1970), p. 423. The views of the group are summarised in Amery's letter to Lord Milner of 26 May 1915 in Amery, *Diaries*, vol. 1, p. 116.

36 Docker, speech of 27 May 1909, reported *Midland Advertiser*, 29 May 1909.

37 *Midland Advertiser*, 7 February and 14 March 1914; diary of Oakeley Arnold-Foster, 19 October 1904. BM Add. MS. 50340. On the bankruptcy of

Griffiths and Co. in 1914, see Department of Overseas Trade memorandum of 1 February 1924, FO 371/10092.

38 Amery, *Diaries*, vol. 1, p. 356; Docker to Hannon, 3 March 1920, H 12/1.

39 Roger Lancelyn Green, *A. E. W. Mason* (1952); Steel-Maitland to Docker, 29 July 1911, Steel-Maitland to Docker, 28 November 1911, Docker to Steel-Maitland, 30 November 1911, ASM 153/4/29, 58 and 68.

40 *Midland Advertiser*, 19 February 1910.

41 Sir Francis Oppenheimer, *Stranger Within* (1960), p. 214. Cf. D. Benjamin of New South Wales Retail Traders Association, 'Where Home Manufacturers Fail', *United Empire*, 13 (1922), pp. 625–7.

42 Thomas G. Patterson, 'American Businessmen and Consular Service Reform 1890–1906', *Business History Review*, 40 (1966), pp. 77–96; Morrison diary, 23 January 1910, Morrison papers 18; Anon., 'The Consular Service and its Wrongs'. *Quarterly Review*, 197 (1903), pp. 598–626; Percy F. Martin, 'British Consuls and British Trade', *Financial Review of Reviews*, 23 (1918), pp. 392–406.

43 Victor Wellesley, evidence of 17 March 1916 to Huth Jackson committee on post-war trade relations, in BM Add. MS. 42245.

44 Capt. J. K. V. Dible, memorandum of 31 May 1929, FO 371/13507.

45 Searle, *Quest for National Efficiency* pp. 36–8, 86–92, 176, 263; Merriman in *Pall Mall Gazette*, 1 December 1884; Lucy Masterman, *C. F. G. Masterman* (1939), p. 160.

46 *Midland Advertiser*, 23 November 1912.

47 *Birmingham Post*, 10 July 1944.

48 Docker's speech to Business League smoker at Wednesbury Town Hall, 21 November 1911, reported *Midland Advertiser*, 25 November 1911; Docker's speech in inaugural meeting of Business League at Tipton, 13 March 1911, reported *Midland Advertiser*, 18 March 1911.

49 W. D. Rubinstein, 'Wealth, Elites and Class Structure in Britain', *Past and Present*, 76 (1977), pp. 121 and 124.

50 S. G. Checkland, 'The Mind of the City 1870–1914', *Oxford Economic Papers*, 9 (1957), pp. 262–4. As to the personal elegance, see the example of that 'impeccable dandy' Lord Revelstoke of Baring Brothers: 'the exquisiteness of his brougham and horse and harness and coachman were such that the police instinctively cleared a way for him, as for royalty, regardless of the traffic': Christopher Sykes, *Nancy Astor* (1972), p. 70.

51 See Hirst's evidence to Tariff Commission, 1904, in TC 32.

52 Docker, letter in *Economist*, 7 February 1914; cf. H. Grahame Richards, 'A Ministry of Industry and Commerce', *Financial Review of Reviews*, 23 (1918), pp. 305–21.

53 Docker, speech to Business League at Wednesbury Town Hall, 3 May 1910, in *Midland Advertiser*, 7 May 1910.

54 For a discussion of the miscomprehension and antipathy between business men and the Foreign Office, see John S. Galbraith, *Mackinnon and East Africa 1878–95* (1972), pp. 33–7, 129 and *passim*; Sir Arthur Nicolson to Sir Gerard Lowther, 23 January 1911, FO 800/347; P. L. Gell to Milner, 16 July 1902, Milner papers 5.

55 Quoted Alfred M. Gollin, *The Observer and J. L. Garvin 1908–14* (1960), p. 103.

56 Gell to Milner, 14 March 1901, Milner papers 5.

57 Docker to Sir Algernon Firth (for forwarding to Asquith), 24 July 1912, printed *Midland Advertiser*, 17 August 1912; cf. Moisei Ostrogorski, *Democracy and the Organisation of Political Parties* (1902).

58 Richard Hyman, *The Workers Union* (1971), pp. 199–200; G. D. H. Cole, *Self-Government in Industry* (1917), p. 52.

59 Steel-Maitland to Grant, 3 September 1910, ASM 148/7/25; cf. Steel-Maitland to Milner, 19 February 1910, ASM 147/1/12.

60 E. H. Phelps Brown, *The Growth of British Industrial Relations 1906–14* (1959), pp. 137–41.

61 Amery, *Diaries*, vol. 1, pp. 64 and 85; K. D. Brown, 'The Trade Union Tariff Reform Association 1904–1913', *Journal of British Studies*, 9 (1969–70), pp. 141–53.

62 *Midland Advertiser*, 28 October 1911.

63 Docker, speech of 23 April 1912, reported *Midland Advertiser*, 27 April 1912.

64 Michael Bliss, '"Dyspepsia of the Mind": The Canadian Businessman and His Enemies', in David S. Macmillan (ed.), *Canadian Business History* (Toronto, 1972), pp. 183–4.

65 Ludford Docker to Hannon, 19 October 1923, H 14/2. Information from John Docker, 1980.

66 Sir Harris Spencer of the Midland Employers Federation speaking of Rogers, quoted *Midland Advertiser*, 21 December 1918. See also my entry on Rogers in *DBB*.

67 Steel-Maitland to Docker, 29 July 1911, ASM 153/4/29; my entry on Manville in *DBB*.

68 *Globe*, 17 July 1914.

69 *Midland Advertiser*, 17 August 1912; cf. Docker's essay in Chapman, *Labour and Capital after the War*, pp. 129–30.

70 William Ashley to Docker, 18 March 1908, Ashley Letterbooks in Birmingham University Collection; Michael Sanderson, *The Universities and British Industry 1850–1970* (1972), pp. 193–7; Docker, essay in Chapman, *Labour and Capital After the War*, pp. 138–9.

71 A. H. A. Knox-Little to Maxse, 17 August 1917, M 474; Thomas J. N. Hilken, *Engineering at Cambridge University 1783–1965* (1967), pp. 153 and 156; Lord Esher, *Journals and Letters*, vol. 3 (1938), p. 215.

72 Steel-Maitland, memorandum of conversation on 25 February 1909 with Councillor H. W. Pooler, ASM 94/2.

73 Steel-Maitland to Docker, 5 January 1911, ASM 164/2/149.

74 Docker to Steel-Maitland, 2 June 1912, ASM 156/319.

75 *Daily Mail*, 8 June 1912.

76 *Midland Advertiser*, 29 June 1912; *Birmingham Gazette*, 2 February 1914. The phraseology of the latter letter resembled a speech of Jesse Collings, the Birmingham Liberal Unionist leader, reported in *Birmingham Daily Post*, 27 October 1893: 'he spoke as a businessman, and all businessmen would agree with him that if they had talent and efficiency they would have to pay for it. It was cheap to pay for it. He was for economy as much as any man, but it was the best economy to have the best quality that they could get.' Quoted Jones, 'Public Pursuit of Private Profit?', p. 244.

77 Ludford Docker to Steel-Maitland, 28 June 1911, ASM 250/8. Dudley Docker to Steel-Maitland, 29 June 1911, ASM 250/61.

78 See, for example, Steel-Maitland to Bonar Law, 18 December 1914, BL 35/5/48.
79 A. J. P. Taylor, *Beaverbrook* (1972), p. 53.
80 Henderson to Steel-Maitland, 17 June 1912, ASM 80/2.
81 Steel-Maitland to Sir Reginald Ward Poole, 13 July 1925, ASM 111; Steel-Maitland to Henderson, 17 June 1912, ASM 80/2.
82 R. D. Blumenfeld to Bonar Law, 8 July 1912, BL 26/5/17.
83 Taylor, *Beaverbrook*, p. 74; Beaverbrook papers K/1; my entries on Dalziel and Henderson in *DBB*.
84 D. P. O'Brien, *Correspondence of Lord Overstone* vol. 2 (1971), p. 832; Stephen Koss, *Rise and Fall of Political Press in Britain*, vol. 1 (1981), pp. 45–6 and *passim*; Madge to Hewins, 3 December 1907, TC 24.
85 Quoted J. A. Spender and C. Asquith. *Life of Lord Oxford*, vol. 1 (1932), p. 32.
86 R. J. Minney, *Viscount Southwood* (1954), p. 178.
87 Cecil H. King, *Strictly Personal* (1969), pp. 85–6, 78.
88 Taylor, *Beaverbrook*, pp. 60–2.
89 Sir Malcolm Fraser to Bonar Law, 26 May 1914, BL 32/3/53.
90 Tom Driberg (Lord Bradwell), *Beaverbrook* (1956), p. 141.
91 Docker to Maxse, 11 February 1918, M 475/193.
92 Docker to Maxse, 20 April 1918, M 474/78. Emphasis in original.
93 Lady Rhondda (ed.), *D. A. Thomas, Viscount Rhondda* (1921), pp. 137–8.
94 *Globe*, 15 June, 24 June and 7 November 1914; 23 February 1915; 5 May 1916; 7 June 1918.
95 Henry Houston, *The Real Horatio Bottomley* (1923), pp. 128, 130–1; Julian Symons, *Horatio Bottomley* (1955), p. 220; House of Commons (hereafter HC) Debates, 75, col. 1393 (11 November 1915). For further details of the *Globe*'s staff and management at this time, see H. Simonis, *Street of Ink* (1917), pp. 96–7.
96 William Sutherland to Lloyd George, 7 December 1915, LG D1/1/10; Docker to Steel-Maitland, November 1915, ASM 165/2/125; Docker to Maxse, undated, M 477/20.
97 Amery, *Diaries*, vol. 1, p. 242.
98 *Globe*, 25 June 1914.
99 *Globe*, 12 February and 7 August 1915. For similar views, see F. S. Oliver, *Ordeal by Battle* (1915), pp. 192–3, 200–4, 217 and 221.
100 Docker, essay in Chapman, *Labour and Capital after the War*, p. 130.

5. The Great War 1914–18

1 Docker, speech of 1 June 1916, reported *Economist*, 3 June 1916; cf. Lloyd George's words to the first meeting of the government's new Reconstruction Committee on 16 March 1917: 'No such opportunity had ever been given to any nation before – not even by the French Revolution. The nation now was in a molten condition: it was malleable now, and would continue to be so for a short time after the War, but not for long' (Edwin Montagu papers AS–1–9). For detailed contemporary discussion of these themes see Adam Whyte and T. C. Elder, *The Underwar: Patriotic Policy in British Trade* (1914), and T. C. Elder, *The Coming Crash of Peace* (1916).

2 Evidence of Sir Clarendon Hyde to Balfour of Burleigh committee, 14 June 1917, BT 55/11.
3 Victor Wellesley, memorandum on Foreign Office Reconstruction, 30 October 1918, ASM 115/3.
4 Evidence of A. H. Preece to Parsons committee on electrical industry after the war, 24 May 1916, BT 55/20. The British manufacturer was 'an individualist in business' according to Whyte and Elder (*The Underwar*, p. 74): 'He finds much more joy in breaking than in making rings. Even when he stands to benefit from the close organisation of his trade, he has to be coaxed, bullied or driven into the fold.' Hugo Hirst's magazine, the *Britannic Review* (July 1915, pp. 309–10) compared German 'obedience to unity of direction' to 'English individualism': 'its procedure is slow, costly, wasteful and un-scientific when the community is ill-informed, but its very defects stimulate growth and initiative'.
5 Burton, I. Kaufman, 'The Organisational Dimension of United States Foreign Policy 1900–1920', *Business History Review*, 46 (1972), pp. 17–44; William H. Becker, *The Dynamics of Business-Government Relations: Industry and Exports 1893–1921* (1982); Burton Kaufman, *Efficiency and Expansion: Foreign Trade Organization in the Wilson Administration 1913–1921* (Westport, Conn., 1974).
6 *Journal of British Electrical and Allied Manufacturers Association*, January 1915, p. 1.
7 *Economist*, 3 June 1916.
8 Wellesley, memorandum of 30 October 1918, ASM 115/3.
9 R. K. Middlemas, *Politics in Industrial Society* (1979), pp. 18–20 and 123.
10 Interview with Lord Barnby, 12 November 1980.
11 Docker, speech of 1 June 1913, reported *Economist*, 3 June 1913.
12 The preceding account is based on a letter of Sir Edmund Wyldbore-Smith to Foreign Office, 16 February 1921, FO 371/6966. On a shipment of steel castings from the Henricot foundry in August and September 1914, see H. J. Farrow to Foreign Office, 11 September 1914, and Lincoln Chandler to Foreign Office, 30 September 1914, in FO 368/937.
13 Metropolitan Carriage to chairman of Defence of the Realm Act Lessees Commission, 2 June 1915; Docker to Steel-Maitland, 10 May 1916; Admiralty memorandum, which Steel-Maitland confidentially loaned to Docker, 14 June 1916; Docker to Steel-Maitland, 15 June and 19 June 1916, ASM 170/1, Mun. 4/5917.
14 See correspondence between Charles Palmer and Harold Smith of the Press Bureau published in the *Globe*, 10 September 1914. For the background to these scares, see David French, 'Spy Fever in Britain 1900–15'. *Historical Journal*, 21 (1978), pp. 355–70. The wartime opinions of a typical *Globe* reader are conveyed in an eccentric book by 'North Country Miner' (the pseudonym of Alfred James), *Six Months in Politics* (privately printed, 1917). A copy given by James to Sir Richard Cooper of the National party is now in the Library of the London School of Economics.
15 *Globe*, 26 and 30 October, and 2 November 1914.
16 *Financial News*, 26 October 1914, reprinted in the *Globe* that evening. See also Whyte and Elder, *The Underwar*, pp. 14, 23–4, 34 and *passim*.
17 HC Debates, 68, cols. 699–700. For the thinking of Lord Desart's pre-war

committee (1911–12) on Ánglo-German wartime trade, see David French,
British Economic and Strategic Planning 1905–1915 (1982), pp. 29–30, 61–4.

18 Docker to Steel-Maitland, 7 December 1914; Steel-Maitland to Bonar Law,
14 December 1914, BL 35/4/34. Further Amendment Acts to the legislation
on trading with the enemy were passed in July 1915 and January 1916, and
as described later the upshot of the latter Act was that the Board of Trade
wanted Docker to take over the previously German-owned Siemens electrical
works at Stafford.

19 Captain R. S. Hilton to Lord Moulton, 11 April 1915, Mun. 5/149. Sir
Hallewell Rogers was at this time chairman of the Gas Committee of
Birmingham Council, and was therefore Hilton's superior. On Hilton, see
Jonathan S. Boswell, *Business Policies in the Making* (1983), p. 101 and *passim*;
and my entry with Boswell on Hilton in *DBB*.

20 Docker to Steel-Maitland, 29 July 1915, ASM 165/1/179. Steel-Maitland
forwarded this letter to Bonar Law.

21 Docker to Steel-Maitland, 25 May 1915, ASM 165/1/536.

22 See Minutes of Deputation of Birmingham Munitions Output Executive to
Lloyd George, 28 May 1915, Mun. 5/149; Addison diary, 28 May 1915.
Officials at this meeting included Lord Elphinstone, G. M. Booth, William
Beveridge and Eric Geddes.

23 Addison diary, 5 June 1915.

24 Docker to Maxse, 10 December 1917, M 474/288. Emphasis in original.

25 Docker to Maxse, 8 April 1918, M 475/243.

26 Docker to Maxse, 8 April 1918, M 475/246.

27 Metropolitan Carriage to Director of Naval Contracts, 26 July 1915, Tennyson-
d'Eyncourt papers, box 45.

28 Churchill to Clementine Churchill, 23 February 1918. Gilbert, *Winston
Churchill*, companion vol. IV, pt 1 (1977), p. 253; Sir John Tilley, *London to
Tokyo* (1942), p. 89.

29 *Globe*, 6 March 1919; Docker to Maxse, 4 October 1918, M 475.

30 Charles Palmer to Bonar Law, 2 January 1914, BL 31/2/9.

31 Lord Birkenhead, *Frederick Edwin, Earl of Birkenhead*, vol. 2 (1935), p. 47. For
the historical background to this disagreement, see P. Towle, 'The Debate on
Wartime Censorship in Britain 1902–14', in Brian Bond and Ian Roy (eds.),
War and Society, vol. 1 (1975), pp. 103–13; Perceval Landon, 'War
Correspondents and Censorship', *Nineteenth Century*, 52 (1902), pp. 327–37.

32 Sir John Edwards-Moss to Lord Willoughby de Broke, 8 November 1915,
Willoughby de Broke papers 11/24. See also Leo Maxse, 'The Panic of
November 5 1915', *National Review*, 66 (December 1915), pp. 600–8.

33 Diary of Sir Maurice Hankey, 1 November and 8 December 1915, Hankey
papers 1/1. A few months later, another Cabinet Minister, Lord Curzon, said
'Kitchener is a nullity but he hangs on to office as it means pay': Lord Bertie
of Thame, memorandum of 12 April 1916, FO 800/175.

34 C. à Court Repington, *The First World War*, vol. 1 (1920), p. 67.

35 It was discussed in the House of Commons on 11 November 1915 (HC
Debates, 75), but Docker assured Steel-Maitland 'he had *nothing* to do with
the Commons debate', ASM 165/2/125. Asquith spoke in the debate, in
which the *Globe*'s case was put by the dissident Scottish Liberals, Pringle and
Hogge.

36 HC Debates, 75, col. 1405.
37 Sir William Sutherland to Lloyd George, 7 December 1915, LG D1/1/10.
38 Docker to Steel-Maitland, January 1916, ASM 170/1/153.
39 *Globe*, 1 February 1917; 'West Country Miner' (pseudonym of Alfred James), *Six Months in Politics* (1917), pp. 119–21.
40 A. H. A. Know-Little to Maxse, 17 August 1917, M 474; Wallace Wright to Maxse. (? August 1917) M 477; Docker to Maxse, 8 September 1917, M 474/191; Docker to Maxse, 1 October 1917, M 474/229; Docker to Mrs Kitty Maxse, 10 September 1918 or 1919, M 456/369; *Times*, 29 September 1917; Kenneth O. Morgan, *Consensus and Disunity* (1980), p. 237; Amery, *Diaries*, vol. 1, pp. 47, 56–7; Lady Donaldson of Kingsbridge, *The Marconi Scandal* (1962), pp. 88–9 and *passim*.
41 Sir Geoffrey Harmsworth and Reginald Pound, *Northcliffe* (1959), p. 585; Randolph Churchill, *Lord Derby* (1960), p. 314; Peter Fraser, *Lord Esher* (1973), pp. 376–8.
42 C. à Court Repington, *The First World War*, vol. 2 (1920), pp. 165, 313.
43 Maxse to Northcliffe, 15 April 1918; Docker to Maxse, 8 April 1918, M 475; Docker to Maxse, 20 April 1918, M 474.
44 Maxse to Derby, *c.* 5 March 1917; Docker to Maxse, 20 April 1918, M 474.
45 Docker to Maxse, 8 April 1918, M 475/245.
46 H. A. Gwynne to Sir Graham Greene, 24 October 1916, Gwynne papers, box 23; Stephen Roskill, *Naval policy between the Wars*, vol. 1 (1968), p. 361; Stephen Roskill, *Documents relating to the Naval Air Service* (1969), p. 81; Geoffrey Till, *Air Power and the Royal Navy* (1979), p. 114. Information for the *Globe* on Sinn Fein in Ireland was supplied by another Conservative MP: see Walter Guinness to Maxse, 21 January 1919, M 476.
47 Docker to Maxse, 11 February 1918, M 475/193; Docker to Maxse, 27 February 1918, M 475/199; Docker to Maxse, 1 April 1918, M 475/227.
48 *Globe*, 16 March 1917; 26 August 1918.
49 Steel-Maitland to Sir John Willoughby, 7 March 1917, ASM 174/484. See Hilaire Belloc's lines on 'The Grocer Hudson Kearley', *Collected Verse* (1970), p. 232.
50 Lord Devonport to Lloyd George, 8 December 1916, LG F15/2/1. Sir Stephen Tallents, *Man and Body* (1943), p. 230. See also José Harris, 'Bureaucrats and Businessmen in British Food Control 1916–19', in Kathleen Burk (ed.), *War and the State* (1982), pp. 139–41.
51 Leslie Hannah, *Electricity before Nationalisation* (1979), p. 68.
52 Lord Derby to Lloyd George, 25 January 1917, LG F14/4/18. Docker, however, welcomed Derby's replacement by Milner at the War Office: Docker to Maxse, 20 April 1918, M 474/78.
53 Steel-Maitland to Bonar Law, May 1916, ASM 170/1/1366.
54 Edwin Montagu to Lloyd George, 1 May 1917, Montagu papers AS/IV/3/687; LG F39/3/11.
55 Lord Reading to Lloyd George, 30 May 1917, LG F43/43/1/4.
56 Addison, *Four and a Half Years*, p. 468.
57 For Lord Kylsant's acquisition of the Elder Dempster group, see P. N. Davies, 'Group Enterprise: Strengths and Hazards', in S. Marriner (ed.), *Business and Businessmen* (1978), p. 147. Objections to cost investigations of books were very common among manufacturers. Lionel Hichens of Cammell Laird, who

was conspicuous for his opposition to all wartime profiteering, complained in 1916 that the accountants' methods were 'inquisitorial': he believed 'enquiry into costs is a new method of negotiating prices...open to abuse, as private and vital information may be conveyed to competitors': Mun. 4/6509.

58 Sir Arthur Duckham to Sir Herbert Hambling, 30 August 1917; Sir John Mann to Sir Herbert Hambling, 31 August 1917, Mun. 4/4175.
59 Sir Herbert Hambling to Sir John Mann, 31 August 1917, Mun. 4/4175.
60 Mann to Sir Laming Worthington-Evans, 27 August 1917, Mun. 4/4175.
61 Special meeting of Executive Council of FBI, 25 September 1918, and meeting of Executive Council of FBI. 9 October 1918, FBI C/3. For Docker's mild public strictures on excess profits duty and the munitions levy, see Chapman, *Labour and Capital after the War*, p. 131. Docker and his associates invested a generous portion of their war profits in government stock specially issued to fund munitions output. For example during Big Guns Week in October 1918, when there was a national campaign (organised on a municipal basis) for the public to buy War Bonds to be spent on heavy guns, BSA and MCWF both subscribed £500,000 each towards the campaign in Birmingham. The Midland Bank subscribed £100,000 there; Dudley Docker took £20,000, while MCWF directors such as Greg and Ludford Docker subscribed £5,000 each. *Birmingham Mail*, 21 October 1918.
62 John Charteris to Maxse, 30 September 1917, M 474/228. Churchill to Docker, telegram 17 April 1918. Churchill papers 15/116. See Gilbert, *Winston Churchill*, vol. 4 (1975), p. 106, and companion vol. IV, pt 1 (1977), p. 303.
63 Cab. 23/6; Gilbert, *Winston Churchill*, companion vol. IV, pt 1, p. 334.
64 Docker, in Chapman, *Labour and Capital after the War*, p. 132.
65 Report of Advisory Committee on Labour, Manufacture and Raw Materials (Employers), 21 May 1917, Mun. 5/53/300/89.
66 Mun. 5/53/300/87.
67 Churchill to Lloyd George, 28 August 1918, quoted Gilbert, *Winston Churchill*, companion vol. IV, pt 1 (1977), p. 379 (where, however, Sir Henry McCardie in mis-identified as Charles McCurdy).
68 Docker to Steel-Maitland, 25 May 1915, ASM 165/1/536.
69 Addison diary, 16 July 1915, Addison box 97.
70 Addison diary, 7 July 1915, Addison box 97. For a more general discussion of this topic, see Peter K. Cline, 'Eric Geddes and the Experiment with Businessmen in Government 1915–22', in Kenneth D. Brown, *Essays in Anti-Labour History* (1974), pp. 74–104.
71 Addison diary, 15 February 1918, Addison box 96.
72 *Globe*, 18 October 1917; Docker to Hannon, 3 July 1922, H 12/4; Docker to Maxse, 20 April 1918, M 474/78.

6. The Federation of British Industries and the British Commonwealth Union 1916–22

1 BEAMA, *The BEAMA Book: A History and Survey* (1926); BEAMA, *Twenty One Years* (1933), p. 9.
2 Sir Charles Macara, *Recollections* (1921), pp. 217–25; *Times*, 4 July 1913.

3 Docker to Steel-Maitland, 16 February 1914, ASM 162/21. See also Docker to Maxse, 20 April 1918, M 474/79: 'I don't often agree with Sir Chas Macara': and my entry on Rylands in *DBB*.

4 *Journal of BEAMA*, April 1915, had listed the purposes of a National Industrial Board as: to cover the world with British commercial representatives, to discuss reconstruction problems with Government, to foster science, industrial education and training, to remove class antagonism, to 'efface false distinctions and link both Science and Art' and generally to 'perform all the functions of a real Minister of Commerce' (p. 87). John Haworth, Secretary of the EPA, advanced similar views in *Journal of BEAMA*, July 1915, and also called for the establishment of industrial banks (pp. 140–2). Cf. the *Globe*, 25 April 1916; 'A completely representative National Industrial Federation would constitute the most effective Ministry of Commerce. A purely Government body for this purpose would be *de trop*.'

5 Docker's speech to BEAMA, at Birmingham and Midland Institute, 23 February 1916. Full text in *Globe*, 24 February 1916.

6 Reprinted in Elder, *The Coming Crash of Peace*, pp. 47–71.

7 *Journal of BEAMA*, July 1916, p. 135; my entry on Tait in *DBB*.

8 See Despatch of 25 January 1903 from Sir Constantine Phipps, Brussels. Text in Reports on the Constitution and Functions of Foreign Ministries of Commerce, Cd 1948 of 1904.

9 Docker, speech of 2 March 1917, reported *Economist*, 10 March 1917. Wallenberg had founded the Industrial Union (Sweden's equivalent of the FBI) around 1911, and was also founding president of the Swedish Taxpayers Union in January 1921. See Despatch 190 of Sir Colville Barclay, Stockholm, 6 April 1921, in FO 371/6953. The quotation about the Wallenberg family's power is taken from L. K. Jones' minute of 14 April 1921 in FO 371/6953. In Britain the Wallenbergs were represented by the British Bank of Northern Commerce.

10 *Economist*, 3 June 1916.

11 *Globe*, 21 July 1916.

12 Sir William White to Lord Salisbury, 15 April 1887, quoted Colin L. Smith, *The Embassy of Sir William White at Constantinople 1886–91* (1957), p. 126.

13 R. P. Hastings, 'Birmingham Labour Movement 1918–45', *Midland History*, 5 (1980), pp. 78–9; for an account of the founding, a list of the founding members and an account of their views, see *Morning Post*, 21 July 1916, and *Globe*, 25 September 1916.

14 Addison diary, 13 March 1917, Addison box 98.

15 For example, Arthur Churchman the tobacco manufacturer sent £10,000 of bearer bonds to Oldham a fortnight before getting his baronetcy in 1917. See Churchman to Steel-Maitland, 17 July 1917, and Steel-Maitland to Churchman, 21 July 1917, ASM 193/270.

16 Lord Barnby, interview 12 November 1980. See also my entries on Locock and Nugent in *DBB*.

17 Docker, quoted *Economist*, 3 June 1916.

18 R. T. Nugent, report of Conference on Overseas Organisation, 8 December 1919, Nugent papers. The title of Consular and Overseas Trade Committee used in the text is bastardised. Initially, in November 1916, it was known as the Consular Committee; in early 1917 it became the Overseas Trade

(Consular) Committee; and in September 1917 the Overseas Trade and Consular Committee. The full run of minutes is in FBI C/26. Aspects of this subject are covered by the evidence of Sir Vincent Caillard, R. T. Nugent and E. F. Oldham to the Balfour of Burleigh committee, 16 February 1917, in BT 55/10. Cf. Sir Hugo Hirst to Sir Edward Holden, 28 June 1916, in BT 55/21; Nugent to Steel-Maitland, 9 July 1919, in Nugent papers. Interesting evidence by Victor Wellesley about his experience as British Commercial Attaché in Spain (1908–10), given to the Huth Jackson committee on post-war trade relations (17 March 1916), is in Sir William Ashley's papers, BM Add. MS. 42245; cf. H. G. Richards, 'Germany and Spain', *Financial Review of Reviews*, 23 (1918), pp. 158–73.

19 Lincoln Chandler to Nugent, 30 October 1919, Nugent papers.
20 Docker, article in *Sunday Times*, 2 September 1917.
21 Nugent to Lloyd George, 15 January 1917, Nugent papers.
22 Docker, quoted *Economist*, 3 June 1916.
23 Rylands to Docker, 17 December 1919, Nugent papers.
24 Sir Joseph Lawrence to Bonar Law, 2 August 1918, BL 83/6/6.
25 Rylands, retiring address as president of FBI, 21 November 1921; cf. Nugent to Frank Moore, 24 April 1917, and Rylands to Chandler, 29 May 1917, all in Nugent papers.
26 Nugent to Sir Richard Vassar-Smith, 11 February 1918, Nugent papers; cf. Stokes to Nugent, 30 October 1916, FBI C/3.
27 Tennyson. *Stars and Markets*, pp. 145–51.
28 Docker, 'The Industrial Problem', pp. 302, 307.
29 The committee stated that the amount paid under profit-sharing schemes in 1901–11 amounted to only 5 per cent on wages paid. For a survey of profit-sharing schemes by the *Globe*'s city editor under Docker's proprietorship, see article by H. H. Bassett in *Financial Review of Reviews*, June 1913; cf. H. H. Bassett, *British Commerce* (1913), p. 153.
30 Report of Labour Committee, 17 November 1917, FBI C/84.
31 Amery, *Diaries*, vol. 1, p. 259.
32 Meeting of representatives of EEF and FBI's Labour Committee, 15 March 1918, FBI C/84.
33 Meeting of EEF and FBI representatives, 10 April 1918, FBI C/84. See lists of member companies of EEF (December 1917) and of NEF (January 1918) in Mun. 5/53/300/81. On the NCEO, see Middlemas, *Politics in Industrial Society*, pp. 113, 128, 146, 160. Docker retained an equivocal view of Smith, and in the mid-1920s advised the Minister of Labour that 'for personal reasons I should discount some of the opinions and advice of Sir Allan Smith': ASM 193/94/2.
34 Rodger F. Charles, *The Development of Industrial Relations in Britain 1911–1939* (1973), pp. 110–11; Addison, *Four and a Half Years*, pp. 434–5; G. D. H. Cole, *Self-Government in Industry* (1917), pp. 38–9 and *passim*. Papers relating to the establishment of Whitley Councils in the Birmingham area are in Sir William Ashley's papers, BM Add. MS. 42250.
35 *Globe*, 22 October 1917.
36 Docker, essay in Chapman, *Labour and Capital after the War*, p. 138.
37 Nugent to Caillard, 25 January 1919, Nugent papers.
38 Minutes of Executive Council meeting, 12 February 1919, FBI C/3.

39 Nugent to Docker, 15 March 1917, Nugent papers.
40 Rylands to Docker, 17 December 1919, Nugent papers. At the Executive Council meeting of 30 July 1919, F. C. Fairholme the managing director of the Sheffield steelmakers, Firths, opposed merging with BEPO as it was 'essentially a political body rather than an industrial, and it would be better for the Federation to build up its own Colonial connection rather than adopt the BEPO as a nucleus', FBI C/3.
41 Hiley to Nugent, 2 August 1919, Nugent papers.
42 Nugent to Rylands, 13 December 1919, Nugent papers.
43 Nugent to Rylands, 16 December 1919, Nugent papers.
44 Rylands to Nugent, 17 December 1919, Nugent papers.
45 Nugent to Oldham, 16 January 1920, Nugent papers.
46 Austen Chamberlain, *Politics from Inside* (1936), p. 43.
47 For Imperial Association of Commerce prospectus, see *North China Herald*, 3 August 1918; Nugent, memorandum of 15 May 1918, Nugent papers.
48 John A. Turner, 'The British Commonwealth Union and the General Election of 1918', *English Historical Review*, 93 (1978), pp. 528–59.
49 Sir Joseph Lawrence to Bonar Law, 2 August 1918, BL 83/6/6. Much other information in this and the next paragraph is taken from the minute books of the London Imperialists in the Hannon papers.
50 Rylands to Chandler, 29 May 1917, Nugent correspondence. The BCU recognised the truth of some of Rylands' criticisms when the General Purposes Committee, on 8 August 1918, laid a condition of 'strictest secrecy' on all parliamentary candidates supported by it. For Manville's public denial on 11 May 1920 that the FBI financed parliamentary candidates, see HC Debates, 129, col. 329.
51 Grant Morden to Hannon, 15 February 1932, H 16/1. For adverse comments on Morden, see Lord Robert Cecil to Steel-Maitland, October 1922, ASM 184/106; Lord Derby to Baldwin, 22 November 1929 (adding 'not a man with whom I would have any truck'), Baldwin papers 30. Other interesting references to Morden are in R. J. Minney, *Viscount Southwood* (1954).
52 Docker to Hannon, 26 December 1919 and 3 January 1920; Hannon to Docker, 30 December 1919, H 12/1. An excellent account of the British Cellulose scandal is D. C. Coleman, 'War Demand and Industrial Supply: The Dope Scandal 1915–19', in J. M. Winter (ed.), *War and Economic Development* (Cambridge, 1975).
53 Sir Richard Cooper, the National MP for Walsall, may have had business connections with Docker, since his letter dated 8 August 1916, to Docker, in FBI C/3, is headed Saltley (a Metropolitan Carriage factory). Though Cooper was a harsh critic of political corruption and the sale of honours, his own financial dealings were not irreproachable. See file of correspondence in BL 83/6/25. See Lord Croft, *My Life of Strife* (1949), and W. D. Rubenstein, 'Henry Page Croft and the National Party 1917–22', *Journal of Contemporary History*, 9 (1974); Lord Ampthill to J. O. P. Bland, 19 December 1917, Bland microfilm 11.
54 Sir Joseph Lawrence to Bonar Law, 2 August 1918, BL 83/6/6.
55 Minutes of General Purposes Committee of BCU, 13 June 1918 and 11 July 1918.
56 Minutes of General Purposes Committee of BCU, 18 July 1918. Docker to Hannon, 6 December 1918, H 11/3. This file contains fulls details of Beck's

candidature, including the early dealings with him, by Docker and Hiley, over Kingswinford.

57 Lawrence to Bonar Law, 2 August 1918, BL 83/6/6. Emphasis in original. The BCU's sponsorship of parliamentary candidates can be compared with those of the National Federation of Discharged and Demobilised Sailors and Soldiers: see Stephen Ward, 'The British Veterans Ticket of 1918', *Journal of British Studies*, 8 (1968) pp. 155–69.

58 On Gritten, see Sir Alexander Fuller-Acland-Hood to J. S. Sandars, 9 June 1910, Bodleian Eng. Hist. C/760; on Goff, see HC Debates, 15 December 1920, 136, cols. 565–6.

59 Gerald D. Feldman, 'German Big Business 1918–29', *American History Review*, 75 (1969), p. 49.

60 Hannon to Sir Hallewell Rogers, 19 December 1921, H 11/13.

61 Harold Duncan to Steel-Maitland, 28 May 1919, H 14/1; cf. Sir Herbert Williams, *Politics Grave and Gay* (1949), p. 74.

62 Docker to Sir Allan Smith, 9 October 1918, quoted Turner, 'The British Commonwealth Union', p. 543.

63 *Midland Advertiser*, 21 December 1918.

64 *Globe* editorials, 7 October, 5 November, 10 December and 12 December 1918.

65 Hannon to Page Croft, 19 August 1918, H 11/1.

66 *Globe*, 13 June 1919. A vivid account of Northumberland is in 'Janitor' (pseudonym of J. G. Lockhart and Mary Lyttleton (Lady Craik)), *The Feet of the Young Men* (1928), pp. 122–33. See also my entry on him in *DBB*.

67 Steel-Maitland to Sir Malcolm Fraser, 8 August 1919, ASM 182/410. Maxse had little interest in economic reconstruction problems, and was only with difficulty dissuaded by Docker from retiring as editorial consultant in January 1919. Docker to Maxse, 4 October 1918, M 475; Maxse to Docker, 15 January 1919; Docker to Maxse, 20 January 1919, M 476. In February 1920 Maxse gave four lectures at Caxton Hall, London, later published as *Politicians on the Warpath* (1920): the meetings were chaired by Sir Edward Carson, Docker, Lord Ampthill of the National Party and H. A. Gwynne, editor of the *Morning Post*.

68 Nugent to Rylands, 21 January 1920, Nugent papers.

69 Docker to Geddes, 11 December 1919, ASM 96/1/15.

70 Docker to Steel-Maitland, 26 December 1919, ASM 96/1/78.

71 Lincoln Chandler to Steel-Maitland, 18 December 1919, ASM 96/1/84.

72 *Times*, 17 December 1919.

73 Nugent to Rylands, 18 December 1919, Nugent papers. The minutes of the Wagon-Builders' committee are in FBI C/66.

74 ASM 276/6–9. For the background, see Michael Bentley, 'Liberal Politics and the Grey Conspiracy of 1921', *Historical Journal*, 20 (1977).

75 Docker to H. J. Fletcher, 4 March 1922, ASM 276/76.

76 H. Verdon Leonard to Steel-Maitland, 15 March 1922, ASM 276/76.

77 Captain Frederick Guest to J. T. Davies, 12 August 1919, LG F21/4/10. For a contemporary left-wing view of the subject, see the Independent Labour party's Information Committee's pamphlet, *Who Pays For The Attacks on Labour?* (1920).

78 Middlemas, *Politics in Industrial Society*, p. 132; Nugent to Rylands, 21 January 1920, Nugent papers.

79 Sir George Younger to Bonar Law, 16 August 1919, BL 98/1/8.

80 *Dictionary of Labour Biography*, vol. 4 (1977), pp. 204–6; H 13/4; Bernard Porter, *Critics of Empire* (1968), p. 124.
81 Caillard to Sir Allan Smith, 11 February 1919, H 11/4.
82 David Mitchell, *Queen Christabel* (1977), p. 272.
83 Hannon to Jessie Kenny, 29 November 1918; Hannon to Manville, 21 March 1919, H 11/5. Christabel Pankhurst to Maxse, 1 January 1919, M 476. See *Globe*, 11 December 1918.
84 Minutes of BCU General Purposes Committee, 25 July 1919; Hannon to Trevor Jones, 5 July 1919, H 11/13. As late as 1920 the BCU financed a feminist newspaper conditional on its right to nominate contributors to write articles attacking liquor nationalisation proposals; see Hannon to Mrs Oliver Strachey, 19 March 20, H 12/1.
85 Hannon to George Crosfield, 4 April 1919, H 11/13; Captain H. Willans to G. D. McCallum of Engineering Employers Federation, 6 March 1920, H 11/10; Hannon to Crosfield, 15 October 1920, H 12/1; Willans to McCallum, 23 October 1920, H 11/10.
86 John Stubbs, 'Lord Milner and Patriotic Labour 1914–18', *English Historical Review*, 87 (1972), pp. 717–54.
87 Victor Fisher to Steel-Maitland, 21 December 1916, ASM 548/2. Cf. Amery, *Diaries*, vol. 1, pp. 64, 85, 161. Fisher also obtained £200 from Walter Long, the Colonial Secretary, in 1918. See David Killingray, 'The Empire Resources Development Committee and West Africa 1916–20', *Journal of Imperial and Commonwealth History*, 10 (1982), p. 208. This interesting article throws other sidelights on the BCU.
88 Hannon, memorandum on Industrial Unrest, nd (1918), H 13/4.
89 Cf. S. R. Ward, 'Intelligence Surveillance of British Ex-Servicemen 1918–20', *Historical Journal*, 16 (1973), pp. 179–88.
90 Sir Hallewell Rogers to Lloyd George, 7 October 1920. Text in BCU minute books, H.
91 Middlemas, *Politics in Industrial Society*, p. 132.
92 Smith and Caillard, memorandum of 1 March 1920, under minutes of General Purposes Committee of BCU, 4 March 1920.
93 M. F. Armstrong to Cunliffe-Lister, 23 October 1925, Swin. 2/6. For a typical example of Hannon's gossipy indiscretion, in 1923, see Amery, *Diaries*, vol. 1, p. 337.
94 Sir Charles Petrie, *Sir Austen Chamberlain* (1940), pp. 150–1. As late as 1921 Docker was privately propounding a 'new scheme to run country on "Board of Directors" plan with big businessmen – non-politicians', Hannon noted in his diary of 26 January 1921, 'Vague – cannot see it possible.'
95 Paul Barton Johnson, *Land Fit for Heroes: The Planning of British Reconstruction 1916–1919* (Chicago, 1968), p. 412.
96 Hannon to Docker, 6 June 1919, H 14/2.
97 George Bowyer to Cecil Harmsworth, 5 April 1921; Oliver Harvey, minute of 8 April 1921, FO 371/6728.
98 Hannon to Horatio Bottomley, 1 November 1918, H 12/1. Interview with Lord Barnby, 12 November 1980.
99 *Globe*, 11 December 1918; the same article also endorsed C. Pankhurst. Lloyd-Greame (Cunliffe-Lister) wrote to Maxse on MCWF notepaper on 18 January 1919 about the government proposals on unemployment donations for discharged soldiers, presumably with a view to directing *Globe* editorial

comment to the subject, M 476. For Lloyd-Greame's views, see his article 'Empire Trade Development', *United Empire*, 13 (1922), pp. 223–30.

100 Hannon to George Hally, 5 February 1948, H 32/1.

101 Information from Mr John Docker and Lord Barnby, 1980.

102 Douglas Vickers' name does not appear, either, among those of the Conservative and Unionist MPs who attended the meeting at the Carlton Club in October 1922 which voted to kill Lloyd George's coalition government. See Robert Rhodes James (ed.), *Memoirs of a Conservative* (1969), pp. 129–33. Among recent British MPs who took their seat in Parliament, Douglas Vickers' record of silence was only surpassed by Sir Herbert Austin, MP for Kings Norton 1918–25, and by Frank McGuire, MP for Fermanagh and South Tyrone 1974–81. Other business men who scarcely uttered a word during their years as MPs included Hallewell Rogers, Davison Dalziel and the property dealer Sir Harry Mallaby-Deeley.

103 Lionel Hichens, quoted *Times*, 31 October 1918.

7. Diplomacy, the British Trade Corporation and the British Stockbrokers Trust 1916–25

1 Lord Faringdon on 5 July 1916, BT 55/32/FFT 1. The three reports of the Huth Jackson committee are in BT 55/121, but the minutes of evidence have not survived. A summary of Docker's evidence, compiled by Lord Faringdon, is in BT 55/32. A copy of these items, together with other working papers of the committee and the evidence of Victor Wellesley, are in Sir William Ashley's papers, BM Add. MS. 42245.

2 Lord Hardinge to Docker, 5 December 1916; Docker to Sir Edward Grey, 7 December 1916; Grey to Docker, 9 December 1916, FO 368/1853. For the context of Docker's wartime Foreign Office committees, see D. C. St M. Platt, *Finance, Trade and Politics in British Foreign Policy 1815–1914* (Oxford, 1976), pp. 378–80, 385–95.

3 There is interesting correspondence between Pennefather and Hewins in TC 18; and the official views of the Association of British Chambers of Commerce on consular reform can be found in Guildhall MSS. 14,476/8 and 14,476/9.

4 Wellesley, memorandum of 25 January 1917, FO 368/1853; Wellesley, minute of 26 April 1917, FO 368/1855.

5 Dudley Docker at committee meetings of 31 January and 13 February 1917, BT 60/1/3/15062.

6 Majority report on Foreign Trade and Consular Service, signed by Docker, Wellesley and Pennefather, 4 April 1917, FO 368/1854.

7 Faringdon to A. J. Balfour and Sir Albert Stanley, 18 April 1917; Wellesley minute of 26 April 1917, FO 368/1855.

8 Oppenheimer, *Stranger Within*, pp. 305, 321. For contemporary criticism of Foreign Office attitudes, see Percy F. Martin, 'British Diplomacy and Trade', *Quarterly Review*, 215 (1911), pp. 442–61.

9 Steel-Maitland to Lord Robert Cecil, 11 September 1917, ASM 115/1.

10 Sir William Clark to Steel-Maitland, 21 May 1919, ASM 115/1. Cf. Sir William Clark, 'Government and the Promotion Trade', *Journal of Public Administration*, 1 (1923).

11 Steel-Maitland to Lord Curzon, 6 and 7 May 1919; Steel-Maitland to Lord Robert Cecil, 13 May 1919, ASM 115/6.

12 Lord Norwich, *Old Men Forget* (1954), pp. 46, 99; Lord Vansittart, *The Mist Procession* (1958), p. 277.

13 Steel-Maitland to Lord Hardinge of Penshurst, 24 February 1919, ASM 115/6; Auckland Geddes to Steel-Maitland, 8 July 1919, ASM 115/7. Cf. Steel-Maitland to George Lloyd, 14 March 1919, ASM 182/319.

14 Report of committee to examine the Question of Government Machinery for dealing with Trade and Commerce, Cmd 319 of 1919. Completion of the report was delayed by the long absence of Sir Eyre Crowe in Paris: Sir Kenneth Lee to Steel-Maitland, 10 July 1919, ASM 174/822.

15 Sir Sidney Waterlow, minute of 6 July 1923, FO 371/8432. The DOT was recommended for abolition, as an economy measure, by the Geddes committee on national economy in 1922, but the proposal was abandoned after manufacturers like Lionel Hichens of Cammell Laird urged that DOT was 'of the greatest value to small and big firms alike' and far preferable to the 'old-fashioned system of muddle and inertia' that had previously prevailed. See his letter in the *Times*, 22 February 1927. Winston Churchill's Budget of April 1927 provided for the abolition of the DOT as a separate department in order to save the minister's salary, but after condemnation by the business community, the motion was withdrawn.

16 Sir Austen Chamberlain, minute of 24 April 1929, FO 371/13876.

17 David Killingray, 'The Empire Resources Development Committee and West Africa 1916–20', *Journal of Imperial and Commonwealth History*, 10 (1982), p. 206.

18 Its members were Lord Faringdon; Sir Basil Blackett, then a Treasury official and subsequently Director of the Bank of England 1929–35; Sir William Clark, then head of Commercial Intelligence at the Board of Trade, and later Comptroller of the Department of Overseas Trade; Gaspard Farrer of Barings; W. H. N. Goschen of the National Provincial Bank; Rt Hon. F. Huth Jackson, Director of the Bank of England 1892–1921; Walter Leaf and Hon. Rupert Beckett of the Westminster Bank; Hon. Algernon Mills of Glyn, Mills; (Sir) James Hope Simpson, of Liverpool and Martins Banks; and Dudley Docker of the Midland Bank. The minutes of evidence of the committee are in BT 55/32.

19 Report of the Departmental Committee on Financial Facilities for Trade, Cd 8346 of 1916. It was welcomed by the *Globe* on 23 September 1916. See also Anon., 'English and German Banking in Relation to Trade and Industry', *Quarterly Review*, 226 (1916), pp. 532–47.

20 *Economist*, 9 June 1917.

21 The list is in BT 13/83.

22 Docker, speech of 7 June 1917, reported in *Economist*, 9 June 1917.

23 Kaufman, 'Organisational Dimension of United States Foreign Policy', pp. 41–3.

24 J. T. Walton Newbold (afterwards communist MP for Motherwell), quoted Donald McCormick, *Pedlar of Death* (1965), p. 174.

25 Steel-Maitland to Lord Robert Cecil, 12 November 1917; minute by H. G. Brown, 2 November 1917, both in BT 60/1/13698.

26 'Industry and Finance', anonymous article in *Round Table*, 25 (1916), pp. 62–3. By 1913 the German dyestuffs industry was twenty-five times as large

as the British, producing 85 per cent of world output. Germany exported 80 per cent of its dyestuff production; 80 per cent of Britain's total domestic consumption of dyestuffs came from Germany.

27 Rubinstein, 'Wealth, Elites and Class Structure', p. 116. See also Checkland, 'The Mind of the City', pp. 265–6.

28 Faringdon, 5 July 1916, BT 55/32/FFT 1.

29 Meeting of Faringdon committee on financial facilities for trade, 5 July 1916, BT 55/32. For English bankers' unenterprising reluctance to open offices in Germany, see Oppenheimer, *Stranger Within*, p. 162. For a trenchant contemporary discussion of British joint-stock bankers' neglect of manufacturers, see Whyte and Elder, *The Underwar*, pp. 97–101. On BTC generally, see Sir Robert Inglis Palgrave, 'The British Trade Corporation', *Quarterly Review*, 229 (1918), pp. 143–53.

30 HC Debates, 93, cols. 1840–1, 1857, 1865 and 1870.

31 Docker, speech to MCWF shareholders, 7 June 1917, in *Economist*, 9 June 1917. The *Globe* attacked the Corporation's parliamentary critics on 18 May as 'carping and inconclusive' and 'malevolent', and on 23 May wrote of 'interested and captious opposition' which 'emanate[d] chiefly in quarters that cannot fairly be described as industrial either in the sense of employers or employed'.

32 *Globe*, 20 June 1917.

33 Sir Edward Carson, memorandum of 21 January 1918, Cab. 21/108.

34 Meade Falkner to Lord Rendel, 4 January 1901, Armstrong papers 1192.

35 Sir Algernon Firth, letter of 25 June 1917, Guildhall Ms. 14,476/9.

36 Steel-Maitland to Reginald Morcom, 30 September 1918, ASM 181/399.

37 BT 13/83.

38 Lord Faringdon to Foreign Office, 14 January 1918; Sir William Clark to Victor Wellesley, 30 August 1918, FO 368/1968.

39 R. P. T. Davenport-Hines, 'Vickers' Balkan Conscience', *Business History*, 25 (1983).

40 Dickson to Foreign Office, 8 April 1919, FO 371/4140; *Economist*, 14 February 1920. A few months earlier, control of the National Bank of Turkey was being sought jointly by Barclays Bank and the Ionian Bank. Steel-Maitland to Clark, 18 October 1918. ASM 115/9.

41 Caillard to Sir Thomas Sanderson, 25 September 1888, FO 64/4264.

42 Marian Kent, 'Agent of Empire? The National Bank of Turkey and British Foreign Policy', *Historical Journal*, 18 (1975), p. 381.

43 Sir Henry Babington Smith to Sir Edward Grey, 11 June 1913, FO 371/1826.

44 This phrase comes from a memorandum by Count Leon Ostrorog, the legal adviser of Vickers, who lived in Turkey, 1893–1914, which was enclosed with Caillard to Lloyd George, 7 October 1918, LG F6/1/19.

45 *Economist*, 8 February 1919.

46 See G. R. G. Allen, 'A Ghost from Gallipoli', *Journal of Royal United Services Institution*, 108 (1963), pp. 137–8.

47 Sir William Clark to Steel-Maitland, 23 August 1918, ASM 115/9.

48 Mun. 4/5739; cf. Severin de Bilinski's three articles, 'Financial and Political Conditions in France', *Financial Review of Reviews*, 21 (1928), 'Financial and Political Conditions in Europe', *ibid.*, 22 (1929) and 'National cum Internationalism', *ibid.*

49 Sir Henry Babington Smith to Foreign Office, 23 March 1920, FO 371/4973; cf. *Documents of British Foreign Policy*, 1st ser., vol. 2 (1948), p. 796. On BTC in Russia see also L. W. M. Kettle, *The Allies and the Russian Collapse 1917–1918* (1981), pp. 176–219, 231–47, and L. W. M. Kettle, *Sidney Reilly, the True Story* (1983), pp. 73–90 and especially 86–8.

50 *Documents of British Foreign Policy*, 1st ser., vol. 3 (1949), p. 797.

51 Lord Faringdon to Lord Curzon, 6 August 1920, FO 371/4973.

52 WO 32/5697; Gilbert, Winston Churchill, companion vol. IV, pt 2 (1977), p. 722; Kettle, *Sidney Reilly*, p. 79.

53 Sir John Tilley to Faringdon, 12 August 1920, FO 371/4973.

54 Despatch 354 of Sir Beilby Alston, former Deputy High Commissioner in Siberia and then British Minister in Tokio, 29 August 1919. *Documents of British Foreign Policy*, 1st ser., vol. 3 (1949), pp. 534–5.

55 Memorandum by Sir John Pratt, 21 August 1929, in *Documents of British Foreign Policy*, 2nd ser., vol. 8 (1960), pp. 154–63; cf. L. H. Drakeford to G. E. Morrison, letter 18 July 1917, in Morrison, *Correspondence*, vol. 2, p. 617; Roberta Albert Dayer, *Bankers and Diplomats* (1981).

56 Steel-Maitland to F. C. Goodenough, 5 November 1919, ASM 182/345.

57 *Economist*, 8 February 1919. Correspondence on the Portuguese Trade Corporation is in ASM 193/252.

58 *Economist*, 14 February 1920; Patrick Hannon, letter in *Times*, 5 February 1925.

59 Kent, 'Agent of Empire?', p. 389.

60 Wallscourt Hely-Hutchinson Waters, *Secret and Confidential* (1926), p. 363. Emphasis in original.

61 Faringdon to Lord Lloyd, 2 February 1925, FO 371/10867.

62 Faringdon to Lord Tyrrell, 11 March 1926; Overseas Trade Despatch 73 from E. Murray Harvey, Belgrade, 18 March 1926; Despatches 418 and 458 of Sir Coleridge Kennard, Belgrade, 26 October and 25 November 1926. All in FO 371/11412.

63 *London and China Telegraph*, 1 and 8 November 1920; *Financier*, 5 November 1920; memorandum of 9 May 1919 by Archibald Rose, Commercial Secretary at Peking Legation, FO 370/5343; Sir James Kemnal to H. E. Metcalf, 8 April 1921, S. Springer to J. O. P. Bland, 5 July 1921, Bland microfilm, reel 10. A summary by Lord Faringdon of Kemnal's evidence to the Huth Jackson committee is in BT 55/32/FFT 2. On Manzi-Fé, see my entry on Lord Cobbold in *DBB*.

64 Steel-Maitland to Docker, 20 December 1922, ASM 193/184/519.

65 Anon., 'Industry and Finance', pp. 53–7; Checkland, 'The Mind of the City', p. 266.

66 Sir Nutcombe Hume, quoted Laurie Dennett, *The Charterhouse Group* (1979), p. 14. The great fraudulent company promotor E. T. Hooley claimed on his bankruptcy in 1898 to have paid £40,000 in 'systematic blackmailing' to one newspaper, and £10,000 for an article in another newspaper: see P. L. Payne, 'The Emergence of the Large Scale Company in Great Britain 1870–1914', *Economic History Review*, 20 (1967), p. 521. More generally on this subject see William Reader, *A House in the City* (1979), pp. 66–122; H. Osborne O'Hagan, *Leaves from My Life* (1929), pp. 103–11; Hugh E. M. Stutfield, 'The Company Monger's Elysium', *National Review*, 26 (1895), pp. 836–48; S. F. Van Oss, 'The Gold Mining Madness in the City', *Nineteenth*

Century, 38 (1895), pp. 537–47; S. F. Van Oss, 'The Westralian Mining Boom', *Nineteenth Century*, 40 (1896), pp. 711–20; Hugh E. M. Stutfield, 'The Higher Rascality', *National Review*, 31 (1898), pp. 75–86; W. R. Lawson, 'Company Promoting à la Mode', *National Review*, 32 (1898), pp. 103–15; Hugh E. M. Stutfield, 'The Company Scandal: A City view', *National Review*, 32 (1898), pp. 574–84; S. F. Van Oss, 'The Limited Company Craze', *Nineteenth Century*, 43 (1898), pp. 731–44; W. R. Lawson, 'The Inventor's Opportunity', *National Review*, 36 (1900), pp. 261–72; W. R. Lawson, 'Stock Jobbing Companies', *National Review*, 35 (1901), pp. 869–81; Anon., 'The Game of Speculation', *Quarterly Review*, 197 (1903), pp. 88–114; 'Whitaker Wright Finance', *Blackwood's Magazine*, 175 (1904), pp. 397–409.

67 *Economist*, 19 January and 9 February 1918. See also William A. Thomas, *The Provincial Stock Exchanges* (1973), pp. 251–2.
68 Diary of Sir Edward Holden, 16 October 1912, MBA.
69 Docker to Hannon, 19 July 1921, and Hannon to Docker, 22 July 1921, H 12/8. The parliamentary chairman of the Asquithians was George Lambert, whom Docker knew 'quite well'. Crammond was Cantor lecturer at the Royal Society of Arts in 1918; his lectures, analysing the effect of war on the British economy and reconstruction possibilities, were published by the Society as a pamphlet in 1918. For a fuller list of his writings see bibliography.
70 By 1920 BST had already underwritten one issue alone worth £16 million, and it was an increasingly prominent issuing house after 1924. See chapter 10 n50 (p. 272). BST's paid-up capital in 1929 was £538,212; it was absorbed in 1954 by Phillips, Hill, Higginson.
71 Docker, in Chapman, *Labour and Capital after the War*, p. 133; Docker, 'The Large View in Business', p. 300.

8. Armaments, electricity and rolling-stock 1917–29

1 Evidence of Sir Clarendon Hyde before Balfour of Burleigh committee, 14 June 1917, BT 55/11.
2 A. L. Levine, *Industrial Retardation in Britain 1880–1914* (1967), pp. 31, 39.
3 Hirst, memorandum of December 1920, Hewins 76/259.
4 Cd 9072 of 1918; minutes of evidence to this committee are in BT 55/20 and 21.
5 The quotations are by James Devonshire, a member of the Parsons committee, examining A. H. Payne on 19 October 1916, BT 55/20. There are various scattered references in the papers of the Parsons committee to Vickers' attempts in 1916 to buy Siemens.
6 R. E. Catterall, 'Electrical Engineering', in N. K. Buxton and D. H. Aldcroft, *British Industry between the Wars* (1979), pp. 241, 251, 256 and 271.
7 Robert Jones and Oliver J. D. Marriott, *Anatomy of a Merger* (1970), pp. 58–60; FBI papers; *Statist*, 17 May 1919.
8 *Times*, 22 March 1915; *Times Engineering Supplement*, 24 May 1905.
9 BT 55/11.
10 Steel-Maitland to Lord Devonport, 6 January 1914, ASM 162/196. In 1913–14 Hiley had sought a new job as manager of the Port of London Authority; Amery, *Diaries*, vol. 1, p. 143; Hannon diary, 20 January 1921.
11 Steel-Maitland to Lord Curzon of Kedleston, 10 July 1919, ASM 121/4/261.

12 Addison, *Four and a Half Years*, p. 468.
13 *Vickers News*, October 1919.
14 Docker to Lord Robert Cecil, 16 December 1918, FO 382/1837.
15 *Times*, 28 April 1915.
16 Trebilcock, *Vickers Brothers*, pp. 27, 30. See the case of Admiral Sir Windham Hornby, chairman of Hotchkiss, who dropped dead aged eighty-seven at their annual general meeting in 1899 whilst explaining the dismissal of their managing director.
17 Alfred P. Sloan, *My Years with General Motors* (1963), p. 4. Sloan was president for twelve years and chairman for nineteen years of General Motors.
18 *Arms and Explosives*, 1 August 1919.
19 W. Seymour Leslie, *The Jerome Connexion* (1964), pp. 117–18.
20 Report to Minister of Munitions by Committee of Enquiry into Royal Ordnance Factories, Woolwich, chaired by Rt Hon. Thomas McKinnon Wood, dated 22 November 1918, Cmd 229 of 1919, p. 8.
21 Alfred D. Chandler, *The Visible Hand*, (1977), p. 414.
22 *Arms and Explosives*, December 1909.
23 Caillard, memorandum to Vickers board on proposed merger with Metropolitan Carriage, January 1919, Vickers (hereafter V) microfilm R 325.
24 Memorandum to Sir V. Caillard on MCWF by auditors, 7 February 1919, V microfilm R 326; Hannah, *Rise of Corporate Economy*, p. 118.
25 Caillard, memorandum to board of Vickers on proposed merger with MCWF, January 1919, V microfilm R 325.
26 Caillard to Hewins, 19 May 1919, Hewins 74/158; meeting of Grand Council of FBI, 18 June 1919, FBI C/1; Repington, *The First World War*, vol. 1, p. 521; *Times*, 25 March 1919.
27 General P. I. Balinsky to Caillard, 30 April 1922, V microfilm R 241.
28 *Statist*, 12 December 1925.
29 Charles Wilson, *History of Unilever*, vol. 1 (1954), pp. 243–54: for the optimistic business forecasts of Lord Weir, Lord Inverforth and Stanley Baldwin in February 1919, see Amery, *Diaries*, vol. 1, p. 257.
30 Col. A. T. Maxwell to J. D. Scott, interview 14 May 1959, Vickers file 269.
31 On his long-term hopes for Metrovic, see Sir Philip Nash, 'Wanted: An Imperial Power Policy', *Empire Review*, 40 (1924), pp. 505–8. On Hiley and Hatry, see the Marquess of Winchester, *Statesmen, Financiers and Felons* (Monte Carlo, 1935), pp. 250–4.
32 J. D. Scott, *Vickers, a History*, (1962), p. 157.
33 *Economist*, 22 December 1928.
34 Sir A. J. Grant, *Steel and Ships* (1950), p. 66; for an account of Charles Spencer, chairman of Cravens, in July 1921, see Charles à Court Repington, *After the War* (1922), p. 351.
35 Alex Richardson, *Vickers Sons & Maxim: Their Works and Manufactures* (1902), p. 1.
36 Scott, *Vickers*, p. 47.
37 Minutes of Evidence to Royal Commission on Private Manufacture of and Trade in Arms, Cmd 5292 of 1936.
38 The head agreement between Vickers and City of Bristol Corporation was dated 1 July 1927, and provided for a complete generating station at Portishead. Vickers' tender price was £605,522. The provisional price for

building work was £128,700, This and subsidiary agreements of 1926–7 are in Vickers papers box of agreements BRA–BRI.

39 Douglas Vickers, speech at River Don Works, Sheffield, 24 March 1919. Text in *Economist*, 29 March 1919.

40 Sir Pierce Lacy to Sir M. W. Jenkinson, letter 31 May 1935, V microfilm R. 275.

41 Sir James Reid Young, interview with J. D. Scott, 26 May 1959, Vickers file 61. HC Debates, 144, col. 1310.

42 Caillard memorandum of 27 April 1920. V microfilm R 275. For fuller details and analysis, see R. P. T. Davenport-Hines, 'British Armaments Industry during Disarmament 1918–36', Cambridge PhD, 1979.

43 Douglas Vickers, speech in *Times*, 20 July 1922; R. H. Selbie to Sir George Beharrell, 19 November 1919; Docker to Selbie, 9 December 1919, Metro. 1/35; board minutes of 8 January and 12 February 1920, Metro. 10/28; Wyldbore-Smith to Selbie, 2 March 1922, Metro. 1/351/36.

44 Vickers' holding in Secheron was written down almost to nothing in 1923. See memorandum on Electric Holdings of 22 February 1927 in V microfilm R 322.

45 At the board meeting of 26 September 1919, it was agreed that the Swiss Bankverein lend Vickers the necessary money at 1 per cent above the Swiss bank rate.

46 BEAMA, *Combines and Trusts* (1927), pp. 45–6.

47 Docker, memorandum of 7 November 1919, V microfilm R 275.

48 Sloan, *My Years with General Motors*, pp. 26–7, 42.

49 Docker to D. Vickers, letter 15 April 1920, V microfilm R 275.

50 Docker to D. Vickers, letter 24 April 1920, V microfilm R 275.

51 Hankey in Minutes of Evidence to Royal Commission on Private Manufacture of and Trade in Arms, p. 721.

52 Winston Churchill, House of Commons, 15 November 1915, HC Debates, 75, col. 1515.

53 Committee on Industry and Trade, *Survey of Further Factors in Industrial and Commercial Efficiency* (HMSO 1928), p. 174. Emphasis in original.

54 *Ibid.*, p. 180.

55 Caillard, memorandum of 27 April 1920, V microfilm R 275.

56 R. A. Church, *Herbert Austin* (1979), p. 185.

57 *Statist*, 8 November 1919.

58 Sir James Reid Young in interview with J. D. Scott, 26 May 1959, Vickers file 4.

59 Church, *Herbert Austin*, pp. 103–5; Z. E. Lambert and R. J. Wyatt, *Lord Austin* (1968), pp. 153–4; P. W. S. Andrews and E. Brunner, *Lord Nuffield* (1955).

60 D. Vickers, speech 15 April 1925, *Vickers News*, May 1925.

61 Zaharoff to McKenna and Docker, letter 24 November 1925, V microfilm R 315.

62 W. Seymour Leslie, *The Jerome Connexion* (1964), p. 117. If the origins of the Advisory Committee seem obscure, it is worth noting that Charles Craven (Vickers' Barrow director) did not know officially of the existence of the committee at the end of November 1925. Douglas Vickers had not told him of it (Craven to Jenkinson, letter 29 November 1925, V microfilm R 315). Vickers' Finance Committee had, since July 1924, comprised Caillard,

Dawson, D. Vickers, Herbert Lawrence and Wyldbore-Smith. Of these, Wyldbore-Smith was an out-and-out Docker man; Lawrence was a City banker, generally in agreement with Docker; Dawson's position is characteristically hard to assess, but he was not as die-hard against Docker as Caillard.

63 Much of the text of the report of the Advisory Committee is in *Economist*, 12 December 1925. See also *Investors' Chronicle*, 12 December 1925.

64 Jenkinson to Zaharoff, letter 16 December 1925, V microfilm R 315.

65 Zaharoff to Docker and McKenna, letter 24 November 1925, V microfilm R 315.

66 See my entries on Birch, Dawnay, Jenkinson and Lawrence in *DBB*.

67 *Vickers News*, December 1929.

68 Jenkinson to Zaharoff, letter 16 August 1927, V microfilm R 333.

69 Zaharoff to Jenkinson, letter 16 August 1927, V microfilm R 333.

70 Zaharoff to Jenkinson, letter 19 August 1927, V microfilm R 333.

71 Members appointed to the Armaments Shipbuilding Board in 1926 were Buckham, Craven, Dawson, Oliver Vickers, George Taylor and Jenkinson. The industrial management board was formed in 1926 comprising M. B. U. Dewar of MCWF, Bernard Docker, Sadler (the general manager of Vickers, who soon retired through illness), Nash of Metrovic, T. L. Taylor of Taylor Brothers, Wyldbore-Smith, Yule and Jenkinson. Dudley Docker was an honorary member. (Wyldbore-Smith and Jenkinson sat on the rolling-stock sub-committee; Yule and Jenkinson sat on the electrical sub-committee.) The finance management board originally appointed in 1926 comprised Caillard, Cartwright, Vincent Vicker, Yule and Webster Jenkinson. The first three of these left the Vickers board in 1926–7, and were replaced by Sim and Lawrence.

72 Sir G. T. Buckham, report on Vickers-Armstrongs, 17 March 1928, V microfilm R 339.

73 Birch to Lawrence, 10 February 1928, V microfilm R 286.

74 George W. Vickers, memorandum on reorganisation of plant, 13 February 1928, V microfilm R 339.

75 Trebilcock, *Vickers Brothers*, p. 21; Scott, *Vickers*, p. 189.

76 PSO 358. Sir H. A. Lawrence to Sir M. P. A. Hankey, letter 7 October 1932, Supp. 3/43.

77 Docker to Lawrence, letter 8 February 1928, V microfilm R 276.

78 BEAMA, *Combines and Trusts*, pp. 96–7.

79 Sir John Pratt, memorandum of luncheon with Docker, 30 January 1929, in FO 371/13897.

80 Lawrence to Docker, letter 13 February 1928, V microfilm R 276. Jones and Marriott, *Anatomy of a Merger*, pp. 94–5. Swope was not the first American with such ambitions. The financier, Henry Villard, associated with the Deutsche Bank of Berlin, Siemens-Halske and American Westinghouse, had long before wanted to create 'a world cartel'. Chandler, *Visible Hand*, p. 427.

81 Docker to Lawrence, letter 8 February 1928, V microfilm R 276.

82 Docker to Lawrence, letter 13 February 1928, V microfilm R 276.

83 Swope to Lawrence, letter 14 February 1928, V microfilm R 276.

84 Sim to Swope, letter 15 February 1928; Swope to Sim, letter 15 February 1928, V microfilm R 276.

85 Swope to Lawrence, letter 16 February 1928, V microfilm R 276.

86 Docker to Lawrence, letter 14 February 1928, V microfilm R 276.
87 *Times* (22 February 1928) stated that it had been 'officially informed that Mr Dudley Docker has acquired from Vickers Ltd the control of Metropolitan-Vickers'.
88 Lawrence to Swope, telegram 14 March 1928, V microfilm R 276.
89 Swope (in Chicago) to Lawrence, telegram 15 March 1928, V microfilm R 276. Jones and Marriot (p. 99) attribute to Swope a telegram of similar meaning but different wording – presumably a version received by Morgan Grenfell.
90 Docker to G. R. T. Taylor, letter 15 March 1928, V microfilm R 276.
91 *Times*, 17 March 1928. Cf. *New York Times*, 2 May 1928. In fact GE of America kept all but 40,000 Ordinary shares, worth £50,500, which were passed to Docker as payment for his help of the American firm, Jones and Marriott, p. 98.
92 Guy Dawnay (of Vickers-Armstrongs), *The Times*, 27 January 1943.
93 G. R. T. Taylor, New York, to D. Docker, letter April 1928. Lawrence considered this a private letter, whose despatch he should not stop, but judged such recrimination to be idle, V microfilm R 276.
94 CP 77 (28). 'Electrical Development and American Capital', by Wilfred Ashley, 9 March 1928, Cab. 24/193. Ashley to Churchill, 15 March 1928, Treasury papers 172/1626.
95 G. Walker, 'The Development and Organisation of A.E.I.', in R. S. Edwards and H. Townshend (eds.), *Business Enterprise* (1958), pp. 307–13.
96 On the Russian arrest of the Metrovic engineers, see *Documents of British Foreign Policy*, 2nd ser., vol. 7 (1958), pp. 300–585, 779–808; a more succinct account is given by Lord Strang in *Home and Abroad* (1956).
97 Sir John Pratt, memorandum of 30 January 1929, with Wellesley's minute of 2 February, FO 371/13897.
98 Jenkinson to Lawrence, letter 23 August 1933, V microfilm R 323.
99 Sir Hugo Cunliffe-Owen to Beaverbrook, 5 April 1934; Beaverbrook to Cunliffe-Owen, 10 April 1934; *Daily Express*, 4 and 5 April 1934; Beaverbrook papers C/107.
100 Jenkinson to Lawrence, letter 4 September 1934, reporting conversation with Sir Guy Granet of AEI, V microfilm R 323.
101 Jenkinson, memorandum comparing financial position of MCWF at 31 March 1919 and 31 December 1927, dated 2 July 1928, V microfilm R 324.
102 Report on capacity of works in rolling-stock group in relation to market requirements, 1928, V microfilm R 325.
103 Lawrence to Jenkinson, letter 11 September 1927, V microfilm R 323.
104 Birch to Craven, letter 16 November 1931, V microfilm K 162. Cf. Winston Churchill, memorandum of 1 November 1918: 'The foundation of the munitions budget is tonnage; the ground floor is steel; and the limiting factor in the construction is labour': quoted *History of Ministry of Munitions*, vol. 2, pt 1, (nd (*c.* 1921–2)), p. 95.
105 G. R. T. Taylor, memorandum of 9 March 1928, V microfilm R 339.
106 Sir G. T. Buckham, report of Vickers-Armstrongs and steel, 17 March 1928, V microfilm R 339.
107 Jenkinson to Lawrence, 12 September 1927, V microfilm R 323.
108 Jenkinson to Lawrence, 22 February 1928, V microfilm R 276.
109 McKenna to Jenkinson, 23 February 1928, V microfilm R 276.

110 Col A. T. Maxwell to J. D. Scott, 14 May 1959, Vickers file 269.
111 Jenkinson to McKenna, 9 March 1928, V microfilm R 276.
112 G. R. T. Taylor to Docker, 14 March 1928, repeating the message from Docker which he had passed on orally to Lawrence, V microfilm R 276.
113 G. R. T. Taylor, memorandum of 9 March 1928, V microfilm R 339.
114 Buckham, memorandum on Vickers-Armstrongs and steel interests, 17 March 1928, V microfilm R 339.
115 *Economist*, 22 December 1928.
116 Birch, memorandum on English Steel Corporation, 4 January 1929, V microfilm R 334.
117 Birch, memorandum of 28 November 1929, V microfilm R 334. Cf. Birch to Lawrence, letter 3 December 1929: the Taylors told Birch 'with some heat that the Vickers-Armstrongs board had nothing whatever to do with the organisation of the English Steel Corporation, and they would be in no way consulted', V microfilm R 334.
118 Jenkinson to Neilson, letter 3 March 1930, V microfilm R 344.
119 Report on works development of English Steel Corporation, 26 November 1931, by Sir George Hadcock and Sir James Cooper, directors of Vickers-Armstrongs, V microfilm R 344.
120 Birch to Craven, letter 16 November 1931, V microfilm K 162.
121 *Economist*, 2 April 1932; Scott, *Vickers*, pp. 193–5.
122 Capt. G. D. Burton, note on capacity of Metropolitan-Cammell factories, 29 April 1929, V microfilm R 325.
123 Standard Steel Cars then had a maximum annual capacity of 60,000 freight cars and 1,200 passenger cars; Pullman shops in 1930 had a capacity of 44,500 freight cars and 1,800 passenger cars. See O'Connor, *Mellon's Millions*, p. 282.
124 Caillard, memorandum on proposed merger with MCWF, January 1919, V microfilm R 325.

9. Inter-war politics 1922–39

1   Hilton Young to Lloyd George, 26 September 1921, LG F28/8/2.
2   His appeal is in H 11/13.
3   Docker at Conference of BCU, 8 November 1923, H 13/3.
4   Docker's written appeal to BCU members, 21 November 1923, H 13/3.
5   Gilbert, *Winston Churchill*, companion vol. V, pt 1 (1980), p. 326; Amery to Baldwin, 10 April 1927, Baldwin papers 28.
6   Hankey to Lloyd George, 24 March 1921, Cab. 63/31; Metropolitan Railway board minutes of 9 December 1920, and 20 January, 10 and 31 March, and 28 April 1921, Metro. 10/28.
7   J. C. C. Davidson to Bonar Law, 24 March 1921, BL 107/1/4.
8   J. C. C. Davidson to Baldwin, 14 May 1940, Baldwin papers 174.
9   Steel-Maitland to Arthur Glazebrook, 27 June 1923, ASM 185/283.
10 Sir G. B. Sansom to Sir Edward Crowe, 12 October 1934, Baldwin papers 32.
11 Docker to Lloyd-Greame, 5 October 1925, Swin. 2/6.
12 There is an immense amount of material on the case in the Hannon, Swinton and Steel-Maitland papers. Harold Duncan (1885–1962) was an undoubted adventurer who nevertheless became Legal Adviser to the Dominions Office and Colonial Office (1943–5), and died a QC and KCMG.

13 Docker to Hannon, 21 July 1925, H 12/6.

14 Amery, *Diaries*, vol. 1 (1980), pp. 18, 439, 449, 542.

15 Steel-Maitland, memorandum on iron and steel industry of December 1928, Baldwin papers 29.

16 Amery, *Diaries*, vol. 1, pp. 571–2.

17 Docker to Sir Hugo Cunliffe-Owen, 15 April 1930, Beaverbrook papers C/107.

18 Caillard to Hewins, 10 October 1921, Hewins 78/4. Docker to Gretton, 21 November 1930, Hewins 83/178. Gretton to Hewins, 23 December 1930. Hewins 93/176. On Gretton, see my entry in *DBB*.

19 Docker to Cunliffe-Owen, 15 April 1930, Beaverbrook papers C/107. Cf. my entry on Cunliffe-Owen in *DBB*.

20 Sir Edward Crowe to Sir George Sansom, 21 June 1934, FO 371/18114; on the FBI mission, see Paul Haggie, *Britannia at Bay* (1981), p. 76; Ann Trotter, *Britain and East Asia 1933–1937* (1975), pp. 115–31, my entry on Barnby in *DBB*.

21 T. C. Barker and Michael Robbins, *History of London Transport*, vol. 2 (1974), p. 279.

22 Steel-Maitland, memorandum of conversation with Dudley Docker on 31 March 1925, ASM 387/24. This interview is mentioned, a little misleadingly, by R. K. Middlemas (*Politics in Industrial Society*, pp. 194, 480), where an incorrect reference to the source in the Steel-Maitland papers is given. There is no evidence that all of the men listed by Middlemas as having been consulted at this time actually did meet Steel-Maitland: for example, P. J. Pybus of English Electric (whom Middlemas misnames Arthur Pybus). As to India, Docker regarded it as a misfortune that the educated pupil there 'turns his back on industry and not infrequently desires to become a "pleader", a profession already overstocked'. Docker, 'The Large View in Business', p. 300.

23 Docker to Steel-Maitland, 6 May 1926, ASM 111.

24 Steel-Maitland to Baldwin, 11 October 1926, Baldwin papers 7.

25 Ramsay MacDonald to Sir John Corcoran of National Union of Manufacturers, 20 November 1929 (a letter which he did not dare send!), MacDonald papers 30/69/672.

26 Foreign Office memorandum, 'Changing Conditions in British Foreign Policy', 26 November 1931, CP 301(31), CAB 24/225. I owe this reference to Dr Patrick Salmon of the University of Newcastle-upon-Tyne.

27 Christopher Thorne, *The Limits of Foreign Policy* (1972), p. 52.

28 Wellesley, minute of 8 June 1923, FO 371/8432.

29 The preceding paragraphs are based upon Sir Walford Selby's minute of a conversation with Docker on 4 February 1931, and on Wellesley's memorandum in FO 371/15671.

30 D. G. Boadle, 'The Formation of the Foreign Office Economic Relations Section 1930–7, *Historical Journal*, 20 (1977), p. 920.

31 Anthony Powell, *Faces in My Time* (1980), pp. 209–11.

32 Norman Rose, *Vansittart* (1978), p. 100. On Sir Warren Fisher's interference in other senior appointments at the Foreign Office, see Lord Avon, *Facing the Dictators* (1962), pp. 319–20, 521.

33 Robertson to Steel-Maitland, 27 January 1929, ASM 253/665.

34 Docker to Cunliffe-Lister, 23 November 1927, Swin. 2/12; Docker to Wargrave, 19 July 1928, Wargrave papers; Docker to Steel-Maitland, 29 July 1915, ASM 165/1/179.

35 Davidson to Cunliffe-Lister, 11 February 1929, Swin. 2/14.
36 Steel-Maitland to Peacock and Weir, 12 May 1929, ASM 121/4/48.
37 Steel-Maitland to Vansittart, 12 May 1929, ASM 121/4/46.
38 Docker to Steel-Maitland, 21 November 1927, ASM 253/225. For the subscriptions of Brotherton and Broughton to party funds, see Robert Rhodes James, *Memoirs of a Conservative* (1969), p. 291. Broughton in fact died before his intended elevation to the peerage, and his son was created Baron Fairhaven later in 1929.
39 Bernard Docker to Hannon, 29 October 1941; Hannon to Ernest Brown, 30 December 1941, H 36/4.

10. International electrical and railway trusts 1914–44

1 *Documents of British Foreign Policy*, 1st ser., vol. 20 (1976), p. 726.
2 Hugo Hirst's evidence to Tariff Commission, February 1921, TC 1.
3 Hannon diary, 8 February 1921.
4 Hirst, evidence to Tariff Commission, February 1921, TC 1.
5 *Documents of British Foreign Policy*, 1st ser., vol. 20 (1976), pp. 683–4.
6 Hannon diary, 26 January 1921.
7 Jones and Marriott, *Anatomy of a Merger*, p. 94.
8 Hannon diary, 8 February 1921.
9 The preceding paragraph is based upon Heineman's obituary in *New York Times*, 2 February 1962; a report on Heineman in 1939 by the British Embassy in Brussels in FO 371/22877; George Gay and H. H. Fisher, *Public Relations of the Commission of Relief in Belgium*, 2 vols. (1929); Count Richard Coudenhove-Kalergi, *Crusade for Pan-Europe* (New York, 1943), p. 123; Ludovico Toeplitz, *Il Banchiere* (Milan, 1963), pp. 54–6; information from Mr John Docker; evidence of W. Rutherford (28 June 1916) and A. W. Tait (13 July 1916) to Parsons committee on electrical trade after the war, in BT 55/20; Simon Katzellenbogen, *Railways and the Copper Mines of Katanga* (Oxford, 1973), p. 113.
10 *Société Générale de Belgique 1822–1972* (1972), p. 55.
11 Material for the preceding two paragraphs comes from the essay on Belgium in Rondo Cameron, *Banking in the Early Stages of Industrialisation* (1967); from the evidence of Baron de Chazal in April 1917 to the Balfour of Burleigh committee in BT 55/11; from Sir Peter Rylands' speech of 1 November 1922 to the FBI sub-committee on foreign exchanges in FBI C/65; and from a memorandum of 22 January 1930 on Belgian rationalisation by N. S. Reyntiens of the British Embassy in Brussels in BT 56/14.
12 Amery, *Diaries*, vol. 1, p. 260. For contemporary attitudes to German economic penetration of Belgium, see Jules Claes and J. Holland Rose, *The German Mole* (1915).
13 BEAMA, *Combines and Trusts*, pp. 43–4, 55, 59.
14 See, for example, Sir Edmund Wyldbore-Smith to Foreign Office, 16 February 1922, FO 371/7376.
15 Lloyd-Greame to Cambó, 25 October 1924; Heineman to Lloyd-Greame, 24 November 1924, Swin. 2/4; Sir Malcolm Robertson to Cunliffe-Lister, 13 April 1927, Swin. 2/12; Cunliffe-Lister to Baldwin, 13 August 1925, Baldwin

papers 18; C. J. W. Torr, memorandum of 12 April 1927, R. L. Craigie, minute of 23 April 1927, FO 371/11959; Sir Malcolm Robertson, memorandum of 16 March 1929; Sir Miles Lampson, minute of 24 December 1929, FO 371/13464.

16 Jacques de Launay (ed.), *Louis Loucheur: Carnets Secrets 1908–32* (Paris, 1962), pp. 5–14, 177, 183–4; Toeplitz, *Il Banchiere*, pp. 139–43.

17 BL 111/20/94.

18 Despatch 261 of Sir Eric Phipps, Paris, 4 February 1924, FO 371/10533; R. K. Middlemas and John Barnes, *Baldwin* (1969), pp. 155, 186; Coudenhove-Kalergi, *Crusade for Pan-Europe*, pp. 119–24; Sir Maurice Hankey to Robin Hankey, letter 5 September 1929, quoted S. W. Roskill, *Hankey, Man of Secrets*, vol. 2 (1972), p. 488; Lord Mersey, *A Picture of Life* (1941), p. 328. On cartel diplomacy generally, see Stephen A. Schuker, *The End of French Predominance in Europe: The Financial Crisis of 1924 and the Adoption of the Dawes Plan* (Chapel Hill, North Carolina, 1976).

19 Despatch 645 from Sir Ronald Graham (Rome), 28 July 1925, FO 371/10914; Despatch 518 from Graham, 1 August 1929, FO 371/13679; Despatch 142 from Graham, 21 February 1930, FO 371/14421. See also Cesare Sartori, 'Giuseppe Volpi di Misurata e i Rapporti Finanzari del Gruppo SADE con gli USA 1918–1930', *Ricerche Storiche*, 9 (1979), pp. 426–38.

20 Hugh Thomas, *The Spanish Civil War* (1961), p. 9; Toeplitz, *Il Banchiere*, pp. 139–43.

21 Minute of H. Brooks, 8 July 1920; Despatch 494 of Sir Esme Howard, 23 July 1920, FO 371/4803. Annual Report on Spanish Personalities (1926) in FO 371/11945.

22 Commercial Despatch 34 of Sir Maurice de Bunsen, 26 March 1912, FO 368/725; John Brooks, *New Yorker*, 21 May 1979, p. 42.

23 Sir George Grahame to Cunliffe-Lister, 10 January 1929, Swin. 2/14.

24 A long and readable account of March's intrigue over Barcelona Traction is John Brooks, 'Annals of Finance', *New Yorker*, 21 May and 28 May 1979.

25 Webster Jenkinson is mentioned very favourably in Docker to Steel-Maitland, 5 February 1920, ASM 96/1/198.

26 BEAMA, *Combines and Trusts*, p. 98.

27 R. E. Catterall, 'Electrical Engineering', in N. K. Buxton and D. H. Aldcroft (eds.), *British Industry between the Wars* (1979), p. 271.

28 Docker to Cunliffe-Lister, 8 April 1927, FO 371/11959. For Docker's introduction to Sofina to the Metropolitan Railway, see R. H. Selbie to Heineman, 29 March 1924; Selbie to Docker, 27 May 1924, with enclosure of Della Riccia's report; Heineman to Selbie, 28 June 1924, with Docker's annotations; Heineman to J. S. Anderson, 24 December 1931. All in Metro. 10/833.

29 Rongé to H. O. Chalkley, 3 May 1927, FO 371/11959.

30 C. J. W. Torr, memorandum of 12 April 1927, FO 371/11959; Sir Malcolm Robertson to Cunliffe-Lister, 13 April 1927, Swin. 2/12; Robertson, memorandum of 16 March 1929, FO 371/13464.

31 Papers relating to Sofina's capital reconstruction of 1928–9, given by Docker to Sir Ronald Lindsay, are in FO 371/13876; *Times*, 31 January 1929.

32 Webster Jenkinson to Sir Herbert Lawrence, 20 September 1929, V microfilm R 329.

33 Sir George Grahame to Sir Austen Chamberlain, 12 November 1927, FO 371/12366; Jack Murray to Chamberlain, 13 February 1928, FO 371/12365.

34 Roskill, *Hankey*, vol. 2, pp. 420–4. It is possible that Docker wanted Chilcott's help in Egyptian business because the latter was known to hold strong private influence on the Foreign Secretary, Austen Chamberlain.

35 Lord Lloyd to Sir Austen Chamberlain, 21 April 1928, FO 371/13140.

36 Lord Tyrrell to Chamberlain, 14 February 1928, FO 371/13140.

37 Docker, memorandum on Production of Hydro-Electric Energy in Egypt, 10 April 1929; Sir Ronald Lindsay's note of interview with Docker, 11 April 1929; Mark Patrick to Lindsay, 19 April 1929 (giving account of an interview with General Nash of Metrovic), FO 371/13876.

38 Sir Edward Crowe to Jack Murray, 21 December 1927, FO 371/12367.

39 Middlemas, *Master Builders*, pp. 294–5; Herbert Addison, *Sun and Shadow at Aswan* (1959), pp. 81 *et seq.*; Lord Lloyd to Sir Ronald Lindsay, 21 April 1929, FO 371/13877.

40 Annual Report of Personalities in Egypt and the Sudan for 1930, FO 371/15421; Lord Woolton, *Memoirs* (1959), pp. 235–7.

41 *Documents of British Foreign Policy*, 1st ser., vol. 22 (1980), pp. 698–9.

42 Vernon Watlington to Dawson, 28 February 1929 (photograph); Watlington to Dawson, 4 March 1929; Watlington to Dawson, 5 March 1929, FO 371/13877.

43 Lloyd to Lindsay, 21 April and 5 May 1929, FO 371/13877; memorandum by Egyptian Department, 6 February 1931, FO 371/15420; see my entry on Pybus in *DBB*.

44 Roland Nugent, memorandum of conversation with Steel-Maitland, 26 October 1917, Nugent papers.

45 Duke of Atholl, speech in House of Lords, 11 December 1929, HL Debates, 75, col. 1176; Gordon Waterfield, *Professional Diplomat* (1973), pp. 146–56.

46 Minute of Sir Lancelot Oliphant, 13 February 1931, FO 371/15420.

47 Cecil (Lord) Farrer to Sir Maurice Peterson, 10 May 1932, FO 371/16125.

48 Despatch 463 of Sir Percy Loraine, Cairo, 7 May 1931, FO 371/15420.

49 Memorandum by Major Ralph Glyn, MP, soliciting a peerage for Dalziel, sent to Sir Austen Chamberlain in May 1926, FO 371/11859. See also my entries on Dalziel and Arthur Grenfell in *DBB*.

50 Jack Murray to Sir Austen Chamberlain, 13 February 1928, FO 371/12365. BST raised £2 million 6 per cent guaranteed first mortgage debenture stock for Cook's in 1927–8.

51 Hyde diary, 10 February 1931, 12 February 1931, 23 February 1931, 24 April 1931, MBA.

52 Despatch 25 from Sir Charles Bentinck (Lima), 28 February 1929, FO 371/13507.

11. Birmingham Small Arms 1918–44

1 BSA 4/5/1; see also George H. Frost, *Munitions of War: Record of Work of the BSA and Daimler Companies 1914–18* (Birmingham, 1921).

2 Geoffrey Robinson, MP, 'The Lessons of Meriden', *Spectator*, 15 July 1978.

3 Addison, *Four and a Half Years*, p. 290; Repington, *The First World War*, vol.

1, p. 494; Amery, *Diaries*, vol. 1, p. 143. All these comments refer to Chamberlain's dismal performance as Director of National Service in 1916–17, but his weakness at business strategy originated from exactly the same faults. For Docker's more favourable assessment of Chamberlain and the manpower problem, see Docker to Maxse, 6 February 1918, M 475/189. This letter is based upon the views of Chamberlain's deputy, Hiley. No reference is made here to his interference in foreign policy during 1938 to 1939, which is best explained by Maurice Cowling, *The Impact of Hitler* (1975), and by *Documents of British Foreign Policy*, 2nd ser. vol. 18 (1980), p. ix.

4 For Rogers, see Hannon diary, 5 January 1921; for Walker see Madders diary, 22 February 1912, MBA.

5 Lord Fisher to Churchill, 2 March 1915, Adm. 116/1681.

6 See Holden's obituary by Professor E. N. da D. Andrade in *Obituaries of Fellows of the Royal Society*, vol. 2 (1938), pp. 367–9.

7 Quoted C. P. Kindleberger, *Economic Growth in France and Britain* (1964), p. 158. Cf. W. J. Reader, *I.C.I.*, vol. 2 (1975), pp. 5, 77, and Leslie Hannah, *Electricity before Nationalisation* (1979), pp. 39, 42, 151, 175, for examples of arrogant and exclusive engineers treating marketing with contempt; W. J. Baker, *A History of the Marconi Company* (1970), p. 156.

8 *Economist*, 11 October 1919.

9 *Economist*, 29 April 1922.

10 *Economist*, 7 January 1922.

11 On Shaw's career, see *Times* obituary, 4 October 1977.

12 Holt-Thomas to Sir Sefton Brancker, 6 May 1926, Baldwin papers 20.

13 In April 1920, Holt-Thomas contributed two serialised articles to *The Times* entitled 'A Year's Commercial Flying', which contain information on the London–Paris service. Under the Post Office vote for 1920, £75,000 was allotted to finance aerial mail; the Post Office charged 2½ shillings per letter forwarded aerially. See also his article 'Commercial Transportation and High-Speed Services by Air', *Ways and Means*, 1, 12 April 1919, pp. 173–4.

14 *Aeroplane*, 8 October 1930.

15 Martin, memorandum of 20 January 1920, BSA 1/2/42. Martin consulted a London accountant, A. W. Tait, who replied ambiguously that the sale price should not be judged in the light of Airco's apparent asset value of £2,082,238, still less of its wartime earnings, but by the future adaptability of Airco's business to BSA's purposes. See Tait to Martin, 21 January 1920, BSA 1/2/42, and my entry on Tait in *DBB*.

16 Holt-Thomas to Sir Sefton Brancker, 6 May 1926, Baldwin papers 20. Cf. Peter Fearon, 'Aircraft Manufacturing', in N. K. Buxton and D. H. Aldcroft (eds.), *British Industry between the Wars* (1979), p. 219; Sir Geoffrey de Havilland, *Sky Fever* (1961).

17 *Economist*, 6 November 1920; see also Robin Higham, *Britain's Imperial Air Routes 1918–39* (1960), pp. 29–34.

18 Quoted *Economist*, 22 April 1922.

19 One of the other appointments to the Birmingham Advisory Committee, in 1933, was Sir William Stratford Dugdale, grandson of the W. S. Dugdale whose election agent in North Warwickshire in 1832 had been Docker's father-in-law, J. B. Hebbert.

20 Astbury diary, 6 July 1932 (this request was apparently unsuccessful), MBA.

21 Sir John Corcoran to Sir Noel Birch, 17 March 1925, WO 32/5660. See also Corcoran to Sir Daniel Neylan, 30 October 1922. Mun. 4/6225.

22 BSA to Cunliffe-Lister, 24 July 1925, FO 371/10975.

23 G. Westel to Hannon, 1 November 1923, H 22/3.

24 Hannon to Sir Laming Worthington-Evans, 31 December 1924, H 31/1; BSA 3/3/22.

25 Hannon to Worthington-Evans, 13 March 1925, WO 32/5660.

26 Record of meeting at House of Commons on 19 March 1925, WO 32/5660; cf. note on BSA and Soley proposals, nd (?1930), WO 32/4956.

27 R. A. Rotherham to Worthington-Evans, 23 April 1925, WO 32/5660.

28 Sir Noel Birch, minute of 2 May 1924, WO 32/4956.

29 Sir Herbert Creedy to Sir George Barstow, 18 November 1925, WO 32/5660. When the Ministry of Munitions had a similar but fruitless agreement for the sale of surplus armaments with Armstrongs and Vickers in 1921, Sir William Larke had minuted to Lord Inverforth on 14 January 1921, 'the Department could not employ the methods of negotiation which are a condition of success in securing this business in many countries'. This tripartite agreement of January 1921 was cancelled by mutual consent in October 1921 after it had failed to yield serious business. The depressed state of the world arms trade was conveyed by J. P. Davison of Armstrongs: 'he regarded hardly any of the enquiries as genuine at the present time: they were nearly all either from Commission Agents who were on the make, or from Governments of poor repute who did not wish to pay for the goods before delivery, which was...unacceptable'. D. H. Hall, minute of 19 September 1921, Mun. 4/6069.

30 Henry Tarrant in interview with Sir John Corcoran, 14 April 1925, WO 32/5660.

31 Bernard Draper to Financial Member of Army Council, 21 April 1925, WO 32/5660.

32 See Ball's evidence to Royal Commission on Private Manufacture of Arms, 6 February 1936. Also Geoffrey Burton to Sir Frederick Bovenschen, 9 July 1935; and Burton to BSA board, 31 October 1935, BSA 3/3/23.

33 BSA 3/3/30.

34 BSA 3/3/22.

35 John Ball to Lord Shinwell, 21 February 1930, WO 32/4956.

36 Quoted Robert Skidelsky, Oswald Mosley (1975), p. 196.

37 Bird and Hutton-Stott, Lanchester Motor Cars, pp. 169, 181–2; Arthur Pollen, memorandum of April 1921, BSA 19A/1/2/43.

38 M. Miller and R. A. Church, 'Motor Manufacturing', in N. K. Buxton and D. H. Aldcroft (eds.), British Industry between the Wars (1979), p. 210.

39 Griffiths to Martin, 8 September 1931, H 31/1.

40 Sir Robert Vansittart and Sir Victor Wellesley, minutes of 2 March 1927, FO 371/11964. Emphasis in original.

41 Sidney Pollard, The Wasting of the British Economy (1982), p. 84.

42 Bird and Hutton-Stott, Lanchester Motor Cars, pp. 179, 184. In June 1929 a London financier called James Dunning (1873–1931) had begun trying to arrange the merger of the Rover, Lanchester and Standard companies, but nothing came of the scheme. He envisaged transferring all production to the Standard works at Coventry, and closing the Rover and Lanchester factories.

See A. P. Young memorandum on proposed rationalisation scheme for British motor industry, 23 April 1930, Bank of England archives, SMT 3/249.

43 Manville to Hannon, 10 April 1931; Hannon to Martin, 13 May 1931, H 31/1.

44 Hon. Barnaby Howard, *Times*, 26 August 1961. Herbert was replaced as managing director of the cycle and motor division by James Leek in 1935, and subsequently entered business at Beira (1943) and Umtali (1948). See also Leo Maxse, 'The *Baralong* Case', *National Review*, 66 (1915), pp. 922–50, which judged that Herbert 'merely appears to have constituted himself the executioner of certain murderers caught *flagrante delicto*' (p. 924).

45 Astbury diary, 1 July 1932, MBA.

46 Pollen to Hannon, 15 August 1932, H 31/1.

47 Pollen to Hannon, 7 December 1932, H 31/1.

48 Hannon to Martin, 10 December 1932, H 31/1. See also S. W. Roskill, *Beatty, the Last Naval Hero* (1980), pp. 63, 66.

49 Astbury diary, 4 July 1932, MBA.

50 Astbury diary, 1 July 1932, MBA.

51 Astbury diary, 3 November 1932, MBA.

52 Hannon to Wood, 4 October 1932, H 31/1.

53 Martin to Hannon, 9 December 1932, H 31/1.

54 Hannon to Martin, 7 December 1932, H 31/1.

55 Hannon to Martin, 10 December, H 31/1. See my entry on Pollen in *DBB*.

56 Addison, *Four and a Half Years*, pp. 96, 207, 442. Dr P. L. Cottrell of Leicester University is preparing a study of the 117 Old Broad Street group and its successors. See my entry on Alexander Roger in *DBB*.

57 Sir Alexander Roger, memorandum on BSA organisation, 13 December 1932; Martin to Hannon, 14 December 1932, H 31/1.

58 Wood to Hannon, 19 February 1933, H 31/1.

59 Wood to Hannon, 26 October 1933, H 31/1.

60 Hannon to Wood, 19 December 1933, H 31/1.

61 Hannon, memorandum on BSA administration, 13 December 1933, H 31/1.

62 Astbury diary, 16 February 1940, MBA.

63 Hannon, aide-memoire of lunch with Burton, 30 June 1944, H 35/4. Lord Woolton on his first meeting with Docker described him as 'a most vigorous personality' (diary, 9 March 1941) and later as 'a grand old man, very influential in the City' (diary, 11 April 1942). Docker in 1942–3 helped organise an attempt to instal Woolton as McKenna's successor as Midland Bank's chairman. Docker believed that Woolton's popularity as 'Uncle Fred', the broadcasting Minister of Food, would enable him to resist post-war attacks from socialists of Stafford Cripp's kidney. See diary 9 September 1942, 3 April and 3 July 1943.

64 Lady Docker, *Norah* (1969), pp. 12, 62.

65 Sir Bernard Docker to Lord Woolton, 18 November 1949, Woolton papers 54/1.

66 Copies of the *The Docker Digest*, of Lady Docker's autographed photograph, etc, are in Woolton papers 54/1. Lord Woolton was a friend of Bernard Docker, and sometime director of BSA, Elrafin and Birmingham Railway Carriage and Wagon Co. Other correspondence on the BSA crisis of 1956 is in H 31/1.

67 Lady Docker, *Norah*, pp. 215–16; private information.
68 Binder Hamlyn to H. C. Rose, 4 October 1960, Woolton papers 54/1.

12. Conclusion

1 W. D. Rubinstein, 'British Millionaires 1809–1949', *Bulletin of Institute of Historical Research*, 47 (1974), p. 221.
2 R. H. Tawney, *The Acquisitive Society* (1961 edn), p. 39.
3 R. Musil, *The Man without Qualities*, vol. 1 (1979 edn), p. 12.

Bibliography

Unpublished papers

Lord Addison (Bodleian Library, Oxford).
Admiralty (Public Record Office).
Armstrong Whitworth and Co. (Tyne and Wear Record Office, Newcastle).
H. O. Arnold-Forster (British Library).
Sir William Ashley (Birmingham University and British Library).
Lord Baldwin of Bewdley (Cambridge University Library).
Lord Beaverbrook (House of Lords Record Office).
J. O. P. Bland (Thomas Fisher Library, Toronto University).
Birmingham Small Arms (Warwick University Modern Records Centre).
Board of Trade (Public Record Office).
Cabinet Office (Public Record Office).
T. A. K. Elliott (Mrs Thea Elliott, Burford).
Federation of British Industries (Warwick University Modern Record Centre).
Foreign Office (Public Record Office).
H. A. Gwynne (Bodleian Library, Oxford).
Lord Hankey (Churchill College, Cambridge).
Sir Patrick Hannon (House of Lords Record Office).
W. A. S. Hewins (Sheffield University Library).
Bonar Law (House of Lords Record Office).
D. Lloyd George (House of Lords Record Office).
London, Brighton and South Coast Railway (Public Record Office).
Ramsay MacDonald (Public Record Office).
Leo Maxse (West Sussex County Record Office, Chichester).
Metropolitan Railway (Greater London Record Office).
Midland Bank (Poultry, London EC2).
Lord Milner (Bodleian Library, Oxford).
Ministry of Munitions (Public Record Office).
Ministry of Reconstruction (Public Record Office).
Ministry of Transport (Public Record Office).
Edwin Montagu (Trinity College, Cambridge).
G. E. Morrison (State Library of New South Wales, Sydney).
Sir Roland Nugent (FBI collection at Warwick University).
Lord Rendel (Tyne and Wear Record Office, Newcastle).

Securities Management Trust (Bank of England).
Southern Railway (Public Record Office).
Sir Arthur Steel-Maitland (Scottish Record Office, Edinburgh).
Stratford-on-Avon and Midland Junction Railway (Public Record Office).
Lord Swinton (Churchill College, Cambridge).
Tariff Commission (British Library of Political and Economic Science).
Sir Eustace Tennyson-d'Eyncourt (National Maritime Museum, Greenwich).
Treasury (Public Record Office).
Vickers (Millbank, London SW1).
Lord Wargrave (House of Lords Record Office).
War Office (Public Record Office).
Lord Willoughby de Broke (House of Lords Record Office).
Lord Woolton (Bodleian Library, Oxford).

The existence at the Harris Museum, Preston, Lancashire, of the papers of the
United Electric Car Company, and of associated electrical businesses in which
Docker was associated with George Flett and others after 1902, came to notice too
late for use in this book. This Preston collection contains much material of direct
relevance to Docker's career.

Books
Place of publication is London unless otherwise indicated.
Addison, Christopher, *Politics from Within*. 2 vols., 1924.
Addison, Christopher, *Four and a Half Years*. 2 vols. in 1, 1934.
Allen, G. C., *The Industrial Development of Birmingham and the Black Country*. 1927.
Amery, Leopold C. M. S., *Diaries 1896–1929*. Vol. 1, 1980.
Barnett, Correlli, *The Collapse of British Power*. 1972.
Bassett, H. H., *British Commerce*. 1913.
Becker, William H., *The Dynamics of Business-Government Relations: Industry and
    Exports 1893–1921*. 1982.
Bird, Anthony and Hutton-Stott, Francis, *Lanchester Motor Cars*. 1965.
Blank, Stephen, *Industry and Government in Britain*. Farnborough, 1973.
British Electrical and Allied Manufacturers' Association, *The BEAMA Book: A
    History and Survey*, 1926.
    Combines and Trusts. 1927.
Byng, Gustav, *Protection: The Views of a Manufacturer*. 1901.
Caillard, Sir Vincent, *Imperial Fiscal Reform*. 1903.
Chapman, Sydney (ed.), *Labour and Capital after the War*. 1918.
Claes, Jules, and Rose, J. Holland. *The German Mole*. 1915.
Coudenhove-Kalergi, Count Richard, *Crusade for Pan-Europe*. New York, 1943.
De Launay, Jacques (ed.), *Louis Loucheur: Carnets Secrets 1908–32*. Paris, 1962.
Dictionary of Business Biography. 1984– .
Docker, Lady, *Norah*. 1969.
Documents of British Foreign Policy. 1947– .
Elder, T. C., *The Coming Crash of Peace*. 1916.
Frost, George H., *Munitions of War: Record of Work of the BSA and Daimler Companies
    1914–1918*. Birmingham, 1921.
Gilbert, Martin (ed.), *Winston S. Churchill*, companion vols. III to V. *1914–1939*,
    8 vols., 1972–82.

Gollin, Alfred M., *The Observer and J. L. Garvin 1908–1914*. 1960.
Hannah, Leslie, *The Rise of the Corporate Economy in Britain*. 1976.
Hannah, Leslie, and Kay, J. A., *Concentration in Modern Industry*. 1977.
Hauser, Henri, *Germany's Commercial Grip on the World*. 1917.
Hewins, W. A. S., *Apologia of an Imperialist*. 2 vols., 1929.
Hinkkanen-Lievonen, Merja-Liisa, *British Trade and Enterprise in the Baltic States 1919–1925*. Helsinki, 1984.
Hobson, J. A., *Imperialism*. 1902.
Johnson, Paul Barton, *Land Fit for Heroes: The Planning of British Reconstruction 1916–1919*. Chicago, 1968.
Jones, Robert, and Marriott, Olivier J. D., *Anatomy of A Merger*. 1970.
Kaufman, Burton I., *Efficiency and Expansion: Foreign Trade Organization in the Wilson Administration 1913–1921*. Westport, Conn., 1974.
Kennedy, Paul, *The Rise of Anglo-German Antagonism 1870–1914*. 1980.
Kennedy, Paul and Nicholls, Anthony (eds.), *Nationalist and Raciclist Movements in Britain and Germany before 1914*. 1981.
Kettle, L. W. M., *The Allies and the Russian Collapse 1917–1918*. 1981.
Sidney Reilly, the True Story. 1983.
Leslie, W. Seymour, *The Jerome Connexion*. 1964.
Levine, A. L., *Industrial Retardation in Britain 1880–1914*. 1967.
Maxse, Leopold J., *Germany on the Brain*. 1915.
Politicians on the Warpath. 1920.
Middlemas, R. K., *The Master Builders*. 1963.
Politics in Industrial Society. 1979.
Middlemas, R. K., and Barnes, A. J. L., *Baldwin*. 1969.
Minutes of Evidence to Royal Commission on Private Manufacture of and Trade in Arms. Cmd 5292 of 1936.
Morrison, G. E., *Correspondence 1895–1920*. 2 vols., Cambridge, 1976–8.
North Country Miner (pseudonym of Alfred James), *Six Months in Politics*. 1917.
O'Connor, Harvey. *Mellon's Millions*. 1933.
Oppenheimer, Sir Francis, *Stranger Within*. 1960.
Platt, D. C. St M., *Finance Trade and Politics in British Foreign Policy 1815–1914*. Oxford, 1968.
Pollard, Sidney, *The Wasting of the British Economy*. 1982.
Price, J. H., *Tramcar, Carriage and Wagon Builders of Birmingham*. Hartley, Kent, 1982.
Repington, Charles à Court, *The First World War*. 2 vols., 1920.
After the War. 1922.
Riesser, Jacob, *The German Great Banks and their Concentration in Connection with the Economic Development of Germany*. Washington, 1911.
Roskill, S. W., *Hankey, Man of Secrets*. 3 vols., 1970–4.
Scott, J. D., *Vickers, a History*, 1962.
Searle, Geoffrey R., *The Quest for National Efficiency*. Oxford, 1971.
Smith, Sir Swire, *The Real German Rivalry*. 1916.
Teichova, Alice, and Cottrell, P. L. (eds.), *International Business and Central Europe 1918–1939*. Leicester, 1983.
Tennyson, Sir Charles, *Stars and Markets*. 1957.
Trebilcock, R. C., *Vickers Brothers*. 1977.
The Industrialization of the Continental Powers 1780–1914. 1981.
Turner, John A. (ed.). *Businessmen and Politics*. 1983.

Weiner, Martin J., *English Culture and the Decline of the Industrial Spirit 1850–1980*. 1981.
Wendler, Gehart Jacob, *Deutsche Elektroindustrie in Latinamerika: Siemens und AEG 1890–1914*. Stuttgart, 1982.
White, Arnold, *Efficiency and Empire*. 1901.
Whyte, Adam Gowan, and Elder, T. C., *The Underwar: Patriotic Policy in British Trade*. 1914.
Williams, Ernest Edwin, *Made in Germany*. 1896.
Winter, J. M. (ed.), *War and Economic Development*. Cambridge, 1975.

Articles, pamphlets and theses

Addis, Sir Charles, 'A British Trade Bank', *Economic Journal*, 26 (1916).
Ainslie, Douglas, 'The Foreign Office and the Consular Service', *Nineteenth Century*, 85 (1919).
Anon., 'The Consular Service and its Wrongs', *Quarterly Review*, 197 (1903).
   'The Game of Speculation', *Quarterly Review*, 197 (1903).
   'British Investments Abroad', *Quarterly Review*, 207 (1907).
   'English and German Banking in Relation to Trade and Industry', *Quarterly Review*, 226 (1916).
   'The Labour Movement and the Future of British Industry', *Round Table*, 23 (1916).
   'Industry and Finance', *Round Table*, 25 (1916).
   'The Proposals for a British Trade Bank', *Bankers' Magazine*, 102 (1916).
   'Shall England Finance Germany after the War?', *Quarterly Review*, 229 (1918).
Ashley, W. J., 'German Iron and Steel', *Quarterly Review*, 227 (1917).
Ball, Albert, 'German Methods in Italy', *Quarterly Review*, 224 (1915).
Barker, J. Ellis, 'Britain's Coming Industrial Supremacy', *Nineteenth Century*, 80 (1916).
Bell, Sir T. Hugh, 'Could We if We Would, and Would We if We Could, Capture German Trade?' *Economic Journal*, 26 (1916).
Bliss, Michael, '"Dyspepsia of the Mind": the Canadian Businessman and his Enemies', in David S. Macmillan (ed.), *Canadian Business History*. Toronto, 1972.
Boadle, D. G., 'The Formation of the Foreign Office Economics Relations Section 1930–37', *Historical Journal*, 20 (1977).
Burr, C. H., 'German Business Methods in the United States', *Quarterly Review*, 232 (1919).
Caillard, Sir Vincent, 'A New Force in Industrial Legislation', *Empire Review*, 32 (1918).
   'Premier's Indefinite Policy: Risk of Disorganising Production', *Times Trade Supplement*, 23 Aug. 1919.
   'Industry and Production', *National Review*, 75 (1920).
Cannan, Edwin, 'British Industry after the War', *Economic Journal*, 26 (1916).
Checkland, S. G., 'The Mind of the City 1870–1914', *Oxford Economic Papers*, 9 (1957).
Cline, Peter, 'Winding Down the War Economy: British Plans for Peacetime Recovery 1916–19', in Kathleen Burk (ed.), *War and the State: The Transformation of British Government 1914–1919*. 1982.

Colvin, Ian D., 'The Germans in England – 1915', *National Review*, 66 (1915).
'A National Policy', *National Review*, 66 (1916).
Crammond, Edgar, 'The Nationalisation of British Railways', *Quarterly Review*, 211 (1909).
'Finance in Time of War', *Quarterly Review*, 213 (1910).
'Gold Reserves in Time of War', *National Review*, 57 (1911).
'British Investments Abroad', *Quarterly Review*, 215 (1911).
'Imperial Defence and Finance', *Nineteenth Century*, 72 (1912).
'The Financial Difficulties of Federalism', *Quarterly Review*, 219 (1913).
'Financial Preparations for War', *Nineteenth Century*, 74 (1913).
'Economic Aspects of the War', *Quarterly Review*, 221 (1914).
'British and German War Finance', *National Review*, 67 (1916).
'The Reckoning', *Nineteenth Century*, 80 (1916).
'British Finance during and after the War', *Quarterly Review*, 230 (1918).
'The Economic Position of Great Britain', *Quarterly Review*, 232 (1919).
Crouzet, François, 'When the Railways were Built', in Sheila Marriner (ed.), *Business and Businessmen*. Liverpool, 1978.
Davenport-Hines, R. P. T., 'British Armaments Industry during Disarmament 1918–36'. Cambridge PhD 1979.
'Vickers' Balkan Conscience', *Business History*, 25 (1983).
Dawson, W. H., 'German Trade after the War', *Quarterly Review*, 228 (1917).
Docker, Dudley, 'The Labour Unrest: The Businessmen's View', *Daily Mail*, 8 June 1912.
Open Letter to Sir Algernon Firth, *Midland Advertiser*, 17 August 1912.
'Foreign Loans and British Industries', *Economist*, 7 February 1914.
'The Port of Finance', *Financial News* and *Globe*, 26 October 1914.
'Causes of Industrial Unrest', *Sunday Times*, 2 September 1917.
'The Industrial Problem', *National Review*, 72 (1918).
Chapter in Sydney Chapman (ed.), *Labour and Capital after the War*. 1918.
'The Large View in Business', *Ways and Means*, 2, 27 September 1919.
Elliott, Sir John, 'Early Days of the Southern Railway', *Journal of Transport History*, 4 (1960).
Fayle, C. Ernest, 'Industrial Reconstruction', *Quarterly Review*, 226 (1916).
Forbes, Ian L. D., 'German Informal Imperialism in South America before 1914', *Economic History Review*, 31 (1978).
Foxwell, H. S., 'The Nature of the Industrial Struggle', *Economic Journal*, 27 (1917).
'The Financing of Industry and Trade', *Economic Journal*, 27 (1917).
Good, E. T., 'Trade after the War', *Bankers' Magazine*, 101 (1916).
'German Dumping', *Financial Review of Reviews*, 16 (1921).
Hauser, Henri, 'German Economic Methods and their Defeat', *Fortnightly Review*, 106 (1916).
Hirst, Hugo, *Some Business Aspects of Tariff Reform*, 1908.
The Manufacturer and the State. 1910.
The Higher Aspect of Business. 1914.
Homer, J. F. X., 'Foreign Trade and Foreign Policy: The British Department of Overseas Trade 1916–1922'. Virginia PhD, 1971.
Horsnaill, W. O., 'British Trade and Manufactures', *Quarterly Review*, 226 (1916).
Jennings, H. J., 'A British Trade Bank', *Fortnightly Review*, 106 (1916).

Jones, Linda, 'Public Pursuit of Private Profit? Liberal Businessmen and Municipal Politics in Birmingham, 1865–1900', *Business History*, 25 (1983).

Kaufman, Burton I., 'The Organisational Dimension of United States Foreign Policy 1900–1920', *Business History Review*, 46 (1972).

Kennedy, J. M., 'The Functions of the Overseas Trade Department', *Fortnightly Review*, 110 (1918).

Kent, Marian, 'Agent of Empire? The National Bank of Turkey and British Foreign Policy', *Historical Journal*, 18 (1975).

Landells, Walter, 'The London Stock Exchange', *Quarterly Review*, 217 (1912).

Lawson, W. R., 'Company Promoting à la Mode', *National Review*, 32 (1898).

'The Investor's Opportunity', *National Review*, 36 (1900).

'Stock Jobbing Companies', *National Review*, 35 (1901).

Lehfeldt, Robert A., 'British Industry after the War,' *Economic Journal*, 26 (1916).

Lowe, Rodney, 'The Erosion of State Intervention in Britain 1917–24', *Economic History Review*, 31 (1978).

McLaren, A. D., 'The German Banks and Peaceful Penetration', *Quarterly Review*, 231 (1919).

Makgill, Sir George (of British Empire Producers Organisation), 'Industrial Organisation and Empire', *Nineteenth Century*, 82 (1917).

'The Law and the Alien', *Nineteenth Century*, 83 (1918).

Marrison, A. J., 'Businessmen, Industries and Tariff Reform in Great Britain 1903–1930', *Business History*, 25 (1983).

Martin, Percy F., 'British Diplomacy and Trade', *Quarterly Review*, 215 (1911).

'British Consuls and British Trade', *Financial Review of Reviews*, 23 (1918).

'Post Bellum Trade – What of Ours?', *Financial Review of Reviews*, 23 (1918).

O'Farrell, H. H., 'British and German Export Trade Before the War', *Economic Journal*, 26 (1916).

Palgrave, Sir Robert Inglis, 'The Great Commercial Banks of Germany', *Bankers' Magazine*, 102 (1916).

'Trade Banks', *Bankers' Magazine*, 102 (1916).

'The British Trade Corporation', *Quarterly Review*, 229 (1918).

Patterson, Thomas G., 'American Businessmen and Consular Service Reform 1890–1906', *Business History Review*, 40 (1966).

Phillips, Gregory D., 'Lord Willoughby de Broke and the Politics of Radical Toryism 1909–14', *Journal of British Studies*, 20 (1980).

Powell, Wilfred, 'Clarifying British Commerce of German Influence', *United Empire*, 8 (1917).

Richards, H. Grahame, 'Amalgamations', *Financial Review of Reviews*, 23 (1918).

'A Ministry of Industry and Commerce', *Financial Review of Reviews*, 23 (1918).

Rubinstein, W. D., 'Henry Page Croft and the National Party 1917–1922', *Journal of Contemporary History*, 9 (1974).

'Wealth, Elites and Class Structure in Britain', *Past and Present*, 76 (1977).

Saul, S. B., 'Motor Industry in Britain to 1914', *Business History*, 5 (1962).

'Mechanical Engineering Industries 1860–1914', in B. E. Supple (ed.), *Essays in British Business History*. Oxford, 1977.

Searle, Geoffrey R., 'Critics of Edwardian Society: The Case of the Radical Right', in Alan O'Day (ed.), *The Edwardian Age*. 1981.

'The Revolt from the Right in Edwardian Britain', in Paul Kennedy and Anthony Nicholls (eds.), *Nationalist and Racialist Movements in Britain and Germany before 1914*. 1981.

Shaw, Christine, 'The Largest Manufacturing Employers of 1907', *Business History*, 25 (1983).

Speed, Harold, 'The Commercial Spirit and Modern Unrest', *Financial Review of Reviews*, 109 (1918).

Steel-Maitland, Sir Arthur H. D. R., 'Government and Foreign Trade', *Nineteenth Century*, 85 (1919).

Stiles, C. R., 'The Industrial Problem of Peace', *Financial Review of Reviews*, 12 (1917).

Stutfield, Hugh E. M., 'The Company Monger's Elysium', *National Review*, 26 (1895).

'The Higher Rascality', *National Review*, 31 (1898).

'The Company Scandal: A City View', *National Review*, 32 (1898).

Tawney, R. H., 'The Abolition of Economic Controls 1918–1921', in J. M. Winter (ed.), *History and Society: Essays by R. H. Tawney*. 1978.

Turner, John A., 'The British Commonwealth Union and the General Election of 1918', *English Historical Review*, 93 (1978).

Van Oss, S. F., 'The Gold Mining Madness in the City', *Nineteenth Century*, 38 (1895).

'The Westralian Mining Boom', *Nineteenth Century*, 40 (1896).

'The Limited Company Craze', *Nineteenth Century*, 43 (1898).

Watchman (pseudonym), 'Some New Facts About German Commercial Tactics', *National Review*, 55 (1910).

Wilson, John F., 'A Strategy of Expansion and Combination: Dick Kerr & Co 1897–1914', *Business History*, 27 (1985).

Wise, B. R., 'The War after the War', *National Review*, 67 (1916).

Wright, Arnold, 'The Breakdown of the Board of Trade, a Suggested Reorganisation', *Financial Review of Reviews*, 7 (1912).

Zollinger, Max von, 'Der Aufbau des Brown, Boveri-Konzerns', *Schweizerische Zeitschrift für Volkswirtschaft und Sozialpolitik*, 29 (1923).

Newspapers and magazines

Arms and Explosives
Britannia Review (subsidised by Hugo Hirst)
Economist
Empire Mail and Overseas Trade (subsidised by Sir Vincent Caillard)
Empire Review
Globe
Journal of British Electrical and Allied Manufacturers' Association
Midland Advertiser
National Review
Nineteenth Century and After
Quarterly Review
Times
United Empire
Vickers News

Index

Aboud Pasha, Ahmed, 208–10
Adams, Stanley, 212
Addison, Viscount: meets DD, 92; becomes
Minister of Reconstruction, 99; finds DD
'most helpful', 100; on 'new monster'
FBI, 110; 'reassured' by DD, 117;
admires Sir A. Roger, 228
Aitken, see Beaverbrook, Lord
Albert I, King of Belgium, 201
Allgemeine Elektrizitäts-Gesellschaft, 7–8,
53–4, 58, 105, 113, 155, 188, 200
Allen, Maude, dancer, 96
Allenby, Viscount, 208
Amery, Leo: influenced by Milner, 4, 55;
'ultra-imperial', 66; on Birmingham
corporatism, 73–4; on Whitley Councils
as new second chamber, 116;
encourages 'patriotic labour', 129; on
imperial protection, 188; opposes GATT,
191
Anglo-Argentine Tramways, 203, 207
Ansaldo, 182
Argentina, 42–3, 49, 196–7, 221, 226
Armstrong, Sir George, blimp, 80
Armstrong Whitworth and Co, 31, 120,
139, 160, 177, 182–3
Ashfield, Lord: Eric Geddes detests, 99;
power-hungry, 136; directorship, 212
Ashley, Wilfrid (Lord Mount Temple), 180,
197–8
Ashley, Sir William, 55, 77, 133
Ashton, Lord, 41
Ashton-Gwatkin, F. T. A., 196
Asquith, H. H. (Earl of Oxford): his
enemies, 72; receives DD's memo, 73,
76; attacked by Globe, 81–2; weary of
Kitchener, 95; wife sues Globe, 96
Astbury, H. A., 10, 33

Aston family, 17–18
Atholl, Duke of, 209–11
Austin, Sir Herbert (Lord Austin), 115,
173
Avery, W. T. Ltd, 47

Babcock and Wilcox, 207
Baguley, motorcar engineer, 50, 52
Baldwin, Stanley (Earl Baldwin of
Bewdley): wartime committees 133–4;
'comparatively unknown', 187;
defeated, 188; 'an attractive simple
fellow', 189; lacks industrial policy,
191; seeks Peace Treaty, 192; offers
barony to DD, 197
Balfour, Arthur (Earl of Balfour): his
script, 13; is DD's antithesis, 56; 'a
loser', 72; 'the champion scuttler',
73
Balfour, Arthur (Lord Riverdale), 142
Balfour of Burleigh, Lord, his committee,
58, 99, 149, 158
Ball, Captain John, swashbuckler, 221
Ballin, Albert, on Germanophobia, 60–1
Baltic states, 131, 143, 220
Barker, Sir Francis: helps found London
Imperialists, 120; director of Electric
Holdings, 157; his methods at Vickers,
160–1; 'not quite normal', 165; DD
condemns his Swiss deals, 169–70; and
Wolseley Motors, 173
Barnby, see Willey, Vernon
Barnes, George, 102
Bassett, H. H., 82
Battenberg, Prince Louis of (Marquess of
Milford Haven), 89
Bayley, W. L., 228
Beard, John, trade unionist, 37, 73, 90

285